Guilty Pigs

*'trespassing bees...
murderous zebras
...reasonable cows'*

Katy Barnett & Jeremy Gans

Guilty
Pigs

The Weird

&

Wonderful
HISTORY
of
ANIMAL
LAW

LA TROBE
UNIVERSITY PRESS

IN CONJUNCTION WITH BLACK INC.

Published by La Trobe University Press in conjunction with Black Inc.
22–24 Northumberland Street
Collingwood VIC 3066, Australia
enquiries@blackincbooks.com
www.blackincbooks.com
www.latrobeuniversitypress.com.au

La Trobe University plays an integral role in Australia's public intellectual life, and is recognised globally for its research excellence and commitment to ideas and debate. La Trobe University Press publishes books of high intellectual quality, aimed at general readers. Titles range across the humanities and sciences, and are written by distinguished and innovative scholars. La Trobe University Press books are produced in conjunction with Black Inc., an independent Australian publishing house. The members of the LTUP Editorial Board are Vice-Chancellor's Fellows Emeritus Professor Robert Manne and Dr Elizabeth Finkel, and Morry Schwartz and Chris Feik of Black Inc.

9781760641849 (paperback)
9781743822159 (ebook)

A catalogue record for this
book is available from the
National Library of Australia

Cover design by Tristan Main
Text design and typesetting by Tristan Main
Cover images from FoxysGraphic / Alamy Stock Vector (pig) and Sergey Pykhonin / Alamy Stock Vector (bible)

Printed in Australia by McPherson's Printing Group.

This book is dedicated to the memory of Lucy 'Tilly' Houghton
(3 October 1992 – 29 June 2020)

CONTENTS

ANIMALS' LAWS

O N A SATURDAY MORNING IN AUGUST 2012, THREE GEN-
erations of the Edward family went shopping at The Basin, a
suburb in the foothills of Melbourne's Dandenong Ranges,
feted for its village atmosphere. En route to the local bak-
ery, Emily Edward noticed two Staffordshire terriers roaming around the
park. Later, her mother, Jennifer, browsing in a store, saw two dogs sprint
through the alley behind the shopping strip. Sensing something was amiss,
she went looking for her daughter, only to find the staffies attacking a Jack
Russell terrier and Emily's four-month-old border collie. While Emily
screamed at the dogs, Jennifer tried to loosen the jaws of the dog that had
latched onto the puppy's neck and ear. The local butcher and a passer-by
came to the rescue and pulled the staffies away, but Jennifer was left with a
puncture mark and a torn finger, prompting a trip to a medical clinic. The
incident led to the life of a four-year-old Staffordshire terrier called Izzy
being put on the line – and, as it happens, this sparked a landmark High
Court judgment three years later.

The question of how the law should respond to this incident and the
many conflicting interests of the parties involved – the staffies, their owner
and the Edward family – gave rise to a decision called *Isbester v Knox City
Council*, probably the most important Australian decision on animal law
in recent years.

Tania Isbester, the staffies' owner, sued the Knox City Council – the
administrative body of a local government area in Melbourne's eastern
suburbs – when it decided that her dog Izzy should be put down. She initially sued them in Victoria's Supreme Court, then in its Court of Appeal
and finally in Australia's High Court. Each of those courts ruled on the
dispute and, importantly, they published the reasons for their rulings. It is
this case that prompted us to write this book. Some years ago, we began to
discuss the many issues it raises about the relationship between animals,
humans and the law.

As we will see, *Isbester v Knox City Council* ostensibly focused on Tania

Isbester and her local council but was really all about Izzy, a four-year-old Staffordshire terrier, and her life and death. Izzy's fate rested on a statute enacted by Victoria's parliament that allowed what could have been a private law dispute about compensation for Jennifer Edward, who was bitten by Izzy, to be initially dealt with as a criminal prosecution of Izzy's owner and then as a government decision about Izzy herself. In short, the case is about a court's decision on a common law rule concerning administrative law, which, in the end, saved Izzy's life.

Non-lawyers may be wondering what we mean when we say that this could have been a private law dispute. Let's consider that first, and then move on to consider the criminal law and public law aspects of the case.

Private Law: Restoring the Edward Family

Private law deals with the legal rights and obligations humans have towards each other as private individuals. Two common types of private law are contracts, by which two individuals agree to reciprocal obligations, and the law of property, which allows us to enforce rights and obligations about what we own – including animals – whether or not others agree. The main sort of private law addressed in this book is tort (from the Norman French word for 'wrong'), which deals with instances of people wronging each other, and what the wrongdoer must do to make it up to the other person. There are many ways in which people may wrong each other: by interfering with another's body, property or business; by being careless; and by destroying someone's reputation.

There are obvious overlaps between tort and criminal law, but what makes tort different is its focus on what the offender can do to make it better for the wronged party (rather than how the state should punish the offender for their actions). In early medieval times, English law often dealt with what we would now consider criminal offences through the law of tort, resolving incidents such as the one that we have been describing through the law governing private obligations.

The initial law that applied to Izzy was property law, which, as we mentioned, is a type of private law that governs what people can do with and to things owned by someone else. Many animals – especially in urban settings – are someone's property, just like a bicycle or a bag. This may be surprising to some readers because of course Izzy was not just a bicycle or a bag. She had special value to her owner, as indicated by how hard Isbester fought on her behalf in court. She also had a relationship with the family who housed and provided for her. Nonetheless, she was, for the purposes of the law, to be regarded as property.

The law of property means that people generally cannot do anything to a companion animal owned by someone else without that owner's permission. But the law is full of (mostly) sensible exceptions, including provisions for people to do otherwise forbidden things – within reason – that are necessary to protect themselves, others and even property. An exception of that sort clearly allowed Jennifer, the butcher and the passer-by to pull the two staffies away from the Jack Russell and the border collie that day. The same exception almost certainly allowed them to place the staffies in a fenced-off area at the back of a bike shop, which they presumably did to stop them attacking more animals or people. In an extreme situation, the law could have allowed the locals to injure or even kill the staffies, but only if they properly thought that there was no other way to keep everyone safe.

Isbester, the staffies' owner, was not at The Basin's shops that morning, and this fact had many legal potential implications for Izzy's case. One example is that property law permits people to seize and deal with others' property if they think that there's no reasonable way to identify the owner. In this instance, however, the dogs' owner could be easily identified, either from the microchip implants that are mandatory for cats and dogs in Victoria or by simply asking around the neighbourhood.

Not for the last time in this case, the relevant private law was overshadowed by Victoria's statute on dogs and cats, the *Domestic Animals Act 1994*, which says that anyone can seize a dog at large, so long as they promptly deliver it to the local council, which in turn must notify its owner if the owner is identifiable. Most Australian law is from statutes such as this. Each state and mainland territory has its own parliament that makes different rules. Over the top of the states (like an umbrella) we have the federal parliament, which can only legislate on certain matters listed in the Australian Constitution. In the federal system, federal laws are only valid if they are within the powers and restrictions set out in the Constitution, but if they are valid, they apply across Australia and override contrary state legislation. Underneath each of these parliamentary systems, there are many other sorts of written rules – variously called regulations or by-laws, orders, codes or instruments – made by other public bodies and even by some private bodies.

As we know, the dogs' owner was identified as Tania Isbester, who lived about a kilometre from The Basin with her five children and three Staffordshire terriers. One of those staffies, a female named Bud, was still in her yard on the day of the attack. The other two dogs, a female named Izzy and a male named Jock, had seemingly escaped and made their way through the streets and a park to the local shops. The *Domestic Animals Act 1994* says that an owner can get back a stray dog that has been delivered to a council within eight days of its apprehension if he or she proves ownership, pays a fee and complies with the council's rules (by registering the dog, for instance). Soon, Izzy and Jock were back in Isbester's yard.

For the Edward family, things were not back to the way they were. The family's border collie puppy was covered in blood after the attack and had to be taken to the vet. Jennifer Edward likewise went to a medical clinic to have her finger cleaned and antiseptic applied. Depending on billing and insurance arrangements, the family may have been out of pocket for those medical expenses. Emily Edward later said that she felt unable to walk her dog at The Basin after the attack and, four months afterwards, gave the puppy away 'for retraining'. She added that, even a year later, her son remained scared of dogs and walking in the area. These events imply further financial costs (a replacement puppy, perhaps) and the potential for ongoing limitations on their lives (for instance, coping with or recovering from physical and emotional injuries, and restrictions on their usual activities).

Tort law offers a remedy of sorts for at least some of these after-effects in the form of financial compensation for the out-of-pocket expenses of the victims and their pain and suffering. There are many different torts, each specifying who can be made to pay for another's expenses and suffering, and when and how much they have to pay. Australian tort and contract laws derive from a form of judge-made or common law that arose in medieval England after the Norman conquest. Medieval kings asked judges from the different regions of England to compile their decisions, establish what was 'common' to all of them and discard anything that was idiosyncratic or regionally specific. Over time, the cases decided by judges gave rise to a giant body of judge-made law, incrementally developed on a case-by-case basis. Occasionally (more and more often in modern times) parliaments decide that the common law needs reform or clarification, and they will pass legislation to adjust or replace it. Criminal prosecutions and administrative actions (which we describe later) were originally common law causes too; however, there are now statutes governing these parts of the law, and today criminal law is almost entirely decided by parliaments.

Many modern tort claims are made under the law of *negligence*, which potentially allows someone who is injured to recover money from someone else who should have foreseen that their actions could cause such injuries. The law of negligence is said to have been developed by judges in the United Kingdom in 1932, when a woman claimed that she had found a snail in her bottle of ginger beer and sued the manufacturer, but the law was soon taken up by the common law world, including Australia.

In *Isbester v Knox City Council*, the charge of negligence clearly could have been applied to Isbester, the adult in charge of Izzy and Jock. But to successfully sue her, the Edward family would have had to prove that she had acted unreasonably and that the Edward family suffered as a result. In practice, the family would have needed to prove that Isbester both could and should have stopped her dogs from getting out of her backyard that day. Proving that would depend on several factors, including how exactly the two dogs escaped, how foreseeable this and subsequent events were, and what practical steps Isbester could have taken to stop them. Proving such things in court can be difficult and potentially costly.

The problem of animals attacking people is one that has existed for millennia. As we will discuss in Chapters 2 and 3, older torts that were developed in English courts centuries before the modern law of negligence might have provided an easier legal remedy for people who found themselves injured by someone else's animal. One older law, now abolished in Australia, allowed people to sue landowners if a dangerous animal escaped from their land and caused injury or damage to someone or something. A different law called *scienter* (after the Latin word for 'knowledge'), which still exists in parts of Australia, deals specifically with people who own dangerous animals that attack people. Importantly, neither of these older doctrines requires the injured person to prove that the animal owner did anything wrong. Instead, owners are strictly responsible for whatever harm their animal causes. Because strict rules often work unfairly in modern settings – they can make owning a dog a financially risky proposition, for instance – many of them have since been abolished.

As we will explain in Chapter 2, there are some very old laws that deal with roaming animals such as cows, goats and horses, but they do not cover dogs and cats, so they would not have applied to Izzy and Jock. But in Victoria, the old doctrine of *scienter* is still part of the law today. The catch is that the main limitation of that old law – that it only covers 'dangerous' animals – is also still part of the current law (in some other places, parliaments have removed or softened that requirement). This means that, in the case of domesticated animals such as dogs, the Edward family would still have to prove that the animals in question – that is, Izzy and Jock – were *known* to be dangerous at the time of their attacks. So, to successfully sue Isbester, the Edward family would have had to prove that her staffies had acted in a dangerous way prior to the Saturday of the attack. This too would have been an uphill battle. Isbester would later tell Knox City Council that her dogs were typically friendly, non-aggressive pets, noting that she willingly let them share her home with her five children.

As it happens, later events cast new light on Isbester's dogs. Nine months after the incident at The Basin, Bud and Jock attacked another dog. More significantly, nine days after that, all three dogs were involved in two attacks near Boronia Mall, a large suburban shopping centre several kilometres from Isbester's house. The first incident occurred on a Sunday morning in early June 2013, when the three dogs attacked a cavoodle, Alfie, and his owner. A second, especially horrible attack occurred later the same morning, and was described this way by the other dog owner involved:

> I rolled onto my left side and saw my left hand. It was at this point that I noticed my little finger was just hanging by a bit of skin. I managed to get up on my knees and tried to put my body over Pugsley. All three dogs were still attacking Pugsley and still had hold of her. They were not deterred by my screaming and my trying to fight them off. I was still hitting the dogs with my hands and my knees but they would not let go.

Alfie's and Pugsley's owners were in a much better position to sue Isbester than the Edward family, not only because the new attacks were seemingly even more frightening and damaging, but also because they came *after* the earlier incident, so it was much easier to prove that Isbester should have recognised, and indeed acted on, the dangers her staffies posed. However, these later incidents would not have helped the Edward family's case had they wanted to sue: both negligence and *scienter* are about foresight, not hindsight.

All of this discussion of private law is hypothetical, as there are no reports of anyone suing Isbester. Most people will not take the step of suing another person for lots of reasons – some simply do not want to, others cannot afford it or fear throwing good money after bad; other people reach their own private arrangement that solves their problem cheaply without having to go to court, striking a deal with someone or relying on insurance to foot the bill. It is also possible that one of the people involved did go to court. We would not necessarily know about this, because most courtroom events are not reported by the media, the courts or law reporting organisations.

What we do know is that Tania Isbester had Jock – the male staffy that was the common element in all three attacks – euthanised on the afternoon of the two incidents near Boronia Mall. As Jock's owner, Isbester was free to have him killed painlessly for any reason – selfish or selfless. Her possibly belated recognition of Jock's dangerous nature could not be used as evidence against her, because courts are loath to discourage people from taking measures to reduce future harm. In any case, it soon became clear that other parts of the law could (and would) be applied to this case.

Criminal Law: Punishing Isbester

Most people will be familiar with the notion of *criminal law*. Broadly speaking, criminal law deals with official punishment. Generally, various government officials seek to punish people for the good of society by first proving people are guilty of crimes. In Australia, punishments include jail and a variety of orders or fines, but in the past, corporal punishments such as whipping and capital punishment also existed – and in some countries they still do. The kinds of crimes for which people may be punished include serious offences, such as murder or rape, usually punished by jail terms, and also much lesser wrongs, such as speeding contraventions, typically punished by fines. For offences that fall between these extremes – including many offences that relate to animals – the courts often impose orders requiring people to behave in a certain way or to be watched closely for a period, sometimes in combination with fines or prison. This book will address both historical forms of criminal law, including the prosecution and punishment of animals, and modern forms of law, which are used against humans, including the law of cruelty to animals.

Evidence law runs beneath all types of law, and deals with how we prove to a court that something did or did not happen, and what the court can and cannot take into account. In non-criminal matters, the test is 'on the balance of probabilities' – that is, if it is more likely than not to have occurred in the way alleged. In criminal matters, proof must be established beyond reasonable doubt. In Chapter 4, we look at the roles animals can play in evidence law, both by providing evidence and proof, and by aiding law enforcement.

Nearly 150 years before Izzy and Jock attacked Emily Edward's puppy, Victoria's parliament enacted its first statute about dogs. (In its thirteen years of existence up till that point, the colony had enacted half-a-dozen statutes about livestock). The *Dog Act 1864* required anyone who owned a dog over the age of six months to register and collar the dog, and it allowed police officers or local officials to seize a registered dog 'found wandering at large' and charge a fee for its return. To encourage local authorities to enforce the statute, the registration fee (five shillings), the return fee (two shillings and sixpence) and the various penalties for noncompliance with registration and collaring rules (up to twenty shillings) were all made payable to those authorities.

The scheme's goal was not just to reunite lost dogs with their owners – the more immediate concern was to control dogs that attacked sheep. This problem was dealt with by a statutory addition to tort law, which allowed sheep owners to claim compensation from dog owners without having to prove that the latter had prior knowledge of their dog's 'mischievous propensity'.

The statute set out a very different rule for dogs that attacked people or other sorts of animals:

> If any dog shall in any public place in Victoria rush at or attack any person or horse or bullock whereby the life or limbs of any person shall be endangered or any property shall be injured, the owner of such dog shall forfeit a sum of not less than five shillings nor more than five pounds over and above the damages which such dog may have occasioned, and such damages shall be recoverable in any court of competent jurisdiction.

Like the rule for dogs that had attacked sheep, this rule drops the *scienter* requirement that the dog's owner would only be liable if they knew their dog was dangerous. It differs from the sheep rule by imposing a fine 'over and above' the compensation payable. That punitive element places the new provision in the category of criminal law not private law. In other words, the Victorian parliament decided in 1864 to treat dog attacks as everyone's business.

This decision meant that anyone could bring an action – a criminal prosecution – against the owner of a dog, regardless of whether the dog's victim wanted to, or did in fact, sue for damages. In practice, however, the criminal law is almost entirely enforced by government officials. There are several reasons for that. Unlike private law actions such as negligence or *scienter*, prosecutors usually have to pay for their own expenses, including their lawyers, even if they win. And winning a criminal prosecution is generally harder than winning a private law action, as the criminal law imposes onerous responsibilities and oversight on prosecutors while granting criminal defendants a bevy of protective rights. In the case of Victoria's statutory action against the owners of attacking dogs, Victoria's courts eventually confirmed that people would have to take on all of these costs in order to access the scheme's sole benefit – not having to prove that the owner had prior knowledge of the dog's dangerous propensities. Unsurprisingly, few, if any, ordinary people took up that option, leaving such prosecutions to police and local authorities.

The same scheme, modernised and expanded (to require the registration of cats, and to cover dog attacks on any animal), is still in place in Victoria and was in place in 2012 to 2013, when it was seemingly breached in multiple ways by Isbester. Apparently, she had failed to properly register her dogs, successfully confine them to her yard and stop them from attacking other dogs and people. But these failures did not necessarily mean she would be prosecuted, much less punished. Government officials, including the police, are bound by budgetary, personnel and resource constraints, as well as general guidelines that limit them to starting prosecutions that have a reasonable chance of success and which are in the public interest. So even though Emily Edward complained about Izzy and Jock to Knox City Council in 2012, no prosecutions were initiated until the dogs attacked again in mid-2013.

The first criminal charges against Isbester were brought eleven days after the dog attacks at Boronia Mall, and they all related to the more recent incidents. In all, Isbester faced twenty-three charges for a variety of offences, including that her dogs had been unregistered, at large and attacking people in May and June of 2013. It was only after these charges were brought that the Knox City Coordinator of Local Laws, Kirsten Hughes, learned about Emily's complaint from the previous August. A few days after, she personally charged Isbester with six more offences relating to events at The Basin, including, crucially, a charge of owning the dog that bit Jennifer's finger.

Isbester's prosecution was quite simple, at least compared to prosecutions for crimes that are much more serious (such as murder) or complex (such as fraud). The offence of being the owner of a dog that injured someone is a 'summary' offence. That means that instead of being tried before a judge and jury, the case was tried by a magistrate. Magistrates are still legally trained, but they are paid less than judges, and often work in small, very busy courthouses in local suburbs, hearing dozens or more cases a day. Isbester's case was simpler still because the basic facts were not in dispute: she owned the three dogs, they were not registered, they had left her property without her and they had bitten people and other dogs. Additionally, regulatory offences such as this do not require the prosecution to prove that the offender had any intention of causing harm, had known they were doing so or had done anything unreasonable.

Nevertheless, the criminal law allowed Isbester some avenues to avoid being punished. She could have argued that her failure to register the dogs was due to an honest misunderstanding (say, about when the registration was due or whether it had been paid, perhaps because a letter did not reach her); however, the prosecution would still win if it could prove that any mistake was unreasonable. She also could have raised a defence – originally developed for farmers whose livestock caused traffic accidents – that the damage inflicted was ultimately caused by someone or something else that she could not have been expected to guard against (such as a stranger opening a gate, or a thunderstorm, fireworks or other unexpected event prompting the dogs to escape and misbehave). Isbester could even have argued that the injured person was at fault in some way – if they had teased or otherwise provoked her dogs, for instance.

While it is likely that Knox City Council could have overcome such arguments, they would have made the prosecution a more costly affair, not only for the council but also for the various victims of Bud, Izzy and Jock, who may have been called on to testify in court and be cross-examined about what had happened. Instead, as occurs in nearly all criminal law cases, the prosecutor and the accused struck a deal: Isbester would agree to plead guilty to various charges in return for concessions from the council. More specifically, Isbester would acknowledge that she was guilty of twenty of the charges, in return for the council dropping its prosecutions for the remaining nine.

As part of the deal, the council agreed not to identify a particular dog in the charges relating to the events of mid-2013 (perhaps because the witnesses to those attacks could not tell which staffy was which). However, the council insisted on one thing: that Izzy be identified as the dog that had bitten Jennifer Edward's finger. Even though Isbester owned all three dogs, the question of which dog had bitten whom affected the orders the sentencing judge could make, which in turn had an impact on not just Isbester but also her dogs. In addition to punishing Isbester and making her compensate anyone injured by her dogs, her sentencing judge could also order that the dogs 'be destroyed' by a local council officer. Unsurprisingly, ahead of striking the deal, Isbester's lawyer wrote to the council's lawyer asking, 'What does council intend about the fate of the two remaining dogs, given the dog Jock has already been voluntarily euthanised?' The next day, the lawyer emailed back: 'Council will not be seeking an order from the court in relation to the destruction of the dogs.' But note those words: 'from the court'!

Two weeks later, Isbester pled guilty to twenty breaches of Victoria's *Domestic Animals Act*, including an offence identified as relating to Izzy under section 29 of the Act:

> If a dog that is not a dangerous dog or a restricted breed dog, attacks or bites any person or animal and causes death or a serious injury to the person or animal, the owner of the dog … is guilty of an offence and liable to a penalty not exceeding 40 penalty units.

Usually, a 'serious injury' under the criminal law means an injury that is permanent or life-threatening, but in this case, Victoria's parliament said that a dog bite requiring medical attention qualified, so long as bodily tissue was torn or there was more than one puncture. That meant that Jennifer Edward's bitten finger, which tore her skin and was treated with antiseptic by a doctor, was serious enough to count. Astonishingly, Isbester could have been charged with exactly the same offence – a charge that would be determined by a local magistrate – if Izzy had killed someone! The maximum penalty for such an offence would have been a $7000 fine. The reason a human death can result in such a low punishment for the animal owner is that the owner can be convicted even if she was completely blameless for what her dog did.

At the sentencing hearing three months after the dogs' latest attacks, Magistrate John Cashmore told Isbester that he would have liked to imprison her for allowing her dogs to repeatedly escape from her property, but in the end, he gave her a twelve-month community correction order. This is Victoria's most serious non-prison sentence, and it typically requires offenders to complete education programs, perform voluntary work and submit to monitoring for compliance. Cashmore also ordered Isbester to compensate the victims of her dogs' attacks and to reimburse the court for its own expenses in sentencing her. But he did not order that Izzy be put to death, presumably because the council did not ask him to. As it turned out, the council did not need the court to make the order, because another part of the law was about to be applied.

Public Law: Killing Izzy

A third kind of law, which some readers may not be familiar with, is public law. Public law deals with the powers and decisions of governments in relation to the people they govern. Most modern countries have laws that limit how their governments can act, dividing particular powers between different parts of government, and recognising and seeking to restrain the immense power the state has over its people. This branch of public law is called constitutional law. A second branch of public law deals with the laws that give governments powers over people, including choices that government officials make about what to do or not do, and about what they let others do. This branch of law is called administrative law, because its intent is to ensure the government stays within the powers it has been given and that the decision-making process of those who administer government power is properly and fairly exercised.

Public law is not usually associated with animals, but this chapter will describe a major instance in which administrative law determined the fate of one animal in particular. The position of animals is also affected by the many specific bodies of law that deal with particular issues or entities, including environmental law, corporations law and so forth, but it is public law that had a pivotal role to play in this case.

The day after Isbester was sentenced, Knox City Council wrote to her about Izzy:

> On 12 September 2013, you pleaded guilty at the Ringwood Magistrates' Court to charges in relation to a serious attack by your dog Izzy

on a person on 4 August 2012 at The Basin. Under Section 84P(e) of the *Domestic Animals Act 1994*, council may consider the destruction of a dog if the dog's owner has been found guilty of an offence under section 29.

Since 1864, Victorian local governments were permitted to 'destroy' stray, unwanted or dangerous dogs if they chose to, but they had a more limited role in relation to dogs with owners where those dogs had not been declared dangerous – they could prosecute the owners, but they left it up to a judge to decide whether the dog should die. That changed nearly two decades before Izzy and Jock went to The Basin. In 1994, Victoria's parliament enacted a more modern and comprehensive statute on dogs and (for the first time) cats. None of the politicians who 'debated' the new law's many innovations even mentioned a novel provision allowing local councils to make a decision on whether to kill a dog themselves.

There is a world of difference between allowing a judge to order a dog's death and permitting a council to do so. Judges, including the magistrates who hear nearly all criminal cases, make their decisions after formal hearings involving lawyers, witnesses and all sorts of laws. But government officials, including councils, routinely make decisions that affect people's lives without the aid of hearings, arguments or even – for some political decisions – rules of any sort.

Victoria's 1994 statute meant that, once Isbester was found guilty of an offence under section 29 – that is, she was the owner of a dog who had bitten someone – the elected members of Knox City Council had the authority to vote on whether to kill Izzy, for whatever reasons they wished. They were also allowed to let someone else – a dog expert, for instance – make the decision for them.

The letter sent to Isbester described how Knox City Council decided to resolve the question of Izzy's life or death:

Knox City Council will be holding a panel hearing on Monday 30 September 2013 at 2 p.m. at the Knox Civic Centre at 511 Burwood Highway, Wantirna South. The panel consists of three council officers who will consider all the information prior to making any decision ... You are invited to attend this panel hearing and provide a written and/or verbal submission to assist council in making a decision with respect to your dog. In making a decision, council will consider the seriousness of the attack, the potential future risk to the community as well as the court proceeding, any response from the victim and your submission.

Two weeks later, the Isbester family went to the council's offices to 'assist' the three council employees in their decision about whether or not to have Izzy killed. The hearing started with two other employees reading out summaries of the dogs' attacks and the magistrate's sentencing remarks. Then Tania Isbester read out a statement prepared by her own lawyer, and also supplied letters from the butcher at The Basin, a neighbour and an animal behaviourist. The Edward family asked to speak too, but insisted that the Isbester family leave the room first. After everyone had had a chance to speak, the panel members privately discussed what they had heard and reached their decision: Izzy would die.

The *Domestic Animals Act* does not require councils to follow any such process and nor does any other legislation. And while the statute allows people to appeal some council decisions to a professional tribunal, it does not allow appeals against a decision to order a dog's death. Nevertheless, the council's decision was subject to Victorian administrative law.

In 1994, when parliament allowed local councils to decide whether some dogs live or die, it presumably did not want councils to make their decisions by tossing a coin, demanding a bribe from the owner or letting a self-declared dog-hater make the call. Based on that assumption, Australia's courts can, if asked, check councils' decision-making practices against these assumed requirements.

Assisted by lawyers with an interest in animal rights, Isbester asked the Supreme Court of Victoria for a 'judicial review' of the panel's decision. She was not asking whether the panel made the right decision or not, but rather whether it reached the decision in the right way. Although Isbester's lawyer identified a number of things that he said the panel did wrong, the judge, Karin Emerton, rejected his criticisms. Isbester claimed she had been tricked into pleading guilty by Knox City Council's lawyers, who gave her the impression that Izzy's life was safe; however, Emerton found that Isbester's own lawyer had warned her that the deal did not affect the council's power to kill her dog. Isbester also argued that it was unfair to send her out of the room before the Edwards spoke to the panel – something that would not be permitted in a criminal trial – but Emerton found that the process was fair enough in this instance, especially as Isbester was told what was said in her absence and given a chance to respond. Isbester pointed out that Jennifer Edward had initially been unable to say whether it was Izzy or Jock who bit her finger, but the judge ruled that the panel members were within their rights to conclude that Izzy was the culprit. Emerton's decisions left Izzy in a very bad spot, which became worse when Isbester asked three more judges from Victoria's Court of Appeal to review the case and they again rejected her complaints.

Izzy had just one slim chance left. The reason that judge-made law is called 'common law' is because it replaced myriad different local legal systems that had developed in medieval England. The thinking behind common law was that it allowed everyone in England to go to a single authority – the king – to ensure that they had been treated in the same way that anyone else would have been. In practice, hardly anyone could afford to go to London for a ruling, and the king had no time to decide every dispute anyway; however, the slim possibility of a final review helped to keep the other decision-makers in line. As England expanded its empire, the same process became available to the United Kingdom and then the whole British Empire (later the Commonwealth of Nations): anyone could ask the Queen's Privy Council (judges who were also lords) for a final ruling. When Australia federated, a new Australian body – the High Court of Australia, consisting of a small set of judges appointed by the Australian government – was given the same role, initially in parallel with the Privy Council and then, from the mid-1980s, on its own. That meant that Isbester could go to Canberra to seek a final ruling on her case.

Izzy's slim chance paid off. Not only did the High Court decide to take on Isbester's case, it ruled that the council's decision about Izzy was unfair – in just one way. The issue that caught the judges' eyes was not what Knox City Council decided, or how or why that decision was made – it was *who* made the decision. The problem was visible in the letter the council sent to Isbester back in September 2013:

> The chairperson of the panel will be Steven Dickson, Manager City Safety and Health, who is delegated to make the decision in relation to your dog. The second panel member is Kirsten Hughes, Coordinator Local Laws. The third panel member will be an officer of council who has not had any involvement in the matters, to provide assistance in the decision-making process. The officer involved in the investigation may be present but they will not be involved in the decision-making.

Kirsten Hughes, the panel's second member, was very much 'involved in the investigation' of the events at The Basin. She was the one who had laid the charges against Isbester, liaised with the lawyers and spoken to some of the witnesses, including Jennifer Edward. And, although she was not actually the one who decided whether or not Izzy should die, she was part of the closed-room discussion as that decision was made.

Importantly, the High Court did not decide that Kirsten Hughes was actually biased in any way. Indeed, Australia's chief justice rejected any such suggestion quite firmly when the case was heard in Canberra and noted that Hughes clearly had no vendetta against the dogs of Knox City: she had sat on seven similar panels and Izzy's was one of only two that had decided that the dog in question had to die. Rather, the problem was one of appearances: it would be quite reasonable for a person watching the proceedings to worry that because of her earlier involvement in Emily Edward's complaint about Izzy and Jock, Hughes might be influenced by that experience. The Victorian courts had dismissed this concern because Victoria's parliament had decided to give local councils dual roles, both as the prosecutor in criminal cases and the judge in administrative decisions. But the five High Court judges said that assigning the same employee to both roles breached a fundamental principle: that no-one can be both a litigant and a judge in the same matter.

The High Court's ruling did not mean that Izzy was safe. Instead, it meant that Knox City Council would have to make its decision again, this time without any participation from someone who had been involved in the earlier prosecution. The council could easily have decided, once more, to kill Izzy, but it did not. There are a number of possible reasons for this. First, having reportedly spent $600,000 in fighting Isbester's legal action, ultimately unsuccessfully, the council would surely have been less willing to fight her a second time. Second, in accordance with the High Court's judgment, a new panel was formed to decide Izzy's fate. This time, the council opted not to put any of its own officers on the panel, instead appointing three justices of the peace who could – unlike the last panel – assure everyone that they had no pre-existing interest in the case. Third, and probably most importantly, Izzy's circumstances had changed during the eighteen months since the first panel's decision.

During the time that the three different courts had mulled over Knox City Council's decision-making process, Izzy had been kennelled at the Melbourne headquarters of the Royal Society for the Prevention of Cruelty to Animals (RSPCA), 20 kilometres from Isbester's house. The RSPCA's shelter manager told the new panel that after the dog had shown signs of depression, she had fostered Izzy in her office for much of that period. Izzy had seen around twenty new dogs each day at the RSPCA but, according to the manager, had 'lunged' just once. An animal behaviourist who assessed Izzy during this time pronounced her of 'little risk to the community', although she also recommended that she be housed in a single-dog home and only let out with a trained handler. Finally, and most crucially, the head of the RSPCA's South Australian branch offered to take full responsibility for Izzy's care, rehabilitation and rehoming. (Victoria's branch said it could not do so, as it was too busy dealing with dogs rescued from puppy farms.)

The panel also heard from Tania Isbester, who asked that the staffy be returned to her – Isbester said how hard the matter had been for her and her children and added that she had poured concrete to stop any dogs escaping her yard again – and from a series of witnesses (including the shelter manager and Isbester's own lawyer), who said they would have been willing to care for Izzy themselves if circumstances had permitted. The panel ultimately decided to take up the South Australian RSPCA's offer. The case was over. But was Izzy safe?

A Dog's Life

The High Court's ruling in *Isbester v Knox City Council* caused a brief flurry of headlines about how 'every dog can have its day ... in court!' But the High Court's decision was not really about Izzy, dogs or even animals more broadly – it was about how a very general legal principle applies to a very specific statutory scheme. This example illustrates a broad point that will come up throughout this book: that a lot of animal law is really just a particular application of human law. The High Court discussed Izzy herself just once, when it described Isbester's particular interest in her dog's life:

> Whether one describes an interest in a dog as a property right, or acknowledges the importance of a domestic pet to many people, the appellant is a person who may be affected by a decision which will require her interests to be subordinated to the public interest.

The judges' ambivalence about whether Izzy was just Isbester's property or something more is a recurring theme in this book. What is striking is that it did not matter either way in this case.

It is very rare for a dog – or any animal, even a human one – to have their day in court. But the law still has the potential to affect every animal. Our aim in this book is to describe these laws, using as many examples as we can. We will do our best to explain why the law is the way it is, but that does not mean that we think the law is always good or correctly applied. There is much about the laws relevant to Isbester's case – the private law's complex rules for compensating dog-bite victims, the criminal law's strictness with dog owners and the public law's vagueness about how officials can decide to kill dogs – that causes us qualms, although we also understand the arguments in favour of those approaches. Even the High Court's ruling, appealing as it is, is open to question – after all, it was favoured by just five of the nine judges who heard the case. Importantly, it could always be changed by the Victorian parliament if, for instance, it decided that it was inefficient to involve outsiders in deciding whether to destroy a dog. Even our natural sympathies for Izzy need to be tempered by those who have a different perspective, such as the Edwards, the owners of Alfie or Pugsley, or someone who might deal with Izzy in the future. Speaking of which ...

The perfect ending to this case would have been for Izzy to live a happy life in Adelaide, but things are more complicated. Before Victoria's panel, the chief executive of South Australia's RSPCA had outlined a process of 'medical and behavioural assessment ... to ascertain the extent to which rehabilitation is required and any risk Izzy posed to other animals and the community'. Six months after the panel's decision, he announced the result: Izzy was a danger to other dogs and 'cannot safely be rehomed in South Australia'. Although he had promised Knox City Council's panel that Izzy would be euthanised if she was 'deemed a risk and unsuitable for rehabilitation or rehoming', he told the media that 'there is no deadline on Izzy's outcome'.

Three months later, the Queensland RSPCA's 'Adopt a Pet' website posted a new ad:

Hello to all my Indie fans! Let me tell you all about me. I am a sweet and calm girl who enjoys my own company and who will need access to inside and outside. I am looking for a special someone who can give me heaps of TLC. My foster mum says I adore pats, belly rubs and sitting in your lap. I could do this all day long if mum would only let me. I love going on walks and am very well behaved on the leash. My manners are beyond incredible. You would think I have attended etiquette training school because I am also polite and very well-mannered but I haven't. Mum says I am just a natural … I am looking to be your one and only with no other dogs or smaller animals as we have different views on things. I am best to be around older kids only as I can find the littlies overwhelming.

Izzy was given not only a second reprieve but a new name and 'a fresh start', according to the chief of RSPCA Queensland. The organisation explained that Queensland had a foster carer experienced in Staffordshire terriers. 'Indie actually had less issues than any other dog she's fostered. It really does appear that Indie was found to be guilty by association,' the Queensland officer said, adding that any new owner would be told of the dog's 'full history'. Just over four years after Izzy went to The Basin shops and one year after her case went to Australia's High Court, the Isbesters' staffy was adopted by an anonymous couple, undeterred by either of those events.

OWNING ANIMALS

O N A COLD DAY IN TORONTO IN DECEMBER 2012, SHOP-pers at the IKEA furniture chain were astonished to see a small, lost-looking monkey, wearing a sheepskin-lined coat, wandering unaccompanied around the store. He quickly became known as the 'IKEA monkey' and was an internet sensation, immortalised in memes, games and cartoons.

In fact, the Japanese macaque was named Darwin, and he was owned by the lawyer Yasmin Nakhuda, who had a penchant for exotic animals. Darwin had escaped from a crate in the back seat of Nakhuda's car in the shopping mall's car park. Once the monkey's presence was reported by agog shoppers and onlookers, Toronto Animals Services (TAS) collected the monkey and took him to their shelter. TAS did not have appropriate facilities for Darwin, for the very good reason that it was illegal to keep monkeys in Toronto. Nakhuda had obtained the monkey from a shady and mysterious exotic-animal dealer called Ayaz, for the sum of C$5000.

Shortly after Darwin was taken to TAS's shelters, Nakhuda rang Ayaz and sought his help in retrieving the monkey, but given the publicity he had already attracted on social media, Ayaz refused. Nakhuda, who later gave evidence that she regarded Darwin as 'a member of her family' and her 'son', was distressed. She went to TAS's offices to demand that TAS return Darwin to her, but they denied her request on the basis that Nakhuda could not prove that Darwin was vaccinated, and he might be carrying diseases. If Darwin tested positive for hepatitis B (fatal to humans) or another disease, TAS said, they would have the authority to euthanise him. If he were disease-free, Darwin would be transferred to a primate sanctuary. Eventually, he ended up at Story Book Farm Primate Sanctuary.

Questions of ownership of animals can arouse strong passions and lead to legal proceedings, as the case of Darwin the Japanese macaque shows. But it is a fair bet to say that many of us – especially non-lawyers and those of us who have not had disputes over ownership of animals – have not thought deeply about what it means when you say that you 'own' an animal.

Ownership is a difficult concept. To say that one owns a thing is to say that one has certain rights and responsibilities in relation to that thing (as a whole, or just certain attributes of it). If you own this book – presuming it is a hard copy – you may scribble all over it, tear out the pages, burn it, give it away to a friend, abandon it, loan it out for a fee or sell it second-hand. Of course, we hope you like it enough that you do not do most of these things, but they are all among the 'bundle of rights' that come with ownership. However, if you do not own this book and, in fact, have borrowed it from a library or a friend, the situation is different. You do not have the same rights over the book: you cannot destroy it, deface it, give it away or so on. Property rights define our relationship with things (including different sorts of property, such as land and copyright), but, crucially, they also define the rights of other people in relation to those things. If you do not own this book, the owner can get compensation from you if you damage or destroy it, through the law of tort (wrongs).

To say we have ownership of animals has certain ramifications. Think about what you could do with this book if you owned it, and apply those same rights to an animal. To own an animal might mean we have the right to control it, to sell, lease or give it to another person, to abandon or kill it, to exclude others from using the animal without permission, to take produce from the animal (its milk, fleece and so on) or take its offspring away.

There is a relationship between controlling something and owning it, but the two concepts do not match up exactly. Sometimes, the law legitimates pre-existing control or allocates control over things to certain people. The easier an animal is to control, the easier the animal is to own. Therefore, the ownership of bees has been a consistently difficult legal question in a number of cultures throughout the ages.

In *Yanner v Eaton*, a 1999 Australian case involving questions of ownership over wild crocodiles, four judges of the High Court noted that it is very hard to define what property is, particularly in relation to wild animals:

'Property' does not refer to a thing; it is a description of a legal relationship with a thing. It refers to a degree of power that is recognised in law as power permissibly exercised over the thing. The concept of 'property' may be elusive. Usually it is treated as a 'bundle of rights'. But even this may have its limits as an analytical tool or accurate description, and it may be, as Professor Gray has said, that 'the ultimate fact about property is that it does not really exist: it is mere illusion'.

In this chapter, we'll see that property rights in animals are different in various cultures and have changed over time. This also reflects the malleability of the concept of ownership itself. Ownership is shaped by law, culture and history.

The linguistic history of our property law reveals how deeply the notion of owning animals is embedded in Western culture. 'Chattel' – the legal word for a 'good' or an article of movable property – is related to the word 'cattle'. The eighteenth-century judge and jurist Sir William Blackstone noted that both words are derived from *catalla*, a Latin word that was primarily applied to farm animals, but also to all movable property. In fact, in some ancient societies, and even some modern ones, productive beasts, such as cattle, functioned as currency and status markers. The ancient Irish saga *Táin Bó Cúailnge* revolves around a planned theft of cattle: Queen Medb of Connacht and her husband, King Ailill, plan to steal a stud bull from King Conchobar Mac Nessa, of Ulster, to ensure Medb's herd is equal to her husband's. Later, in Irish Brehon law, cows, pigs and horses were effectively units of currency, with dairy cows the most prized item.

This leads us to consider *why* human animals might want to own other animals. There are many reasons, which shows us that ownership is complex and not the expression of one single desire or policy. People may wish to own animals for their companionship, to protect or take responsibility for them, to eat them, to use the resources they produce, for self-protection, warfare, labour, transport, sport or profit, as an exemplar of status or, in the case of certain wild animals, as objects of fascination or symbols of human domination over nature.

Although Mesopotamian laws clearly contemplated property rights in animals, the first ancient legal system to outline a complete and structured notion of such rights was Roman law. It distinguished between ownership of wild animals (*ferae naturae*) and domestic animals (*mansuetae naturae*). Only qualified ownership of wild animals was possible, but domestic animals could be owned completely. The distinctions and principles present in Roman law have since been adopted and adapted by the common law, including modern Australian law, and the Latin terms for wild and domestic animals continue to be used in legal cases and textbooks to the present day.

The distinction between wild and domestic animals is complex. Indeed, Fabrice Teletchea, an ecologist and zoologist, says that 'wild and domesticated animals should not be considered as complementaries (such as true/false, dead/alive) but rather as antonyms (such as long/short, fast/slow), because they represent the extremes of a process and not a simple dichotomy'.

There is a further difference to note between domesticated and tame animals. Domesticated animals are animals that are selectively bred to have certain genetic characteristics, including a tolerance of humans. Even when they are reintroduced to the wild and have been feral for thousands of years, like the Australian dingo, they are genetically distinct from their wild counterparts. Conversely, tame animals are wild animals that have been taught by exposure to be tolerant of, and useful to, humans, but they otherwise remain indistinguishable from their counterparts in the wild. Thus, for example, elephants in a zoo are genetically no different to wild elephants, whereas domesticated dogs are genetically quite different to wolves, even if they return to the wild.

In this book, we see that the law does not consistently apply these distinctions between wild and domestic animals and domesticated and tame animals: it applies them in a particular way to ownership of animals and in another way when establishing whether an animal keeper is strictly liable for damage caused by animals for the purposes of *scienter*, a law that covers owners of intrinsically dangerous animals.

Parallels with Slavery

Owning a Japanese macaque such as Darwin is clearly not the same as owning a ballpoint pen: he is not just a *thing* in the same way your pen is. But is there a sense in which owning and controlling other living beings is akin to slavery? Some US scholars have drawn parallels between human slavery and ownership of non-human animals, but these efforts have been controversial. Historical slavery cases have also been used to argue that non-human animals should be freed from captivity.

Many societies, at different times, allowed humans to own other humans as slaves. As we noted above, the ancient Irish generally used animals as a unit of currency, but sometimes slaves were also used. Roman law famously allowed for the ownership of other humans and had complex rules for how people could be freed from slavery and how people could become slaves (they could be born into slavery, sold into slavery as children, captured and enslaved, or enslaved as punishment). It is not so long ago that slavery was also permitted by English common law, which compared fellow humans of a distinct 'racial' group to animals. For this reason, analogies between humans and animals are used with great care by courts today. We, too, do not raise the matter of slaves lightly.

In a recent case before the Washington Court of Appeals, Chief Justice Pennell argued that not all analogies between humans and animals are inherently dehumanising or racist:

> The use of animal analogies at trial is problematic. Many animal comparisons operate as racist code. Others are simply dehumanizing. But there is no hard and fast rule. Not all animal analogies are inherently improper. When a particular analogy does not clearly convey an improper message, an appellate court should not be quick to find offense …
>
> Joseph Richmond has filed a petition for relief from conviction, arguing for the first time that the state's prosecutor used an improper animal analogy during closing argument. Mr Richmond fails to show the analogy was patently racist or dehumanizing. The analogy, which compared Mr Richmond to a hornet's nest, was plausibly aimed at describing Mr Richmond's erratic behavior.

Richmond's request for relief was denied, as the court did not think that the specific animal analogy used was dehumanising.

We might compare the analogy used in Richmond's case to the racist analogy between human slaves and cattle used by Lord Hardwicke in an English case from 1749, *Pearne v Lisle*. The plaintiff in this case had leased fourteen African slaves to the defendant for £100 per year and alleged the defendant failed to pay him and failed to deliver the slaves to his agent upon request. He sought specific performance of the contract in the Court of Chancery. 'Specific performance' means that the party who is not complying with the terms of the contract must fulfil his or her obligations or be punished for contempt of court.

Hardwicke held that the owner of a slave could bring an action for wrongful possession of a slave, because 'it [the slave] is as much property as any other thing', contrary to the suggestions of Lord Holt in two earlier cases. But ultimately, Hardwicke refused to specifically enforce the contract on the basis that the slaves were not sufficiently 'unique':

> The Negroes cannot be delivered in the plight at which they were at the time of the demand, for they wear out with labour, as cattle or other things; nor could they be delivered on demand, for they are like

stock on a farm, the occupier could not do without them, but would be obliged, in a case of sudden delivery to quit the plantation.

One reason we find this analogy repugnant is that it reflects a mistaken belief that some humans are less human than others.

In 1772, twenty-three years after *Pearne v Lisle*, Lord Mansfield threw the legality of slavery contracts into doubt in the famous case of *Somersett v Stewart*, refusing to allow the owner of an escaped slave to recapture him and take him abroad. It took legislative intervention spanning from 1807 to 1833 to fully outlaw trading in slaves in Britain.

Notoriously, slavery was legal in the United States until 1865, when the thirteenth amendment to the US Constitution was passed, in the wake of the bitter Civil War between the Northern and Southern states, which was partly fought on this issue.

Unlike the slave trade that sparked the American Civil War, Roman slavery was not imposed on the basis of 'race', making manumission (the act of freeing a person from slavery) more common and allowing former slaves to obtain full citizenship and status. Indeed, former slaves in Roman times sometimes proclaimed their manumission proudly on their gravestones.

But *all* slavery is offensive to modern eyes, wherever, whenever and in whatever circumstances it existed. This is because (contrary to *Pearne v Lisle*) humans are not 'fungible' – that is, one person is not simply replaceable by another – nor are people simply 'tools' or things to be used. To say that a human being is property is to deny their dignity and self-determination, because ownership allows another person to control what happens to them, and suggests that they do not have the capacity to look after themselves or make their own decisions. Indeed, in Australia today, acts that resemble legal slavery – such as exercising property rights over a person or reducing them to slavery, even with that person's supposed consent – are among the country's most serious federal crimes.

By contrast, the law treats animals as property, even if they are unique and have their own personalities, wishes and needs. When Judge Mary Vallee of the Ontario Superior Court of Justice was asked in 2013 to rule on what would happen to Darwin the Japanese macaque, she said:

The parties agree that the court does not have jurisdiction to determine what is in the best interests of the monkey. ... The monkey is not a child. Callous as it may seem, the monkey is a chattel, that is to say, a piece of property. The court may apply only property law principles when considering the issues in this case.

Consequently, Darwin's needs were not under consideration by the court in any explicit sense. The sanctuary that took in Darwin reported that he was interacting with other primates in his new home and receiving high-quality veterinary care. It seems likely that the monkey was better off in the sanctuary than with Nakhuda; however, his wellbeing was not the basis upon which the case was decided. The question was simply who owned him.

Judge Vallee was aware that describing Darwin as a chattel might sound callous, because – as anyone who has owned a companion animal knows – non-human animals can possess distinct personalities, often have a capacity to feel pain and emotion (in times past this was sometimes doubted) and have varying degrees of sentience, which implies that a living being has desires and needs, and that those desires and needs should be recognised. For this reason, many countries and regions have passed legislation recognising this sentience and the unique status of non-human animals, albeit with more rhetorical than practical effect. Some scholars propose a middle-ground solution: in order to protect animals and prevent or minimise their abuse, they argue the law should recognise that animals are a different sort of property – 'sentient property'.

Nonetheless, the global prevalence of notions of ownership of animals, particularly in societies that have domesticated animals, suggests that *some* rules of permanent ownership may be inevitable once animals are domesticated, even if those rules vary according to culture and time. Conversely, societies that have not domesticated animals may have different notions of ownership. For instance, while indigenous societies may have rules about who has an entitlement to an animal that is hunted (as is evident in Australian native title law), the concept of confining an animal and thereby owning it permanently may not exist. This shows us that laws regarding ownership of animals are contingent and very much affected by the culture, history and time in which they arise.

Ownership of Wild Animals

In the case of Darwin the Japanese macaque, it turned out to be very important to the judge's reasoning that Darwin was a wild animal. Darwin was found to be wild because he could not be domesticated: he bit people repeatedly, he had to be harnessed and leashed at all times, otherwise he would try to escape (as he eventually succeeded in doing), and he was not toilet trained (he wore a diaper). Because Darwin was wild, Nakhuda could only hold what is called 'a qualified ownership' over him, and Judge Vallee found that Nakhuda immediately lost ownership once he escaped and had no right to have Darwin returned to her.

What does it mean to have qualified ownership? Again, we must go back to the Romans. As we noted earlier, the Romans were the first to systematically outline the distinction between wild animals and tame or domesticated animals. This was significant, because under Roman law, people could not own wild animals in the same way they owned domesticated animals. As the Roman jurist Gaius is quoted as saying in *The Digest of Justinian*, 'All animals taken on land, sea, or in the air, that is wild beasts, birds, and fish, become the property of those who take them ... [but] when they escape from our control and return to their natural state of freedom, they cease to be ours and are again open to the first taker.'

Many modern European countries were influenced by Roman law and their current laws reflect that. Scotland, for instance, continues to have a 'hybrid' legal system, combining Roman law and the common law. From the time of Napoleon onwards, European countries often enacted all-encompassing civil codes that summarised the law, making it more readily understandable to the populace. These civil codes originated from and were partly based on Roman legal codes. Civil codes still remain in operation in many parts of Europe, and in other areas of the world such as Japan and South America.

The German Civil Code has provisions dealing specifically with wild animals, and you can see how Roman notions of ownership are reflected in them:

(1) Wild animals are ownerless as long as they are free. Wild animals in zoos and fish in ponds or other self-contained private waters are not ownerless.

(2) Where a captured wild animal regains freedom, it becomes ownerless if the owner fails to pursue the animal without undue delay or if he gives up the pursuit.

(3) A tamed animal becomes ownerless if it gives up the habit of returning to the place determined for it.

While England was less influenced by Roman law than many other European countries were, Roman ideas about the ownership of wild and domestic or tame animals also flowed through into the English common law, which was later exported to Australia.

According to the common law, a person cannot own a wild animal unless they take possession of the animal by capturing or killing it. This has been part of English law for hundreds of years. The thirteenth-century jurist and cleric Henry de Bracton said of wild animals:

> When they are captured they begin to be mine, because they are forcibly kept in my custody, and, by the same token, if they escape from it and recover their natural liberty, they cease to be mine and are again made the property of the taker. They recover their natural liberty when they escape from my sight into the free air and are no longer in my keeping, or when, though still within my view, their pursuit is no longer possible . . .
>
> The taking of possession also includes fishing, hunting and capture. It is not pursuit alone that makes a thing mine, for though I have wounded a wild beast so severely that it may be captured, it nevertheless is not mine unless I capture it; rather it will belong to the one who next takes it, for much may happen to prevent my capture of it.

The notion of *control* is an important factor of ownership – if you control an animal to a sufficient degree, you may come to own it – but although some animals are impossible to control (such as bees and cats), they may still be owned. However, the question is still raised: what level of control must be shown before a wild animal can be said to belong to a particular person?

In the eighteenth century, William Blackstone noted in *Commentaries on the Laws of England* that according to common law, ownership of a wild animal is necessarily limited or qualified, but there are three ways in which it may occur.

First, a person may own a wild animal by capturing or keeping the animal, so that the animal stays on the person's property or becomes tamed. The latter is known as ownership *per industriam*, or 'by industry'. If the animal is apt to leave the property, the owner will continue to own the animal if there is an *animum revertendi*, or tendency to return to the owner. It is this aspect of the law that meant Nakhuda no longer owned Darwin when he escaped: he apparently showed no tendency to return to her, hence she lost any right to him.

Second, a person may temporarily own a wild animal that lives on their property and cannot leave because it is young, injured or looking after young. This is known as *ratione impotentiae et loci*, meaning 'by reason of incapacitation and location'.

Third, a person may own a wild animal if they have the right to capture, hunt or kill the animal. This right may arise as part of the exclusive rights associated with owning land, known as *ratione soli*, meaning 'by reason of the soil or land'. Alternatively, the right may be granted a privilege, known as *ratione privilegii*, meaning 'by reason of privilege'. This privilege is generally granted by the Crown, as with the right of swan marks, discussed later in this chapter. This is, in effect, a law of hunting.

It is possible that rules and norms regarding ownership, hunting and who owns the catch predate the evolution of humanity as a species. Chimpanzees, our closest relative, have rules about who gets the most meat from a hunted animal. Male Taï chimpanzees, for instance, cooperatively hunt red colobus monkeys, but it takes twenty years of practice for male chimpanzees to become successful at ambushing them. Those chimpanzees who hunt the monkeys consistently receive more meat than males who do not participate in the hunt. The actual captor typically receives the most meat, but those who anticipate the monkey's movements or ambush the prey also receive generous shares, and those with lesser roles receive lesser shares.

There is a rich and varied law on what constitutes ownership of wild animals at common law. A landowner owns the body of a wild animal that dies upon his or her land. Moreover, while a wild animal is on a person's land, that animal is effectively a resource of the landowner, who may grant the right to hunt or take the animals on their land to others. Ownership of land is thus intimately tied up with the right to own, hunt, use and profit from wild animals – thus we return to the idea that property rights essentially govern relations between individuals. The right to hunt or take animals from the land is a property interest itself (showing one way in which the 'bundle of rights' of ownership can be divided up). It is called a *profit à prendre* (Middle French for 'right of taking'). *Profits à prendre* may also be granted in relation to other valuable resources like gravel or oil, subject to the prerogative rights of the Crown.

People who do not own the land upon which wild animals are found, or do not have a right to hunt from that land, may not access wild animals from it or even buy wild animals from others who have taken it from that land without permission. In *Blades v Higgs*, an English case from 1865, the parties went all the way up to the House of Lords (which had a committee that acted as England's top court) to ascertain the ownership of some conies (adult rabbits), which were taken from the land of the marquess of Exeter by a poacher and sold at market to Blades. Higgs and several other men in the service of the marquess subsequently seized the conies from Blades. The question for the House of Lords was who owned the conies: Blades or the marquess?

Ultimately, it was found that the marquess owned the conies, because a trespasser (the unnamed poacher) took them from his land without permission. It followed from this that property in the conies had not been given to Blades, because the poacher had no right to give it. The Latin name for this principle is *nemo dat quod non habet*, meaning 'no-one gives what they do not have'. In other words, if you do not have a property right to something in the first place, you cannot sell it to someone else. If Blades had been a 'bona fide purchaser for value without notice', he might have had property in the conies, but presumably he was aware that they were poached. While Blades had control of the conies temporarily, his ownership of them was not legitimated by the law, and hence the marquess could seize the conies back by means of 'self-help'.

What then of an animal, such as a wild bird, which may fly away from the nest during the day, and then return? The law holds that animals of this kind can be owned too (*animum revertendi*). These principles date back to Roman times, as with so much law in this area. *The Digest of Justinian* said:

> In the case of these animals which habitually go and return, the accepted rule is that they are held to be ours so long as they have the instinct of returning; but if they lose that instinct, they cease to be ours and are open to the first taker. They are deemed to have lost that instinct when they abandon the habit of returning.

In the following section, we look at the situation of several different types of wild or semiwild animals: crocodiles, wild fish, shellfish, bees, foxes, peacocks, pigeons, swans, whales and exotic animals.

Crocodiles

In Australia, the state's 'ownership' of native fauna potentially conflicts with the right of Indigenous Australians to hunt and take native animals.

In *Yanner v Eaton*, a case mentioned at the beginning of this chapter, Gangalidda man Murrandoo Yanner used a traditional form of harpoon to spear two juvenile estuarine crocodiles in Queensland. He and other Gangalidda people ate some of the crocodile meat and froze the rest.

The relevant state legislation that was then in force, the *Fauna Conservation Act 1974* (Qld), states in section 7(1):

All fauna, save fauna taken or kept otherwise than in contravention of this Act during an open season with respect to that fauna, is the property of the Crown and under the control of the Fauna Authority.

The legislation also said that a person must have a licence to take fauna in section 54(1)(a) of the Act.

Yanner did not have a licence. However, Indigenous Australians have native title interests recognised at common law – in the famous decision of *Mabo v State of Queensland (No. 2)* – and by the *Native Title Act 1993* (Cth). At that time, section 211 of the *Native Title Act* specified that a state law would not apply if it prevented an Indigenous person from otherwise enjoying a traditional activity, such as hunting, gathering or fishing, or any cultural activity that was part of their personal, domestic or communal needs and which reflected their native title interests.

Yanner claimed his clan had a connection with the land that pre-existed colonisation, and that hunting crocodiles remained a traditional custom. Therefore, he claimed, the *Fauna Conservation Act* did not apply insofar as it conflicted with his native title rights. However, the state claimed that the *Fauna Conservation Act* extinguished any native title rights to hunt animals because the state had taken ownership of any fauna before the federal law was enacted.

Chief Justice Gleeson, and Justices Gaudron, Kirby and Hayne (a majority of the seven judges), found that the rights held by the Queensland government in native fauna was not what is called 'full beneficial' or 'absolute' ownership. In other words, the government did not own the native fauna in the same way that you might own a book, in part because it did not have the powers over native fauna that you might have if you owned something fully. It lacked absolute ownership of fauna for several other reasons.

First, it was impossible to identify exactly which native animals were owned by the Queensland government. Second, as we have discussed earlier in this chapter, it was a long-held principle at common law that people could not fully own wild animals. Third, the kind of ownership the Queensland government had in the fauna was not equivalent to a person who owned a domestic animal: the native fauna came and went, and the government had no responsibility for the behaviour of the fauna. Fourth, it seems that the origin of the provisions for ownership of native fauna were geared towards imposing a royalty on skins of animals or birds taken in Queensland.

While the *Fauna Conservation Act* said that the Queensland government 'owned' the native fauna, this was simply an expression of the fact that the state had power to conserve and regulate wild animals. Consequently, the majority found that the Act did not extinguish any native title interests Yanner or other Gangalidda people held.

Fish and Shellfish

Cases about the ownership of wild fish have come before the courts several times in different ways. Imagine a situation where a fisherman has an open net from which fish could escape, and another fisherman comes and takes the fish. Has the second fisherman taken fish belonging to the first fisherman? In fact, this question has come up before the courts twice (once in England and once in the United States) and the answer was different in each case!

In the English case, *Young v Hitchens*, which was decided in 1844, the plaintiff had drawn a net partially around a school of pilchards, leaving a small opening which he was going to close with a 'stop net'. The defendant rowed up to the opening, threw his own net within the partial enclosure and took some of the fish. The plaintiff sued the defendant for damages. The court held that the plaintiff could not show sufficient control, and that the fish were not his property.

In 1902, a very similar case, *State of Ohio v Shaw*, arose in the United States. It had quite a different outcome. Some fishermen had set up an open-ended net in Lake Erie from which fish could escape. The defendant took fish from the net, and the court held that the defendant was liable for theft. The level of control (which involved reasonable precautions against the fish escaping) and the demonstrated intention to possess was enough to establish the plaintiff's ownership. The exertion of greater control over the fish seems to have been the determinative factor that swayed the American court in a different direction than that taken in *Young v Hitchens*.

Disputes about fish ownership still arise in the twenty-first century, such as in *Borwick Development Solutions Ltd v Clear Water Fisheries Ltd*, an English case decided in 2020. Borwick had bought considerable stocks of fish, and it maintained and kept them in man-made lakes in a disused gravel mine. It ran a fishery business from the site, where customers paid to fish and then returned any catches to the lakes. When Borwick defaulted on a loan secured over the land by a charge, receivers for Borwick sold the land on which the fishery was located to Clear Water. The receivers told Borwick that they had not considered the fish to be subject to the charge under which the land was sold, and nothing was said in the contract of sale as to who they belonged to. Borwick asserted that it still owned the fish, a valuable resource, and that as Clear Water had improperly interfered with its right to possession, it was entitled to the value of the fish.

The trial judge found that Borwick retained ownership in the fish, but the English Court of Appeal overturned that decision. The court held that the fish were wild, and as a result, the only ownership that could be asserted was a 'qualified property right'. In making its decision, the court referred to ancient jurisprudence, including Roman law; in fact, the court quoted Gaius in *The Digest of Justinian* on the principle that wild animals could only be temporarily owned and when they escaped control became free again. The only way Borwick could assert ownership was to show contin-ued possession of them – either *per industriam* (through exerting effort to possess and keep them) or *ratione soli* (through possession of the land on which they were kept). Once the land had been sold, in this instance at least, Borwick no longer had qualified rights in the fish, because it could not actually control or maintain the fish anymore, nor could it access the land upon which they were kept.

This case might have been more easily resolved in Italy, as article 926 of the Italian Civil Code specifically covers migrating pigeons, rabbits and fish:

> Rabbits or fish which go from one warren or fish pond into another warren or fish pond belong to the owner of the latter, provided such rabbits or fish have not been attracted there by fraud or artifice.
>
> The same provision is applicable to pigeons migrating to other pigeon houses, except for the various provisions of law with respect to carrier pigeons.

While the fish here were not 'migrating', it seems that whoever owned the land on which they live would be the owner of the fish under this provision.

What, then, of fishing? Australian common law originally gave the public a right to fish, inherited from the English common law; however, this has mostly or wholly been overridden by statute in modern times and, particularly since the 1980s, fishing has become highly regulated. In 2008, the Australian High Court decided that Northern Territory fisheries legislation had wholly abrogated the public right to fish. And in Victoria, the *Fisheries Act 1995* explicitly asserts in section 10(1) that the Crown 'owns' all wild fish 'found' in state waters. It seems likely that this would abolish any public right to fish, regardless of whether the concept of the Crown 'owning' all wild fish is workable.

In 1898 – much earlier times – several men were charged with theft for taking oysters from the National Park of New South Wales (now known as Royal National Park). Justice O'Connor found that because oysters are wild animals, they could not be the subject of property until they were captured (the judge acknowledged that the concept of capturing an oyster was somewhat odd). Although legislation purported to give ownership of oysters to the Crown in certain circumstances, it was not properly in force, and the regulations made under the statutes were thus beyond power (*ultra vires*, in Latin). Accordingly, the men were found not guilty of theft. The reports note that, thereafter, the governor declared the National Park to be a 'Public Oyster Reserve', to avoid any doubt in future.

As already noted, *Yanner v Eaton* provides that Indigenous Australians can retain a native title right to hunt, notwithstanding certain state or Commonwealth laws. However, whether or not Indigenous people retain a specific right to take abalone depends upon showing a continued tradition of their doing so. Consequently, two separate Australian cases came to different conclusions on this matter. In 1993, in *Karpany v Dietman*, the High Court of Australia held that the South Australian *Fisheries Management Act 2007* did not prohibit Indigenous Australians from taking undersized Greenlip abalone if they could demonstrate this was a subsisting native title right and if their conduct was for the purpose of satisfying personal, domestic or non-commercial communal needs. However, in a 1994 case from New South Wales, *Mason v Tritton*, Mason, an Indigenous Australian who did not have an abalone fishing licence, was found to have contravened the *Fisheries and Oyster Farms (General) Regulation 1989* (NSW) by possessing more than the permitted quantity of abalone. He argued he had a native title right to collect abalone, but failed to prove that this had been a specific right of his people.

Conflict between native title laws and fishing more generally arose in a 1995 case from Western Australia, *Sutton v Derschaw*, in which Derschaw and other Indigenous Australians had caught mullet with nets that were prohibited due to their size. The defendants argued they had a native title right to fish, but the court found they did not establish native title to that area, and that the activities they had engaged in were prohibited for the good of all Australians, Indigenous or non-Indigenous.

Bees

Human coexistence with bees has a long history: evidence of beekeeping has been discovered at the Neolithic site of Çatalhöyük, dating back to 8000–7000 BCE, but the first evidence of beekeeping in legal codes is found from the time of the Hittites, thousands of years later.

The importance of bees in ancient times stemmed from the fact that sugar was rare and expensive: honey was used to sweeten food instead, and beeswax was used to make candles. Mead, one of the oldest known alcoholic drinks, could be made from fermented honey. Aristotle, Pliny the Elder and the Welsh bard Taliesin all mention mead.

Bees provide a particular challenge to any legal system, even a modern one. A property right in bees is difficult to establish for several reasons. First, whereas cattle and horses can be branded, there is no way of marking a particular bee as 'your' bee, and its value depends upon being part of a hive. Second, bees can go wherever they please, and while they usually return to their hive, they can swarm onto different land at unpredictable times; a hive can also split into a separate swarm. Third, bees can sting people, and sometimes they can even kill. This raises the question of who is responsible if someone's bee stings another.

In *The Digest of Justinian*, Gaius's opinion on bees is set out at length:

Bees, again, are wild by nature and so those which swarm in our tree are, until housed by us in our hives, no more regarded as ours than birds which make a nest in our tree. Hence, if another should house or hive them, he will be their owner. Again, honeycombs which they make can be taken by anyone with no question of theft, though, as said earlier, one entering upon another's land can be lawfully barred by the owner who becomes aware of it. A swarm which flies away from our hive is deemed still to be ours as long as we have it in sight and its recovery is not difficult; otherwise it is open to the first taker.

While Gaius regarded bees as wild, other Roman authors, such as Pliny, regarded them as occupying an intermediate position between wild and tame. The modern law treats them as one or the other, depending on context.

Romans were not the only ancient people to have elaborate theories regarding the ownership of bees. The medieval Irish Brehon law devoted an entire section of law to 'bee judgments' or *Bechbretha*, in Irish Gaelic. (*Bech* was the word for bee in Old Irish; rather delightfully, bumblebees are called *bumbóg* in Gaelic.) The *Bechbretha* said that if bees swarmed, ownership was only retained if the owner tracked or pursued the bees and kept them in sight.

How the honey was to be shared if the bees swarmed to another's land was determined by complex laws, based on who tracked the bees, who originally owned the bees, on whose lands the bees settled and on whose land the bees fed. For instance, if bees swarmed onto the land of a dignitary, and the original owner tracked them there, the original owner was entitled to one-third of the honey for three years, even if the bees were looked after by the dignitary; one-third of the honey went to the dignitary who owned the land; and the final third went to the owner of the land upon which the bees fed. Different kinds of land gave rise to different kinds of shares.

Interestingly, in relation to bees, the Anglo-Australian law, and the British law that preceded it, has not changed much in over 600 years. Cleric and jurist Henry de Bracton discusses bees in his famous thirteenth-century legal treatise *De Legibus et Consuetudinibus Angliae* (*On the Laws and Customs of England*), as does William Blackstone in his eighteenth-century *Commentaries on the Laws of England*. Both treat bees in a similar way to Roman law, arguing that no property in bees arises until they are hived, and that an owner may only reclaim bees that have flown away if he can keep the bees in sight.

In some jurisdictions there is an exception to this rule, which still persists: a landowner can prevent the original owner of the bees from trespassing on his or her land. This came to the fore in a 1939 case from England, *Kearry v Pattinson*. Kearry's bees swarmed and settled in his neighbour Pattinson's property. Although Kearry could still see the bees and identify them, his neighbour would not allow Kearry onto his land to collect the bees. The King's Bench Division held that because Kearry had no legal right to enter the land, he lost ownership, and the bees reverted to being wild.

Of course, there is always the question of whether or not the bees are actually identifiable! In 1911, Lynam found some bees swarming on a rail in his Queensland cattle yard and hived them in a box, thus successfully claiming ownership of them. When the box went missing, Lynam claimed it was stolen by a man called Gadd, in whose yard Lynam found the bees. Gadd was charged with theft, but the jury was not convinced beyond a reasonable doubt that the bees on Gadd's land were the same bees that Lynam had originally hived, and Gadd was acquitted.

European countries with civil codes approach the matter of pursuit differently, allowing bee owners to pursue their bees onto the land of others. The German Civil Code, particularly detailed on the topic of bee ownership, not only gives the owner the right to pursue their bees onto land belonging to another, but if the bees have entered into an unoccupied hive belonging to someone else, it allows the bee owner to break open the hive, paying compensation if he causes any damage to it.

If two or more swarms merge, the total swarm becomes co-owned in proportion to the number of people who originally owned the separate swarms. If a swarm moves into a hive already occupied by other bees, the owner of the hive obtains ownership of all of the bees, and any other person's ownership or rights to the swarm are extinguished.

If the common law approach seems less fair than the civilian approach – if it seems unjust that Kearry lost his bees because Pattinson would not allow him to pursue them – it may reflect the traditional common law insistence on the primacy of property rights in land.

Foxes

The famous US case of *Pierson v Post* is often used to teach American law students property law. Lodowick Post, his friends and hounds were chasing a fox on foot across an uninhabited beach in New York when Jesse Pierson intervened, clubbing the fox to death with a fence railing. At the time, the two men were both in their twenties and well-off sons of prominent New York families. There seems to have been some tension between the families about whether 'sporting' of this nature was appropriate, or whether foxes (beasts that preyed on chickens) should be dispatched swiftly and without sport.

The legal question was whether Post had 'owned' the fox and Pierson had taken his property. A majority of the court decided that pursuit was not enough: Post did not own the fox. While it may have been unsporting of Pierson to kill it – Justice Livingston described Pierson as a 'saucy intruder' – it was not theft.

Justice Tompkins, who delivered the main judgment, said:

> We are the more readily inclined to confine possession or occupancy of beasts *feræ naturæ*, within the limits prescribed by the learned authors above cited, for the sake of certainty, and preserving peace and order in society. If the first seeing, starting, or pursuing such animals, without having so wounded, circumvented or ensnared them, so as to deprive them of their natural liberty, and subject them to the control of their pursuer, should afford the basis of actions against others for intercepting and killing them, it would prove a fertile source of quarrels and litigation.

Legal historian Angela Fernandez summarises the logic behind the majority decision in *Pierson v. Post, The Hunt for the Fox*, her book detailing the history behind the case:

> In a hunt ... the animal can and often does escape; so the clearest manifestation of control is to kill it (as Pierson did). Killing the animal constitutes best possession. This is sometimes referred to as a 'bright line' rule, said to be clearer and easier to apply than the allegedly 'fuzzy' standard of an imminent taking that might still go awry.

Justice Livingston dissented, and would have given Post the fox, saying ownership did not depend on actually touching or capturing the animal, 'provided the pursuer be within reach, or have a reasonable prospect (which certainly existed here) of taking, what he has thus discovered an intention of converting to his own use'. His dissent seemed to have an uncharacteristically humorous flavour.

It is, in fact, possible to tame and breed foxes (typically for their fur), but there is conflicting case law on this issue from Canada. In a 1917 case where a 'ranch'-bred fox escaped and was killed by someone, the fox was held to be a wild animal that had regained its freedom: the court found the fox had no intention of returning to the ranch. In a later, similar case from 1932, the court held that the foxes in question were sufficiently tamed to have become domesticated animals, capable of being owned, and the person who killed the escaped fox was liable to compensate the owner for its value.

Famously, Soviet scientist Dmitri Belyaev and his colleagues were reputed to have domesticated silver foxes over forty generations in Novosibirsk by selectively breeding the tamest foxes. The foxes apparently demonstrated 'domestication syndrome': their legs, tails, snouts and upper jaws were shorter; they had floppy ears, curly tails and brindled or dappled coats, with a star pattern on the forehead; their mating became more frequent, without seasonal limits; and they were friendlier and wagged their tails. However, it was recently suggested that the foxes were not entirely wild to begin with, and were originally taken from Canadian fur farm populations, which had those characteristics before the experiment was undertaken. Consequently, some think 'domestication syndrome' may have been overstated, and more experiments are needed to establish it.

The status of tamed foxes under Australian law became an issue in New South Wales, when a charity called Sydney Fox Rescue, formed in 2012, began rescuing captured foxes, domesticating them and placing them with families. However, in 2014, the New South Wales government declared foxes to be a pest, and said owners had to apply for a permit in order to keep them. It has refused to change its stance on this, despite lobbying from Sydney Fox Rescue in 2016.

Peacocks and Pigeons

Some tamed birds have wild characteristics. Again, this was recognised by Roman law in *The Digest of Justinian*:

> The wild nature of peacocks and doves is of no moment [not important], because it is their custom to fly away and to return; bees, whose wild nature is universally admitted, do the same.

This was contrasted with the tamer characteristics of domesticated poultry and geese. While wild geese that flew away were no longer owned, domesticated geese that flew away still belonged to the owner, and anyone who took them was liable for theft. Although Gaius seems to have thought of peacocks as intrinsically wild (despite their being introduced to Italy), Pomponius suggests they could be regarded as tame on some occasions:

If, when my tame peacock escaped from my house, you chased it so that it disappeared, I could have the action for theft against you if someone else should take it.

While it may seem extraordinary that the theft of tame peacocks was prevalent enough to require a specific rule, the Romans had a predilection for keeping exotic animals and thus had specific rules about owning them.

Interestingly, in English law, as historian and academic Krista Kesselring explains, there was doubt at one point as to whether someone could steal a peacock, because they were animals meant for pleasure, not profit. However, views began to change in the sixteenth century:

An Act of parliament passed in 1539 signals the shift: in making it a capital offence to steal the king's hawks or their eggs, the Act insisted that a man ought to be able to assert his rights 'as well in things of high pleasure as in things commonly valuable … and in especial things of pleasure'. In arguments that have their echoes today, some people started to say that pleasure – that the comfort and good health that came from, for example, hearing a caged bird sing – was itself profitable. Judges had applied the pleasure vs profit distinction even to objects such as musical instruments and tried to do the same with diamonds, things deemed to be of no intrinsic value beyond the pleasure they brought.

In the present day, economists call a good that is valuable simply because of its high price a 'diamond good', but historically speaking, a 'peacock good' would have been just as apt.

Pigeons and doves were not 'diamond goods' in medieval Europe, although in England, only lords of the manor were entitled to put dove cotes on their properties. Pigeons and doves were eaten, as were their eggs, and their dung was collected for fertiliser, tanning and making gunpowder. Homing pigeons, of course, were used to deliver mail and to communicate in wartime, because of their exceptional ability to return to their nest, which is believed to be related to magnetoreception. Thus, the 1948 English case of *Hamps v Darby* established that an escaped racing pigeon remains the property of the owner as long as the animal retains an intention to return to the owner (*animus revertendi*). Modern law regarding the ownership of pigeons and doves has not changed much since ancient times.

Swans

The ownership of swans in England and Wales has an extraordinary history. Swans are useful in some ways – they can be eaten, and their feathers are used as quills – but they are also a symbol of status and royalty. It is sometimes said that only the queen may eat swan, and that she owns all the swans in Britain. This is not strictly correct. The truth is far more interesting.

First, the monarch of England only has rights in relation to a particular species of swan native to Britain, the mute swan (*Cygnus olor*). Secondly, it seems the monarch only owns the *unmarked* swans in British waters.

The first mention of mute swans being a 'royal bird' comes from Gerald of Wales (Giraldus Cambrensis) in the late twelfth century, but the monarch's right to own mute swans is now generally deemed to be part of the royal prerogative. It only extends to England and Wales, not to Scotland, Northern Ireland or any other realms still governed by the queen.

At some point, the monarch began to grant ownership of swans to nobles. In the thirteenth century, owners of swans started to place 'marks' on the swans' beaks (*cigninota*, in Latin) with the permission of the king. A declaration in 1405 to 1406 reiterated that only the king could grant this right. Until that time, ownership of swans was governed by customary law.

In 1361, the king made Thomas de Russham responsible for 'the supervision and custody of all our swans, as well as in the water of the Thames as elsewhere within our Kingdom'. Thereafter, the king had a Master of the King's Game of Swans, also known as the Royal Swan-herd, Royal Swan-nerd or Royal Swan-master. The swan master was also responsible for keeping swans safe in inclement weather.

In 1482 and 1483, Edward IV's *Act for Swans* was passed to prevent unlawful keeping of swans by 'Yeomen and Husbandmen, and other persons of little reputation'. Accordingly, the only people who could have swan marks or own swans were nobility and rich people: those who 'have Lands and Tenements of Estate of Freehold to the yearly Value of Five Marks above all yearly Charges'. If the Act disqualified a person from owning swans, they were to divest themselves of ownership, and if this was not done before Michaelmas, those qualified for ownership were entitled 'to seize the said swans as forfeit; whereof the king shall have one-half, and he that [shall seize] the other half'. This is what is known as a 'sumptuary law': a law that restrains certain social classes from owning or consuming something and is designed to enforce social hierarchies.

Formal registration of swan marks became a practice around this time. Additional codes and ordinances were enacted specifying who should own swans and cygnets in particular areas. Only the monarch could claim unmarked mute swans, although the monarch also had several of his or her own marks.

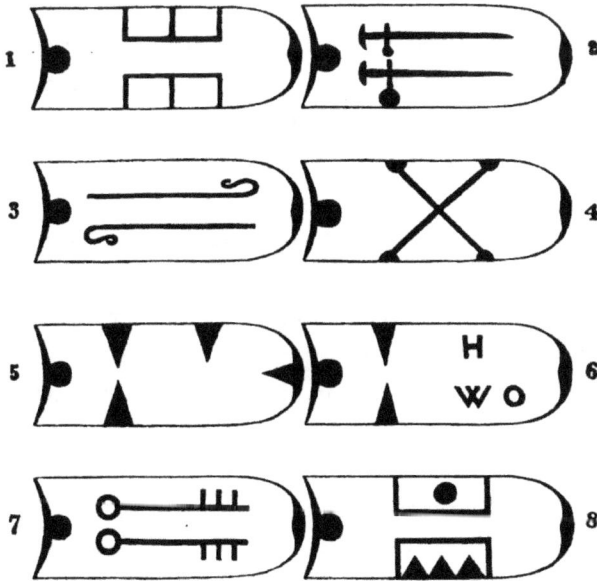

Examples of swan markings

Today, the only other people who are still legally allowed to hunt and eat unmarked mute swans are the fellows of St John's College, Cambridge, a privilege granted for royalist support in days gone past. They no longer exercise this right, but swan traps remain within the walls of the college.

The marking, recording and disposal of swans was known as 'swan upping', and was overseen by the swan master. People would catch the swans, record the ownership of the birds and their offspring, and place markings upon the beaks of the birds. It seems that the marks were inscribed with a knife or branded with a hot iron. The swan master was to meticulously maintain the marks in an 'upping book'.

Why were swans such a big deal? They were regarded as luxury goods, and their association with royal favour gave them high status in medieval times. The precise reason for this association is unclear, but it may relate to their beauty, their solitary nature, the way they fiercely protect their cygnets and the fact that one needs a large property to keep swans. Swans were also eaten, and in 1247, Henry III ordered forty swans for his Christmas banquet at Winchester.

Once the process for marking swans was established, the king formed special courts to apply the law of swans, called the Courts of Swan-mote or Swan-moot, to settle swan-related disputes. The swan master was responsible for enforcing the king's rights in the courts. The swan master's office became profitable, and regional deputies were appointed. Strict rules promulgated by local swan owners protected the monarch's swans from being harmed. The 1523 *Ordinances Made in Respect of Swans on the River Witham in Lincoln* set out a number of rules, including the following:

> No fisher, or other man that hath any ground butting on any water, or stream, where swans may breed, or of custom have bred, shall mow, shear, or cut any thackets, reed, or grass within 40 feet of the swan's nest, or within 40 feet of the stream, on pain of every such default to forfeit unto the king, or his deputy, xl [40 shillings] ...

> No manner of person or persons [shall] hawk, nor hunt, fish with dogs, or set nets, or snares, or engines, for no fish, or fowl, in the day time, or shoot in hand gun, or cross bow, between the Feast of Philip and James and the Feast of Lammas, in pain for every such default, to forfeit unto the king or his deputy, the thing that is set, and in money the sum of 6s. 8d.

> No hemp or flax [shall] be steeped in any running waters, nor within 40 feet of the water, nor any other filthy thing be thrown in the running waters, whereby the waters may be corrupt, nor no man to encroach on the running water, whereby the waters may be hurt, by any kind of means, in pain of every such default, to forfeit unto the king, or his deputy, xl [40 shillings].

Stealing swan eggs was forbidden, under pain of imprisonment and fines. During the reign of Henry VII (1485–1509), stealing 'the eggis of any faucon, gossehauke laners or swannes out of the neste' was punishable by a year and a day's imprisonment and a fine, half to be paid to the king, and half to the person on whose land the nest was. During the rule of James I (1603–25), anyone who took 'the Egges of any Phesant Partridge or

Swan upping on the River Thames

Swannes out of the Neasts, or willinglie breake spoile or destroy the same in the Neaste' was punished by three months' jail without bail, or a fine of twenty shillings (used to aid the poor of the parish) for each egg taken or destroyed.

In 1592, the *Case of Swans* established the principles for swan ownership and confirmed the general principles of the ownership of wild animals and the rights of the monarch. The dispute on which the case was based arose when Dame Joan Young and Thomas Saunger were directed by the sheriff of Dorset to round up 400 unmarked swans from the rivers of Dorset, because Queen Elizabeth I sought possession of them. Young and Saunger argued that the swans belonged to them. The right to these swans had once been held by the Abbey of St Peter at Abbotsbury, an order of Benedictine monks that no longer existed. It might seem extraordinary that monks had rights to such a delicacy, but the description of the monk in the prologue to Geoffrey Chaucer's *Canterbury Tales* suggests it was not unusual:

> Now certainly he was a fair prelaat;
> He was nat pale as a forpyned goost.
> A fat swan loved he best of any roost.

45

The grandfather of Dame Joan's first husband had assisted in the dissolution of the monastery, and Henry VIII had allowed him to purchase the estate. The estate had then passed to his grandson and heir (Young's late first husband, Giles Strangeways). Young and Saunger claimed they had been given rights to the swans for one year by Strangeways. However, because swans were 'royal birds', the right to these swans could only be granted *ratione privilegii* (by the Crown). Thus, the monarch can technically claim all *unmarked* mute swans in English waters. As it happens, the Abbotsbury Swannery continues to belong to the descendants of the Strangeways family today, and many swans still live there, but the queen chooses not to claim them.

As the *Case of Swans* observes, there was an elaborate system of ownership of cygnets. If the parents of cygnets were owned by two different people, the cygnets were divided between them: an equal number went to the owner of the cob (the male swan) and the owner of the pen (the female swan), with the owner of the cob having the first pick. Alternatively, if only one cygnet was disputed, one owner might pay half the value to the other or might be promised the next bird from the match. If there were three cygnets, the person upon whose land the nest was built might have an entitlement to the third one, although the value would be less than the other two, as long as he paid a fee to the monarch.

The ownership system for cygnets is different to that which applies to the ownership of most other baby animals, which at common law belong to the mother's owner. In the *Case of Swans*, Edward Coke explains this as follows:

> The law thereof is founded on a reason in nature; for the Cock Swan is an emblem or representation of an affectionate and true Husband to his Wife above all other Fowle; for the Cock Swan holdeth himself to one female only; and for this cause nature hath conferred on him a gift beyond all others; that is, to die so joyfully, that he sings sweetly when he dies; upon which the Poet saith,
>
> > *Dulcia defecta modulatur carmina lingua,*
> > [The swan, chanter of its own death,]
> >
> > *Cantator, cygnus, funeris ipse sui, &c*
> > [modulates sweet songs with failing tongue]

And therefore this case of the swan doth differ from the case of Kine, or other brute beasts.

The Latin quote in the judgment is from the Roman poet Martial, and reflects the classical belief that swans were generally silent but sang a beautiful song upon their death. In fact, the 'swan song' is entirely mythical, but there is a germ of truth to the idea that swans are pair bonded: swans mostly do stay together (they rarely 'divorce'). The female Australian black swan, however, is distinctly less faithful to her mate than her European relatives.

Queen Elizabeth II has chosen not to exercise her rights in relation to unmarked swans, with the exception of those in certain stretches of the River Thames. The only private parties to now own marked swans are the Dyers Company and the Vintners Company. Dyers, Vintners and the queen still conduct annual swan uppings on the Thames for the purposes of swan conservation.

It remains generally illegal to eat swans in England, but for different reasons. Mute swans are protected as a 'wild bird' by the *Wildlife and Countryside Act 1981* (UK). Under this Act, it is an offence to kill, injure or take a wild bird, or to disturb, destroy or take its eggs. The only person who could presumably eat swan in England is the queen, but this is simply because she would have sovereign immunity, not because of any deeper principle.

'Royal Fish'

The *Case of Swans* also noted that all whales and sturgeon are 'royal fish', owned by the monarch of England. This was stated in 1322, by an Act of Edward II called *Prerogativa Regis* or *Of the King's Prerogatives*. It provided:

The King shall have Wreck of the Sea throughout the Realm, Whales and [great Sturgeons] taken in the Sea or elsewhere within the Realm, except in certain Places privileged by the King.

Porpoises and dolphins are also regarded as falling under this law, which extends to Scotland and Northern Ireland.

The monarch's entitlement to the 'wreck of the sea' (goods that had been washed ashore by a shipwreck) was removed in 1894 by the *Merchant Shipping Act 1894*, but the rest of this particular section of *Prerogativa Regis* remains in force. Consequently, when a Welsh fisherman named Robert Davies caught a 10-foot long sturgeon in 2004, he offered the fish to the Receiver of Wrecks, the official presently appointed to dispose of 'royal fish' in England, Wales and Northern Ireland on behalf of the queen. The queen declined it and said that Mr Davies was entitled to dispose of the sturgeon as he wished.

Of course, the fact that whales are called 'royal fish' raises the inevitable objection that whales, porpoises and dolphins are not in fact fish at all. In his 1935 book *Uncommon Law*, A.P. Herbert invents a humorous case in which a dead whale has washed ashore in an English town. As the whale starts to decompose and smell, the townspeople and the monarchy both disclaim liability for disposing of it. Eventually, the Ministry of Agriculture, Fisheries and Food points out that the whale is a mammal, not a fish, and the case against the monarchy is adjourned.

There is also genuine case law describing who owns wild whales from the days when whales were routinely hunted – almost to extinction in some cases. Melville's famous novel *Moby-Dick* summarises the legal difference between a 'fast-fish' and a 'loose-fish':

Yes; these laws might be engraven upon a Queen Anne's farthing, or the barb of a harpoon, and worn around the neck, so small are they.

i. A Fast-Fish belongs to the party fast to it.

ii. A Loose-Fish is fair game for anyone, for anybody who can soonest catch it.

But what plays the mischief with this masterly code is the admirable brevity of it, which necessitates a vast volume of commentaries to expound it.

First: What is a Fast-Fish? Alive or dead, a fish is technically fast when it is connected with an occupied ship or boat, by any medium at all controllable by the occupant or occupants, – a mast, an oar, a nine-inch cable, a telegraph wire, or a strand of cobweb, it is all the same. Likewise a fish is technically fast when it bears a waif [a long poled flag used to locate a floating carcass], or any other recognised symbol of possession; so long as the party waifing it plainly evince their ability at any time to take it alongside, as well as their intention so to do.

This passage accurately describes the common law as it applied to whalers in Greenland, as stated in the eighteenth-century cases *Littledale v Scaith* and *Hogarth v Jackson*. Again, control and the ability to impede movement were pivotal.

Greenland's rule was not applied uniformly, however. Property law scholar Robert C. Ellickson notes that different jurisdictions had different rules, based on the behaviour of the whales that occupied them. The 'fast-fish' rule applied in Greenland, which is inhabited by right whales. They are relatively slow, mild-mannered whales, and are unlikely to break the harpoon line. Therefore, a 'bright line' rule that required attachment was suitable. Whales in other parts of the world were faster and more likely to break the line or capsize a boat if whalers attempted to hold onto them. Accordingly, a different rule was necessary.

Thus, in the 1881 US case of *Ghen v Rich*, when Ghen shot a fin whale with a specially marked 'bomb lance', Ghen was still able to claim it as his when the fin whale sank and its carcass washed up 17 miles away on a local beach. A third party, Ellis, found the whale and subsequently sold it to Rich, but Ghen brought evidence that the local custom around Cape Cod was that whales belonged to the person who had 'first iron', and that any-one who found it was to notify the fisherman and receive a salvage fee. The court accepted this custom, finding that Ghen retained ownership. Rich had already processed the whale, shipping off the blubber and trying out the whale oil, but had to pay Ghen damages for the tort of 'conversion' or 'trover', because he had interfered with Ghen's right to possession.

The court said that there were sound reasons for applying local custom, not the common law rule:

> Unless [the custom] is sustained, this branch of industry must neces-sarily cease, for no person would engage in it if the fruits of his labor could be appropriated by any chance finder. It gives reasonable sal-vage for securing or reporting the property. That the rule works well in practice is shown by the extent of the industry which has grown up under it, and the general acquiescence of a whole community inter-ested to dispute it. It is by means clear that without regard to usage, the common law would not reach the same result.

The local custom of alerting the hunter and paying a salvage fee to the finder allowed for the efficient disposal of a large, soon-to-be rotten carcass, while preserving the hunter's labour. In the 1901 New Zealand case *Baldick v Jackson*, local custom was applied to similar effect.

Incidentally, the sovereign's right to 'royal fish' is highly unlikely to apply to Commonwealth countries. The question was raised in *Baldick v Jackson*, and Chief Justice Stout said of New Zealand:

> Whaling was common in New Zealand prior to New Zealand being proclaimed a part of the British dominions. After it was declared part of the British dominions, and whilst under the dominion of New South Wales, no claim was ever made to the whales caught in New Zealand as royal fish, and whaling was very active in New Zealand after 1829 ... I am of opinion that this statute has no applicability to New Zealand, and that though the right to whales is expressly claimed in the statute of 17 Ed II, c 2, as part of the Royal prerogative, it is one not only that has never been claimed, but one that it would have been impossible to claim without claiming it against the Maoris, for they were accustomed to engage in whaling; and the Treaty of Waitangi assumed that their fishing was not to be interfered with – they were to be left in undisturbed possession of their lands, estates, forests, fisheries, &c.

It is therefore unlikely that this right to 'royal fish' ever extended to Australia either.

Exotic Animals

People have always wanted to own exotic animals. The Romans even had a specific dock just for unloading them. Throughout history, exotic wild animals have been kept in menageries, zoos and homes, or used in events such as circuses, whether the Roman sort – in which gladiators or prisoners sometimes fought to the death with wild animals – or more modern circuses that feature animals performing tricks.

The ownership of a sea lion was at issue in *Mullett v Bradley*, an American case from 1898. Mullett was in the business of capturing sea lions off the coast of California and selling them to exhibitors in New York. When he injured a sea lion during its capture, the prospective buyer rejected the sale. Mullett placed the sea lion on an island while he looked for another purchaser, but the sea lion escaped and disappeared. One year after the sea lion's disappearance, Mullett discovered that it was in the possession of

Bradley. Bradley had bought him from a fisherman who had caught him 70 miles off the coast of New York.

Once again, the question was whether the original pursuer (Mullett) still owned the wild animal, even though he had subsequently lost control over it. The Supreme Court of New York decided that sea lions were wild animals, and when they escaped, they therefore regained their liberty and became wild again. Mullett attempted to argue that sea lions could not regain their liberty until they reached their home waters, but the court rejected this argument. Therefore, when the fisherman caught the escaped sea lion, he established a qualified property right to the animal and could sell it to Bradley.

This discussion brings us back to the case of exotic-animal collector Yasmin Nakhuda. Undeterred by losing her legal case to retain ownership of Darwin the Japanese macaque, Nakhuda moved to a different area in Canada, which at that time did not have by-laws against owning exotic animals, and purchased a large farm. In 2015, the *Toronto Star* reported that she had obtained two more Japanese macaques, named Tibet and Sumo, whom she kept in separate enclosures. Somewhat mysteriously, a 2016 *Huffington Post* article reported that she had a Japanese macaque named Caesar and another monkey named Diva, as well as two miniature donkeys, a wallaroo, alpacas, two marmosets, two ferrets and a black-and-white fox. It is not clear if Tibet and Sumo had been renamed or replaced. In 2017, the area to which Nakhuda had moved passed a by-law banning ownership of exotic animals, but allowing residents to keep their existing animals.

Ownership of Domesticated Animals

What if Judge Vallee had held Darwin to be a domesticated animal, capable of being owned in an unqualified way by Yasmin Nakhuda? As it happens, it would not have made a difference in this particular case. TAS had the authority to detain Darwin on the basis of its power under by-laws prohibiting people from keeping monkeys and various other animals in Toronto. Moreover, when Nakhuda turned up to TAS's offices and demanded that Darwin be returned to her, she signed a form surrendering Darwin to TAS. Nonetheless, the situation with regard to ownership of domestic animals is more straightforward than that of wild animals.

Before we go any further, it is necessary to consider what domestication means and what it entails. It has been theorised that domestication of animals arose in three different ways. First, the 'commensal pathway' of domestication arose when wild animals (including dogs, cats and chickens) were attracted to human settlements by the presence of food and developed a partnership with people. Second, the 'prey pathway' of domestication arose when actively hunted animals (including cows, goats, sheep and pigs) began to be managed by humans. Third, the 'directed pathway' arose when humans made a deliberate effort to capture, domesticate and use certain animals (including horses, camels and donkeys).

Humans and animals have lived and worked together for a very long time, hence the ancient nature of some laws regarding ownership and control of animals, but it is not precisely clear when domestication began. It may have occurred in multiple places at different times.

The dog appears to be the first animal to be domesticated, but again it is unclear exactly when this started: it could have been anywhere between 40,000 and 14,000 years ago. Dogs coexisted with humans, and in effect, domesticated themselves.

The earliest archaeological evidence may have been found in the Chauvet Cave in France, which is estimated to have been blocked by a rockfall about 25,000 years ago, before the last ice age. The cave floor shows the preserved imprints of the feet of a human child, aged about ten years old, alongside those of a dog. The dog's footprints were distinguishable from wolf footprints, which were also found in the cave, by the shorter middle toe of the front paw.

There is also early evidence of affectionate relationships between humans and dogs. In 1914, the bones of a puppy with distemper were discovered along with the bones of humans, buried in a quarry in Germany 14,000 years ago; the puppy could not have survived without tender care.

Archaeological evidence shows that some Neolithic people seemed to bury dogs with or near the dead, and fed them the same food as humans, indicating a profound attachment. In early Mesopotamian epic poems *The Descent of Inanna* and *The Epic of Gilgamesh*, characters keep dogs on collars and leashes.

The next animals to be domesticated were goats, sheep and chickens. What then of cats? They are relative latecomers in the chronology of domestication. It appears that they coexisted with humans in a wild state for some time (hunting rodents and so forth once we began to store grain) until they consented to become domesticated.

In Rudyard Kipling's story 'The Cat that Walked by Himself', the human characters invite a dog, horse and cow to join them, which each animal does, submitting to domestication, but upon every invitation, the cat says to the humans, 'I am not a friend and I am not a servant. I am the Cat who walks by himself and all places are alike to me.' The story ends with the cat being partly, but not fully, tamed:

[The Cat] will kill mice and he will be kind to babies when he is in the house, just as long as they do not pull his tail too hard. But when he has done that, and between times, and when the moon gets up and night comes, he is the Cat that walks by himself, and all places are alike to him. Then he goes out to the Wet Wild Woods or up the Wet Wild Trees or on the Wet Wild Roofs, waving his wild tail and walking by his wild lone.

The reason Kipling's tale resonates is because, like all good fables, there is truth to it, a truth that is reflected in history and the law. Although cats are genetically domesticated (tabby coats are not found in wild cats), they still retain a distinctive tendency to roam. They cannot be controlled in the ways we often associate with possession and ownership of other domestic animals. Hence, as Justice Hammond of the New Zealand High Court put it, 'Dogs are rigorously controlled, whilst, if I may be permitted the expression, cats are entitled to ponce about town, completely unregulated.'

American judges have a similar opinion. Thus in the US case *McDonald v Jodrey* [1890], in which a domestic cat killed a neighbour's canary, the judge said:

Cats attach themselves to places rather than to persons, and are rather harbored than owned. They are not subject to direction like dogs, nor can they be put under the same restraint as most other domestic animals. To such extent, they may be regarded as still undomesticated, and their predatory habits as but a remnant of their wild nature.

Cats' tendency to wander may raise issues if, when their owners are out, they frequent the homes of other people. In England, a couple in Hammersmith, London, recently accused their neighbour of attempting to claim their cat Ozzy as her own. The neighbour was feeding Ozzy, who regularly visited her home. The neighbour then asserted Ozzy would be better off with her, resulting in a four-year legal battle, in which the couple sought injunctions restraining the neighbour from feeding or interacting with the cat. The case settled in January 2020, just before it was due to be heard in the Central London County Court, after the neighbour gave copious undertakings not to interact with the cat anymore. Apparently disputes involving wandering cats are not unusual.

Many people think of domestic animals as being members of their families (particularly companion animals). However, other domestic animals are used for labour and to produce food and other products, such as fleece. As noted at the outset of this chapter, domestic animals are property, and are generally treated at law accordingly, subject to legislation about animal cruelty and certain criminal laws, which we discuss further in Chapter 5.

Forms of Ownership

Domestic animals can be subject to many forms of ownership. They can be held in partnership (a form of joint ownership), held on trust or mortgaged. Stock liens can be imposed over sheep, cattle and all kinds of agricultural animals. There is even an English case involving the mortgage of a dog! Racehorses are often jointly owned. They can be a very valuable asset, because they provide entertainment for those who enjoy racing, and if they win races their owners receive prize money. Racehorses can even be used as security for loans.

Saltoon v Lake, a 1978 New South Wales case, dealt with several of these forms of ownership. The question was whether a mortgage over a racehorse called Mighty Khan was valid. Saltoon had loaned Scali $20,000, secured by a mortgage over four horses, one of which was Mighty Khan. Scali sold Mighty Khan to three people (all members of the Lake family), but he did not tell them about the mortgage. Saltoon's solicitor mailed a letter informing the new owners of the mortgage, but they did not receive it. When Scali went bankrupt and could not repay the loan, Saltoon attempted to seize the horse to repay his debts. The new owners of Mighty Khan were unsuccessful in resisting this.

It is possible to become the owner of an animal that has been given as a gift. However, in order to be legally valid, the gift must comply with certain requirements – for instance, an intention to give the animal as a gift should be demonstrable.

In *Glaister-Carlisle v Glaister-Carlisle*, a husband and wife disputed the ownership of a white miniature poodle named Springtime Ballyhoo. The poodle had originally been owned by the husband, but when she mated with his wife's black poodle and conceived puppies as a result, the couple argued, and the husband threw Springtime Ballyhoo at his wife, saying, 'She is your responsibility now.' The wife alleged that in doing so, her husband gifted her with the pregnant poodle. Later, unsurprisingly, the parties were estranged, and the husband sought to have Springtime Ballyhoo returned to him, going so far as to kidnap the poodle from his wife. The Court of Appeal held that, while possession of the dog had been delivered to the wife, there had been no intention to give her to the wife as a gift (quite the opposite).

Conversely, in an Australian dispute in 2021, *Chow v Chang*, the court found that one of the parties had intended to gift a pet to the other. Maurice Chow and Marina (Siwen) Chang, former de facto partners, were in a dispute about the ownership of a Pomeranian dog, Kobe. After their relationship broke down in 2019, Chang retained the dog, and Chow sued to obtain ownership of him. Chow argued that he had paid for the dog, and that Kobe belonged to him. Chang argued that Kobe was a gift to her. Magistrate Hoare held that Chow had intended to give Kobe to Chang as a gift:

> The weight of evidence, particularly of Ms Chang and corroborated by the content of the contemporaneous text messages such as 'buy me a dog lol' and 'b'day gift please', satisfied me that, as a matter of fact and law, Mr Chow purchased the Dog with the intention of gifting it to Ms Chang. I find that Mr Chow purchased the Dog at her request and to accede to a dearly held wish of hers in the context of a then loving relationship … In my opinion, when weighing the oral evidence and the content of the contemporaneous text messages, it is simply implausible that he purchased the Dog for himself intending Ms Chang merely to have enjoyment of it.

The fact that Chow, an astute businessman, had put Chang's name on the ownership documents and on the receipt (notwithstanding the fact that he paid the purchase price) further strengthened the magistrate's conclusion. After the decision was handed down, Chang said to the media, 'I have invested a lot of time looking after him and training him; essentially he's my baby. Which is why I spent the time and effort to go to court – I didn't want to lose him.' Meanwhile, Chow said that he would not appeal the decision, but he missed Kobe every day. 'Despite whatever the court says, I still think that dog should be mine. He is amazing. He's fast for his size, he's brave and he's very playful.'

Even corporations can become embroiled in passionate battles about dogs. New Yorker Barry Myrick was drawn into a series of legal battles with his employer, the cleaning company M&M Environmental, over the ownership of a pit bull cross called Roxy. Roxy was owned by the cleaning company, and her job was to sniff out bed bugs. However, during the four years that Myrick was partnered with Roxy at work, Myrick and his wife paid for her food and vet bills, and Roxy lived with them when she was not working. Myrick was laid off in March 2020 as a result of COVID-19, but while he returned other items and equipment to the company, as he was required to do under his contract, he did not give Roxy back. The dispute arose because the company regarded Roxy as a useful and valuable piece of equipment that belonged to them, whereas Myrick regarded Roxy as part of his family. The company alleged he had stolen the dog, and he spent fifteen hours in jail in August 2020. The company also filed civil proceedings against Myrick and sought to stop his supporters from raising money to assist him with legal fees. In May 2021, the company settled its dispute with Myrick, and ownership of Roxy has now been transferred to him.

'Defective' Animals

Animals with defects are treated as defective property. One prominent New South Wales case from 1976 involved a claim about a defective bull. McBride had paid $21,000 for stud bull, Midgeon Supreme, after the auctioneer employed by Elder Smith Goldsborough Mort Ltd had said he thought the bull was the best shown. The contract of sale had an exclusion clause, which provided that because the bulls had been made available for inspection, they would be purchased with all faults, for which the vendors would not be liable. However, Midgeon Supreme turned out to be infertile, a fault which could not have been discerned upon inspection.

The judge held that the sale of Midgeon Supreme was governed by the *Sale of Goods Act 1923* (NSW), and was thus subject to an implied term that the goods would conform with their description. Midgeon Supreme was described and sold as a stud bull, but he was not capable of siring offspring.

The judge awarded McBride the difference in price between what he had paid for the bull ($21,000) and the value of the bull if he was sent for slaughter ($500). The bull's meat was clearly thought to be his only value, and McBride was expected to slaughter him if he so chose. There is no evidence of what eventually happened to Midgeon Supreme.

The way damages are measured for defective animals depends on the animals' purpose and the circumstances of their purchase. In *Vieira v O'Shea*, a 2012 case involving the sale of a racehorse, Vieira purchased an interest in a racehorse on the advice of O'Shea, a horse trainer, who said the horse was free of any health problems that would inhibit its ability to race. In the event, the horse had a pre-cystic lucency in a joint in its left hind leg, which required surgery and two years' recovery before the horse could race again. The New South Wales Court of Appeal again treated the case as one where a person has bought defective property on the basis of misinformation. And again, the value of the animal was deemed to be the difference between its price at the time of sale and its true value (in this case, that value was measured at the time the horse recovered from the injuries, at which point it would have been reasonable to expect Vieira to reduce his losses by selling his interest, a legal principle called mitigation). Vieira was also allowed to recover certain costs he had incurred in treating the horse.

Judging an animal's value is obviously more difficult when a person's interest in an animal is not financial, but emotional. Monty Python's famous 'Dead Parrot Sketch' deals with a situation in which a man complains to a pet shop owner that the parrot he purchased from the shop is dead:

MR PRALINE: I wish to complain about this parrot what I purchased, not half an hour ago, from this very boutique.

SHOP OWNER: Oh yes, the, uh, the Norwegian Blue ... What's, uh ... What's wrong with it?

MR PRALINE: I'll tell you what's wrong with it, my lad. 'E's dead, that's what's wrong with it!

SHOP OWNER: No, no, 'e's, uh ... he's resting.

MR PRALINE: Look, matey, I know a dead parrot when I see one, and I'm looking at one right now.

SHOP OWNER: No, no, he's not dead, he's, he's restin'! Remarkable bird, the Norwegian Blue, idn'it, ay? Beautiful plumage!

MR PRALINE: The plumage don't enter into it. It's stone dead.

SHOP OWNER: Nononono, no, no! 'E's resting!

While this sketch is one of Monty Python's most hilarious, a sick companion animal may be no laughing matter for owners. If an animal turns out to be unwell or to have health problems, it is treated as a form of defective property.

In *Davy v Kidwai*, a Canadian case from 2020, Michael Davy bought an eclectus parrot called Tiberius from Akhtar Kidwai for C\$2100. According to Davy, Kiwai said Tiberius was moulting and had clipped wings, but was otherwise healthy. One month after purchase, Tiberius was diagnosed as having psittacine beak and feather disease (PBFD), and his condition deteriorated rapidly after that. The Civil Resolution Tribunal of British Columbia, which heard the case, found that Tiberius was a 'chattel' for the purposes of the British Columbia *Sale of Goods Act*, under which there is an implied warranty guaranteeing that the goods sold will be durable for a reasonable period. The expected lifespan of an eclectus parrot is normally thirty to forty years, but a veterinarian said that Tiberius's life span would be greatly reduced by his incurable PBFD, and that he may not live long (between several months and several years). The tribunal member ordered Kidwai to refund 75 per cent of the purchase price and to pay for veterinary care expenses in relation to Tiberius.

Similar cases have occurred in Australia. In one matter, the Bird family (with the assistance of the Animal Law Institute and pro bono legal representation) sued a breeder for selling them a dog that turned out to be neither purebred nor dewormed as claimed. Less than a week after buying Nala, the Birds realised she was very unwell and infested with worms, probably contracted in utero from her mother. The Birds sought immediate veterinary treatment for Nala, which saved her life, but she had ongoing health issues. The Birds were able to sue Nala's breeder under certain consumer guarantees, non-excludable mandatory standards of quality in the supply of goods and services to consumers under the Australian Consumer Law. Section 54 of this law provides (among other things) that goods supplied to a consumer must be of acceptable quality, fit for purpose, free from defects and durable. The decision was unreported, but the Victorian Civil and Administrative Tribunal awarded the Birds \$15,521.96 for past and future veterinary fees to treat Nala's health problems.

These cases can be contrasted with a 2021 case from Wales, *Pendragon v Coom*. Judy Coom bought an Old English sheepdog named Lady for £1000 from a professional breeder, Anette Pendragon. The breeder sold Lady to Coom at a reduced price, as she was the product of an accidental mating and was not registered with the Kennel Club. Coom was happy with this deal – she did not want to show Lady as a pedigree dog, she wanted her as a pet. However, some months after Coom bought Lady, the dog developed hip dysplasia and diabetes insipidus, and required significant medical attention, including hip replacements. Coom sought payment of the medical costs of treating Lady. Pendragon refused, but offered to refund Coom's money if Lady was returned to her. Coom did not want to return the dog, and instead sued Pendragon under the *Consumer Rights Act 2015* (UK), on the basis that the goods sold were not of 'satisfactory quality'.

At the first hearing, Deputy District Court Judge Wilson found that Lady's hip dysplasia rendered her of unsatisfactory quality. While Lady's mother did not have hip dysplasia, measurement of her hips had shown that her puppies were highly likely to develop the condition and, although there was some dispute as to whether Pendragon became aware of it before or after the sale, Wilson found that she should have informed Coom of the risk. Among other things, Pendragon was required to pay the 'costs of repair', being the vet bills for the treatment of the hip dysplasia not covered by insurance (over £4000).

However, on appeal, Judge Keyser held that the defect was a latent one, which could not have been known at the point of sale, and that there had been no misrepresentation. Keyser found Coom was not entitled to be reimbursed for any of the costs of Lady's treatment that Coom incurred after April 2019, on the basis that it had been unreasonable for her to keep Lady and seek to 'repair' her:

> In my judgment, the reasonable course for Ms Coom was to exercise her statutory right to reject Lady. She would then have been entitled to recover the price paid for the dog. She might also have been entitled to recover some damages. She would, anyway, have avoided substantial expense that was quite out of proportion to the value of the dog…
>
> Ms Coom advances two further reasons why it was reasonable not to reject Lady. First, she says that she was attached to her pet. That

may be so, but I do not accept that it made it reasonable to retain the animal at an expense that was disproportionate to its value and that she is most unlikely to have considered incurring without recourse to insurance and to a third party to pick up the bill. Second, she says that she was concerned that Ms Pendragon would have tried to breed from Lady. I do not accept that this is a valid reason for acting in a manner that resulted in such significant financial outlay, especially on the tenuous evidence supporting such an alleged belief.

Judge Keyser simply treated Lady like any other faulty chattel, which could be readily exchanged for a new chattel. Barrister Rosalind English said that the decision, 'though consistent with consumer and contract law, strikes a discordant note in current times'.

This case leads into our next topic: how do we compensate people when another person harms their animal? As we will see, the law again vacillates between treating the animal as a chattel and treating the animal as something with special value.

Harming Other People's Animals

If a person harms or kills a domestic animal belonging to someone else, then the person will be liable for interfering with another's property (through the torts of trespass to goods or conversion) or for failing to exercise reasonable care (through the tort of negligence). This principle has an ancient history, and even the Code of Hammurabi, a set of Babylonian laws dating back to c. 1754 BCE, has stipulations for dealing with harm to oxen and asses:

> If anyone hire an ox or an ass, and a lion kill it in the field, the loss is upon its owner.

> If anyone hire oxen, and kill them by bad treatment or blows, he shall compensate the owner, oxen for oxen.

> If a man hire an ox, and he break its leg or cut the ligament of its neck, he shall compensate the owner with ox for ox.

> If anyone hire an ox, and put out its eye, he shall pay the owner one-half of its value.

If anyone hire an ox, and break off a horn, or cut off its tail, or hurt its muzzle, he shall pay one-fourth of its value in money.

If anyone hire an ox, and God strike it that it die, the man who hired it shall swear by God and be considered guiltless.

Echoing these laws, St Thomas Aquinas later opined that when another person wrongfully killed an ox belonging to someone else, they committed theft, because the ox was property.

Even indirect actions can cause harm to animals, giving rise to damages for owners. Recently, a Dutch owner of two rare hyacinth macaws (collectively worth €40,000) and a yellow-naped Amazon parrot (worth €1250) successfully sued a hot air balloonist for €62,000, after it was established that his parrots died of shock when the balloonist fired his main burner just 50 metres from the parrots while competing in a race. Apparently, balloonists typically mark where animals are and take care not to scare them, but the presence of the parrots had somehow been missed in this instance.

On the other hand, in the 1951 Canadian case of *Nova Mink v Trans-Canada Airlines*, the airline was not held liable for negligence when a low-flying aeroplane so scared the mink in a commercial mink farm that they ate their own young, causing the farm owner considerable financial loss. The difficulty in this case was that the airline could not have foreseen the consequences of its pilot's actions – in legal parlance, it was not a 'reasonably foreseeable' event that the plane might fly over a mink farm and cause mink to eat their young.

The law struggles to provide compensation for companion animals above and beyond their value as an item of property – note that the owner of the parrots was compensated according to the parrots' considerable market value. When someone tortiously damages property, generally the damages are measured by the market cost of a replacement, but this presumes that the property is replaceable and had no special meaning to the owner.

This rule is difficult to apply in the case of companion animals, where the owner may suffer significant distress as a result of an injury to, or the death of, a companion animal. For instance, in a Tasmanian case from 1927, *Davies v Bennison*, Davies sought damages after Bennison (her neighbour) shot and killed her cat. Davies sought £150 as compensation, not only for the value of the cat but also for the extreme distress and physical health problems she had suffered as a result of seeing her cat killed. The court found that Bennison had committed trespass by shooting into Davies' yard, but the measure of damages was simply the market value of a replacement cat (£2). At that point in time, even if Davies had witnessed a person being killed, she would not have been entitled to damages for distress.

In recent times, a similar approach has been taken in the United States. In a Texan case, Carol Schuster's dog, Licorice, was taken to a dog store to be groomed. Licorice escaped from the custody of a store employee when she was taken outside to relieve herself, and could not be found. Schuster and the store employees spent several days looking for Licorice, but, sadly, her body was found four days later, after she had apparently been run over. Schuster claimed damages for lost wages during the time she was searching for Licorice, loss of companionship, mental anguish and exemplary damages (designed to punish for malicious wrongdoing). While Justice Pemberton acknowledged that 'there are myriad examples that Texans today view dogs more as companions, friends, or even something akin to family than as an economic tool or benefit', he said was not free to depart from previous cases which said that the subjective value of a companion animal was not recoverable. The animal was simply property, and Schuster was only entitled to the fair market replacement value of the dog (US$500).

Conversely, in a 2004 Australian case, *Beaumont v Cahir*, the court recognised the unique bond between a human and a horse. When Beaumont negligently landed his hot air balloon in a paddock, the balloon startled Cahir's horse, Yhani, causing her to impale herself on an uncapped star picket. Cahir did not want to buy a replacement horse, because she had an affectionate and unique relationship with Yhani. She instead sought the costs of restoring Yhani to health, which the magistrate awarded her. Beaumont appealed the judgment on the basis that the desire to reinstate Yhani to health was unreasonable, and that he should only be required to pay Cahir the value of a replacement horse and the cost of euthanising Yhani. On appeal, Justice Cooper rejected Beaumont's argument, saying:

> It was a relevant circumstance that the horse was an animate chattel, was a horse which the respondent had put substantial time and money into since she acquired it in order to improve its general condition and to train with it as a horse upon which she could compete in dressage horse riding, and was a horse which suited her particular requirements as a rider ...

What the learned magistrate did was to treat the fact that the horse was an injured suffering animal which required an immediate decision as to its treatment as one of the relevant circumstances against which reasonableness was to tested.

Cahir was entitled to the costs of restoring Yhani to health. However, if Yhani had died, it is unlikely Cahir would have received damages under Australian law for the distress this would have caused her.

In Canada, damages for the distress caused by the loss of a companion animal were awarded in *Ferguson v Birchmount Boarding Kennels Ltd.* A dog named Harley was placed in boarding kennels while his owners, the Fergusons, were on holiday in Hawaii. Harley escaped the kennels by squeezing through two boards in the enclosed play area while he was being exercised. He was never seen again. Mrs Ferguson was particularly badly affected by Harley's escape – she was emotionally distraught and hysterical after she heard the news, and later suffered from insomnia and nightmares, and had to take time off work. Later, the Fergusons obtained another dog of the same breed as Harley. When the case was first heard in the Small Claims Court, Deputy Judge Yee awarded damages not only for the cost of a replacement animal, but also to compensate for the pain and suffering the Fergusons experienced as a result of Harley's loss. The kennel appealed, but Justice Chapnik held that the deputy judge had been right to award damages for pain and suffering given 'the evidence of the [Fergusons'] relationship with Harley, and Harley's unique abilities and nature'. Hence, Harley could not simply be treated as equivalent to inanimate property.

Companion Animals and Family Breakdowns

As we have already seen, when a marriage or de facto relationship breaks down, the ownership of any shared companion animals may be disputed. Sometimes animals can even cause the break-up! Every now and then, it is reported in newspapers that one person in a relationship taught a parrot owned by both parties to say rude things about the other, leading to the couple's subsequent divorce.

Companion animals are regarded as 'property' for the purposes of the distribution of assets. Consequently, in Australia, animals are covered by provisions in the *Family Law Act 1975* (Cth) that determine how property is to be divided between spouses. However, while money is easy to divide, a living companion animal is indivisible. There is not much case law in Australia regarding custody of companion animals. For children of a marriage or a de facto relationship, there may be shared residence and contact regimes between parents, but there is no express provision for a court to award such arrangements for companion animals. Generally parties seek to settle any dispute about animal custody outside court.

One rare case in which the custody of a companion animal was considered extensively is *Downey & Beale*, a 2017 decision of the Federal Circuit Court of Australia. Downey and Beale, who were formerly married, were arguing about the ownership of a dog. Before they were married, the couple had gone together to purchase the dog in question, and the husband had paid for him. The couple did not cohabitate before their marriage, and the dog lived at the wife's parents' home after he was purchased. The wife paid for his veterinary bills and other needs, and was also listed on veterinary bills as the 'owner'. Upon the breakdown of the relationship, the dog stayed with the wife, but the husband later registered himself as the dog's owner and asked the judge to transfer ownership to him.

Judge Joe Harman was aware that the parties might not regard the dog as property, but as something more important:

> I am conscious of that, opined by Roger Caras, 'Dogs are not our whole life, but they make our lives whole.' I am completely empathetic with the importance this issue holds for the parties, and conscious that the parties ... may consider this sentient creature, this living being, as fundamentally important to them.

The judge noted that 'neither party seeks to apportion a value to [the dog] and appropriately so. They do not argue that his worth is monetary. His worth is their love and affection for the creature as they express it.' However, despite the feelings of Downey, Beale and the judge, the dispute over ownership of the dog was to be resolved according to property law principles, because that is how our law categorises animals. In the event, it was decided that the wife was the dog's owner, and it was not appropriate to remove him from her possession.

In the 2020 decision *Davenport & Davenport*, a husband sought 'shared custody' of the dog owned by him and his wife during their marriage. The wife was the registered owner and had the dog in her possession. There was a dispute over which of the parties had purchased the dog. Judge Tonkin concluded that because the husband had sought custody of the dog (rather than a division of property), she did not have the power to deal with the matter and dismissed the application. The court would, however, have had the power to deal with the ownership of the dog with as a matter of property, as in *Downey & Beale*.

The rare circumstance in which a court may rule on the custody of a companion animal is when it is tied to the custody of a child, if it is deemed to be in a child's best interests that the companion animal accompany them. For instance, in the 2007 case *Jarvis & Weston*, a child expressed fear that his dog would not be looked after if it was left at his father's house while he stayed with his mother. The judge determined that the dog should go with the child.

The inability of courts to deal sensitively with the custody of companion animals in the event of family breakdowns has led Australian legal academic Tony Bogdanowski to argue that legislation should be enacted to deal with this issue, recognising the importance of companion animals as family members.

In the United States, it is a different story: there have been a number of high-profile cases involving divorce and custody of companion animals. Some US states take a 'best interests of the animal' approach, which means that in appropriate cases, joint custody can be awarded regardless of who has legal title to the animal. Other US states take a property-based approach to animal disputes. Decisions made in those states have generally held that possession should follow the legal title, custody agreements are not enforceable and that the interests of animals are not relevant (in fact, courts have been known to be dismissive of the suggestion that they should be). Exceptions may be made if there is evidence that the legal title holder has abused the animal in question.

The Israeli Family Court considered a 'best interests of the animal' approach in *Ploni v Plonit*, as described in legal scholar Pablo Lerner's helpful article on the case. A de facto husband and wife had rescued a blind street cat named Jane Eyre and a dog named Shayna during their five-year relationship. The dog had suffered from a tick infestation and numerous infections, and had to have a hysterectomy. The couple's relationship broke down in an acrimonious way, and the wife took the animals with her when she left. The husband sought visitation rights, but the wife said he did not care about the animals and was seeking visitation as a means to harass her. The main animal in issue was the dog, Shayna. The court did not reject the idea that the animals were property, but it did determine that they were 'creatures with a soul', somewhere in between objects and rational beings. Under a property approach, the animals would simply have stayed with the wife (who had been their primary carer). However, the judge decided to seek evidence from an expert on the best interests of the animals. The expert said that the dog was strongly attached to both the cat and the wife; she also clearly recognised the husband, but was a little nervous with him. The expert therefore recommended that the wife be granted custody, and the husband visitation rights. Ultimately, the judge declined to grant visitation rights to the husband, which he said would cause stress to the wife. He held that the wife's emotional health prevailed over the interests of the dog or the husband, particularly given that the dog's happiness seemed to be linked to the wife's.

A Singaporean case has also considered the best interests of the animal, with the added complication that the estranged parties lived in different countries at the time of the dispute. Mr and Ms Tan had adopted a dog named Sasha while living together in the United States. After the parties' relationship broke down, Ms Tan had taken Sasha back to Singapore with Mr Tan's knowledge. However, Mr Tan then sought to assert that he was the sole owner of the dog and entitled to custody. Justice Chan Seng Onn said that the evidence disclosed that they were (and had always intended to be) joint owners of the dog. In considering who should have custody of the dog, he considered the best interests of Sasha, and noted that in order for Sasha to be returned to Mr Tan, she would have to be sent back to the United States. Mr Tan was a surgeon who lived alone, worked long hours and did not have the capacity to look after Sasha. Conversely, Ms Tan had looked after Sasha for the previous two and a half years, and she and her family members had a very strong bond with the dog. In the circumstances, it was in the best interests of Sasha to be left in the possession of Ms Tan.

Generally speaking, if someone tortiously takes a good or chattel, or refuses to deliver goods by a contract, courts hold damages to be an adequate remedy unless the good or chattel is 'unique'. This raises particular issues for animal owners, who may prefer 'specific' enforcement, particularly in the context of custody arrangements for companion animals. 'Specific performance', as we noted earlier, is when the court orders a noncompliant party to fulfil the obligations contained in a contract. In the United States, courts are sometimes prepared to specifically enforce post-divorce custody arrangements for animals if there is evidence of an enforceable custody contract.

In the US case *Houseman v Dare*, Mr Dare and Ms Houseman, after breaking off their engagement, made an oral agreement that Ms Houseman would have primary custody of the dog, but Mr Dare would have access to the dog too. Ms Houseman went on holidays and left the dog in Mr Dare's possession. When she returned from her holiday, she asked for the dog back, but Mr Dare refused. At first instance, the trial judge awarded Ms Houseman US$1500, representing the amount originally paid for the dog (reflecting the notion that damages are usually an adequate remedy for breach of contract). However, when Ms Houseman appealed, the Superior Court of New Jersey agreed that Mr Dare should be forced to return the dog to Ms Houseman. The court noted that, traditionally, contracts for unique goods are specifically performed, and Ms Housman's affection for the dog rendered it unique.

It is unclear how this would apply in Australia. While we have a similar law regarding unique goods, up to this point there have been no cases of this nature – any cases involving specific performance of a contract for an animal have focused on animals as valuable assets, rather than animals with sentimental value.

Treating Animals as More than Property

The courts vacillate between treating animals as mere 'things' and treating them as living beings, with agency and needs of their own. We saw this ambivalence in the case of Izzy the Staffordshire terrier, discussed in the introduction. In that case, the High Court of Australia noted that one could see ownership of a companion animal as simply a property right, or one could acknowledge that animals can be very important to people, but it did not resolve the question of which conception of animals should be applied to Izzy.

It seems clear to us that, depending on the circumstances, animals cannot be property in the way that an inanimate thing can be property. But by the same token, the notion of ownership of animals is so deeply ingrained in many societies that it would be difficult to dismantle.

Would it have made a difference to the case of Darwin the Japanese macaque if Canada had a legal provision similar to that which exists in the Australian Capital Territory? The Australian Capital Territory recognised the sentience of animals by making the following amendments to the *Animal Welfare Act* in 2019:

(1) The main objects of this Act are to recognise that –

    (a) animals are sentient beings that are able to subjectively feel and perceive the world around them; and

    (b) animals have intrinsic value and deserve to be treated with compassion and have a quality of life that reflects their intrinsic value; and

    (c) people have a duty to care for the physical and mental welfare of animals.

(2) This is to be achieved particularly by –

    (a) promoting and protecting the welfare of animals; and

    (b) providing for the proper and humane care, management and treatment of animals; and

    (c) deterring and preventing animal cruelty and the abuse and neglect of animals; and

    (d) enforcing laws about the matters mentioned in paragraphs (a), (b) and (c).

With such a provision, the judge in Darwin's case might have been able to treat Darwin not only as property, but as a sentient being with a right to a quality of life reflecting his value, perhaps taking into consideration what Darwin's best interests were. But, here, the judge would have run into some difficulty – which we will return to at different points in this book – what exactly were the best interests of Darwin? Since animals cannot tell us directly, we have to guess as best we can.

It comes as no surprise to learn that the sanctuary claimed it was in Darwin's best interests to be with other primates that recognised he was a wild animal, while Nakhuda continued to insist that it was in his best interests to be uncaged, in her custody, with human contact and affection. Really, it would have been best for Darwin if he had not been separated from his family and others of his species in the first place. He is now unable to live with other Japanese macaques because there are no reserves for this species in Canada, and the lack of detail about his origins meant he could not go to a specialist reserve in the United States.

The sanctuary that Darwin lives in reported in 2019 that he was doing well, despite having difficulty socialising with other primates and keep-ers because he had been separated from his mother at a very young age. He had been put in his own enclosure, but had been befriended by two olive baboons named Sweet Pea and Pierre in the neighbouring enclosure. Unusually, Darwin had eventually been able to move into their enclosure – usually primates of different species do not get along well. After Sweet Pea died, Pierre acted as a surrogate father to Darwin. The story of the 'IKEA monkey' seems to have ended as well as it could in the circumstances.

2

CONTROLLING ANIMALS

Little Lamb who made thee
 Dost thou know who made thee
Gave thee life & bid thee feed.
By the stream & o'er the mead;
Gave thee clothing of delight,
Softest clothing wooly bright;
Gave thee such a tender voice,
Making all the vales rejoice!
 Little Lamb who made thee
 Dost thou know who made thee

'The Lamb', by William Blake, 1789

NOT ALL PEOPLE REJOICE IN LAMBS AS WILLIAM BLAKE apparently did. In 1885, American billionaire William Louis Winans was furious when he found a lamb on the edge of Morvich Forest, part of the huge Scottish estate he had leased for twenty-one years from J.T. Mackenzie in 1882. The lamb belonged to Murdoch Macrae, a shoemaker and cottar who lived on the estate with his wife and children. A cottar was a landless tenant who was given possession of a cottage in return for his labour. For many years, the previous owners and tenants of the estate had allowed the Macraes to graze their sheep on the edge of the forest, but Winans wanted to turn Morvich Forest into a deer forest and found the cottars on the estate irritating. When he told the Macraes that their sheep were trespassing, the Macraes removed them. But when the Macraes rescued and hand-reared an injured lamb, it became a companion animal for the family and sometimes strayed into the forest. Winans brought legal proceedings to prevent the lamb from trespassing, and in the first instance was granted an 'interdict', the Scottish equivalent of an injunction.

What should happen to trespassing animals? We'll see that different cultures and eras produce several legal solutions. In *Winans v Macrae*, one solution would have been to allow Winans to kill or take the lamb for himself. Many legal systems operated this way in ancient times, but over the years they generally moved away from this solution (with odd statutory exceptions where animals were particularly prone to causing harm). A second solution would have been to allow Winans to keep the lamb until Macrae paid for any damage done, but there are generally statutory limitations placed on impounding animals today. A third solution would have been to order Macrae to keep the lamb away from the forest by means of an injunction, or, if that seemed too draconian, to make him pay for any damages. But what damage could a lamb do to wild land at the edge of the forest, and how much would that be worth in monetary terms?

As it happens, it was these questions that caused the Court of Sessions to refuse the interdict requested by Winans, because the damage done by the lamb was not serious enough to warrant a coercive remedy. Lord Young said:

> If we take 200,000 acres of rough grass land, with a public road running through it and a cot on the side of it, the land being unfenced – to fence that land against children or against a pet lamb by the interdict of a Court of Justice would, I think, be an outrageous proceeding. It is impossible that children could be confined to the high road; it is impossible that a pet lamb can be confined to the high road, any more than a cat or a dog. Life in that country would not be possible if these unenclosed lands were fenced by interdict of this court against trespasses of that description. Interdict is granted by this and other courts of law where appreciable wrong was done, whether a man's property or other right was threatened or apprehended. Here there was no appreciable wrong whatever ... We will protect a man against his right being trespassed on, but not against children toddling on the land at the roadside, or against a dog or kitten going on it.

There is something delightful about the Scottish case: the impoverished shoemaker and his little lamb winning against an American billionaire. As Andrew Steven, professor of property law at Edinburgh University, said to *Scottish Legal News*, 'It has echoes of David and Goliath.'

It is worth observing that Scottish law treats these matters a little differently to English and Australian law, because the former is partly derived from Roman law, and as we have already noted, Roman law required some loss for an interdict to be granted in such a situation. Conversely, English and Australian law tend to treat property rights in land very strictly: injunctions and substantial damages have been awarded even where scaffolding or overhanging cranes infringed on someone's airspace. So, there is a possibility that Winans' injunction would have been granted in Australia.

Winans v Macrae vividly illustrates the fact that we share this world with animals but seek to control the ways they impinge on our world. Humans use some animals and indeed bring them into our world, but we want to keep our distance from others, sometimes forcibly. One of the ways we do this is through the law. In this book's introduction, we explain that wrongdoing can be punished by the state (by criminal law) or by individuals suing for damages (by private law, according to the law of tort). The state may also step in to regulate the ways in which animals are kept. The focus of this chapter is on civil wrongdoing (tort), with some nods at crime and governmental regulation.

As we have already seen when looking at the issue of owning animals, the law treats wild animals and domestic animals differently. However, in the context of controlling animals, the division works in another way again. Consider bees. For the purposes of ownership, the law generally regards bees as wild (or semiwild) animals, capable of being owned in a qualified way when they are hived, as long as they return to that hive. This view relates to the fact that bees are not easily controlled or kept to a certain area. However, the position of the law with regard to someone's liability for their failure to *control* their bees reflects the fact that bees are useful to humans and plants, and contribute to the common good. Thus, they are regarded as 'domesticated' animals, not 'pests', as wasps sometimes are. Consequently, when considering whether a beekeeper should be liable if they do not control their bees, the law recognises that bees have considerable benefits and does not consider bees an intrinsically dangerous animal, despite the fact that bees may sting humans.

Such laws focus on the competing interests of humans, rather than the interests of non-human animals, but in some respects they do take into account the characteristics of non-human animals – either as species or as individuals. In some areas of the law, the behaviour of a non-human animal is judged according to what a 'reasonable' animal of that particular species would be expected do. The idea of a 'reasonable animal' resembles the legal mechanism of the 'reasonable person', which is often used to determine the tortious actions of humans. Thus, courts slip between seeing animals as things and seeing animals as sentient or living creatures with individual wants and needs.

In the first half of this chapter, we look at domesticated animals. Uncontrolled domesticated animals can potentially cause harm to land, property and people in three broad ways. First, domesticated animals might stray and enter onto privately owned land, destroying valuable crops or property. Second, domesticated animals might annoy humans who live nearby, owing to their smells, dung or noise, for instance. Third, domesticated animals might harm humans when they interact with them in public. All of these situations potentially involve wrongdoing.

In *Read v J Lyons & Co Ltd*, Lord Simonds said:

> The law of torts has grown up historically in separate compartments and ... beasts have travelled in a compartment of their own.

This reflects the fact that there are several ancient causes of action that arose *specifically* to deal with straying and dangerous animals. 'Distress damage feasant' and 'cattle trespass' are causes of action designed to deal with straying animals that produce milk, meat, fleece or eggs. *Scienter*, mentioned in the introduction, is designed to deal with dangerous animals that cause harm to humans. There are also several general tortious causes of action that apply to wrongful conduct more broadly, including trespass (wrongfully entering someone's land), nuisance (interfering with someone's right to quiet enjoyment of their property) and negligence (carelessly causing harm to someone owed a duty of care).

In the second half of this chapter, we focus on how the law seeks to control wild animals, mainly insofar as they are 'pests' (which generally means that they cause more problems for humans than they benefit them). There are three legal issues that arise here.

First, government regulations sometimes state that certain animals are pests because they interfere with human flourishing, perhaps if they disturb or eat crops, pass disease or cause harm to people, other animals or ecosystems. Often a pest animal interferes with a human-defined use of the land – agriculture, for instance, or animal conservation. Generally, the law authorises and even encourages people to control or kill pest animals in these circumstances.

Second, there can be private disputes between individuals or businesses if one party maintains a habitat for wild or semidomesticated animals that are determined to be a nuisance or a public health and safety risk. Here, the law must set rules that prevent disputes between neighbours. The term 'nuisance' is used when we can identify a party who can be held responsible for the existence of the animals and their effects. The law's focus is on ensuring that the responsible party stops the animals from being a nuisance.

Historically, there was a third possibility: in continental European, the law could prosecute the pest animals themselves by anathematising them. Anathematisation was the process whereby the Catholic Church excluded 'heretics' from the society of the faithful. We briefly discuss one such case in this chapter, and in Chapter 6 we look at this history in more detail.

We have already seen that the laws governing the ownership of wild animals are more complex than those governing the ownership of domesticated animals. However, the reverse is true of laws for controlling animals. The control that humans exert over domesticated animals means it is easier to show ownership over them, but the accompanying obligations to control them are detailed and ancient. Conversely, the control that humans exert over wild animals is limited – meaning it is harder to demonstrate ownership – but the obligation to control them is also limited.

Domesticated Animals

Trespassing Animals

The Western notion of land ownership generally means that if you own land, you have exclusive possession of that land and can choose who or what comes onto it, including domesticated animals. If a person comes onto your land without your permission, the person is a trespasser. However, if a domesticated animal goes onto your property, its owner can also be liable for trespassing.

When animals were domesticated and farming became common, disputes about trespassing animals arose. Many ancient legal systems had laws to deal with this. In Roman law, the *actio de pastu*, which dealt with cattle that wrongfully grazed on another's land, survived the general amalgamation of laws regarding wrongful damage to property and remained a separate action. In Irish law, the system of *comaithches* required people to give 'fore-pledges' to their neighbours that they would pay compensation for damage caused by their farm animals if they trespassed.

When Australia was colonised, it inherited two ancient English torts: distress damage feasant and cattle trespass. Some states subsequently abolished these old torts, and others instituted statutory responses to the problem of straying animals, particularly dogs, goats, geese and pigs, which could presumably do the most harm to other farm animals or crops.

Distress Damage Feasant

Remember that a possible legal remedy in *Winans v Macrae* was to allow Winans, the estate owner, to seize and hold Macrae's lamb until he paid damages. This is what the tort of distress damage feasant – an ancient English tort dating back to Anglo-Saxon times – allows people to do. Holding the animal was called 'impounding', and the animal that was held as security was called the 'gage'. The name of this tort derives from the Norman French *faisant dommage* ('doing damage').

The earlier custom seems to have been to kill rather than hold straying animals. Thus, the law of the Anglo-Saxon king Ine (688–95) states:

> [If] any beast breaks hedges and wanders at large within, since its owner will not or cannot keep it under control, he who finds it on his corn land shall take it and kill it. The owner [of the beast] shall take its hide and flesh and suffer the loss of the remainder.

However, the next paragraph of this law contemplates monetary compensation and seizure of the animal in other circumstances, including where a landowner has not properly maintained a fence or has failed to fence his land.

Traces of the right to kill a straying animal survived for some time in English law. Thus, in Canterbury, Bristol or London, wandering pigs could be killed if they were repeatedly caught in the act. In Portsmouth in 1272, a wandering 'hogge' could be 'smyte of the snowte be the eyen' (deprived of the snout right back to the eyes) on its third offence. Wandering ducks could be taken by anyone in Southampton, Bristol and Coventry. In the four Scottish boroughs in 1295, the law was somewhat more vicious:

> If any one finds geese or goats damage feasant [out doing damage],
> he may take the heads of the geese and fasten their beaks in the soil

and eat their bodies, and he may kill goats and have their bodies as his escheat [taking them as unclaimed property].

The notion of punishing animals for their actions originates from the laws of ancient European societies (Greek, Roman, Teutonic, Celtic and Scandinavian), which provided that if a domestic animal caused someone death or injury, the animal had to be given to the victim or the victim's family as reparation or to allow retribution to be exacted on the animal. This is known as 'noxal surrender', from the Latin *noxa*, meaning 'guilty body'. Ancient European societies had a general horror of animals that killed people, which meant the animal's remains would not be consumed or used.

Later Roman law stipulated that the owner of a domestic animal that had injured a person was obliged to either surrender the animal (*noxae dedere*) or pay compensation for the damage it caused (*pauperies*). It seems that surrender was initially the usual remedy, but damages came to be regarded as more appropriate. Noxal surrender was applied only if the animal had harmed someone in a way that was out of character, not as a result of it being teased or in pain. It applied to the actions of not only animals but also slaves and sometimes children, which suggests a legal equivalence was drawn between animals and people who lacked legal capacity to make decisions on their own behalf.

There was a similar progression in English law. Noxal surrender was also present in Anglo-Saxon laws of Alfred the Great (from c. 899). If a 'neat' (probably an ox or cow) injured a person, the owner was to hand over the beast or compensate the victim. Similar penalties were applied to animals who strayed and caused damage to property. There were also provisions for the noxal surrender of trees: the wood was to be given to a victim's family if a tree fell on a man and killed him while it was being felled. In this sense, animals were seen either as things, like falling logs, or as part of the general environment.

Glanville Williams, the eminent English law professor, hypothesised that laws moved naturally from noxal surrender towards damages: first, the owner of a straying animal bargained with the landowner for return of the animal rather than allowing the landowner to destroy or keep it. Then, in a particular area of England, it became customary for the owner to pay a fine, which gave them the right to retrieve the animal from the other person's land (an action known as *replevin*). Eventually, the victim's right to take vengeance on the animal vanished completely, and the owner was simply liable to pay for damages.

As an illustration of this progression, the Anglo-Saxon law of King Ine evolved into the tort of distress damage feasant in medieval England. The advantage of distress damage feasant is that it is not fault-based; the difficulty is that animals have to be caught in the act of causing harm and distrained or impounded for the action to work. Moreover, it only applies to animals known as *avers*, a Norman French word for farm animals, including oxen, cows, goats, sheep, pigs, horses, donkeys, ducks, chickens, turkeys, fowl and geese – in short, animals kept for primary production of some kind.

Another difficulty is that one has to be sure they had the right to impound the animal, as wrongfully taking someone's animal also gives rise to disputes. On 18 September 1844, in Newtown, Sydney, three men, Daniel Ripley, William Dawson and Thomas Perigo, were fined ten shillings for rescuing Ripley's goat from their neighbour, John Booth, who was attempting to take the goat to the pound for trespassing on his land. (Perigo was, in fact, the great-great-great-great-grandfather of Katy Barnett, one of the authors of this book.) However, all was not as it seemed, and in October 1844, Ripley asserted that he and his companions had not attempted to rescue the goat at all. He claimed that he had simply said, within earshot of his neighbours, 'Can you stand by taking the goat here?', meaning that Booth had impounded the goat when it was on Ripley's property, not Booth's. Bystanders gave evidence that Ripley's account was more accurate, and Booth was committed for trial for perjury by Justice Windeyer. It is unclear what happened after this: nothing more is reported in the newspapers or law reports of the day.

When animals are difficult to control, it is hard to see how they can be restrained. For this reason, most laws do not provide for bees to be seized and held. Medieval Irish law was the exception. Its *Bechbretha* ('bee judgments') had a provision for *athgabál bech* or 'distraint of bees' if they repeatedly trespassed on someone's land. Identifying the bees was, of course, difficult, but Thomas Charles-Edwards and Fergus Kelly, the editors and translators of the modern edition of the text, hypothesise that the wronged landowner would sprinkle flour on the trespassing bees so that they could be identified when they returned to the hive. The philosopher Aristotle had noted this as a means of identifying bees in the ancient world. It is not entirely clear how the *athgabál bech* law worked, but the remedy for the landowner appears to have been to 'shut in' and seize the bees, and if the owner of the bees did not recognise the wrong done, the landowner could safely destroy any trespassing bees in future.

Dogs and cats are not *avers* and generally have not been impounded for distress damage feasant. This historical division persists to the current day, with dogs (and some cats) being governed by separate statutes to other domesticated animals. Under Victoria's *Domestic Animals Act 1994*, the owner or occupier of a private property that a dog or cat has entered onto on 'one more than one occasion without … permission' can 'seize' it, but must tell their local council that they have done so. After the animal's owner is notified – and can recover the animals for a fee – the owner becomes liable for a fine any time the dog or cat 'enters or remains on' that property in the future.

Distress damage feasant has been abolished in relation to animals in the United Kingdom, the Australian Capital Territory and New South Wales, and its application is limited in Tasmania. However, it still applies in other Australian states. That being said, in some jurisdictions it has probably been rendered effectively inoperative by statutory regulation for handling straying livestock. For instance, there are strict legislative provisions in Victoria for the right to impound livestock, and there is no right to destroy animals found straying. New South Wales law also has provisions as to when animals may be impounded.

Although the common law does not authorise a person to destroy an animal found straying on their property, statutes sometimes allowed this in the past. In late-nineteenth-century and early-twentieth-century New Zealand, legislation permitted a person who found an unregistered dog on their premises to destroy the dog.

In the 1890 case *Thompson v Burling*, Burling and his dog trespassed onto property owned by Thompson's father, who warned Burling to get off his property or he would ask his son to shoot the dog. When Burling did not comply and Thompson shot and wounded Burling's dog, Thompson was charged with malicious injury to property. On appeal to the New Zealand Supreme Court, the conviction was overturned because the relevant legislation empowered Thompson to 'destroy' the dog (a definition that was found to include wounding the dog). The fact that the dog was unregistered was irrelevant, as no registrar or registration office existed in New Zealand.

In *Robinson v Wagner* (1911), which took place after the relevant statute was updated, Wagner castrated Robinson's dog, which was also unregistered, after finding it on his property. When the dog subsequently became lethargic and was no longer useful as a work dog, Robinson sought damages – the dog had been worth £10 before its castration, but now Robinson could only sell it for £3. Chief Justice Stout found that Robinson had been permitted to castrate the dog because the legislation allowed someone to 'destroy' an unregistered dog, and 'destroy' meant 'ruin' as well as 'kill'.

Not to be outdone by the law of its antipodean cousin, Australian law has its own statutory oddities, primarily regarding the destruction of goats that stray onto another's land. Section 7 of New South Wales' *Inclosed Lands Protection Act 1901* (still in force) provides that the owner or occupier of enclosed land may 'destroy' any goats found trespassing on that land:

(1) Any owner, occupier, or person in charge of inclosed land may destroy any goat found trespassing thereon.

(2) Subsection (1) does not authorise the destruction of any goat that –

(a) is legibly branded, or

(b) has around its neck a collar with the name and address of its owner legibly engraved on it, or

(c) has an ear mark, or

(d) is wearing an ear tag.

The relevant law in the Australian Capital Territory has an almost identical clause.

These provisions are a hangover from early colonial times. Wandering goats and pigs were an issue from the first days of the Australian colonies, and in 1811, the governor of New South Wales issued an order demanding that stray goats and pigs be impounded. If you search for 'stray goat' on Trove (the historical newspaper database of the National Library of Australia), it will give you some idea of how big a problem goats were: you will be inundated by news stories – right up till the mid-twentieth century – about straying goats destroying gardens and farms.

The first version of the New South Wales *Inclosed Lands Act*, which was passed in 1854, only allowed for the destruction of goats (a statutory exception was later made for Angoras, which were exempted from destruction), but the equivalent Victorian and Queensland Acts from the 1870s (now no longer in force) also provided for goats, pigs and geese to be destroyed if they were found trespassing, as did the relevant Papua New Guinean ordinance. These laws did not, however, give farmers the right to destroy trespassing turkeys or bulls (even when a bull was dangerous), as two Queensland cases confirmed.

Cattle Trespass

Another possible remedy in *Winans v Macrae* was for Macrae, the owner of the lamb, to pay damages to Winans, the landowner. Yet another possibility was for Winans to ask for an injunction requiring Macrae to ensure the lamb did not stray again (which is essentially the option Winans sought). 'Cattle trespass' is a tort that can give rise to both of these remedies. It is a 'strict liability' tort, meaning that the owner will have to pay for any damage caused by their animal if it strays onto someone's else's land, regardless of whether it is their fault that it strayed. The tort only applies to straying animals: if animals are deliberately driven onto another land, the normal law of trespass will apply.

Like distress damage feasant, cattle trespass is an ancient tort, though it has somewhat later origins. Glanville Williams said that cattle trespass did not really begin appearing in English law until 1214, during the reign of King John. Despite its name, the action applies not only to straying cattle but also to the category of animals called *avers* – basically, any domesticated animal kept for its meat, milk or fleece.

The tort of cattle trespass has been abolished in the Australian Capital Territory, New South Wales and South Australia, but is still occasionally used in other states. In fact, in a Queensland case from 2005, *Lade & Co Pty Ltd v Black*, the Lades went to the Queensland Supreme Court to sue their neighbour Black for cattle trespass (in a case that did actually involve cattle). Black's cattle had strayed onto land owned by the Lades, who grew sugar cane near Proserpine in Queensland. The Lades obtained an injunction for cattle trespass, restraining Black from allowing the cattle to stray again. In the month after this, the Lades said that the cattle had continued to stray and that Black had committed contempt of court. Justice Cullinane held that Black should be fined $500 and be made to pay for any income lost by the Lades as a result of the trespasses.

The matter did not end there, however. The case came back before the Queensland Supreme Court in 2007, with a different judge. The Lades sought compensatory damages not only for the 2005 trespasses but also for other cattle trespasses they alleged had taken place in October to November

2002. Chief Justice De Jersey found that the Lades did not establish that the trespasses in 2002 had been committed by Black's cows, nor did they prove that they had suffered any loss as a result of the 2005 trespasses. Accordingly, they were not entitled to damages in relation to those incidents.

In light of this case, it is interesting to contemplate how an English or an Australian court would have dealt with *Winans v Macrae*. As the Queensland Supreme Court's decision shows, courts are reasonably ready to award injunctions to restrain animals from trespass or cattle trespass. On the other hand, Winans seems to have been an unsympathetic character, and perhaps an Australian court would have had a similar reaction to the Scottish Court of Sessions for this reason.

Similarly to distress damage feasant, cattle trespass does not apply to dogs or cats, and has never done so – perhaps because we do not eat them, milk them, use their fleece or take their eggs, and therefore do not count them as *avers*. In medieval times, liability for straying dogs (particularly vicious ones) was dealt with under several different doctrines, including an ancient form of trespass, a nascent *scienter* doctrine and incitement to harm.

Several theories as to why cats and dogs were not *avers* were raised by Justice Willes in the 1864 case *Read v Edwards*, in which a pointer dog had escaped and scattered or killed 160 pheasants on someone else's land:

> Reasons were offered, which we need not now estimate, for a distinction in this respect between oxen and dogs or cats, on account, first, of the difficulty or impossibility of keeping the latter under restraint, secondly, the slightness of the damage which their wandering ordinarily causes, thirdly, the common usage of mankind to allow them a wider liberty, and lastly, their not being considered in law so absolutely the chattels of the owner, as to be the subject of larceny.

Glanville Williams noted that Willes' last point is not quite right: it seems clear that cats and dogs can be both owned and stolen (subject to concerns about cats roaming).

You might think that there is no place for bees in the law of cattle trespass, given that they are very difficult to control and are not covered in modern legal systems. As Justice Legoe said in the 1978 Australian case *Stormer v Ingram*, 'Bees are not cattle. No strict liability under the head of cattle trespass can arise ...' He noted that the situation might be different if a person purposefully 'drove' bees onto someone's property: that might be ordinary trespass.

However, the medieval Irish *Bechbretha* had a very idiosyncratic approach to bees, treating them as capable of cattle trespass. As we have already mentioned, the medieval Irish law of *comaithches*, or neighbourhood, required people to pledge to their neighbours that they would compensate them for any damage caused by their trespassing farm animals. The author of the *Bechbretha* applied this same legal structure to bees. Charles-Edwards and Kelly admit that the author's 'determination to treat a bee as if it were not so different from a cow ... lands [him] in absurdity', but they encourage readers to consider his motivations:

> Like many lawyers, perhaps, he has two ends in view: first, he wants to secure a certain solution to possible disputes or legal problems; and secondly, he wishes to do so at a minimum cost in terms of disturbance to established principles or institutions.

According to the *Bechbretha*, the four neighbours whose property bordered the land of the beekeeper were not entitled to damages for the first three years that the beekeeper was establishing a hive (the first year was to allow the bees to settle, the second year was exempt because bees are generally scarce after being moved and the third year was to allow the hive to regenerate fully). After the hive was established, the landowner on whose territory the bees fed would be entitled to one-third of the honey. In addition, the four neighbours surrounding the bee hive were entitled to the first swarms sent out by the original hive. Their order of entitlement depended upon whether any of the neighbours were kin and whose land was best and closest, but guards had to be put on the bees to ensure the swarms did not escape to other properties, as then the neighbours would not be entitled to them. Charles-Edwards and Kelly say this law was evidently a compromise to stop neighbours and kinsmen pressing the owner of the original hive for a share of his honey: in due course the neighbours would be able to get their own hives and were, in turn, entitled to a three-year immunity from the law of *comaithches*.

While the *Bechbretha* were likely unique in treating bees like cattle to the degree that they did, even in modern times the wide-range foraging of bees has created issues. In 2011, a Bavarian amateur beekeeper, Karl Heinz Bablok, successfully sued a neighbouring landowner who was growing a genetically modified form of maize. Bablok's bees had produced honey that showed traces of pollen from the maize. The pollen was not capable of fertilising other plants. The European Court of Justice held that substances derived from genetically modified organisms required authorisation to be placed on the market as food. It held that pollen is an ingredient of honey, and if honey contained pollen collected from a genetically modified plant it could not be placed on the market as food, regardless of how slight the contamination or whether it was intentional or not. Later that year, however, an EU directive said that 'residues' did not count as 'ingredients'.

Numerous cases involving the impact of pesticides on bees have arisen in the United States. If landowners spray pesticide on their land, are they liable if bees from neighbouring hives come onto their land and die from exposure to that pesticide? One factor is whether or not the bees are 'trespassers': if they are, landowners typically have no responsibility for them unless they are alerted to the bees' presence. Thus, in *Lenk v Spezia*, the landowner was not liable for harm to foraging bees on the basis that they were 'trespassers'. The decision that the bees were trespassers may reflect the notion that bees are privately owned. A better way of viewing the matter might be that bees are a common good, and it is in all of our interests (being in the interest of the environment) that they should be able to forage freely.

A fourteenth-century illustration of beekeeping

In another US case, *Bennett v Larsen Co.*, the Wisconsin Supreme Court decided that bees were *not* trespassers because of the impossibility of keeping them off land they want to forage on (here, the wild nature of bees comes to the fore again). By this reasoning, landowners who fail to comply with instructions not to use a certain pesticide if bees are foraging on their land are liable for harming bees.

Fencing Animals

What then of farmers who fail to properly fence their properties, allowing their animals to escape? The common law holds that they are *not* liable if a non-dangerous animal accidentally gets out and wanders onto a public highway, causing injury. This is known as 'the rule in *Searle v Wallbank*', after one of the seminal cases on the issue. However, if landowners know the animal to be dangerous or deliberately allowed livestock to enter onto the road, they will be liable. In many Australian jurisdictions, the rule in *Searle v Wallbank* has been statutorily abolished. However, it still applies in the Northern Territory and Queensland, where it can have an unfair effect.

The rule was applied in a 2006 Queensland case, *Smith v Williams*. Williams was injured when he attempted to avoid cattle crossing the Kennedy Highway near Innot Hot Springs: he swerved to avoid the cattle and the loaded fuel tanker he was driving overturned. The Smiths were the farmers who owned the cattle. Because they did not *deliberately* allow the cattle onto the highway, they were not liable for Williams' injuries. The operation of the rule in *Searle v Wallbank* meant Williams could not bring a claim against them for failing to fence the cattle.

In a 2016 Queensland case, *Hutton v RLX Operating Company Pty Ltd*, the injured person was luckier, because the Queensland courts had developed various exceptions to the *Searle v Wallbank* rule. Hutton suffered serious physical injuries when, driving on the Capricorn Highway, he ran into a small group of horses that had escaped from the Gracemere Saleyards Complex. The horses belonged to Muscat, who had brought them to the Saleyards Complex for an event organised by Rockhampton Performance Horse Inc. The Saleyards Complex was leased by RLX Operating Company Pty Ltd. Hutton sued all three parties for failing to adequately secure the horses. The judge decided that an exception to the rule in *Searle v Wallbank* was applicable, namely that those responsible for securing livestock should be liable if those animals escaped. Consequently, Hutton was able to obtain damages.

It has been suggested that the rule in *Searle v Wallbank* should be entirely abolished across Australia, not just in relation to the tort of negligence, but in relation to nuisance as well. The Northern Territory, South Australia and Western Australia have gone even further, making the owners of cattle 'found straying, or at large, or tethered, or depastured in any street or public place' guilty of a crime and liable for a fine. Courts have held that this is an offence regardless of whether the owners knew that their cattle had strayed or wanted them to, or even if they reasonably thought their cattle were properly secured. A New Zealand court, reading a similar provision, said that this is because the provision's purpose is to increase the 'safety of those who go upon the roads'. However, South Australia's courts baulked at holding an owner liable when the evidence suggested that a cow had escaped as a result of a trespassing stranger opening a gate. In *Snell v Ryan*, Chief Justice Napier declared the alternative 'tyranny and injustice':

> I have too much respect for the legislature to suppose that it could have intended to penalize the owner of cattle, which are found straying, through no default or neglect on the part of anyone for whom the owner is responsible, but as the result of the wrongful and possible criminal act of a stranger.

Napier's view was later endorsed by his fellow judges, but it did not help the farmer whose lamb was struck and killed by a car on a public road. The court heard that the farmer's workers had driven 650 sheep from a paddock on one side of the road to a paddock on the other side. The trial court had found that the workers had diligently shepherded the flock and that no-one knew how the lamb escaped, but the judges held that this was not enough to exonerate the farmer. Nor was it enough that 'sheep will by reason of their nature escape through [sheep-proof] fences unbeknown to the owner thereof or the servant employee or agent', as the magistrate observed. Rather, the owner can only escape liability if it is shown that an animal's escape was the fault of another person or an act of God – not just an act of sheep. The judges surely had at least a little doubt that the employees had been as diligent as the trial court had found.

After that decision, South Australia amended the offence to provide a defence for owners and their employees who acted 'with all reasonable diligence' to confine their animals – owners who could not be expected to know their animals had escaped or who took all steps to confine them once they realised. The exception developed by the courts has also been applied in South Australian courts in cases that have nothing to do with animals (for instance, a truck driver whose truck was overweight because a petrol station filled it with the wrong fuel was found not be liable). The exception to criminal responsibility is now part of Australia's federal criminal code, and versions of it apply in much of Australia, as well as in Fiji and Nauru.

Trespass, Negligence and Nuisance

Returning to *Winans v Macrae*, let's suppose that Macrae had deliberately driven the lamb onto Winans' land or had recklessly or carelessly allowed it to stray. Trespass is a tort that protects our 'exclusive possession' of land: we have the right to say who can enter onto our land, and it is wrongful if someone enters without permission. Likewise, if someone deliberately herds or recklessly allows animals onto our property without permission it is trespass (as opposed to cattle trespass, which just deals with straying). In such cases, the animal is essentially seen as an extension of the owner. If Macrae had deliberately or recklessly let his lamb stray onto Winans' property, an injunction might have been awarded by an Australian court, unless the court was similarly unsympathetic towards demanding American billionaires.

In *Read v Edwards*, which dealt with a pointer dog that drove away or killed 160 pheasants, the judge held the owner liable for trespass because he knew the dog had a mischievous disposition and liked to chase and destroy game, but he nonetheless allowed it to roam in the wood.

These days, a roaming dog in England and Wales would be covered by section 4 of the *Animals Act 1971* (UK), which states:

> Where a dog causes damage by killing or injuring livestock, any person who is a keeper of the dog is liable for the damage, except as otherwise provided by this Act.

The same statute also provides for liability for trespassing livestock under certain conditions. However, there is a domestic animal glaringly absent from the Act: the cat is not mentioned at all. It is sometimes said that the cat has a 'right to roam'. This may be because roaming cats that catch vermin are regarded as a public good. Or it may be because it is impossible to stop cats from roaming unless they are kept in the house or otherwise enclosed.

This has caused difficulties in Australia, where cats must be prevented from roaming in order to protect native animals.

There have been several cases of cat owners being sued after their pets killed birds belonging to other people, with varying results. In a Scottish case from 1878, Webb sued McFeat for allowing his cat to kill Webb's carrier pigeon. The animals were on neither Webb's nor McFeat's properties at the time of the incident. Had McFeat's cat been trespassing on Webb's property the result might have been different, said the court, but given that both animals were on someone else's land, 'it was the duty of [Webb] to take the guardianship of his bird, said to be so valuable, and therefore both owners are in equal blame, and the case must be viewed as arising from natural law, for which neither owner without *culpa* [fault] can be answerable'. While neither was liable, McFeat had to pay Webb's costs because, initially, he had 'not sympathized with [Webb], but rather put him at defiance, and forced him to prove that it was [McFeat's] cat who slew his bird'.

Conversely, in the 1890 US case *McDonald v Jodrey*, Jodrey was not held liable for his cat killing McDonald's singing canary. While the judge was under no doubt that canaries could be valuable property, he noted that cats were not able to be restrained and possessed in the same way as other domestic animals, and thus it was not possible to stop them from trespassing:

> The depredations which they commit in their wanderings are to be ascribed to this and may be compared to the damage done by other animals of a partially wild nature, such as rabbits or pigeons escaping onto the land of another for which no action lies.

A cat owner might still be liable for nuisance or negligence in relation to the actions of their cat, even in jurisdictions where 'cat trespass' is not possible. Moreover, under Victoria's *Domestic Animals Act 1994*, owners of cats found at large have committed an offence if their local council has ordered a cat curfew. However, the maximum fines for this offence are half of those applicable for dogs.

The tort of nuisance prevents interference with a landowner's right to quiet enjoyment of their property. In *Winans v Macrae*, Winans might have argued that the lamb interfered with his quiet enjoyment of the forest, although given the extent of the land he leased and the apparent inoffensiveness of the lamb's conduct, it seems unlikely this argument would have been upheld, unless it could be shown that the lamb was irrevocably destroying the forest's prospects of being adapted for the keeping of deer.

Winans might also have sued Macrae for negligence: a failure to properly look after the lamb and exercise reasonable care to prevent the lamb from straying onto his property. Negligence holds that someone who fails to exercise reasonable care will be liable for 'reasonably foreseeable' losses if an animal of theirs escapes. However, it is hard to see what the actual loss would have been in this case (unless there was proof that Winans' prospects of establishing a deer forest were ruined) and without being able to show one, it is likely a negligence claim would have failed.

Annoying Animals

When we own or possess land, we have what is called a right to 'quiet enjoyment' of that land – in other words, we have the right to be free of unreasonable interferences from our neighbours. The tort allowing us to prevent people from interfering with this right is the tort of nuisance, which, as the name implies, deals with all kinds of annoyances, including smells, loud noises, running water, pollution, the undermining of land and so forth.

With regard to domestic animals, the law protecting 'quiet enjoyment' is reasonably clear (excepting cats or dogs, for which legislative intervention has been necessary). If a neighbour keeps domestic animals such as horses or pigs that smell, make noise or pollute a neighbour's land, this can be restrained by means of an injunction. This was not always the case. The introduction to the Southampton *Court Leet Records* paints a vivid picture of the kinds of issues created by animals in English towns during Elizabethan times and earlier:

> Hogs strolled about the streets; ducks followed their impudent example; cattle stood there meditatively and thither came men to milk them; butchers used the streets as slaughterhouses, and into them threw the offal from their shops. Fishmongers poured forth their fishy water 'to the great annoyance of the quenes subjects wth the stink thereof'.

Glanville Williams notes that the original law of nuisance was not ideal for dealing with such issues, because it was designed for nuisances created by buildings of a permanent nature, and because distress damage feasant overlapped with nuisance. However, the law of nuisance was then adapted to deal with the smell of pigs, which, as Williams put it, was evidently 'too much even for hardened medieval nostrils'.

In a famous case from 1610, William Aldred alleged that his Norfolk neighbour Thomas Benton had piled up so much wood on his property that no light could enter Aldred's windows. Aldred also alleged that Benton had maliciously built a pigsty so close to Aldred's house that Aldred and his servants had to move out to escape 'the foetid and insalubrious odours of the muck of the aforesaid sows and pigs ... penetrating and flowing into the hall and parlour and other parts of the messuage [a dwelling with attached outbuildings and land]'. The pig muck and lack of light were so severe that the court classified the sty as a public nuisance, but it is clear that a private nuisance action would also have been justified in this situation.

An example of a nuisance law being used in relation to semiwild, semidomesticated animals can be seen in an Australian case from 1949, *Fraser v Booth*, which established that a large number of pigeons can be a nuisance. Booth kept around 350 pigeons on his property in Sydney. Fraser, his next-door neighbour, sought an injunction restraining Booth from keeping the birds, complaining that they were noisy and swooped close to her and her house. For his part, Booth said Fraser and her husband had harassed his pigeons, shouting at them, clapping, blowing tin whistles, letting off firecrackers and squirting them with a hose, among other things. He counterclaimed that he was entitled to an injunction against her and her husband. The judge, Chief Justice Knox of the New South Wales Supreme Court, held that Fraser was 'not unduly difficult or odd' – although perhaps not *particularly* sanguine on the topic of pigeons after her experiences – and that the pigeons were a serious nuisance to her and her family. An injunction was awarded preventing Booth from keeping the birds on the property, but it was postponed for two months to allow Booth to organise alternative accommodation for them.

It is evident that noisy domesticated animals are also capable of being nuisances. Thus, in several old English cases, neighbours were able to restrain people from running noisy horse livery stables, presumably because the horses' whinnies and snorts were so loud. Perhaps the sound of hooves and stamping was also disturbing.

Roosters are another domesticated animal that can create noise disturbances. In the 1936 case *Leeman v Montagu*, Leeman sought an injunction restraining his neighbour Montagu, a poultry farmer in Surrey, from keeping loud cockerels that crowed from 2 a.m. to around 7 or 8 a.m. Leeman asked someone to record the sound of the cockerels on a gramophone record, but the judge decided not to listen to it. The witness who made the recording said the noise was like 'three cornets, two of which were out of tune'. The previous owner of Leeman's cottage compared the sound to 'a football crowd cheering a cup-tie'. There was also evidence that the poultry farm could have been rearranged fairly easily to ensure the cockerels were further from the cottage. Justice Greaves-Lord allowed an injunction, which was suspended for a month to allow the farmer to rearrange the poultry.

Even in the modern day, there are disputes about crowing cockerels. Famously, a disagreement arose in 2019 on the Île d'Oléron, France, regarding a cockerel named Maurice, owned by Corinne Fesseau. Her neighbours, elderly retirees who owned a holiday house on the island, complained that Maurice's loud crowing at dawn created an 'abnormal noise disturbance'. Ultimately, the court in Rochefort held that Maurice's noise was not a nuisance, and Maurice became an unlikely hero for those who wished to preserve the French rural way of life. Sadly (but perhaps not for his neighbours), Maurice died, aged six, in May 2020. This is not the only French case involving rural noise. Such cases have become more common as city dwellers move to the French countryside for 'peace and quiet' and are displeased by the various noises of country life, including lowing cows in Haute-Savoie, quacking ducks and geese in Soustons, loudly trilling cicadas in Provence and croaking frogs in Grignols.

Not all new arrivals to the country object to animal noises. Several years earlier, English publisher Edward Elgar, who had a summer house in Tornac, a village in the south of France, allowed local farmer Claude Mesjeans to graze his cattle on the land around his villa. However, Yves Meignan, a Frenchman who had also moved to the area from the city, complained about the noise of the cowbells causing him 'exhaustion and anxiety' and creating much angst among local villagers. He sued Elgar and Mesjeans to restrain the cows from grazing in the area, but the outcome of the case was not reported.

On 29 January 2021, after widespread complaints about the prevalence of such cases in France, legislation was passed providing that the sounds and smells of the countryside are part of France's 'sensory heritage' and should be preserved. The French government is also considering amending its civil code to better deal with neighbourhood disputes of this type.

Almost ten years earlier, a French couple from Grignols, in the Dordogne, found themselves in an unenviable position. Their neighbours had sued them for the disturbance created by the loudly croaking frogs in the natural pond in their garden, and the court had ordered them to fill in the pond. However, some of the frogs were a protected species, and the couple risked two years in jail and fines of €150,000 if they moved the frogs or filled the pond. Eventually, in March 2021 – after a nine-year legal battle that went all the way to the highest court in France – the Cour de Cassation ordered the pond drained and the frogs moved elsewhere. It seems happy endings for frogs only happen in fairytales.

Frogs have caused problems in Australia too. In *Gales Holdings Pty Ltd v Tweed Shire Council*, the nuisance started with pooling water. Gales Holdings bought some land with a view to developing it. Tweed Shire Council had constructed drains and stormwater outlets on this land, causing water to pool and eventually create a pond, which a colony of endangered wallum froglets came to inhabit. When Gales Holdings sought to develop the land, it was told that the part occupied by the froglets was not to be developed and had to be set aside as a perpetual habitat for them. Gales Holdings sued the council for nuisance (allowing water to run onto the land was a clear nuisance) but also for the losses that it incurred as a result of a portion of its land being ineligible for development. However, in 2013, the New South Wales Court of Appeal held that it was not a reasonably foreseeable risk that the council's drainage works would cause the froglet habitat to develop.

While bees are very useful to the environment and to humanity, their sting is painful, and their tendency to swarm makes them capable of being a nuisance. Beekeepers are expected to prevent them from unreasonably annoying neighbours. If a neighbour is annoyed by the bees, she will often argue both nuisance and negligence. Sometimes nuisance will succeed, particularly in severe cases.

A 1906 case involved rival English beekeepers named Parker and Reynolds, who lived next door to each other. Parker complained that Reynolds' beekeeping was unreasonable. According to the evidence disclosed, Reynolds kept around 500,000 bees within 20 feet of Parker's house, and they invaded his home, stinging his wife, children and servants. Parker's own bees were kept much further away from his dwelling.

Justice Phillimore, another beekeeper, instructed the jury that 'the plaintiff could not lead his ordinary life or eat his ordinary food without the household being in danger of constant stinging', and that if the jury also thought that 'the plaintiff could not live at home in the ordinary way in August according to the simple English ideas, and that his reasonable comfort was substantially interfered with owing to the defendant's bees, they might come to the conclusion that there was a nuisance'. The jury agreed that the bees were a nuisance, and Reynolds was ordered to move the bees 200 yards away from Parker's house.

Another case in which at least one judge was prepared to find nuisance was the Irish case of *O'Gorman v O'Gorman*, in which a man was severely injured after he and his horse were stung by a large swarm of bees. Another judge observed that the situation might have been different if the man was only occasionally stung by a small number of bees: this would not have given rise to liability.

In the South Australian case *Stormer v Ingram*, Justice Legoe was disinclined to hold a beekeeper liable for either nuisance or negligence. The Stormers complained that the bees kept by their next-door neighbour Ingram stung their children and companion animals, drowned in their three fishponds and left yellow bee-droppings on their washing. However, the judge held that merely keeping bees was not a nuisance and that the Stormers did not show that there was any 'unreasonable' interference with the enjoyment of their property.

In his ruling, Justice Legoe cited an old case from the United States, *Earl v Van Alstine*, in which Justice Selden said:

> In modern days, the bee has become almost as completely domesticated as the ox or the cow. Its habits and its instincts have been studied, and through the knowledge thus acquired, it can be controlled with nearly as much certainty as any of the domestic animals ... I apprehend that such a thing as a serious injury to persons or property from its attacks is very rare, not occurring in a ratio more frequent, certainly, than injuries arising from the kick of a horse or the bite of a dog.

Moreover, Justice Selden said:

> The utility of bees no-one will question, and hence there is nothing to call for the application of a very stringent rule to the case. Upon the whole, therefore, I am clearly of the opinion that the owner of bees is not liable *at all events* for any accidental injury they may do.

Justice Legoe agreed, and felt that the bee was of sufficient utility for society in general that the odd sting was not unreasonable. There are several other Australian cases, however, in which people have been restrained from keeping bees, in one instance because a neighbour had a severe allergy to their stings.

It may not be surprising at this point to learn that the law's position on dogs and cats is a little different to other animals. Historically, at common law, there was some doubt about whether a noisy dog was a nuisance. These days, legislation provides that dogs and cats may be nuisances in certain circumstances and that their owners can face criminal fines. For example, under section 32 of the Victorian *Domestic Animals Act 1994*, dog and cat owners can be fined if their animals fail to meet a number of criteria:

(1) The occupier of any premises where a dog or cat is kept or permitted to remain must not allow that animal to be a nuisance.

Penalty: 1 penalty unit.

(2) A dog or cat is to be regarded as a nuisance for the purposes of this section –

(a) if it injures or endangers the health of any person; or

(b) if it creates a noise, by barking or otherwise, which persistently occurs or continues to such a degree or extent that it unreasonably interferes with the peace, comfort or convenience of any person in any other premises.

(3) If a person is found guilty of an offence against this section, the court may order that person to take that action (if any) to abate the nuisance which is specified in the order.

(4) A person must comply with an order made against him or her under subsection (3).

Penalty: 3 penalty units.

Normal barking (or yowling, for that matter) is not a nuisance. It must be persistent and unreasonably interfere with the peace, comfort or convenience of a neighbour. Typically, this is proven by keeping a diary of how often and why the dog barks.

Dog owners are also responsible for picking up their dog's faeces. In New South Wales, either the dog's owner or any person over sixteen who is in charge of the dog must, if the dog defecates in a public place, 'immediately remove the dog's faeces and properly dispose of them'. The relevant statute imposes a duty on the local council to provide an appropriate receptacle anywhere where dogs commonly exercise. Other Australian jurisdictions require that dog owners carry bags for collecting dog poo when they are out with their dogs. Noncompliance is an offence that likely applies whether or not the owner notices that the dog had defecated, but some jurisdictions allow for reasonable mistakes and most provide blanket exceptions for owners of assistance dogs. Standard principles of criminal responsibility would likely exempt dog owners if the faeces were impossible to dispose of – for instance, if the dog had diarrhoea.

Such offences are notoriously difficult to enforce. A 2006 observational study of 400 dog walkers in Northern Ireland parks (where the weather was fine, prominent signs directed owners to clean up after their dogs, and bags and bins were freely available) found that almost half of dog walkers did not pick up their dogs' faeces. The study also found (based on information later supplied by the walkers) that most noncompliant owners were young, male, of lower socio-economic status or walked their dogs off-leash. The author concluded:

> Although this profile is somewhat of a generalization, and additional factors may be related to dog litter management, it nonetheless provides useful information on what sector of the population is most likely to let their dogs foul in public areas. Targeting these particular people with appropriate educational campaigns and law enforcement may be one step in the right direction toward a cleaner and healthier environment.

Somewhat more desperately, local authorities in Australia regularly publicise the unlikely claim that they intend to investigate unsolved cold cases via DNA analysis of the dog poo.

Harmful Animals

Animals may harm people or property in a multitude of other ways. In terms of the harm animals can inflict on humans, they can bite, scratch or otherwise attack them, collide with them on the road, chase them and more. Sometimes an animal may also harm another animal. The liability of the animal's keeper or owner depends upon several factors: whether the animal is intrinsically dangerous, whether the keeper knew it was dangerous, whether the keeper was negligent and what statutory rules exist regarding the animal's keeping.

Dangerous Animals and Scienter

We quoted William Blake's poem 'The Lamb' at the beginning of this chapter, but Blake's explicit counter to this was 'The Tyger', quite a different beast:

> Tyger Tyger, burning bright,
> In the forests of the night;
> What immortal hand or eye,
> Could frame thy fearful symmetry?
>
> In what distant deeps or skies.
> Burnt the fire of thine eyes?
> On what wings dare he aspire?
> What the hand, dare seize the fire?
>
> And what shoulder, & what art,
> Could twist the sinews of thy heart?
> And when thy heart began to beat,
> What dread hand? & what dread feet?
>
> What the hammer? what the chain,
> In what furnace was thy brain?
> What the anvil? what dread grasp,
> Dare its deadly terrors clasp!
>
> When the stars threw down their spears
> And water'd heaven with their tears:
> Did he smile his work to see?
> Did he who made the Lamb make thee?

Just as Blake does, the law approaches tigers very differently to lambs. Again the origins of this are Roman. Natural philosopher Pliny the Elder reports that the Roman Senate initially prohibited people from bringing animals from Africa to Italy, but this changed in BCE 670, when Aufidius, the tribune of the people, allowed African animals to be brought over for the circus. It seems that there was a particular prestige in capturing wild animals from afar and bringing them to Rome. The appetite for such spectacles was voracious: when the famous orator and lawyer Marcus Tullius Cicero was governor of Cilicia (Sicily), his former client the Roman Marcus Caelius Rufus repeatedly begged Cicero to supply him with 'Greek panthers' (leopards from Sicily). Cicero ignored the requests, despite Rufus's warning that 'It will be a disgrace to you if I have no Greek panther'.

It probably comes as no surprise to learn that the Romans, known for their predilection for exotic animals, developed different rules for dangerous animals under the 'Edict of the Aediles' (legal pronouncements by officers called *aediles* who sought, among other things, to ensure the city of Rome was properly run). The Roman laws state:

> No-one is to have a dog, any wild boar, wolf, bear, panther, lion … : and generally any dangerous animal, whether at large or so bound or chained that it did not inflict harm … where there is frequent traffic and it might injure someone or cause damage. The penalty for any contravention of this provision is, if a freeman's death result from it, two hundred solidi; if a freeman be said to have been injured, what a judge regards as right and proper; in all other cases, double the value of the damage done.

This was a 'strict liability' wrong: it did not matter whether or not the keeper of the dangerous animal was at fault or not. The fact that the dangerous animal had killed or injured someone was what established its owner's liability. The Romans were a very pragmatic people – if someone was doing something intrinsically dangerous that might harm members of the public, then they should be made to pay for any damage inflicted.

Strict liability was also present in the Anglo-Saxon laws of Alfred (from c. 899). See for example, the penalties for owners of dogs that injured a human:

> 23. If a dog tears or bites a man, 6 shillings shall be paid for the first misdeed. If the owner continues to feed the dog, 12 shillings shall be paid for the next misdeed, and 30 shillings for the third.

23.1 If the dog is lost or disappears after committing any of these misdeeds, the owner must still pay.

23.2 If the dog commits more misdeeds and the master keeps it, he must pay compensation for whatsoever wounds may be inflicted, according to the amount of [the victim's] full wergeld [literally 'man-payment'].

Similarly strict liability made its way into various modern legal systems, including civilian systems, such as the modern German Civil Code, which states:

If a human being is killed by an animal or if the body or the health of a human being is injured by an animal or a thing is damaged by an animal, then the person who keeps the animal is liable to compensate the injured person for the damage arising from this. Liability in damages does not apply if the damage is caused by a domestic animal intended to serve the occupation, economic activity or subsistence of the keeper of the animal[;] ... the keeper of the animal, in supervising the animal, has exercised reasonable care[;] or the damage would also have occurred even if this care had been exercised.

In Australian (and English) law, we have historically dealt with dangerous animals in a different way, through the doctrine of *scienter*, which, as we noted in the introduction, only imposes strict liability on those who keep 'dangerous' animals. The doctrine arose in England in 1358, developed in the years after the Black Death swept Britain in 1348–49. The name *scienter* comes from the Latin words in the old English writ used for these kinds of actions: *scienter retinuit* ('knowingly retained'). The medieval historian Robert Palmer argued that *scienter* reflected the period's general belief that people should abide by their ethical obligations, including in relation to keeping dangerous animals. Initially, *scienter* was particularly concerned with dangerous dogs, which bit sheep and people, and wild boar, which were accustomed to strike animals. Ironically, as we will see, *scienter* later became inapposite for dealing with dangerous dogs.

The doctrine of *scienter* provides that if an animal is categorised as intrinsically dangerous, then the person possessing it (the keeper) will be strictly liable for any damage done by it, regardless of whether the keeper was at fault. Conversely, if the animal is not placed in the category of being intrinsically dangerous, it must be shown that the keeper knew of that particular animal's vicious propensity before he or she can be liable. Liability will be imposed regardless of where the injury occurs: on the victim's land, on a highway or on the keeper's land.

With *scienter*, we again see that courts make a distinction between wild and tame or domesticated animals, but this distinction does not operate in the same way as it does in regard to ownership. The law of *scienter* distinguishes between intrinsically harmful animals on the one hand (mostly wild animals, but also some tamed animals, such as elephants) and animals that are generally harmless on the other (mostly domesticated animals, but also some wild or semiwild animals, such as rabbits).

Thus, some animals that are regarded as 'wild' for the purposes of ownership will not be regarded as 'wild' for the purposes of *scienter*, because the animals in question are not regarded as intrinsically harmful. For instance, bees are generally not held to be *ferae naturae* for the purposes of the *scienter* doctrine, although they *are* held to be wild for the purposes of ownership. The reason for this seems to be that, while bees can be dangerous en masse, that is only as a result of their hive being threatened or interfered with. It also reflects the recognition that bees are socially and environmentally useful to humans, so we do not want to hold people strictly liable every time a bee injures someone. In *Stormer v Ingram*, Justice Legoe also noted that bees die after they sting someone, and this contributed to his decision to hold that they were not *ferae naturae* – because they die, they do not pose an intrinsic danger to anyone other than the person or animal they sting.

Other animals that are regarded as 'wild' for the purposes of ownership – such as monkeys – can also be regarded as 'wild' for the purposes of *scienter*. In a famous 1846 case, *May v Burdett*, Burdett was found liable when her monkey bit May, leaving her 'greatly terrified and alarmed', as well as 'sick, sore, lame and disordered'. Burdett knew of the monkey's vicious propensity, but he would have been liable even had he not known.

The seminal case involving dangerous animals is *Behrens v Bertram Mills Circus Ltd* in which the Behrenses were injured by stampeding elephants. The Behrenses were a married couple who performed at funfairs and circuses. Standing 2 feet 6 inches and, according to the judge, 'perfectly proportioned', Mr Behrens billed himself as 'the smallest man on Earth'. His wife, Mrs Behrens, was 3 foot and played the accordion. They performed an act together, along with their cat.

On the day of the stampede incident, the Behrenses were performing in a booth annexed to the circus. The manager of the circus, Mr Whitehead, sat in a booth nearby, taking money and attracting visitors. Although no animals belonging to strangers were to be taken onto the premises, Mr Whitehead was looking after his twelve-year-old daughter's Pomeranian dog, hiding it under the booth and attaching its leash to the leg of the chair he was sitting on.

After performing in the circus's opening parade, the elephants passed through the passage in which Mr Whitehead's and the Behrenses' booths were situated. The dog ran out, barking and snapping at the elephants, which startled one of them, causing it to trumpet. When the dog tried to retreat to Mr Whitehead's booth, two elephants followed it. Although the trainer quickly got the elephants back under control, both Mr Whitehead's and the Behrenses' booths collapsed, the dog was killed and Mrs Behrens was severely injured, reducing Mr Behrens to a state of shock. They were unable to work for two years and three months afterwards, and Mrs Behrens could not play the accordion to her previous standard. The Behrenses claimed damages under the doctrine of *scienter*, both for Mrs Behrens' injuries and for their inability to work.

In reaching his decision, Justice Devlin had to consider whether elephants were *ferae naturae* (intrinsically wild). The circus argued that Bullu, the elephant that was startled by the dog, was tame, not *ferae naturae*. Devlin noted that the categorisation of animals according to *scienter* was somewhat illogical:

> The particular rigidity in the *scienter* action which is involved in this case ... is the rule that requires the harmfulness of the offending animal to be judged not by reference to the general habits of the species to which it belongs. The law ignores the world of difference between the wild elephant in the jungle and the trained elephant in the circus. The elephant Bullu is in fact no more dangerous than a cow; she reacted in the same way as a cow would do to the irritation of a small dog; if perhaps her bulk made her capable of doing more damage, her higher training enabled her to be more swiftly checked. But I am compelled to assess the defendants' liability in this case in just the same way as I would assess it if they had loosed a wild elephant in the funfair.

The elephant was judged to be *ferae naturae*, and thus the question was whether the owner had maintained control over it. When the accident occurred, control was lost, albeit for a brief moment, and the circus was therefore held strictly liable for the accident. The barrister representing the circus tried to argue that this was unfair and might impose liability on owners of dogs known to be vicious if they were to accidentally knock down a child, for instance. Justice Devlin held that wild animals that were savage by nature should not be put on the same footing as domesticated animals that were known to be savage by disposition. The barrister argued that the rule was illogical, because so much turned upon the categorisation. While Justice Devlin conceded that the rule lacked logic, he said:

> If a person wakes up in the middle of the night and finds an escaping tiger on top of his bed and suffers a heart attack, it would be nothing to the point that the intentions of the tiger were quite amiable. If a tiger is let loose in a funfair, it seems to me to be irrelevant whether a person is injured as the result of a direct attack or because on seeing it he runs away and falls over. The feature of this present case which is constantly arising to blur the reasoning is the fact that this particular elephant Bullu was tame. But that, as I have said, is a fact which must be ignored. She is to be treated as if she were a wild elephant; and if a wild elephant were let loose in the funfair and stampeding around, I do not think there would be much difficulty in holding that a person who was injured by falling timber had a right of redress. It is not, in my judgment, practicable to introduce conceptions of *mens rea* [intention to harm or kill] and malevolence in the case of animals.

Other animals that have been considered wild (or *ferae naturae*) for the purpose of the doctrine of *scienter* include monkeys, chimpanzees, bears, elephants, lions, zebras, raccoons, tigers, wild dogs and dingoes.

Marlor v Ball was a 1900 case involving zebras. When Ball visited a menagerie with his wife and brother-in-law, the door to the stables had accidentally been left open. Ball came upon four zebras in separate stables, and gently patted one. This turned out to be an exceptionally bad idea. The zebra kicked Ball so hard that he went through the wooden stable partition into the next stable, whereupon a second zebra bit Ball's hand so badly that it had to be amputated. The court held that zebras – like elephants – are intrinsically dangerous wild animals. Zebras are very difficult, if not impossible, to tame. Although they look like striped horses, they are temperamentally different:

> Zebras are aggressive. They have not evolved in tamer, temperate regions, they have instead evolved to survive as a species in Africa where lions are their main predator. There are many recorded cases of zebras killing lions. This is usually caused by a kick to the head, causing death or a broken jaw, thus causing the lion to starve. To give an idea of the power of a zebra's kick, one need just point out that no horse has ever broken a lion's jaw. Furthermore, few people have ever walked away after being kicked by a zebra. A zebra doesn't just kick with the leg. Instead it looks between its legs in order to accurately place its kicks and then bucks and kicks violently with both back legs. Zebras also inflict nasty bite wounds on each other and on people when they are habituated or 'tame' and people get too close.

The Zimbabwean government once attempted to move a herd of sixteen zebras to a different location. To the horror of park employees, when the truck arrived at the new location, only one zebra was still alive. The other zebras had kicked each other to death during the journey.

Australian readers may be interested to know that Australian courts have held that camels and kangaroos are not intrinsically dangerous for the purposes of the *scienter* doctrine. Thus, for an owner of either one of these animals to be liable for an injury it has inflicted, the owner must know that the animal has vicious propensities.

In the 1979 case *Lake v Taggart*, a kangaroo at a nature reserve escaped and attacked Lake as she rode past on her bicycle. A passer-by had warned her that the loose kangaroo was spoiling for a fight and advised her to 'pedal like hell' if she saw it. The kangaroo chased her, but when Lake got to a hill, she 'ran out of puff' and got off the bicycle. In her evidence, she explained what happened next:

> I got off my bike and I automatically just held the bike up in front of me to protect myself. The kangaroo was on the other side of my bike. I could see its front teeth, and it was making a hissing sound. Then all of a sudden it stood on its tail and knocked the bike away from me. I put my head down to protect my face and next I knew I was doing a complete somersault and my neck gave a great crack, and I remember

thinking I had had it. It is going to break my neck. As I went over I remember seeing grey fur over me – I somersaulted and think he must have thumped me because I had two scratches on my thigh in almost identical places. I got up and realised I must get some help so I opened my mouth to call 'help' and squeaks came out and the kangaroo started coming at me with his claws out. My voice came. I was screaming 'help' – I grabbed the kangaroo's paws in instinct I suppose. I just held on. I found I couldn't scream loud enough to call for help. I just opened my mouth and screamed as loud as I could. I could see his back legs thrashing at me. We stumbled backwards but I didn't go down ... All this time I was screaming. We both regained our balance when he started to come at me again. I knew what he was going to do this time. All the time I was screaming. I grabbed its paws again and I pulled down with all my might as I knew he was going to attack me with his back legs. Its head was on my shoulder as I was pulling so hard. I was screaming as hard as I could and stumbled backwards into the bush. I fell backwards, and the kangaroo was on top of me. It was sitting on my thighs, I couldn't move at all. It was pawing at me with its front paws – I was knocking it away. I was screaming as loud as I could. Then I heard a car coming along Thomas Road. I tried to scream louder. And as I was pushing its paws away all the time, the car went past. I started to think I had had it. Then it [the kangaroo] suddenly stopped. I couldn't believe it. I started scratching it under its chin and telling it it was a good boy.

A man and a dog came running down the hill and chased the kangaroo away. Lake suffered a lacerated forearm, which required stitches, as well as bruises and scratching to her arms, leg, back and face. A park ranger later shot a male kangaroo in the area, matching the description of the one that had attacked Lake. The owner of the kangaroo did not know about its violent propensity – he had only just acquired it the day of the attack – and since it was not intrinsically dangerous, he was not liable. If he had known about the kangaroo's nature, the case might have been resolved differently.

Camels – unlike kangaroos – are not native to Australia, though they are well suited to Australia's arid conditions. Harry, a dromedary, was the first camel to be imported to Australia, but he suffered an unfortunate fate. Early on, it might have seemed as though Harry was a lucky camel. He was one of several camels the Phillips brothers tried to import to Australia in

1840, but he was the only camel to survive the voyage. An explorer, John Ainsworth Horrocks, decided to take Harry on an expedition around South Australia. In his final letter before his death – to the organisation that had funded his expedition – Horrocks explained how he had been wounded on 1 September 1846:

> In going round this lake, which I named Lake Gill [after S.T. Gill, the artist who accompanied Horrocks on his expedition], Bernard Kilroy who was walking ahead of the party stopped, saying he saw a beautiful bird, which he recommended me to shoot to add to the collection. My gun being loaded with slugs in one barrel and ball in the other, I stopped the camel to get at the shot belt which I could not get without his laying down.
>
> Whilst Mr Gill was unfastening it I was screwing the ramrod into the wad over the slugs, standing close alongside of the camel. At this moment, the camel gave a lurch to one side and caught his pack on the lock of my gun, which discharged the barrel I was unloading; the contents of which first took off the middle finger of my right hand between the second and third joints, and entered my left cheek by my lower jaw, knocking out a row of teeth from my upper jaw.

His companions tried desperately to get Horrocks home so that he could be properly treated. On the journey, Gill painted a picture entitled *Invalid's Tent, Salt Lake 75 Miles North-West of Mount Arden*. Harry the camel can be clearly seen grazing in the background. Despite his companions' efforts, Horrocks died twenty-three days later, on 23 September 1846, after his wounds became infected. Before he died, he requested that Harry be killed. Horrocks's friend Paddy Gleeson attempted to shoot Harry in accordance with Horrocks's final wishes, but he was so distressed that he did not shoot the camel cleanly. Harry reared up in pain and bit the head of Jimmy Moorehouse, the Indigenous stockman who was holding him at the time. Another bystander had to put poor Harry out of his misery.

Notwithstanding the inauspicious introduction of camels to Australia, a Western Australia case in 1917 held that camels in Australia were domesticated and not *ferae naturae* for the purposes of *scienter*. Accordingly, the owner of a camel that had allegedly attacked and killed a bullock was not strictly liable for the camel's actions. Additionally, there was no evidence that the camel was vicious – or had even caused the bullock's death.

S.T. Gills' depiction of John Horrocks's 'invalid's tent'

A particular problem arises with the *scienter* doctrine and dogs. Dogs are generally *not* held to be intrinsically dangerous, and thus for the owner of any dog to be held liable for the dog's actions at common law, it must be shown that the owner was aware the dog had vicious propensities. As a result, elaborate statutory regimes governing dangerous dogs have replaced the common law. Interestingly, however, dingoes are *ferae naturae*, even though they are a species of dog, probably derived from domesticated dogs brought over by the First Peoples of Australia. This shows that the line between domesticated, tame and wild is not easy to draw.

Careless Owners

In Roman law, if the strict liability laid out in the Edict of the Aediles for keeping dangerous animals by a highway did not apply, it was possible to establish the *actio de pauperie* against the owner. To establish this tort, it was necessary to show that the animal had behaved in an unpredictable manner that would not have been expected by the victim. A person could also be liable under the general 'umbrella' law of tort, or *lex Aquila*, for other injuries – say, for instance, that a mule driver let a mule-drawn cart get out of control, and someone was hit by it.

The *actio de pauperie* is still applied in South Africa, which is a 'hybrid' jurisdiction, combining common law and Roman law. A South African case from 2020, *Van Meyeren v Cloete*, recently led the country's Supreme Court of Appeal to consider the nature of *pauperien* liability. Cloete, a gardener and garbage collector, was savagely attacked by Van Meyeren's three pit bull crosses. Cloete did nothing to cause or provoke the attack. The attack was so severe that neighbours who came to Cloete's rescue initially thought he was dead, and his left arm was subsequently amputated.

The Supreme Court of Appeal of South Africa found that because the *actio de pauperie* is part of South African law, owners of domesticated animals are strictly liable for any injuries they cause, unless the animal in question is acting out – as any animal would be expected to do – because it is frightened, in pain or provoked. The onus of establishing this rests on the animal owner. As German jurist Reinhard Zimmermann explains, 'What this boils down to, effectively, is the judicial creation of the "reasonable cow" or "reasonable duck" as a criterion to determine the owner's liability.'

In this particular case, Van Meyeren was held liable, notwithstanding his claim that a third party had left his gate open. Judge Wallis (with whom the rest of the court agreed) concluded:

> Many people in South Africa choose to own animals for companion-ship and protection. That is their choice, but responsibilities follow in its wake. Whatever anthropomorphic concepts underpin *pauperien* liability, the reality is that animals can cause harm to people and prop-erty in various ways. When they do so and the victim of their actions is innocent of fault for the harm they have caused, the interests of jus-tice require that as between the owner and the injured party it is the owner who should be held liable for that harm ... If anything, with the growth of urban living, the vastly increased number of pet ani-mals, especially dogs, in our towns and cities and the opportunities for harm that they pose, that view of where the interests of justice lie has been strengthened. People are entitled to walk our streets without having to fear being attacked by dogs and, where such attacks occur, they should in most circumstances be able to look to the owner of the dog for recompense.

Negligence was suggested as an alternative offence, but it was not necessary to consider in the circumstances of this particular case.

Australia also has an 'umbrella' law of negligence covering general wrongdoing. Negligence extends to all wrongs: it applies to many financial injuries as well as injuries to people, land and personal property. Although it only emerged as a separate tort in the early twentieth century, it has since engaged in an 'imperial march', superseding many older torts. The basic concept of negligence is that a person may owe a duty of reasonable care to others, and if they breach that duty, they may be liable for any reasonably foreseeable damage caused to others.

Negligence may apply in cases where animals have wandered onto highways (so long as the rule in *Searle v Wallbank* has been abolished in the jurisdiction) or strayed onto another's property as a result of negligence, and so forth. There is obviously a limit to how far negligence can extend in regard to animals. Thus, in *Trend v Trend*, when a wild kangaroo hopped out in front of a motorcyclist, causing a collision that injured the pillion passenger on the motorcycle, no-one was responsible.

Like the Romans, Australians have a tendency to consider what a 'reasonable animal' would do. In South Australia, it is necessary to take into account the nature and disposition of the particular animal in question, pursuant to section 18(2) of the *Civil Liability Act 1936* (SA):

> In determining the standard of care to be exercised in relation to the keeping, management and control of an animal, a court shall take into account –
>
> (a) the nature and disposition of the animal (which shall be determined according to the facts of the particular case and not according to any legal categorisation); and
>
> (b) any other relevant matters.

Again, negligent behaviour by beekeepers has given rise to a significant body of case law going back to early times. An old Irish king, Congal Cáech ('Congal the One-Eyed'), was said to have been stung by bees, which blinded him in one eye. The *Bechbretha* states that he had to stand down as King of Tara after being blinded (physical imperfection of this kind was not permitted in a king). There is also some suggestion that the bees belonged to King Domnall mac Áedo, and that the blinded king demanded that the eye of one of Domnall mac Áedo's sons be put out in recompense for his injuries.

A later Irish case from 1900 (mentioned earlier) provides an indication of how negligence might operate in relation to injuries caused by swarming bees, although only one judge chose to apply it in this instance. Michael O'Gorman was smoking his father's hives to collect honey, causing bees to swarm. The family owned twenty or twenty-two hives, which they kept in a very small garden, right next to the neighbour's house. Next door, the farmer's son, Patrick O'Gorman, was tackling his horse at the usual time and in the usual place (presumably to attach it to a cart or plough). The swarming bees landed on the horse and it took fright. Both the horse and Patrick were stung repeatedly, and the horse bolted with Patrick's foot caught in the long reins. Patrick was thrown over a low wall and crushed by the horse's chest and head, damaging his spine permanently. The jury found that the bees were kept negligently, in unreasonable numbers, in an unreasonable location, and that Michael and his father ought to have known of the risks the bees posed to Patrick, who ultimately died as a result of his injuries.

Michael and his father appealed against the verdict to the Irish King's Bench Division. Justice Kenny chose to treat it as a case of injury caused by nuisance (perhaps because, at that time, the law of negligence was in its infancy) and allowed the jury verdict to stand. Justice Barton, on the other hand, was doubtful that it was a case of nuisance, and decided that the real wrong here was negligence (a lack of reasonable care on Michael and his father's part). He said that he would not have held the beekeeping O'Gormans liable if it were a simple matter of a bee sting, but this was something different: Michael knew Patrick was likely to be there, knew the bees were going to swarm and knew they could sting (he was garbed in protective gear himself). Justice Wright simply agreed with the jury's verdict.

Unfortunately, there are cases from all over the Commonwealth in which beekeepers have been held negligent, although no other case is as tragic as *O'Gorman v O'Gorman*.

In the Australian case *Stormer v Ingram*, which we have already discussed, Justice Legoe found that the beekeeper owed his neighbours a duty of care, but he was unable to find that the beekeeper had breached his duty in any way because he had kept and handled the bees in the proper manner according to the relevant statute. This reflects the fact that originally, the keeping of bees was regulated as part of private law – that is, it was dealt with through private disputes between parties who contested ownership of a hive or claimed injuries of some sort.

Today, as we saw with *Isbester v Knox City Council* in the introduction, the government tends to have elaborate regulations regarding the keeping of various animals, and bees are no exception. In Victoria, for instance, the

Livestock Disease Control Act 1994 provides that anyone who keeps bees must register as a beekeeper and mark their hives with the beekeeper's brand. Part of the reason for this is concern about the exposure of bees to disease (such as American Foulbrood). Beekeepers must also comply with the Victorian Apiary Code of Practice, which, among other requirements, specifies the conditions in which bees should be kept (in terms of water supply, density of the hives, measures to prevent of swarming and so forth).

Another way animals may cause injury to humans is by road accidents, which were more common when animals were regularly used for transport. In a Victorian case from 1918, *Tucker v Hennessy*, Hennessy had left his horse and cart unattended, and the horse bolted and hit Tucker, who was walking down William Street in the centre of Melbourne. It seemed Hennessy had secured the horse, but the horse had broken the 'McColl strap' that secured it, perhaps because the strap was old. A majority of the court held that Hennessy was liable for negligence, because it was foreseeable that a horse that was not properly restrained might knock a pedestrian down. Justice Cussen dissented on the basis that it was potentially unfair to make drivers liable for the unexpected actions of an animal that was ordinarily docile and well behaved.

Some people have incredibly bad luck. In an English case from 1938, *Fardon v Harcourt-Rivington*, Fardon was walking past a parked 'saloon motor car', in which Harcourt-Rivington's dog was secured, as he and his wife went to the market. The dog, a generally docile Airedale terrier, became excited upon seeing Fardon walk past, and barked and jumped against the rear window of the car, smashing the window and sending a splinter of glass into Fardon's eye. The court found that the accident was not foreseeable and Harcourt-Rivington should not be expected to guard against such an extraordinary event.

Complaints with regard to injurious dogs have been rather more successful. As noted earlier, the *scienter* doctrine is not a good way to deal with dangerous dogs; because dogs are not an 'intrinsically dangerous animal', an owner will only be liable if he or she knew the animal had a vicious propensity. Nonetheless, people may be liable for negligently failing to secure their dogs. Two cases involving injury to children illustrate this.

The English case *Draper v Hodder* dealt with an incident in which three-year-old Gary Draper was attacked in his backyard by six or seven Jack Russell puppies, which had escaped from the home of his parents' next-door neighbour, an experienced breeder. No-one saw the attack, but

Gary was severely injured – he suffered 100 dog bites, and he lost a large part of his scalp and some skin from his left cheek. The dogs had previously visited the yard without injuring any children, but evidence was given that it was dangerous to let Jack Russell terriers roam freely in packs because it could overexcite them, and they might attack any moving thing as a result. The English Court of Appeal held Hodder liable for a lack of reasonable care – it was found that was it foreseeable that the animals might harm someone and that he had failed to secure them adequately. It was not necessary to foresee precisely the kind of injury that occurred, only that injury of some sort might occur. The puppies involved in the attack were put down.

A similar case in Australia, *Galea v Gillingham*, dealt with an incident in which a twelve-year-old girl was attacked by a German shepherd. The girl, who had accompanied her father to a building site, was confronted by the escaped dog, which put its forepaws on her shoulders, bit her chest and stomach, and scratched down her body. The dog's owner, Gillingham, came running out to restrain the dog and said words to the effect that he had asked his wife to tie the dog up. The Queensland Court of Appeal applied *Draper v Hodder* and found that Gillingham was negligent for failing to properly secure the dog. It was sufficient to foresee that the dog might injure a child in *some* way (by knocking them down, for example); it was not necessary to show that the dog was vicious or known to be vicious. Therefore, Gillingham was still liable.

It is evident how tinges of *scienter* creep into negligence – even the notion that there is a 'reasonable dog'. Once again, we see that the qualities of the species and the animal itself are assessed in ways that are quite inconsistent with an animal being a 'thing'.

Dangerous Dogs

Contemporary legislation provides a way to manage dangerous dogs before they injure someone (or injure further people if they have offended before). It allows courts or government officials to make declarations or orders about particular dogs, requiring their owners to control them in particular ways. For example, Victoria's *Domestic Animals Act 1994* allows authorised officers to declare a dog to be 'menacing' if it has rushed at or injured a person or animal without causing them serious injuries. The officers may then require the dog's owner to muzzle the dog and control it with a leash or chain when it is outside. If an owner repeatedly fails to comply with these requirements, or if a dog seriously injures someone or has been trained as an attack or guard dog, then it can be declared 'dangerous', and steps must then be taken to ensure that it cannot leave the owner's premises (and children cannot enter them) without permission. The owner is also required to erect warning signs outside their property. Owners of dogs in these categories face much higher penalties if their dogs are found at large or attack someone. Declaring a dog to be 'dangerous' can affect their owners in other ways too. For instance, when Izzy the Staffordshire terrier was declared dangerous, her owner could no longer keep her, as she lived in public housing that banned such dogs from its premises.

Who has to obey the special rules that apply to some dogs? The dog? The person who walks the dog? Or the dog's owner? Over eighteen months, a kelpie–rottweiler cross named Bailey bit three dogs outside its owner's Sydney property and was declared 'dangerous' by a local council ranger, which would have barred the owner from leaving it in the sole care of her children and required her to keep it in an enclosure when left in her yard.

Bailey's owner successfully appealed the declaration to a court, which instead issued a five-year 'control order', requiring the owner to take various 'actions'. These included muzzling Bailey when he was outside and keeping him 'under effective control of some competent person by means of an adequate chain or leash that is attached to the dog and that is being held by (or secured to) the person'.

The owner arranged for a reliable friend to walk Bailey for an hour each morning. She showed the friend the control order with particular requirements highlighted and checked that the muzzle and leash were in place every time the dog left the house. However, in 2010, a council worker approached the friend and noticed that the leash was on the ground and that Bailey's muzzle was not properly secured. The council opted to prosecute the kelpie's owner, who was found guilty and placed on a good behaviour bond.

But the first judge to review the finding of guilt said that it was clearly part of the control order scheme for dog owners to let others walk their dogs. Observing that 'it would be a most unusual result in a case such as this, where the [owner] had taken every reasonable step to ensure that the terms of the order were complied with, to then say that she was nonetheless guilty of committing this offence', the judge decided that the prosecutor had to prove that Bailey's owner actually wanted to breach the control order.

In the end, a still higher court decided that requiring such proof was too onerous for the purposes of the scheme and would make it unenforceable.

As with many relatively minor offences that do not carry a possible prison sentence, the prosecutor only has to prove that the owner had not made an honest and reasonable mistake of fact. The owner would have had trouble establishing such a mistake in this case, because it was not reasonable for her to believe that that the muzzle would *never* become unsecure or that the leash would *never* be put down. But the appeals court found a different answer: the fact that the scheme and order expressly allowed others to take care of Bailey meant that the owner had complied with their requirements by taking 'all reasonable steps' to communicate the order to the carer and directing him to comply.

In a tragic case in August 2011, a pit bull terrier with no prior history of violence escaped a backyard in the northern suburbs of Melbourne after a roller door failed to close. The dog attacked a person on the street and then followed her as she retreated into a neighbouring house. Inside the house, the dog attacked a four-year-old girl, Ayen Chol, biting her face and neck as her mother struggled to intervene. The girl was dragged into the kitchen and only freed after the dog's owners arrived. She died from her injuries. The man in charge of the dog – who was minding the terrier while his son was overseas – was convicted of the same offence that Tania Isbester was convicted of a year later, and received the maximum fine.

Two months after Ayen Chol's death, Victoria's parliament made it a criminal offence for a person to fail to keep a dog that is dangerous, menacing or a restricted breed under control if a reasonable person would appreciate that such a failure could expose someone to the risk of death. If that failure results in the dog killing someone, the offence is punishable by up to ten years in jail.

The Australian government bans the importation of several dog breeds, including pit bulls, and the state of Victoria had banned keeping such breeds a year before Ayen Chol's death. However, there were two problems. The first was that the ban did not apply to dogs owned prior to the ban's introduction, although owners had to comply with conditions similar to those for declared dangerous dogs, and councils could refuse to register particular dogs, which as result had to be moved elsewhere or destroyed. The greater problem was that the scheme was difficult to enforce, as it was often hard to prove that a dog was of a particular breed.

After police seized a dog named Axel during an altercation with its owner, a Victorian tribunal was asked to review a council's determination that Axel was a pit bull terrier. The tribunal heard from a veterinarian, who testified that there was no such breed. The most he would say was that the dog was a crossbreed of the 'pit bull type' that 'might look like' a pit bull. Following this testimony, the tribunal considered whether or not Axel fell within a detailed government standard for the breed, which required a finding of at least three out of five 'confirmation criteria':

- Height at withers from the ground for bitches and dogs is 43 centimetres–53 centimetres.

- Weight for bitches and dogs is 14 kilograms–36 kilograms.

- Muzzle is slightly shorter in length to the skull, being a 2:3 ratio of muzzle to skull.

- The overall outline of the breed indicates it to be slightly longer in length (point of shoulder to buttocks) than height (withers to ground). Bitches may be slightly longer than males.

- The distance from withers to the elbow and the elbow to the ground is generally equal.

The tribunal found that at least some of these criteria were not proved, noting that several measurements were recorded unprofessionally (the dog's height, for example, was measured by placing a manila folder on the dog's head, which, according to some witnesses, was sloping).

The following year, a parliamentary inquiry into the legislation heard evidence that breed was a poor proxy for dangerousness and ultimately recommended permitting Victorians to keep restricted breed dogs in future, while still placing conditions on how they are kept. The parliament implemented that recommendation the next year.

Wild Animals

Throughout history, some wild animals have caused harm to humans, and humans have sought to control or kill those animals. 'Plagues' of animals are mentioned as far as back ancient times. Several of the ten plagues of Egypt mentioned in the book of Exodus involved what might now be known as 'pest' animals, including a plague of frogs, which teemed into people's houses and ovens, a plague of lice, which bit people and livestock, a plague of flies, afflicting both people and livestock, and a plague of locusts, which ate everyone's crops and led to starvation. Consequently, particularly in agrarian and settled cultures, there is a belief that some animals are harmful and should be controlled or killed.

Sometimes animals also carry disease. Black rats have been blamed for spreading the bubonic plague throughout the world, via the fleas that infested them, although it is now considered possible that the fleas actually spread from human to human, so perhaps the fleas and the humans were the pests rather than the rats.

Views on whether certain animals are useful or not are culturally and historically determined. As we will see, some animals in Australia that were previously regarded as useful are now regarded as pests. The Australian Department of Agriculture and Water Resources has defined 'pest animals' as 'those animals that cause more damage than benefits to human-valued resources and social wellbeing. It recognises that some species may also have positive impacts.' This does not have legally binding status but provides a useful definition.

Pest Species

The law has dealt with pest species by allowing for their legal eradication or reduction. Sometimes, governments may put in place positive incentives to encourage people to kill animals regarded as pests. For instance, during China's Great Leap Forward from 1958 to 1962, the government introduced laws to incentivise the elimination of rats, flies, mosquitoes and sparrows. The ecological consequences of this campaign were disastrous. Sparrows ordinarily ate locusts and other pest insects, and with their numbers reduced, plagues of locusts destroyed the harvests and led to the starvation of millions of people. The sparrow was driven to near extinction in China, and the government had to import sparrows from Soviet Russia. Many other countries have also suffered the lasting effects of laws against pest species.

Tudor Laws

Animals such as bears, wild boars, beavers and wolves had already been exterminated in Britain prior to Tudor times, but in the sixteenth century, significant population growth, coupled with disastrous harvests, led to the enactment of laws to eradicate pest species and put bounties on their destruction.

In 1532, King Henry VIII passed *An Acte Made and Ordeyned to Dystroye Choughes, Crowes and Roks*. Choughs, crows and rooks, which all belong the crow family, evidently consumed 'a wonderfull and mervelous greate quantitie of Corne and Greyne of all kyndes, as well in the sowyng of the same Corne and Greyn, as also at the ripynge and kernelynge of the same'. Apparently, they also destroyed the thatch used in houses and buildings. Laws passed by the king introduced a number of requirements for the control of crows: all landowners were to do their best to destroy these birds, all parishes were to use crow nets and all farmers were to meet over the next ten years to discuss their destruction. Any man could give a licence for someone to remove crows and other birds, and landowners were to pay those who destroyed them two pence for every dozen birds they removed. Doves or pigeons were not to be harmed.

In 1566, Queen Elizabeth I, Henry VIII's youngest daughter, vastly expanded her father's legislation against pest animals with *An Acte for the Preservacion of Grayne*. Again, landowners were to destroy birds from the crow family, but also a range of other birds, including 'Martyn Hawke, Fursekytte [kestrels], Moldkytte [a species of kite], Busarde, Schagge, Carmerante [Cormorant] or Ryngtayle [hen-harrier]' and more. Bounties were to be made for the head or eggs of these creatures by parish wardens. Mammals were also targeted, including, 'Foxe or Gray [badgers]', 'Fitchewe, Polcatte [polecats], Wesell, Stote Fayre bade [all weasel-like creatures] or Wilde Catte', 'Otter or Hedgehogges', 'Rattes or Myce', 'Moldwarpe or Wante [moles]', with different bounties placed on the quantities of heads collected in each category, again to be paid by parish wardens. This Act was renewed several times.

Roger Lovegrove, former director of the UK Royal Society for the Protection of Birds, has explained that these laws had a severe impact upon many native British species, which is still felt today. Payments for the killing of animals continued until around 1800 in some districts. From the late 1700s onwards, there were concerns about the impact of certain predatory species of British animals on sporting estates, and the measures introduced to address these concerns lasted until World War II. The enclosure of common land also had a huge effect on wildlife. Commons had previously been unfenced, allowing free passage of animals, but 'enclosure' meant that this land was fenced and devoted to farming or other purposes. Eventually, the sea eagle and the osprey were exterminated entirely, and the wildcat, pine marten and red kite were almost reduced to extinction.

Australian Laws

Australia's geological and climatic history makes its situation unusual: it is an island that separated from Antarctica 50 million years ago, and it was relatively isolated until the Indo-Australian Plate and Asia collided 5.3 million years ago. Because Australia was largely separate from the rest of the world, it has a huge variety of native animals and plants that are found nowhere else in the world. Many of these species have died out or become threatened as a result of the proliferation of species since introduced from other areas of the world.

The first animals to be introduced here were dingoes (which came with Indigenous people), but once the British arrived, many different foreign species followed, including rabbits, foxes, pigs, camels, cats, dogs and horses. The success of the rabbit in Australia inspired some to develop 'acclimatisation societies', which introduced non-native species to Australia from all over the world, either to improve Australia's beauty or as food sources. While some introduced animals failed to survive, others flourished, with devastating consequences for native fauna and flora. Many of these introduced animals also became pests to humans.

Native animals have also been judged as 'pest animals' at times. The thylacine or 'Tasmanian tiger' (a carnivorous marsupial) was the subject of a particularly notorious bounty, which seems to have ultimately driven it to extinction. Thylacines disappeared from the mainland some 2200 years prior to European colonisation, perhaps as a result of competition from the dingo, but they still existed in Tasmania. The Van Diemen's Land Company placed a bounty on them in 1830, because they were concerned about thylacines preying on sheep. In 1887, after intense lobbying, the Tasmanian parliament passed a law allowing for payments of £1 for full-grown thylacines and ten shillings for partly grown thylacines, to be paid if a municipal warden or police magistrate certified that the thylacine had been destroyed. The bounty was ended in 1909. By 1910, thylacines were rare in Tasmania, and the last known thylacine died in captivity in 1936.

At one point, Australia also had a bounty on the head of emus, one of our national emblems. In Western Australia, this culminated in a bizarre 'Emu War'. In 1923, after World War I, emus were taken off the protected list of animals in a particular area of Western Australia, and a law was passed that placed a bounty on their heads – partly because they destroyed crops and partly because they spread the seeds of the noxious prickly pear (itself an introduced species). However, the law did not operate effectively enough for farmers, and in 1932, defence minister Sir George Pearce was persuaded to send in the Australian Army to cull them. The emus proved formidable foes – they were agile, split into small bands, and withstood heavy fire – but eventually a large number were culled. Following the ineffective 'Emu War', the legal solution (a bounty for culling the birds) was reinstated and remained in effect until 1947.

Kangaroo-hunting is still legally permitted in Australia to this day. Following colonisation, kangaroo populations flourished on land cleared for agriculture. According to the National Code of Practice for the Humane Shooting of Kangaroos and Wallabies for Commercial Purposes (2008), kangaroo and wallaby hunters are required to hold a permit under state laws, and they must shoot the animal in a way that is humane, ensuring that joeys are also shot if the mother is killed.

Introduced animals have also been subject to culls. This has been controversial, because many of these animals were introduced to benefit humans but have now come to be regarded as pests. Australian feral horses, known as 'brumbies', are found in the Alpine National Park, where they are damaging habitats and waterways, and threatening native animals and plants. However, some have objected to the culling of brumbies because they are part of Australian folk legend, as the famous Australian poem 'The Man from Snowy River' by A.B. 'Banjo' Paterson exemplifies:

> There was movement at the station, for the word had
>   passed around
> That the colt from old Regret had got away,
> And had joined the wild bush horses – he was worth
>   a thousand pound,
> So all the cracks had gathered to the fray.

The 'cracks' were the best riders. In the end, the eponymous 'Man from Snowy River' takes his horse down a steep hill in a terrifying ride to recover the colt. The origin of the word 'brumby' is unclear, but Paterson seems to have been responsible for its popularisation in a later poem called 'Brumby's Run'.

The tensions between those who want to preserve the brumby as part of Australia's cultural heritage and those who see the brumby as a pest gave rise to a 2020 legal dispute between the Australian Brumby Alliance and Parks Victoria, with the Australian Brumby Alliance seeking to restrain Parks Victoria from trapping and removing feral horses from the Bogong High Plains and the Eastern Alps. However, Justice O'Bryan found that removing or culling brumbies to preserve the biodiversity, ecosystems and unique habitats of alpine Australia was appropriate and would not have a significant impact upon the national heritage values of the Australian Alps. After the bushfires of early 2020, Parks Victoria indicated that it may be forced to cull brumbies rather than remove them.

The introduction of the cane toad (*Bufo marinus*) has had particularly disastrous consequences for Australia. Introduced to control several native species of beetle that feed upon cane plants and to minimise pesticide use, the cane toad spread rapidly through northern Australia but failed to control the beetles. It has natural toxins, and thus kills native animals who attempt to eat it, and it competes with native frogs and toads. Federal senator Pauline Hanson has suggested passing a law that places a bounty on cane toads, paying welfare recipients ten cents for each toad they bring to the local council, which would then euthanise them in freezers. At the moment, a cane toad bounty is only theoretical, but it is worth noting that bounties can sometimes produce perverse incentives, as when the local colonial government in Delhi offered a bounty for cobras, and locals began to breed them to increase their profits.

Nuisance Animals

Another way that wild animals can give rise to disputes is when landowners create the conditions that enable wild animals to thrive, and their neighbours become irritated as a result. The legal position on nuisance is more difficult with regard to wild or semiwild animals, because obviously they are harder to control.

Notoriously, a landowner is not under a duty to restrain wild rabbits on his property from making burrows, and a person cannot seek to 'abate' the nuisance by killing the rabbits. From the thirteenth century onwards, lords of the manor in England would stock their grounds (particularly common grounds) with rabbits (which, as noted earlier, were then called 'conies' or 'coneys' as adults). This was highly profitable because their meat and fur were useful. However, the rabbits could not be confined to one area of land, and they multiplied and spead out, eating crops and undermining land with their burrows. Typically, if rabbits from a lord's burrow were destroying a commoner's crops and the commoner attempted to kill the rabbits as a result, the court found in favour of the lord.

In the famous 1597 case of *Boulston v Hardy*, a dispute about rabbits arose between two commoners. Hardy had created two 'coney boroughs' on his land, and the rabbits increased to a great number and ended up destroying his neighbour Boulston's corn. Hardy was not liable for several reasons. First, as we learned in Chapter 1, any property right in wild animals was necessarily qualified, and second, the court found Hardy could not exercise control over rabbits in the same way as someone who ran a lime-kiln or dye-house could control the products of his industry.

For the purposes of the law of *scienter*, the wild rabbit is not regarded as intrinsically dangerous, perhaps because they are generally not ferocious or directly harmful to humans. However, while rabbits are relatively harmless in England, they have devastated the Australian countryside and wildlife, and several attempts to cull them, to prevent them from devastating the land or to completely eliminate them have failed. We have inherited laws from England that are not entirely logical, because they developed from historical and geographical conditions quite different to those of present-day postcolonial Australia.

Flies are most definitely wild creatures and generally not capable of being owned, but a landowner can be liable for nuisance if he keeps his land in such as state as to attract them. In an English case from 1914, the Blands lived next door to Mr Yates, who had a market garden that he cultivated using a method known as French gardening, 'which required the use of an excessive quantity of manure'. The Blands complained about the smell and the large number of flies infesting their house, which they said bred in the manure. The judge found that the Blands 'had suffered serious inconvenience and interference with their comfort as occupiers of the house and garden according to notions prevalent among reasonable English men and women'. Mr Yates's use of manure was excessive, and accordingly, he was restrained from using it to that extent in the future.

There was a similar Australian dispute, litigated in several cases over several years, in which multiple neighbours complained to their local council about a mushroom farmer who used a compost made from stable straw, horse manure and horse urine, which attracted flies and created a foul smell.

In the first decision, handed down in 1988, it was decided that the situation was so bad as to constitute a public nuisance and the council was therefore entitled to send a notice demanding that the mushroom farmer 'abate' – or reduce the effects of – the nuisance. The dispute was still ongoing in 1994, when it came before a different judge, with the farmer's neighbours and the council again seeking an injunction to restrain the farmer from using the compost, this time simply because of the smell. Justice Brownie did not consider the flies relevant, saying that the flies added 'emphasis and colour' to the case, but were not 'of any enduring significance.'

Brownie's decision shows that private actions such as nuisance have been complemented by overlaying public regulation (by councils who regulate neighbourhood behaviour, for instance). It may also be possible that Australian cultural attitudes to flies are different to English attitudes. Flies are vastly more prevalent in Australia – especially the native 'bush fly' – and thus may be regarded as a normal, everyday annoyance that must be tolerated.

Conversely, in an English case from 1919, *Stearn v Prentice Brothers Ltd*, it was held that a landowner was not responsible for nuisance caused by rats, mainly because the landowner's practices were not excessive and had not altered prior to the rats' proliferation – a plague of rats had simply arisen for unknown reasons. The landowner was Prentice Brothers, which manufactured bone manure for fertiliser. Prentice Brothers collected heaps of bones on its property as part of its business, and this attracted rats. One year, there was a particularly greater number of rodents, which ate the corn of neighbouring farmer Mr Stearn. Mr Stearn subsequently tried to obtain an injunction restraining Prentice Brothers from piling up bones on the basis of *Bland v Yates* (the English fly case discussed above). The court declined to award an injunction, finding that while Mr Yates's practices had been unusual, Prentice Brothers' recent practices were normal for the business – the amount of bones on the premises was the same as it had been for the last thirty years – and it had done nothing to increase the rat population.

Recently, it was reported that the New Zealand suburb of Titirangi in Auckland was overrun by feral chickens and rats, the latter of which were drawn to the food left out for the chickens by one soft-hearted individual. The case has caused conflict between the suburb's neighbours:

'It's reignited old divisions in the village,' said Greg Presland, the long-suffering chair of the Waitākere Ranges community board, which is tasked with addressing the problem. Some Titirangi residents have said on social media that the chickens bring a quaint and charming character to the village. Others say they're 'like something out of a Stephen King movie'.

Presland, who said 'about 15' of the birds have taken up residence 50 metres from his house, said the problem began in 2008, when a resident had released two domesticated chickens in the village and they had 'gone rogue'.

The flock's numbers swelled in the years since, peaking at as many as 250 in 2019.

'A combination of being sleep deprived and seeing the neighbourhood wrecked made some people really hate them,' said Presland, adding that the chickens had also harmed the roots of kauri trees, an endangered New Zealand native.

But the last straw came when the suburb was 'terrorised' by a pestilence of rats 'the size of cats', he said, which were attracted by food left out for the birds. Residents were finally united: the chickens had to go.

Such a situation is not unusual. Even where chickens are not wild, complaints sometimes arise because their feed attracts rats. In this case, the council attempted to round up the birds, but they could not capture them all, and after the COVID-19 shutdown occurred, the chicken population burgeoned again. Some residents have now suggested eating the chickens, whereas another neighbour continues to leave out grain for them. This kind-hearted neighbour might be liable for creating a nuisance, as per Mr Yates, the gardener who caused a local fly infestation by leaving out manure.

The Strange Ambivalence of the Law

When considering whether certain animals should be controlled or not, and whether people should be liable for damage they cause, the law's focus is generally on harm to humans and their interests. However, there is an inevitable slippage of the law's focus when questions arise about whether the conduct of the animal in question is reasonable.

The apogee of this is probably the bizarre anathematisation of pest animals in late medieval and early modern Europe. In such instances, locals prosecuted rats, mice, locusts, weevils and other vermin in ecclesiastical courts, pronouncing a verdict of anathema upon recalcitrant animals that refused to leave their fields and houses. The individual qualities of the animals were considered in detail, with almost surprising tenderness.

Thus, in 1519, the Stelvio commune in Tyrol, Austria, instituted proceedings against local *lutmäuse* (a species of vole), which were damaging crops with their burrowing, thus apparently preventing the locals from paying their tithes. When the judge, Wilhelm von Haßingen, handed down the verdict in the court of Glurns in 1520, he banished the rodents upon pain of anathematisation. He also ordered that the *lutmäuse* be given

> free safe-conduct and an additional respite of fourteen days ... to all those which are young and to such as are yet in their infancy; but on the expiration of this reprieve each and every must be gone, irrespective of age or previous condition of pregnancy.

The judge's statement recognises that it is natural for rodents to burrow and look after their young, and it also the recognises the individual circumstances of the rodents. It is said that a bridge was built to allow the *lutmäuse* safe conduct across the river, although no trace of it remains. The locals of Glurns apparently remember this 'Mäuseprozess' (mouse trial) proudly and have developed mouse-shaped confectionary called the 'Glurnser Mäuse' (chocolate coating over a marzipan filling).

These 'vermin trials' will be considered in more detail in Chapter 6 (including the startling trials of rats and weevils). For now, it is sufficient to note again how the law exhibits an ambivalence in the way it treats animals, and oscillates wildly between solely considering the needs of humans on the one hand and treating animals as groups or individuals with particular tendencies, wants and needs on the other. This theme will continue in the next chapter, which considers the laws that deal with blaming animals.

3.

BLAMING ANIMALS

I N 1386, THE TRIBUNAL OF FALAISE, IN FRANCE, SENTENCED a criminal defendant to death for murdering a child. Before her execution, the defendant was dressed in new clothes, and to reflect the injuries she had inflicted on the child, her head and legs were wounded. She was then hanged before a crowd.

What was so remarkable about this tragic case? The defendant was a female pig, tried and found guilty as if she were human. The event was so memorable that the Church of Sainte-Trinité in Falaise once featured a fresco of the execution, although it was painted over in 1820. But while the trial was considered unusual by the residents of Falaise, prosecutions against animals have in fact been reported all over the world, including in Europe, India, South-East Asia, New Zealand and Africa.

In this chapter, we look at how we sometimes punish or blame animals personally for their behaviour. The way we treat animals for harming or killing humans is revealing: it shows us something about the human psyche, our rationalisations for punishing criminal behaviour and how the law reflects our biases and beliefs.

In order to understand why animals would be treated as criminal defendants, we need to briefly consider the complex mix of motives, purposes and policies behind the punishment of crime more generally – among them retribution, deterrence, rehabilitation, public declarations of rights and maintenance of public safety.

The retributive principle stipulates that someone who injures a victim should be treated in the same way: 'an eye for an eye, a tooth for a tooth'. This is sometimes known as the *lex talionis*, or 'law of the claw'. While this seems violent, one of the functions of criminal law is to prevent the blood feuds and vendettas that characterise societies without strong legal systems, leading to cycles of revenge that can extend for years. The notion that retribution is achieved once the state penalises the perpetrator was designed to stem this problem.

Deterrence is another motive for criminal punishment – of both the specific criminal being punished and other would-be criminals. In the case of animals, however, deterrence is unlikely to play a strong role, unless one believes that animals have the capacity to understand why punishment is meted out.

The performative aspect of criminal justice largely exists so that the public can see that justice has been done, as this enables the other intended effects of the punishment.

In modern times, punishing animals that kill or maim other animals or humans is generally justified as necessary for public safety, rather than as an aspect of retribution, deterrence or performative justice. Nonetheless, the questions raised by the animal trials of the past still exist today. If an animal kills a human or commits another serious crime, should it be held responsible for the act? And if so, what should the response be?

As we discussed in the introduction, in 2015 Knox City Council made the decision that Izzy the Staffordshire terrier should be 'destroyed' after she injured Jennifer Edward. Was Izzy herself being 'punished' for her role in biting another person? Should the law perhaps consider whether non-human animals can be rehabilitated instead of sentenced to death?

The legal response to dangerous or killer animals varies from culture to culture and animal to animal, depending on the historical period in question. The discussion that follows distinguishes between domesticated animals and semidomesticated and wild animals – a distinction that flows through this book more generally. Domesticated animals are generally treated more harshly for their wrongdoings than semidomesticated or wild animals, which are expected to be wild or vicious by their very nature. Domesticated animals, on the other hand, are expected to be controllable and docile, and consequently there is more law relating to their control.

Domesticated Animals and Crimes

When a domesticated animal kills or harms another person, there are at least two possible wrongdoers: the animal and the owner of the animal. Sometimes the owner is blamed; in other cases, the animal itself is held culpable; and sometimes both are blamed. How the animal is treated by the law varies. Under some laws, the animal is treated like a blameworthy inanimate object; under others it is treated more like a blameworthy human (when it is given legal representation, for instance).

The Goring Ox

Laws that seek to ascertain legal responsibility for animals that harm others have an ancient history. Both the Laws of Eshnunna and the Code of Hammurabi, Mesopotamian legal codes dating back to around 1850 BCE and 1754 BCE respectively, contain laws providing that the owner was liable to pay blood money if his ox killed another person. If an ox was known to be dangerous, and the owner did not bind the ox's horns or tie the ox up, the owner was liable to pay for any human death it caused. The fine was higher for the death of a freeborn man than for the death of a slave. The Laws of Eshnunna also mention dogs, with similar pecuniary penalties for their owners. So far, so good: these laws are not very different from modern laws or the laws of Ine, discussed in Chapter 2.

The later Jewish laws contained in the book of Exodus provided that *both* the owner and the goring ox could be punished for a death caused by the ox. If an apparently innocuous ox killed a freeborn person, the ox was stoned to death, and its flesh was not eaten, but the owner of the ox went unpunished. Conversely, if the owner was forewarned that the ox was dangerous, both the ox and the owner could be stoned to death. However, the owner might be allowed to pay the full amount for the value of the deceased's life to save his own (this was not an option for the ox). If the ox gored a slave, the ox was stoned, and the owner had to pay the value of the slave to the slaveowner. Despite the express words used, it is not clear whether the death penalty for the owner was ever meted out: certainly there is no record of it.

In *Bava Kamma*, one of the ancient books of rabbinical commentary on biblical law, the rabbis considered the difference between oxen who were known to be dangerous and those who were apparently innocuous:

> The Sages taught: In the case of an innocuous ox that killed a person and subsequently went and caused damage, the court judges it as a case of capital law [criminal wrongdoing] and the ox is killed, and the court does not judge it as a case of monetary law, despite the damage that it caused.
>
> By contrast in the case of a forewarned ox that killed a person and subsequently went and caused damage, the court judges it as a case of monetary law [civil wrongdoing], and the owner is liable to pay for the damage it caused, and then the court goes back and judges it again as a case of capital law [criminal wrongdoing] and the ox is killed.

This has been taken to mean that the animal was to be tried separately for his actions, because he was subject to the death penalty.

The commentary in the *Mekhilta de Rabbi Shimon bar Yoh. ai* suggested that the ox should not be executed for causing a death unless the case was heard before a rabbinical court of twenty-three, with many of the same procedural protections that would have been accorded to a human. However, rabbinic student Gabriel Kanter-Webber notes that there is no record that explicitly describes an ox being on trial before such court.

In ancient rabbinical commentary, it is reported in several places that the law regarding oxen was once extended to a rooster in Jerusalem, which was purported to have killed a baby by pecking it on the head. The rooster was duly stoned to death – presumably after the legally mandated trial. Therefore, Rabbi Judah ben Bava extended these rules to other killer animals. In fact, Rabbi Akiva held that even killer wolves, lions, bears, tigers, hyenas and serpents should have the benefit of a hearing before a full rabbinical court (Rabbi Eliezer would have said it was right for more ferocious beasts to be summarily killed).

One may wonder where the obsession with oxen in Jewish law stemmed from! It appears that these laws were at least partly inspired by the earlier laws of Mesopotamia because of various overlaps in both this and other areas. There were also good reasons for the law's obsession with oxen. Jeremy Brown, a medical doctor who runs the *Talmudology* blog, notes that even today, cows can be surprisingly dangerous:

> In 2009, orthopedists from Our Lady of Lourdes Hospital in Ireland published a fascinating paper entitled 'Cow-Related Trauma: A 10-Year Review of Injuries Admitted to a Single Institution'. Over a decade, the hospital admitted 47 people with cow-related trauma, most of whom sustained their injuries from kicking ... And next time you feel like walking across a field containing some gentle-looking cows, remember this: one of the patients was admitted with a head injury, a hip fracture and hypothermia after being trampled on by his herd of cattle in a field and found a number of hours later ... Cattle look gentle, and for the most part, they are. But they are large beasts with incredible strength. Hikers (and farmers) beware.

In fact, in 2015, a herd of stampeding cattle, killed a sixty-year-old Irishwoman and injured another woman very seriously.

There are other instances of cattle trials outside Jewish law. In 1641, Thomas Johnson, a Protestant vicar in County Mayo, Ireland, reported that rebels took cattle belonging to English plantation owners and put them on trial for unspecified offences. The rebels apparently held full trials, subjecting the cattle to an ancient English common law procedure known as 'the benefit of clergy', by which an accused could get the trial transferred to an ecclesiastical court, where the death sentence was less commonly handed down. The procedure involved a literacy test, which required the accused to read from the Bible. Purportedly the judge said that the cattle 'looke as if they could speake English, give them the booke, & see if they can read'. Unsurprisingly, the cattle 'stood mute & could not read' and were sentenced to death and duly slaughtered. It is unclear whether the trial was a mockery of English procedure or a genuine attempt to give the cattle a chance at mercy.

Even in modern times, bulls have been subjected to a sort of 'death penalty' for killing humans. In July 2016, Spanish matador Víctor Barrio was killed by a bull called Lorenzo, which speared Barrio through the chest with a horn, puncturing his right lung and thoracic aorta. According to Spanish tradition, Lorenzo was killed so that his lineage would not continue. It is unclear whether he was put to death as punishment, to ensure that his characteristics were not passed on to other cattle or because his actions had 'tainted' him. Tradition dictated that Lorenzo's mother also be killed to fully extinguish his lineage, but she had already died of old age.

Interestingly, Jewish law held that an 'ox in the arena' was not to be subject to a death penalty if he killed someone, because the situation compelled him to gore against his will. In this instance, the rabbis took the individual circumstances of the ox into account.

There is no question of violent bulls being punished in modern Australian law. Neither the bull nor the owner is generally judged to be criminal in the case of an attack. Rather, the question is whether the owner of the bull was negligent in his or her control of the animal. As a result, the approach taken by Australian law is not that far from the Code of Hammurabi and the Laws of Eshnunna: rather than punishing the bull, these laws held that the better response was to demand that the owner of the animal paid for the injury caused if he knew it to be dangerous. The only difference is that under Australian law, the owner's obligation to compensate the victim is subject to the victim's obligation to take reasonable care if he knows a dangerous bull is present.

A 2004 Australian case, *Smith v Capella State High School Parents and Citizens Association*, dealt with the victim's obligation to take reasonable care. The plaintiff, Smith, was injured at a rodeo fundraiser by a bull named Ridgy Didge, which caught Smith in the right hip area with his horns and tossed him into the air, causing Smith severe injuries. Although Ridgy Didge was obviously aggressive, Justice Peter Dutney refused to classify him as an intrinsically dangerous wild animal for the purposes of a *scienter* action, and so the bull's owner, Curran, was not strictly liable for Smith's injuries. The question was then whether Curran had been negligent in letting Ridgy Didge into the arena without warning Smith. In the event, Curran and Smith were held equally negligent: Curran knew the bull was particularly dangerous and should not have let him out without warning; Smith, a bull owner himself, knew that Curran was fetching another bull and should have been aware of the risk. Smith was awarded damages for his past and present losses, including loss of income, medical treatment, and pain and suffering.

Other Ancient Legal Systems

Other ancient legal systems also punished animals for crimes, but less is known about specific historical cases. The ancient Greeks prosecuted both animals and inanimate objects (including spears and statues) that caused people injury or death, but these cases are only mentioned in passing by Aristotle. It is not known what happened to the animals who were prosecuted, but the inanimate objects were banished – that is, they were removed from the territory in question. Killer animals can still be banished today, as we discuss later in this chapter.

In his dialogue on laws, Plato also contemplated placing animals and inanimate objects on trial in a fictional colony called Magnesia:

> If a beast of burden or other animal kills someone ... let the relatives
> open actions at law for homicide against the killer, let judgment be given
> by those of the land-stewards whom the relative selects and as many of
> them as he selects, and when the animal has been defeated in the trial, let
> them kill it and throw it beyond the borders of the land. If an inanimate
> thing deprives a man of life, except for a thunderbolt or any other missile
> of supernatural origin, but among other things if any object kills a man,
> whether by falling itself or because something fell on it, let the relative by
> descent appoint the nearest of the neighbors as judge for the occurrence;

let him thus acquit himself and his whole kin of obligation, and when the
thing has been defeated in the trial, let it be expelled beyond the borders
just as in the case of animals.

In most ancient European societies, a domestic animal that caused
someone death or injury was subject to laws requiring 'noxal surrender',
meaning it had to be given to the victim or the victim's family. There were
also taboos around eating or using produce from any animal who killed
a person. Over time, noxal surrender gradually turned into an obligation
to pay damages. Thus, eighth-century Frankish laws contemplated that an
owner would pay weregild (compensation) for horses, cows or pigs that
killed people or for pigs that desecrated corpses by eating them.

Noxal surrender arguably involves a notion that the animal itself must
be punished or is somehow responsible: when an animal was given to the
victim or their family it was to allow them to exact retribution on it. It also
has a civil flavour: in some ways, the owner was also punished by being
forced to give up ownership of the animal – the replacement of noxal surrender with the punishment of damages cements this.

Killer Animals on Trial

Animal trials seem to have become particularly prevalent in late medieval Europe, although cases of retribution against criminal animals were
recorded in other societies too, including in Africa, Asia and New Zealand. In continental Europe, when an animal caused injury or death to a
human, they were sometimes brought before secular courts and apparently
tried as people would have been. These trials continued until the end of the
early modern era, and were recorded in legal archives and histories across
Europe, to the extent that we have records of the sentences pronounced
upon murderous animals, receipts from the hangmen of killer pigs claiming expenses, and pictures of murderous pigs being tried.

It is possible that the biblical provisions for punishing 'goring oxen' led
some jurisdictions to consider prosecuting animals for crimes as legitimate. The historian Peter Dinzelbacher has noted that animal trials do not
seem to have gained purchase in non-Catholic countries, and that most
cases occurred in a narrow band of countries. Many of the trials dealt with
roaming pigs who killed infants or young children, particularly in the parts
of Europe now recognised as France, Switzerland and Germany. Italy and

Spain do not seem to have held such trials. After the Reformation, Protestant areas did not tend to hold animal trials either. In 1666, a council of the Protestant Geistlicher Covenant of the town of Bern stated: 'Since the ox did not receive any law, he cannot, by breaking one, commit a sin.'

During the trials, animals were occasionally sentenced to death for crimes including killing or maiming people, participating in bestiality or witchcraft. The animals punished in this way included not only pigs, but bulls, cows, horses and even bees. In 864, after a swarm of bees stung a man to death, the Council of Worms decreed that the bees should be suffocated in the hive before they could make any more honey, lest the honey be tainted. It appears that there may have been more trials of this kind than have been discovered so far: the literature of the time demonstrates that people were well accustomed to trials of various animals, both wild and domestic.

Killer Pigs

Why were pigs so prevalent in the annals of killer animals who were prosecuted? Edward Payson Evans, an American scholar and linguist, who wrote what remains the most detailed book on medieval animal prosecutions, offers the following explanation:

> The frequency with which pigs were brought to trial and adjudged to death, was owing, in a great measure, to the freedom with which they were permitted to run about the streets and to their immense number. The fact that they were under the special protection of St Anthony ... conferred upon them a certain immunity, so that they became a serious nuisance, not only endangering the lives of children, but also generating and disseminating diseases.

The Order of Hospitallers of St Anthony was an order of monks that arose in Grenoble in around 1100 to care for people suffering from disease; they were particularly adept at treating ergotism, which arises from eating fungus-infected grain. As a show of gratitude for their good deeds, it became traditional to donate the runt of a litter of pigs to the Hospitallers, St Anthony the Great being the patron saint of pigs and other domestic animals (he reportedly had a faithful companion pig during his time as a monk). The Hospitallers put bells around the neck of their pigs and let them scavenge in the city. 'Tantony pigs' became notorious for following anyone who seemed to have food, although English medieval towns, at the least, tried to control them.

As medieval historian Jamie Kriener notes, pigs were routinely cultivated in antiquity and early medieval times, and their meat was prized among many societies, including by the Romans. However, pigs are very intelligent and physically strong – they are capable of jumping up to 4 feet high and swimming for miles. They learn from other pigs and have an excellent spatial sense. They also love puzzles and enjoy trying to escape if held captive. Ancient and medieval people knew this, and attempted to keep them in check, enlisting swineherds to control them.

In early medieval times, swineherds tended to graze pigs in forests, and landowners even levied a tax on pig owners (called *pannage*) for the use of their land. However, in late medieval times, when animal trials began to arise, pigs were more commonly kept in cities, giving rise to increasing complaints about their smell and dung.

One wonders if small children were easy targets for hungry pigs? It is well known that pigs are omnivorous, and will eat dead animals, rotten garbage and human excreta. We also known that stressed and uncomfortable domestic sows can eat their own piglets. Moreover, pigs occasionally do eat farmers who collapse in the pigpen, or babies or small children: several such incidents have occurred around the world in the last ten years, including in the United States. These incidents do not occur in Australian suburbia today because pigs largely live in industrial farms and do not wander our streets – although we do have feral pigs in the Australian bush.

The homicidal sow of Falaise, whose story we told at the start of this chapter, was far from alone – many pigs were charged with killing children in the past. In 1457, a sow was convicted of causing the death of a five-year-old boy, Jehan Martin of Savigny. The sow's six piglets, found stained with blood, were initially charged as accomplices, but as Evans notes, 'in lack of any positive proof that they had assisted in mangling the deceased, they were restored to their owner, on condition that he should give bail for their appearance, should further evidence be forthcoming to prove their complicity in their mother's crime'. It is fascinating that their age and a lack of evidence of their complicity were considered relevant when making the decision to spare the piglets' lives, just as they would be if a human were on trial. While the piglets were spared the death penalty, their original owner declared he did not want them, and thus they were forfeited as ownerless property to Katherine de Barnault, Lady of Savigny.

TRIAL OF A SOW AND PIGS AT LAVEGNY.

The trial of a sow and her piglets

In another case, in 1494, a pig was arrested for having 'strangled and defaced a young child in its cradle'. During the trial, several witnesses said that 'on the morning of Easter Day, as the father was guarding the cattle and his wife Gillon was absent in the village of Dizy, the infant being left alone in its cradle, the said pig entered during the said time the said house and disfigured and ate the face and neck of the said child, which, in consequence of the bites and defacements inflicted by the said pig, departed this life'. The persons who brought the charges were the friars who lived in the farm next door to the family. In sentencing the pig, the judge said:

> We in detestation and horror of the said crime, and to the end that an example may be made and justice maintained, have said, judged, sentenced, pronounced and appointed, that the said porker, now detained as a prisoner and confined in the said abbey, shall be by the master of high works hanged and strangled on a gibbet of wood near and adjoignant to the gallows and high place of execution belonging to the said monks, being contiguous to their fee-farm of Avin.

131

Sometimes pigs were pardoned for their involvement in crime. In 1379, in Saint-Marcel-le-Jeussey, two herds mingled, one of which was communally owned and one of which belonged to the local priory. Three sows, enraged by the squealing of a piglet, knocked over Perrinot Muet, the son of the swineherd, killing him. The sows were condemned to death. It was said that 'as both the herds had hastened to the scene of the murder and by their cries and aggressive actions showed that they approved of the assault ... they were arrested as accomplices and sentenced by the court to suffer the same penalty'. However, the friar who owned one of the herds sought pardon for all of the pigs except the three perpetrators, and the duke of Burgundy granted this.

On some occasions owners were also punished, as were Jehan Delalande and his wife, whose pig mauled and killed a child called Gilon in 1499. The pig was sentenced to death, and a fine was imposed on the Delalandes because they had been negligent in looking after the child, not because of any negligence in relation to the pig. Evans notes that, in general, 'the owner of the blood-guilty beast was considered wholly blameless and sometimes even remunerated for his loss'. As we will see, English law took quite a different view of this.

The punishment of the killer animals varied. Sometimes, animals were tortured, apparently in order to extract 'confessions' from them (although it is not clear how confessions were made. Evans recounts thirteen instances of European pigs being hanged, three more of them being buried alive and one of a pig being burnt at the stake, all for the crimes of killing infants and children. Interestingly, it appears that following proper procedure remained important. In Schweinfurt, a sow that had bitten off the ear and torn the hand of a local child was jailed. When a hangman hanged the sow without legal authority, it enraged the local populace, and he was forced to flee. The phrase *Schweinfurt Sauhenker* (Schweinfurt sow-hangman) later came to mean a ruffian who ignored the law.

As we have mentioned, killer animals were generally not eaten – even if their species was normally consumed by humans – because the flesh was deemed to be tainted. Evans recorded an instance in 1553, in which some pigs that had killed a child in Frankfurt am Main were executed and thrown into the river. Similarly, a cow that killed a woman in Machern, Saxony, in 1621 was killed and burned, and neither the cow's meat nor hide was used. However, in Ghent, in 1578, a cow that had killed a person was slaughtered, and her flesh was sold, with half the proceeds given to the victim's family and half to the city's poor. The cow's head was struck off and put on a stake near the gallows to indicate that she had been punished.

What Was the Motivation behind Animal Trials?

Romans loved to watch criminals being executed by gladiators and wild animals, and *panem et circenses* (bread and games) satiated the public need for such spectacles. In imperial Rome, the public's right to vote on who lived or died in the arena gave them a sense of power without threatening the emperor. The English public also enjoyed the spectacle of criminals being hanged, put in stocks and pillories or subjected to various forms of humiliation, such as branding. Erected in 1571, and in use until 1783, the 'Tyburn Tree' at Tyburn, near London, was a notorious gallows that allowed multiple criminals to be executed at the one time. There was surely a performative aspect to animal trials as well: they provided just as much of a spectacle as the trials and executions of people.

From a distance, it is easy to think that the existence of animal trials reflect a more superstitious time; however, historian James McWilliams suggests that it was related to the fact that in pre-industrial times – from the medieval era till the nineteenth century – people had a much more intimate relationship with animals:

> People living in pre-industrial agrarian societies interacted almost constantly with domesticated animals. Seventeenth-century farming account books suggest that farmers of that era spent up to 16 hours a day observing and caring for domesticated beasts. They watched these animals make choices, respond to human directives, engage in social relationships, and distinguish themselves as individuals with unique personalities. This observational intimacy lasted well into the 19th century, until feedlots and packing plants consolidated the business of animal agriculture, eventually superseding the practices that kept animals and farmers in close and relatively long-term proximity. A change in mentality followed this consolidation. Humans began to think and talk about animals as objects. 'The pig,' explained one agricultural manual from the 1880s, 'is the most valuable machine on the farm.' Today, with nearly 99 percent of animal products deriving from these 'factory farms', this view of animals-as-objects persists as the dominant perspective.

While there may be something to this, McWilliams' argument ought not be overstated. In medieval societies, animals were still regarded as property, despite their constant proximity to people. St Thomas Aquinas clearly believed that oxen could be owned, and that killing an ox was in no way equivalent to killing a person. Moreover, many medieval people regarded humans as superior to animals and believed that humans were entitled to command them. Indeed, it has been suggested that domestic animals were tried not because they were regarded as equivalent to human murderers, but because they had inverted the natural order of things: they killed humans who were supposed to have mastery over them.

Conversely, the historian Peter Dinzelbacher suggests that animal trials began to flourish due to the conditions present in the late Middle Ages and early modern era: insecurity from epidemics, economic depression and social conflict; the existence of Roman law and court procedure in the relevant areas; the comfort derived from seeing legal process and justice enacted; the profit lawyers, lords and the judiciary made from holding such trials; and the tendency to personify animals in extreme circumstances. Dinzelbacher hypothesises that these trials only took place

> under extremely unusual circumstances in order to help the local community cope with an otherwise recalcitrant threat – not because they were proven to work but because they created the impression that the authorities were assiduously maintaining law and order in a cooperative and decided manner, even if the delinquents were not human beings.

The tendency to legally punish animals seems to have been more common in areas that were predominantly Catholic and had inherited Roman law. However, as we noted earlier, Roman law did not blame animals for crimes *per se*; rather, the paterfamilias was responsible for any harm caused by the actions of their slaves, children and animals via the *actio de pauperie*. Thus it is evident that a shift in philosophy took place, for reasons that remain unclear, although perhaps the legal punishment of animals is consistent with the fact that Roman law likened animals to children and slaves, not things.

We speculate here that the first French trials may also have been inspired by rabbinical writings: in the late medieval period, an esteemed school of rabbinical commentary flourished in the area of northern France where the trials first arose. Of course, both Christians and Jews accepted the book of Exodus, and perhaps, at least, there was a discussion about the rules regarding 'goring oxen' and how they might be enforced when an animal killed a child.

Today, we may not be as far from the medieval mindset as we think. Psychologist Geoffrey Goodwin and legal academic Adam Benforado recently undertook a fascinating psychological study to ascertain what triggers our desire for retribution, specifically in relation to animals. They presented study participants with several different hypothetical animal attacks: in some instances, the victims were human – in various iterations they included a ten-year-old girl, a fifty-five-year-old homeless man and a forty-eight-year-old paedophile who had not been punished for his crimes – and in other instances, the damage was done to property or another animal (such as a domestic dog). The perpetrators included both wild and domesticated animals.

The study showed that when an animal killed a young child, participants were significantly more punitive towards the animal than they were if it killed an older person or another animal. This reaction was replicated several times. Goodwin and Benforado called this the 'victim identity' effect. They noted that the effect was present even though an animal is no more dangerous if its victim was sympathetic. Accordingly, the participants' preferred punishment seems to be based on the view that the crime of killing a child demands a more severe punishment than killing another, less sympathetic, person.

Goodwin and Benforado also presented participants with scenarios in which authorities killed an 'innocent' shark and a shark that was 'guilty' of causing a human death. They discovered what they refer to as a 'targeted punishment effect', which was again replicated several times: participants indicated that only by killing the correct shark could proper amends be made for the victim's death; they were less likely to support killing the 'innocent' shark. Moreover, participants were more likely to support inflicting pain upon 'guilty' animals than 'innocent' animals, particularly when the victim was a child, but less so when the victim was a paedophile. This suggested a retributive motive predominated.

Goodwin and Benforado hypothesise that even in modern times, retributivism can extend to animals:

> In general, people presumably do not think that sharks (and most other animals) have the moral capacity to be able to distinguish right and wrong actions, yet we nonetheless observed responses to shark attacks that indicate retributive motives ... We surmise that they

might, in part, be explained by participants' ascribing relevant mental states (and attributes) to animals (e.g., some kind of low-level purposefulness or intentionality). While these mental states may fall short of the traditional 'guilty mind' (*mens rea*) standard required for criminal culpability under the law, the ascription of such states may enable participants to view animals as appropriate targets of retribution.

This hypothesis ... is consistent with a large body of recent findings on anthropomorphization and mental state attribution. Researchers have shown, for instance, that individuals are liable to attribute human-like traits and capacities to non-human agents, including animals under certain conditions. . . Individuals appear to be especially prone to find agency following moral events – that is, instances in which harm has occurred or a benefit has accrued ... This suggests that one reason why our participants were retributive toward animals is that, following a bad event, they attributed mental states relevant to blameworthiness (e.g., some degree of intentionality or purposefulness) to animal offenders.

Although we no longer hold trials for or hang killer animals, contemporary people appear to be just as likely as medieval people to judge an animal as 'guilty' and deserving of punishment.

Perhaps one of the factors that made medieval trials of killer pigs more common was the fact that their victims were mostly babies or children under the age of seven. Although the French medieval scholar and historian Philippe Ariès argued that childhood did not exist in medieval times in Europe and that society simply saw children as miniature adults, later medieval historians such as Shulamith Shahar, Barbara Hanawalt and Nicholas Orme have strongly refuted this, arguing that there were distinct stages of childhood and that children were seen as valuable, despite (or perhaps because of) the high infant mortality rate at that time.

Goodwin and Benforado's research shows that, today, the death of a child is particularly apt to trigger a demand for a retributive response (a death for a death). It may well be that a similar psychological response occurred in medieval times. Perhaps one reason we no longer hold animal trials for animals is simply that our current legal systems generally do not accommodate it, for all that the psychological impulse to punish an animal may still be present.

English Exceptionalism

Medieval English law did not accommodate animal trials in the same way as continental European law. In the late thirteenth century, Henry de Bracton said that in English law, the law of homicide was limited to humans who killed other humans:

> Homicide is the slaying of man by man. If it is one by an ox, a dog or something, it will not properly be termed homicide.

Hence, England dealt with killer animals as a kind of 'dangerous thing', and trials were unnecessary. English medieval coroners' reports tell us that English domesticated beasts also killed people sometimes; it was the legal response that was different.

England's approach to animal violence links into another odd area of common law inherited by Australia: the law of deodands ('deodand' means 'given to God'). English and later Australian law allowed injured people to force the owners of killer animals or inanimate objects to forfeit them to the state or pay a fine representing the value of the thing, which was usually used for charitable purposes. It was derived from the Anglo-Saxon laws of noxal surrender, mentioned earlier. Under noxal surrender, however, the victim's family received the forfeited animal, not the state.

Animals subject to the laws of deodand included killer pigs and horses whose riders had died through falls or drowning. Inanimate items that were 'deodanded' included cauldrons, boats, ladders, bowls, carts, wheels and rope. The law of deodands was abolished in 1846 in England and Wales, after a train carriage was deodanded because the relatives of the dead passengers could not obtain relief in any other way (contractual liability had been excluded by the train tickets). The New South Wales parliament followed suit.

In 1396, Thomas Hokyn held an inquest into the death of a six-month-old child called Agnes Perone in the Parish of St Giles in Oxford. It was reported that 'a sow ate the head of the said Agnes even to the nose, and so the sow was arrested; value 2s. 4d'. The arrest of the pig does not mean that it was tried: rather, it seems the pig was forfeited and the owner had to pay its value to the king as well. According to the commentary on the modern translation of the records,

> accidents of this kind were not uncommon in the Middle Ages. In the episcopal registers at Lincoln is a copy of a certificate issued by

the bishop at the request of a certain woman, informing the world that the woman had lost an ear by the bite of a sow when as a baby she was lying on the floor, and that it was not cut off for any misdeed on her part.

Legal historian Sara Butler discovered a similar case involving a killer pig from 1370 that had a different outcome for the owner: an inquest into the death of a child called Alice Clerk, daughter of Alan Clerk, in Sheffield. Jurors estimated the value of the pig that killed Alice at twelve pence. The owner was only required to pay the value of the pig, but presumably he was humiliated by the inquest, which was a highly public spectacle played out in front of people from neighbouring villages.

As Butler notes, owners of animals did not always want to surrender their animals: a 'miracle story from the canonization trial of Thomas de Cantilupe recounts how Robert and Letiticia Russell actually hid their own son's body rather than have it discovered and risk having their oxen confiscated for misadventure'.

Sometimes in English law, it was said that the owners of killer animals should be held liable for murder. In a 1329 case dealing with a mare that had killed a child, the court seemed willing to do so:

It was presented that a mare struck a child under the ear so that he died. The court asked the jurors whether the mare had been accustomed to misbehave dangerously. They said that she had. The court asked whether the owner of the mare was still alive. The jurors said that he was not. It was said that if he had been alive he would have been arraigned of homicide and amerced, for after he learned of the mare's bad temperament he should always have kept her tied up in a safe place.

Sir Matthew Hale, the seventeenth-century barrister, jurist and judge, said that if the owner of a domesticated beast had properly secured it, but it got loose and killed someone, the owner would not be punished, but the animal would be deodanded. He also said, in remarks that were later echoed by Sir William Blackstone in the eighteenth century, that if 'thro negligence the beast goes abroad after warning or notice of his condition, and kills a man, I think it is manslaughter in the owner'. If the owner let the animal loose with the intention of frightening people and amusing himself, he also judged this to be murder, even if the owner did not mean it to kill anyone. Thus, in 1865, when an innkeeper let loose a horse that he knew to be dangerous onto the common, and the horse killed a child by kicking her, the innkeeper was convicted for murder. The English view towards parents who put their children in harm's way was just as strict. In a case from 1628, Justice Dodderidge noted in passing that if the mother of a bastard child were to hide her child in a pigsty and the child was eaten, the mother would be hanged for murder.

Interestingly, Scots law, a 'hybrid jurisdiction' combining facets of English common law and Roman law, fell somewhere in between the Continent and England. There were Scots cases where 'wylde or head-strang' horses had to be forfeited to the Crown if they 'caryis and castis the rider aganis his will, over ane craig, or ony uther heich place, or in ane water, quairthrow he deceissis [dies] or drownis'. However, if the rider of the horse caused his own death through folly and rashness, then the horse was not forfeited. When Thomas Bullock spurred a horse to cross the Avon River and drowned, the horse (owned by Bullock's master, one James of Durham) was not forfeited to the sheriff, because the decision to cross the river was foolish. Consequently, there was a notion that a horse may be 'not guilty' if there was good reason for the behaviour that killed the person. Unlike the English deodand, however, the state was under no duty to use the money derived from forfeiting the animal for charitable purposes.

Prosecutions for Witchcraft

A final aspect of animal trials that should be mentioned is the tendency to associate animals – particularly cats, toads and hares – with witchcraft and devilry. Thus, animals that committed crimes were sometimes accused of being possessed by demons, just as people who committed crimes were accused of the same. In some cultures, witches were also thought to have 'familiar' animals that fed from their blood and assisted them in evil deeds.

In 1474, the magistrates of Basel sentenced a cockerel to be burned at the stake 'for the heinous and unnatural crime of laying an egg', as Evans puts it. When the executioner cut open the bird, three more eggs were found within. Although Evans suspected that it was 'framed', the unfortunate bird may have been a female chicken that sported more masculine plumage, as several other instances of 'cockerels' laying eggs occurred in the early twentieth century. A chicken with an ovarian tumour may temporarily grow male plumage, and will continue to lay eggs when she recovers. The 'Rooster of Madison' was one such bird. She later moulted her plumage and regained her female appearance.

A number of dogs were executed for witchcraft during the notorious Salem witch trials in the Massachusetts Bay Colony between 1692 and 1693, along with fourteen women and five men. The execution of the dogs was summary rather than judicial. In October 1692, a girl in Andover accused a neighbour's dog of trying to bewitch her, and the villagers shot the dog immediately. The minister in Andover declared the dog posthumously innocent, on the basis that if it had been possessed by the devil it would not have died. Later, when a dog began behaving strangely in Salem, the girls alleged that a local, John Bradstreet, was 'riding' the animal and tormenting it with his spirit. The dog was killed, and Bradstreet fled to the neighbouring county.

Domestic Dogs on Death Row

We began this book by looking at the modern-day case of Izzy, a dog on death row, but the problem of dogs that harm or kill humans or other animals is ancient. The age of the Vendidad, the Persian Zoroastrian code, is unknown, but it is thought to date back thousands of years. The code contains specific provisions to deal with dogs that wounded people or animals. A mad dog that bit a sheep or a man without barking was to be treated as a wilful murderer: the dog was to be progressively mutilated for each bite it took after the first: each ear was cut off, then each foot, then the tail (presumably the lack of a warning bark made such an attack particularly blameworthy). The Laws of Eshnunna also contain stipulations providing that if a dog bit a man, the owner of the dog would be liable, and Alfred the Great's Anglo-Saxon laws (in use in the 800s) detailed a sliding scale of liability for dog bites, depending on how many times the dog had bitten someone.

Today, domestic dogs pose more of a problem than oxen or pigs, particularly in urban environments. The common law (which Australia inherited from England) has traditionally treated dogs as domesticated animals that are to be presumed tame for the purposes of an action in *scienter*. This means that in order to hold the owner liable, the victim of a dog bite would have to prove that the owner knew the dog was dangerous. Obviously, this was not ideal for victims, and most states in Australia now have specific laws providing that owners are strictly liable for any injuries caused by a dog.

Returning to the story of Izzy, we might consider whether there is a sense in which the dog herself was punished for her 'crime' as much as, if not more than, the human responsible? While we frame our criminal laws as punishing humans, the modern-day connection to medieval animal trials is sharpest when the criminal prosecution of the person responsible for a dog is a prerequisite to that dog's state-ordered 'destruction', as is provided for under Victoria's *Domestic Animals Act 1994*.

This provision covers several quite different offences, from owning a dog that kills or causes a 'serious' injury to a person or animal to owning a dog that attacks without causing much if any harm or merely 'rushes at or chases' someone. The penalties for the human who is prosecuted for such an offence are relatively mild compared to the penalties that apply to those who directly commit violent acts: a fine is the most common penalty, although theoretically the offender could face prison if the dog had previously been declared dangerous or is a restricted breed. But it is a different matter for the dog. So long as the owner is found guilty, and regardless of the severity of the offence, the sentencing judge can still require a local council to kill the dog, and a local council can order the dog's destruction if the judge does not.

As mentioned, the main condition for the exercise of this power is that the person responsible for the dog must be prosecuted and found guilty. In Victoria, the prosecution can target the dog's legal owner or 'a person who keeps or harbours the animal or has the animal in his or her care for the time being whether the animal is at large or in confinement'. In the Australian Capital Territory, the relevant culprit is the dog's 'keeper'.

In 2001, Pamela Elliot pled guilty to being the keeper of Hodesh, a dog of an unspecified breed that was unregistered and had menaced a human and attacked an animal. While Elliot later registered the dog, her de facto partner, who was the sole human to visit Hodesh in the pound, claimed that the dog was his. The ACT's chief justice, asked to rule on the identity of Hodesh's keeper, noted that Elliot would not have been alone in assuming that owning and registering Hodesh made her the dog's keeper. However, riffing on a world-famous English judgment from the 1930s about the duties each human owes her 'neighbour', Chief Justice Miles provided a social test for identifying a dog's keeper:

> The social and humanitarian rule that you are bound to look after your dog becomes in law [that] you have a duty to comply with the Act, and the lawyer's question, 'Upon whom lies the duty?' receives a restricted

reply. You, as the keeper of a dog, must comply. Who, then, in law, is a dog's keeper? The answer seems to be a person who is so closely and directly affected that he or she has (or, perhaps, should have) taken upon himself or herself the responsibility of caring for and exercising control over the dog, feeding, watering and otherwise so caring for it that he or she may expect to receive in return an appropriate measure of loyalty and affection.

Because Elliot's de facto partner was Hodesh's keeper under this test – and because no-one had argued that Hodesh had more than one keeper – Elliot's guilty plea was found wrong. In turn, that meant that no-one had the power to order Hodesh's destruction, unless Elliot's de facto partner was prosecuted and found guilty.

Some jurisdictions have placed further conditions on dog destruction orders. Prior to 2000, Tasmania only required a judge to find that the dog in question was either a killer, dangerous or 'unduly mischievous'. In 1998, after convicting the owner of Missy, a cream labrador cross that had 'harassed' four people and 'attacked' two more people as well as a poodle over the course of eleven months, the magistrate concluded:

> I think it is the general rule that everybody likes to try and give a dog a pretty fair run, just to ensure that what is occurring is perhaps just a little one-off situation, of nothing more than a bit of doggy playfulness, but I think it is fairly clear here that we have gone way beyond that situation … Having regard to all of the circumstances, I think it is appropriate on each and every complaint before this court that I have found proved, that I have the dog declared to be a mischievous dog.

He opted not to fine the owner, but 'as part and parcel of the penalty' to order the dog's death. However, the Supreme Court overturned that order:

> It is clear that a 'one-off situation' or behaviour amounting only to 'doggy playfulness' would not in the normal course of things demonstrate that the dog was either mischievous or dangerous. The fact that the learned magistrate found the behaviour of the dog over a period of some eleven months 'way beyond that situation' does not demonstrate that he was satisfied that the dog, in addition to being mischievous as he declared him to be, was unduly so. Indeed, he pointed out that

although some of the complainants had been apprehensive that the dog might bite them, none of them had in fact been bitten, nor had the poodle, although that may have been due to its owner, Mrs Fletcher, wielding a rake in its defence.

Tasmania subsequently changed the conditions for dog destruction orders: rather than requiring a dog to be 'dangerous' or 'unduly mischievous' before such an order was made, the dog had to have 'attacked' a person or animal. 'Attack' is defined quite broadly to include a dog that bites, 'menaces' or 'harasses', so this requirement clearly would have been met in Missy's case.

Although dog destruction orders are formally made during the sentencing of the owner, they can resemble a criminal trial of the dog. Returning to the ACT case of Hodesh, the chief justice also had to rule on the fate of Indiana, Hodesh's puppy, who, 'in a neat conformity with the blood lines' was owned and kept by Nathan Elliot, the son of Hodesh's owner. The incident that sparked the prosecutions of Nathan and his mother occurred when the two dogs, Hodesh and Indiana, roamed unaccompanied on a suburban street, barking at other dogs and setting off a car alarm, before growling and snarling at two people and, finally, attacking Pepper, a Maltese cross, and Rosie, an Australian Silky Terrier, killing the latter in front of her horrified owners. Two inspectors later caught Hodesh and Indiana and took them to the pound, where the owners of Pepper and Rosie identified them as the dogs that had attacked their pets.

The chief justice sardonically observed that that identification of Hodesh and Indiana did not conform to the elaborate rules laid down by the High Court for identifying suspects being held in custody, which generally require police line-ups to avoid the risk of confirmation bias. This would not have been a problem under federal and national uniform legislation that applies in the Australian Capital Territory, which only imposes these rules for *people* accused of criminal offences. Victoria has a broader statutory rule requiring a warning about the dangerous of misidentifying any 'person or object', but even that seems to exclude animals. To deal with cases where the identification of an animal is disputed, some jurisdictions expressly presume that all dogs involved in an attack were the attacker – a rule that could (or at least should) never be applied to human suspects.

Dog identification was not in dispute in the case of Hodesh and Indiana. Rather, the problem was that the prosecutors' misidentification of

143

Hodesh's keeper had saved the keeper from conviction and the dog from death row, while Indiana still faced a destruction order for her role in the pair's 'rampage'. Chief Justice Miles was not sympathetic to Indiana's keeper, Nathan Elliot, and endorsed the magistrate's reference to his (unspecified) 'character, antecedents and age', and the 'high onus' that ACT law places on dog owners. But Indiana was another matter. The magistrate, while acknowledging that each dog's case was different and that Hodesh was 'more aggressive', had nevertheless held that 'the two dogs appeared to act to some extent together'. The chief justice ruled that this wrongly applied human justice to animals:

> That involves what I might call the anthropomorphic fallacy of look-ing at the behaviour of an animal as if it were that of a human being. It is trite to say that animals do not have any capacity for moral judg-ment, but the point needs to be kept in mind. It is common when assessing the culpability of joint offenders for the purpose of sentenc-ing to have regard to their respective positions with respect to the allocation of individual moral responsibility for the joint offence. It is also common that in such circumstances a court is not able to say that one offender is more or less culpable than the other. But in the case of animals, such principles and considerations simply do not apply.

Instead, three other considerations peculiar to animals were applied. The first was that Indiana was Hodesh's 'pup':

> It is possible, if not likely, that Indiana was so much under the mater-nal influence [of Hodesh] that if the two dogs were to be separated the danger they presented when together would be diminished or even eliminated.

The second was that Indiana, like Hodesh, was kept by a human:

> The fact that they were at large on the day in question was not neces-sarily the fault of the dogs, or of Indiana in particular. If the keeper was at fault in letting them escape and to that extent allowing them to behave as many dogs might do, why should Indiana stand to lose her life?

The third was that there are other options for dealing with animals (beyond a destruction order) that are not available for dealing with humans:

> Banishment orders are almost always inappropriate if made against human beings, but I do not think considerations of the liberty of the subject and the rights guaranteed under the Australian Constitution of freedom of movement of persons within Australia apply to animals.

Rather than leaving 'the younger dog in effect to shoulder the blame for the greater harm done by her mother', Miles adjusted Nathan Elliot's sentence to include a requirement that he take the dog to Queensland, as he had promised to do if the dog was not destroyed.

As we have mentioned, sentencing judges are not the only officials who can order a dog's death after a criminal trial: Victoria and other jurisdictions give local councils – the main enforcement agencies – the same power. The overlapping roles of courts (when punishing dogs' owners) and councils (in managing dangerous dogs) affect each other: councils cannot destroy some dogs unless their owners are brought to court and found guilty by a judge. And, as the Victorian Supreme Court ruled in 2004, a court will often need to know whether council plans to destroy a dog, as the judge will take this into consideration when sentencing the owner – if the owner is already facing the loss of her dog, the court may give her a lighter sentence. It is likely that this information also affects the judge's own decision as to whether to order the dog's death.

The difference between courts and councils is that the point of a criminal trial is to do justice – hence Chief Justice Miles' concerns about not punishing Indiana for the failings of her mother and keeper – while a council's role is to govern, by developing broader policies about dangerous dogs and enforcing them in an efficient way. In the 2004 case *Gubbins v Wyndham City Council*, Wyndham City Council gave the owner of pit bull terrier named Jock a statement of its dog destruction policy before he pled guilty to offences relating to Jock's lack of registration, being at large unaccompanied and biting three horses. The policy laid out the criteria for deciding which dogs to destroy:

1. Restricted breed dog, which has attacked either human or animal, considering they are not to be outside the premises unless muzzled and attached to the owner by chain, cord or leash;

2. Dangerous dog, which has attacked either human or animal, considering they are not to be outside the premises unless muzzled and attached to the owner by chain, cord or leash;

3. Attack on human, providing visible harm is done, e.g. bite wounds, bruising, sutures;

4. Any attack with lesser effect on a child or vulnerable person such as the frail, elderly or disabled;

5. Attack on animal providing the animal is either killed outright or as a result of the attack requires veterinary attention of a serious nature; and

6. Following being found guilty of an offence under the Act in a Magistrate's Court, such other facts and circumstances that it is in the public interest to destroy the dog to protect the public.

Providing that there is enough evidence and no defence available under the Act for the dog's actions.

Note that criterion 4 of the policy specifically mentions children and vulnerable people and that this ties in with our earlier discussion about how attacks on children and vulnerable people are viewed as 'moral events' and as more 'blameworthy'.

The council soon informed the owner that it had decided to destroy Jock under criteria 1 (Jock being a restricted breed) and 6 (because he had a history of chasing horses). Clearly, the council's policy is much stricter than the considerations applied by Chief Justice Miles in Indiana's case. As Jock's owner later complained, it ignores details that might be raised in an animal's defence – which in Jock's case included his otherwise good behaviour, his being disturbed by fireworks that week, his escape being due to works being carried out on a fence, and the owner's willingness to have the dog declared dangerous. Moreover, the council's decision-making process – simply writing a letter to Jock's owner explaining its thinking – is very different to the to-and-fro of a court hearing.

But the Supreme Court ruled that none of that invalidated the council's decision. It was enough that it met minimum standards of rationality and that the two things that did sway the council against Jock had been raised in the earlier criminal prosecution in the presence of Jock's owner. However, the court ruled that the council's process went awry in one respect. When the council permitted the owner to make further submissions to an appeal panel, his entreaties on behalf of Jock were rejected in part because Jock had been unregistered for the past five years. The problem was that Jock's owner wasn't told that the lack of registration would be considered in this way. While the court accepted that this was a minor point, it nevertheless ordered the panel to hold a further hearing in case the owner had an explanation that might change the panel's ruling. Alas, Jock's ultimate fate has not been reported.

These modern cases of blaming and punishing dogs lack the public spectacle of the trials and executions of pigs in medieval Europe, and the main motivation for contemporary destruction orders is public safety rather than the punishment of the dogs. However, it is again notable that the law slides between the notion of dogs as property and the notion that they are something more – at the very least, an important companion animal and perhaps a member of the family.

Wild and Semidomesticated Animals

It seems that in late medieval and early modern Europe, wild animals were also executed or punished for their behaviour at times. In Shakespeare's *The Merchant of Venice*, there is a fictional reference to this practice when Gratiano says to Shylock:

> O, be thou damn'd, inexecrable dog!
> And for thy life let justice be accus'd.
> Thou almost mak'st me waver in my faith,
> To hold opinion with Pythagoras,
> That souls of animals infuse themselves
> Into the trunks of men: thy currish spirit
> Govern'd a wolf, who, hang'd for human slaughter,
> Even from the gallows did his fell soul fleet,
> And, whilst thou lay'st in thy unhallow'd dam,
> Infused itself in thee; for thy desires
> Are wolvish, bloody, starved and ravenous.

In 1685 (almost 100 years after *The Merchant of Venice* was written), the locals of the town of Neuses, Ansbach, in modern Germany, hanged a wolf that had been preying on local livestock and people. The town's cruel and unpopular Bürgermeister (mayor) had just died, and the locals decided that he must have returned, reincarnated as a werewolf. They chased the wolf until it leaped into an abandoned well, and then slew it. The locals severed its muzzle, dressed it in man's clothing and placed a mask, wig and beard upon its head, giving it the appearance of the former Bürgermeister. They then hung it from a gibbet. After that, the corpse was preserved and displayed in a local museum.

The wolf of Ansbach

The Lynching of Elephants

In the earlier twentieth century, there have been several bizarre (and somewhat distressing) instances of hanging or executing circus elephants for their 'crimes' in the United States. As we discussed in Chapter 2, elephants are deemed to be intrinsically dangerous animals for the purpose of the law of *scienter* because of their size and wildness, and because they can inflict grievous injuries when they stampede. The startling extrajudicial executions of murderous elephants show that the impulse for humans to punish killer animals (particularly intelligent animals who appear to know what they are doing when they kill) continued to exist in modern times.

On 13 September 1916, Mary, a thirty-year-old African elephant, was hanged from an industrial derrick mounted on a railcar in Tennessee.

A day earlier, she had killed her new trainer, Walter 'Red' Eldridge, during the elephant parade at Sparks Circus in Erwin, Tennessee. Eldridge was a drifter who had been hired the day before his death and was inexperienced with elephants. The local newspaper reported that Mary

> collided [her] trunk vice-like about his body, lifted him 10 feet in the air, then dashed him with fury to the ground ... and with the full force of her biestly fury is said to have sunk her giant tusks entirely through his body. The animal then trampled the dying form of Eldridge as if seeking a murderous triumph, then with a sudden ... swing of her massive foot hurled his body into the crowd'.

An eyewitness named Coleman said that the elephant threw Eldridge into a drink stand and then stepped on him, and that Eldridge was not gored. A report ten years later simply said that Mary had killed Eldridge by hitting him in the head with her trunk. In the immediate aftermath of Eldridge's death, Coleman reported that a local blacksmith, Hench Cox, attempted to shoot Mary. 'The crowd kept hollerin' and sayin', "Let's kill the elephant, let's kill him ...", but the elephant was unfazed by the shots, and in fact, performed in her usual evening show.

It remains unclear who was responsible for sentencing Mary to death. Some locals said that Tennessee state authorities charged Mary with first-degree murder (inviting parallels to be drawn with the medieval executions of murderous pigs), whereas others said that the decision lay with the management of the circus. Unfortunately, Mary was too heavy for the first chain used to hang her, and fell to the ground, sending the watching crowd scattering. The second chain was stronger, and she died. She was buried in an unspecified spot in the railway yard. The photo purporting to show her hanging from the railway derrick has an unclear provenance, and some suspect it was doctored.

Mary was not the only elephant to be summarily executed. On 4 January 1902, Topsy, a female Asian elephant aged about twenty-eight, was electrocuted at Coney Island, New York, with the help of the Edison Manufacturing Company (Edison himself was not involved with or present at the time of her death). Topsy had killed at least one person and injured several more. The owner decided to kill her, making a spectacle of the process. Topsy knew that something was wrong on the day of her execution and refused to move. Eventually, she had to be executed where she stood. Although electrocution may seem cruel, it had in fact been requested by the

American Society for Prevention of Cruelty to Animals, who had thought that death by hanging would be needlessly painful and prolonged. A film, *Electrocuting an Elephant*, was made by the Edison Manufacturing Company, but it did not prove popular.

George Orwell wrote a an essay from the perspective of British colonial police officer in Burma – a position Orwell had held himself – who is required to shoot a male elephant that, in a state of 'musth', had killed an Indian labourer by stepping on him. Male elephants in musth experience a spike in testosterone and can become extremely aggressive towards other elephants (even their own offspring) and humans while in that state. In Orwell's essay, the elephant is exceptionally difficult to kill by shooting, but the narrator's actions are judged legal. However, it is not clear whether or not the essay is based on real events.

Great Apes and Personhood

For the last thirty years or so, there have been calls for apes – as our closest living relative – to be accorded the same legal rights as humans. Thus, the Great Ape Project argues that laws should be passed to protect all of the great primates, including laws to prohibit the killing of primates, except in self-defence; to protect the right of primates to live in their own habitat with members of their own species; and to protect primates from torture.

However, the legal rights conferred by personhood are generally accompanied by responsibilities, and these might be difficult to apply to some species of great ape, despite their similarity to us. Chimpanzees, for instance, may behave in ways that could be regarded as criminal if a human were to behave in the same way. Chimpanzees kill other chimpanzees from rival tribes, kill and cannibalise tyrants in their own tribe and have a generally 'Machiavellian' approach to social organisation. Moreover, chimpanzees have been held to be intrinsically dangerous animals for the purposes of the *scienter* doctrine; they can never be entirely tamed. In the case that established this, an enraged male chimpanzee bit off the finger of a zookeeper at Wellington Zoo.

Nothing better illustrates the danger chimpanzees can pose than the grievous injuries Charla Nash suffered in 2009 at the hands of Travis, a male common chimpanzee. Nash lived at the back of the house of Travis's owner, Sandy Herold, who, with husband, Jerry, had 'adopted' Travis in 1995, when he was three days old. Travis knew Nash well, but due to a new hairstyle, he may not have recognised her on the day he attacked her, tearing away her face and scalp, and chewing off both her hands. Astoundingly, Nash survived. She eventually received a face transplant, but was permanently blinded. Travis also attacked the police officer who responded to the 911 call, who then shot and killed Travis in self-defence.

The consensus seems to be that Travis was a danger to others because he had been put in an unnatural situation. This was through no fault of his own – he was simply behaving as a male chimpanzees would in the wild. But if Travis had lived and been conferred with 'personhood' rights, should he have been prosecuted for attacking and almost killing Nash? Or should he have been treated as though his responsibility was diminished by the state of captivity in which he found himself? Travis seems to have had a high level of intelligence and to have grieved the death of Sandy Herold's husband, Jerry, in 2004. But the argument that apes are similarly sentient to humans could conceivably be used against chimpanzees such as Travis to claim that they should be treated as human adults, or perhaps as minors, who have committed crimes. Arguments that animals should be treated as legally equivalent to humans raise difficult questions when animals commit wrongs – even in the modern day.

Modern Prosecution of Wild Bears

In 2008, a Macedonian court in the city of Bitola convicted a wild bear of theft and criminal damages after it repeatedly stole honey from a frustrated beekeeper. The beekeeper had attempted to dissuade the bear by playing loud music and using bright lights, but to no avail. Because the bear had no owner and was classified as a protected species, the court ordered the state to pay the beekeeper US$3500 for the damage to the hives. The bear was not jailed and remained at large.

A bear named Katya in Kazakhstan was less lucky. She was convicted of mauling two campers in separate incidents in 2004, and sentenced to fifteen years in prison. She was placed in a prison with human inmates because there was nowhere else to put her at the time. She served her sentence, and in 2019 she was placed in a zoo instead, with the eventual intention that she would be able to live with another bear. Her prison inmates, who had looked after her, said they missed her when she was released.

More Lenience Towards Wild Animals

Ultimately – despite the hair-raising examples of elephant executions – people are seemingly more willing to be lenient towards wild animals that harm people than domesticated animals, perhaps because a certain element of volatility is to be expected from the former. Even in the modern day, we have seen that domesticated animals who harm people are often put down for their actions – for the benefit of public safety, certainly, but perhaps to satisfy some hidden notion of retribution towards the animals as well, particularly if they have harmed vulnerable people.

Courts have also shown leniency and understanding towards wild animals – just as they did to the *lutmäuse* mentioned in the Chapter 2 – and seemed to appreciate the animals wanted to find sustenance and safety. In many cases, as with the *lutmäuse*, there was concern about the difficulty of the vermin in attending court and about giving vermin a fair chance to flee before they were anathematised. This may look odd – but it also shows that people believed that the natural environment should be shared fairly with wild animals, who, after all, were regarded as God's creatures too.

An exception to this occurred in the 1479 trial of a kind of beetle known as *inger* in Lausanne: the beetles devastated the crops and were declared to be 'unclean' and 'not called animals nor mentioned as such'. Accordingly they were called 'accursed' and were told that it was hoped that they would 'daily decrease whithersoever you many go, to the end that of you nothing shall remain save for the use and profit of man'. On the face of it, a reader might think that insects are less close to humans than voles or rats, and therefore offered less sympathy, but in Chapter 6 we'll describe a case where weevils were treated courteously and offered a separate field of their own, so that they could flourish. Edward Payson Evans hypothesises that the *inger* suffered from a problem familiar to humans as well as non-human animals: their lawyer was simply not very good. (He does not tell us whether the *inger* did, in fact, suffer as a result of the malediction pronounced upon them.)

4.

UNDERSTANDING ANIMALS

ARLY IN 2013, THE JUSTICES OF THE SUPREME COURT OF the United States – the world's most closely watched and consequential court – debated the historical relationship between dogs and humans. 'Dogs have been domesticated for about 12,000 years,' wrote conservative justice Samuel Alito. Yes, replied his liberal colleague Elena Kagan, but the dog in the case before the court, a chocolate labrador retriever named Franky, 'was not your neighbor's pet, come to your porch on a leisurely stroll'. Rather, he was a 'highly trained tool of law enforcement', assigned to the narcotics canine handler Sergeant Doug Bartelt. Alito pointed out this was nothing new, quoting a 1318 Scottish statute that prohibited 'disturb[ing] a tracking dog or the men coming with it for pursuing thieves or seizing malefactors'. 'Dogs' keen sense of smell has been used in law enforcement for centuries,' he added. Yes, but not for drug detection, retorted Kagan, which goes back 'only a few decades'.

The justices' debate touches on a number of important themes in this book: that many non-human animals are a part of human society, that animals' interactions with humans vary not only from species to species but also over time, and that human laws both reveal and react to those changes. The relationship between humans and other animals is especially difficult to assess because most of it is prehistorical and we take much of the rest – such as our relationship with our companion animals – for granted. As will be seen in this chapter, the Supreme Court's analysis of that history – limited, as it had to be, to the submissions of the parties before it and various *amici curiae* ('friends of the court') – was incomplete. Indeed, for their historical claims, the justices mostly relied on an unreferenced 1955 article written by a retired police officer to fete the use of dogs in war and policing.

In Chapter 2, we noted that the domestication of dogs may have begun up to 40,000 years ago and would have involved the coexistence of dogs and people, and changes in both of them. There are many ways to describe this relationship: most positively, as humans and dogs helping, protecting and working with each other; less positively, as humans exploiting dogs (and perhaps, sometimes, the reverse); more neutrally, as humans and dogs using and influencing each other in various ways. This chapter is concerned with these more neutral forms of interaction between the two species and, in particular, the legal significance of how humans understand other animals. That is not to say that the legal significance is only neutral or benign. As we will see, animals are often given little choice in their use in the legal system, and sometimes suffer through that use. Some humans can also find themselves victims of the legal system's use or misuse of animals.

In the case that came before the Supreme Court of the United States, the labrador Franky had an immediate effect on Joelis Jardines, who an anonymous caller to a 'crime stoppers' hotline alleged was growing cannabis in his home. At issue was the legal significance of the Florida police's decision to take a dog with them when they knocked at the Jardines' door, and their understanding of Franky's sensory abilities (specifically, his ability to smell cannabis plants), and his trained and innate behaviour (specifically, his tendency to go 'wild' and to hunt if triggered by certain cues). As Justice Antonin Scalia put it, 'It is not the dog that is the problem, but the behavior that here involved use of the dog.' That is, the issue was the legal system's use and understanding of animals.

The main area of law discussed in this chapter is the law of evidence, which governs how courts find the facts to which they apply the law. For instance, in the case of the Staffordshire terriers Izzy and Jock, the law of evidence would govern any dispute about whether it was Izzy or Jock who bit Jennifer Edward's finger. The law's main requirement is that courts only hear evidence that is relevant to the dispute (and not, for instance, how much Tania Isbester's children love Izzy). A second requirement is that courts do not hear evidence that is of little consequence but could prejudice the court (for example, evidence about Izzy and Jock's later attacks on other dogs and people). The law of evidence also limits how particular evidence – such as 'hearsay' or 'opinion' – can be used. This ensures judges and juries are mainly restricted to evidence sourced from humans who testify in court and not the views of others. Finally, the law of evidence is sometimes used to enforce other laws, such as laws that regulate the police. In the United States, courts will not receive evidence obtained through a breach of the US Constitution, including through unreasonable searches, which are barred by the Bill of Rights. That was the issue before the Supreme Court in 2013.

This chapter will consider three overlapping uses that humans can make of their understanding of animals in legal settings: first, animals can witness events that are important to a legal dispute; second, some animals can be trained to play a role that is useful in enforcing the law, notably in policing criminal suspects; and third, animals' trained behaviour can produce useful, even determinative, evidence in particular legal settings.

Animal Witnesses

Certain animals are so ubiquitous in parts of human society that humans not only tolerate their presence but behave as if they were not there. In 1967, the United States Central Intelligence Agency attempted to leverage this situation in an unusual way:

> Our final examination of trained cats [REDACTED] for [REDACTED] use in the [REDACTED] convinced us that the program would not lend itself in a practical sense to our highly specialised needs. Repeated checks on the state of training and equipment showed us that it was indeed possible to train [REDACTED] locations; we were not able to visualize [REDACTED] use for this technique under conditions that prevail.

Why would cats potentially be of use to an intelligence agency? Because they are the largest animal to routinely occupy contemporary urban spaces unaccompanied by humans, without alarming them either. That means they could be useful hosts for covert listening devices. Why did the CIA decide they were unsuitable for this purpose in 1967? Because cats are largely resistant to human direction, a characteristic that is both their main utility to investigators –people will not recognise them as agents of humans – but also the main barrier to their use. The CIA's 'Operation Acoustic Kitty' struggled to overcome the latter barrier with 'training', but remarkably, as we will later discuss, it had some success.

There are three other ways that animals can act as useful witnesses in legal proceedings: they can identify familiar things or people; they can react in recognisable ways to things that are unfamiliar to them; and they can mimic things they have witnessed.

Animals' Reactions to Familiar Things

We opened this chapter by looking at the now ubiquitous use of police dogs, which are the product of careful training and continuous supervision. But people act differently in the presence of other humans, especially police, which limits what police dogs and their trainers can learn as witnesses. The CIA did not consider using dogs for covert intelligence operations, because humans do not generally tolerate dogs being in public places without their owners. Instead, the CIA sought to use untrained animals for this purpose. As it happens, animals without specific training have often been used as witnesses by the courts, which rely on evolved or domesticated behaviours to determine what the animal knows or has seen.

An example of such a case from a century ago is an American private law dispute in Washington, DC. Keeley Moore, the owner of a hat shop, emerged from the store one day to find a woman petting his dog, Prince, and claiming that the dog was hers. After he told her that he had purchased Prince from a peddler in New York City, he was threatened with arrest and eventually sued by the woman's father, Eli Helmick, the inspector-general of the US Army. Helmick insisted that Prince was actually Buddy, a dog he had bought from Kansas years earlier and which was stolen from him four months ago. Faced with the testimonies of Helmick, his wife and daughter (backed up by a photo of the daughter and Buddy), Moore gathered a formidable array of witnesses to defend his own claim to Prince. These included four customers who had seen Prince at the hat shop before Buddy was stolen and a vet who testified that Prince was a mongrel, rather than Helmick's prize-winning Samoyed.

When King Solomon faced a similar dispute about a human baby, he threatened to kill it as a ruse to make the parties reveal their true relationship to the child. Solomon wisely awarded the baby to the woman who immediately dropped her claim in order to save the baby's life. Judge Edward Kimball saw a different, less alarming and perhaps more reliable way to make use of the object of the dispute before him. A Washington newspaper gave the following summary of events in the courtroom:

'And now call the dog,' His Honor commanded the court officer. The animal had been held in confinement in Judge Kimball's private room while the testimony was being taken in the court room. In another moment, the court officer returned, leading the dog by the collar. Officer and animal approached the witness stand and suddenly the dog's ears rose and his nostrils quivered as he evidently caught a scent which was familiar and grateful to his keen senses. With a turn of his head and a swish of his tail the animal bounded to the chair where Mrs Helmick sat and raising his forepaws to her knees, pressed his nose to her cheek and licked it, while the delighted animal continued to wag his tail with enthusiastic joy.

Kimball immediately awarded the dog to Helmick, pronouncing the evidence 'unequivocal'. As can be seen from this example, the dog was very much used by Kimball. On the other hand, this was not just for the humans' benefit but also for the dog's, assuming – as seems clear – he wanted to be reunited with his true owner.

Moore later told *The Washington Times* that he planned to appeal, arguing that 'no evidence was offered to identify the dog as the Helmicks' dog other than mere say so'. He was right. Indeed, while the three Helmicks gave evidence under oath and were cross-examined, the dog, the decisive witness in the case against Moore, did neither. Alas for Moore, evidence law's rule on hearsay, which bars a court from accepting unsworn words or conduct as evidence of what someone witnessed, only applies to human witnesses.

This point, while never controversial, was confirmed in a more recent US decision from the other side of the country. In 2007, the Court of Appeals of Washington State rejected an argument by convicted murderer Roy Russell that his jury should not have heard his neighbour's claim that 'her dog barks every time she sees' him. The judges ruled:

Hearsay is a statement made by someone other than the witness offered into evidence to prove the truth of the matter asserted. But the reference to a person rules out the possibility that the hearsay rule might apply to sounds that animals make. A witness may testify that a dog was barking without violating the hearsay rule. Here, [Christine] Bisson was the declarant and not her dog, as Russell argues. Thus, the trial court did not deprive Russell of his constitutional right of confrontation when it allowed Bisson's testimony.

Russell might have been on safer ground if he had simply questioned why the dog's barking was relevant or argued that the dog's apparent dislike of him might have unfairly turned the jury against him.

In another modern case, this one in Namibia, a party successfully appealed against using an animal in this way. A magistrate, asked to determine whether Jonas Hepute had stolen a cow, relied on evidence from a tribal council that had attempted to resolve competing claims to the cow. The council had placed the disputed cow in a kraal with cattle owned by each party, including cows that they claimed were the disputed cow's dams. When the cattle were released, the two dams went their separate ways and the cow followed the complainant's dam, rather than the accused's. Hepute was initially convicted of theft, but Namibia's High Court was less impressed by the tribunal's evidence than the magistrate had been:

> There is no evidential basis to suggest that the disputed cow followed the complainant's cow because of some instinctive urge. It should be borne in mind that the disputed cow was weaned some years before the 'test' and there is no scientific evidence on record showing what, if any, is the capacity of weaners, or, for that matter, mature cattle, to recognise their dams by smell or sight. But even if they do, there is no suggestion that there is some residual bond which instinctively and invariably causes a desire of the one to associate or be herded together with the other.

Indeed, the judges noted, 'even the headman's councilors, who presumably have some acquired knowledge about the behaviour of cattle through keen observation ... remained sharply divided on what significance could be attached to the disputed cow's behaviour'. Reasoning that the cow may have simply preferred the pastures in one direction and rejecting an argument that the council's test has special status as a customary tradition, the High Court overturned the conviction.

While these later cases were the subject of published rulings, the earlier case from Washington, DC, was only informally reported in newspapers. Alas, we do not know the fate of Keeley Morse's plans to appeal the initial ruling about the ownership of his dog. Although he announced that he would take the matter all the way to the US Supreme Court if necessary, there is no further record of the dispute. All we know is that his hat shop closed later that year, seemingly following bankruptcy proceedings. *The Washington Times*, noting the evident sincerity of all of the witnesses in Kimball's court, concluded: 'Are Buddy and Prince one dog or two dogs? Sherlock Holmes, with all the evidence in the case before him, would surely find the problem puzzling.'

Animals' Reactions to Unfamiliar Things

Three decades earlier, in this exchange between a police inspector, who speaks first, and Sherlock Holmes, the fictional detective makes famous use of a dog's ability to show that it recognised its owner:

'Is there any other point to which you would wish to draw my attention?'
'To the curious incident of the dog in the nighttime.'
'The dog did nothing in the nighttime.'
'That was the curious incident,' remarked Sherlock Holmes.

This detail allowed Holmes to determine that whoever caused the death of a horse trainer was not a stranger to the trainer's dog; in fact, he deduces that the trainer was likely killed by his own horse (which he was trying to maim). As always, author Arthur Conan Doyle was able to make an unusual clue determinative by positing a very particular set of circumstances: a furtive, dishonest owner meets a cryptic demise in the vicinity of interested, useful witnesses (sleeping stable boys who would hear a dog bark) and a dog that was trained to only bark at prowlers. His fictional detective also seemingly ignores other explanations, such as the dog or workers being drugged or bribed (as indeed another stable boy was that night). Real court cases are not usually so neat.

A century later, one of the most famous criminal trials of all time provided a real, more equivocal example of a court using a dog's bark as evidence. On Sunday, 12 June 1994, Steven Schwab took advantage of the gap between *The Dick Van Dyke Show* (which ended at 10.30 p.m.) and *The Mary Tyler Moore Show* (which began at 11) to walk his dog, Sherry, in the Los Angeles suburb of Brentwood. On the return leg, he came across an unattended dog on a street corner, which was alternating between barking at a doorway and turning to him. Figuring the dog was lost, Schwab approached him. He saw that the dog had no identification, but he recognised him as an Akita, an expensive breed (with an expensive collar to match), and noticed that one of his paws was bloody. Testing the waters, Schwab moved away and the dog followed him, stopping to bark and howl at each house it passed, but eventually accompanying him to his second-storey apartment. Reluctant to bring him inside (where Schwab kept a nervous cat) or to place him in a pound overnight, he convinced the couple next door to take him in. The dog's scratching at their door prompted Schwab's neighbours to take him on a midnight walk, during which he pulled them to 875 South Bundy, the home of Nicole Brown

Simpson, former wife of celebrity ex-athlete O.J. Simpson. As the dog finally went quiet, the couple peered into the house's darkened walkway.

It turned out that the dog was named Kato and had belonged to Nicole Brown Simpson. He played a pivotal role not only in the discovery of her body and that of Ron Goldman, but also in the 1995 trial of O.J. Simpson for their murder. Simpson presented an alibi for part of that evening, including undisputed evidence ruling out his murdering the pair earlier than 10 p.m. or later than around 10.40 p.m. that night. The prosecution countered with evidence that Kato had witnessed something unusual at around 10.15 p.m. A next-door neighbour said she was woken by barking sometime after 10 p.m. but was unsure how many dogs were involved or when the barking started. She believed that the barking – 'very, very intense, nonstop and very, very loud' – had persisted for around thirty minutes, until her boyfriend returned home at 10.45 p.m. Her boyfriend said he actually saw Kato on the street, seemingly just before Schwab. Other neighbours also heard continuous barking in the same span of time, prompting one to call the police 'because it barked for so long without anyone trying to quiet it'. But none of that proved that Kato saw anything *unusual* at 10.15 p.m. Rather, that evidence came from a more distant neighbour, who had been watching the 10 p.m. news:

Fifteen, twenty minutes into it, I heard a very distinctive barking coming from somewhere to the south of where I live and I was aware of it for maybe five, six, seven minutes; and at that point, I stopped watching the news and I left the master bedroom ... It was a – you know, it was fairly persistent, it was a significant pitch, and as you may recall, I described it at the time as a plaintive wail. Sounded like a, you know, very unhappy animal.

This evidence – 'A dog has announced that murder was occurring at 10.15', as the defence attorney sardonically put it – could readily have been accepted by the jury as adequate, albeit far from conclusive of Simpson's guilt. Neither side of the case relied on a further Holmesian detail – that Kato apparently had not barked *before* then – but the dog's behaviour was picked over on television during the trial:

'Akitas are not very barky dogs. They normally are very quiet,' said Betty Liittschwager, who has bred, trained and shown Akitas for

30 years in Southern California. 'They are very sensible dogs, and this one must have sensed that something was very wrong' ... Liittschwager described the type of sound as an instinctive call of the wild, similar to the cry a dog makes when another dog is wounded and helpless. 'The wail is half a bark and half a howl,' Liittschwager said. 'It means something out of the ordinary has happened.'

Although Kato's barking would not be barred by the rule against hearsay, peoples' interpretations of those barks would typically be subject to limits. Liittschwager's view could probably have been put to the jury as a permitted 'expert opinion', and the neighbours' 'lay opinions' of what lay behind the dog's barks might also have been allowed if the prosecutor had asked for them, given that there was no other way (short of each witness imitating the wailing in court) for the jury to learn exactly what these witnesses heard. A further opinion that evening would not have been covered by the rules on opinions at all, because it was not a human opinion: the neighbour who heard the 'plaintive wail' added that 'our own dog was on the bed and he was reacting to the barking by growling a little bit'.

The American media speculated about two further ways to read Kato's mind:

Julie Sterling, a trainer at the Kennel Club in West Los Angeles, believes that if the dog were brought to a channeler [someone who claims to know what animals are trying to communicate], it might respond to visual imagery that would reveal what caused the wailing that night. 'Animals have feelings,' said Carol Gurney, an animal channeler. 'They know things.' If they put Kato on the stand in the case, could Gurney get to the bottom of what really happened that night? 'It is possible,' Gurney said. 'Depending on whether the animal wants to talk.'

Although Gurney described putting Kato 'on the stand', her method would require her to give evidence on Kato's behalf, based on what she believed Kato was thinking. It is doubtful that her opinion would satisfy a long-standing requirement under Californian law that scientific or technical expertise be 'generally accepted' in the scientific community in order for it to be admissible. Nor would it be likely to meet the standard for scientific evidence introduced by the US Supreme Court two years before the

Simpson trial, which assesses the reliability of evidence based on considerations such as falsifiability and peer review.

The Kennel Club trainer also suggested showing Kato pictures of possible suspects, including Simpson himself, to see how the dog would respond,
an approach similar to Judge Kimball's method of determining the ownership of Buddy/Prince. However, it seems unlikely that Kato's reaction to
seeing Simpson, in pictures or in person, would be similarly 'unequivocal',
or even useful.

There have been two attempts to prompt such evidence from dogs in
French murder trials. In what was said to be a 'first' in 2008, a Paris judge
cleared a court so that a vet could lead a dog named Scooby into the courtroom during a preliminary hearing in a murder prosecution. Scooby, who
had lived for two years with a woman who was found hanging in her apartment, reportedly 'barked furiously' at an alleged murder suspect. While
the judge thanked the dog for its 'invaluable assistance', later reports said
that the barking was regarded as inconclusive. Six years later, French prosecutors sought to repeat this process in another homicide prosecution,
bringing in the deceased's labrador, Tango, to view the suspect in a fight
that the dog was said to have witnessed. 'So, if Tango lifted his right paw,
moved his mouth or his tail, is he recognising my client or not?', the suspect's lawyer asked, branding the experiment 'very troubling for the French
legal system'. As it happens, neither Tango nor a control labrador, Norman,
showed any discernible interest in the suspect.

In a recent South Australian prosecution for attempted murder, the
parties relied on evidence about the behaviour of the victim's cocker span-
iel, Rusty, in multiple ways. The prosecution argued that blood found at
the scene – which matched that of the accused, a family friend of the home
owners – was likely shed during the crime. The key evidence to support
this was that the housetrained dog's urine and faeces were also present,
suggesting that the dog had witnessed distressing events and had perhaps
bitten the assailant. The prosecution also put forward evidence that Rusty
later barked at a shed where tools that had seemingly been used in the
crime were found. Additionally, the prosecution said, the dog had run away
the day after the crime and was found at the door of the accused's house.
The accused, meanwhile, testified that he had looked after Rusty in the
weeks after the event and that the dog happily sat with him, prompting his
lawyer to argue that 'it would be quite remarkable that if the dog had witnessed some person attack his or her master or mistress that they might

not show an aversion of that person or fear of that person'. The prosecution responded by calling a vet to the stand, who gave a variety of possible explanations for Rusty's behaviour that could support either party. The jury convicted the accused and the state Supreme Court later dismissed his complaints that the judge at the trial should have either excluded the evidence related to Rusty as too tenuous to rely on or warned the jurors about the dangers of doing so. Instead, the appeal judges ruled that the explanations given for Rusty's actions offered were properly in the mix in a complex circumstantial case. They added that the accused's counsel 'very wisely adopted the forensic approach of the less said by the [trial] judge about the indefatigable Rusty, the better'.

Animals Mimicking Things They've Seen or Heard

Some non-human animals are able to communicate with humans about events they have witnessed. This does not permit them to actually *testify* at a trial, as they cannot satisfy the requirement that they understand the obligation to be truthful and could scarcely be cross-examined by the opposing party. However, a court could still be told (by a human witness or via a recording of the animal itself) what the animal communicated. While human courts are yet to confront the prospect of evidence delivered in animal sign language – by chimpanzees, for instance – the media occasionally claims that animals may have something to contribute to legal proceedings.

In 2010, a police officer investigating a case of elder abuse told the media he felt a 'chill' when he heard the victim's parrot saying the words 'help me' and then laughing. In 2014, the family members of a murdered man, who believed that the man's partner was the perpetrator, published a recording of the couple's parrot allegedly mimicking an argument between the two. In late 2018, a police officer guarding a crime scene near Buenos Aires was startled to hear a woman screaming inside. The sound turned out to be the victim's parrot. Argentinian media recently reported that statements about the parrot's alleged utterances were included in the prosecution's file on the murder charges against her housemates: the officer claimed the parrot had said, 'Ay, no, Por favour, soltame!' (No, please let me go!), and more damningly, a neighbour claimed the parrot had once said '¿Por qué me pegaste?' (Why did you beat me?) as one of the victim's housemates left the house.

Neither of the court cases resulting from the first two incidents appears to have made use of the 'evidence' attributed to the parrots to decide if someone was guilty or innocent. Listening to the recording of the parrot belonging to the man who was murdered in 2014 makes it easy to see why: it just sounds like a parrot repeatedly saying 'fuck' and 'fucking', words the bird had clearly heard a lot, but the relevance of which is unclear. While the victim's partner was eventually convicted of his murder, there is no sign that the recording played any role in the prosecution. However, media reports suggest that the police officer who reported the third incident, from Buenos Aires in 2018, testified accordingly at the trial of the victim's house-mates in September 2021. The prosecution's case against the murderers was mainly circumstantial, but featured DNA and bite mark evidence.

Decades ago, US media reported an earlier attempt to introduce a parrot's words into testimony during a murder prosecution:

> Max was found dehydrated and hungry in its cage when the body of Ms Gill, 36, was discovered two days after her death in November 1991. After Max was coaxed back to health at a pet shop, the shop's owner said the bird began to cry out, 'Richard, no, no, no!' The man charged in the case is Ms Gill's business partner, and his name is not Richard. He is Gary Joseph Rasp, and he says he is innocent.
>
> Mr Rasp's lawyer, Charles Ogulnik, brought up the parrot in court when he was questioning the defense's private investigator, Gary Dixon. 'Why did I ask you to follow up on the bird?' Mr Ogulnik asked. Mr Dixon began, 'The bird was making some spontaneous statements to its keeper –' An emphatic objection by the Sonoma County deputy district attorney, Phil Abrams, was sustained by Judge Raymond Giordano of Superior Court.

Unfortunately, there is no record of what the objection was and why it was sustained. One problem may have been that although parrots are not subject to the hearsay rule, the rule would still have applied to whomever Max was mimicking. For those words to be admissible, Rasp would have to prove that a hearsay rule exception – such as the dying declaration or spontaneous utterance exceptions – applied to whoever said those words in Max's presence. A second problem may have been a Californian rule that bans criminal defendants from implicating a third party in a crime without sufficient evidence against that third party. Either way, the difficulty Rasp faced was a lack of context for whatever it was that Max was mimicking.

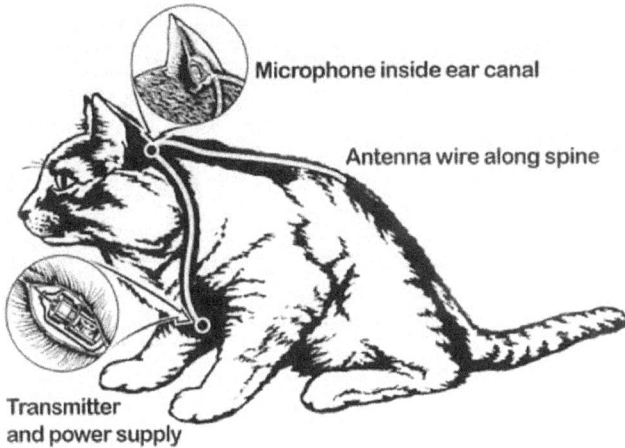

Microphone inside ear canal

Antenna wire along spine

Transmitter
and power supply

Operation Acoustic Kitty

This brings us back to where we began our discussion about using the behaviour of animals as evidence: the CIA's bizarre attempt to use cats to gather intelligence. The aim of the 'Acoustic Kitty' project was to turn a cat into a better parrot:

> The techs produced a three-quarter-inch transmitter for embedding at the base of the cat's skull, where loose skin and flesh provided a natural pocket. Implanting the transmitter proved viable, once a device was packaged to withstand the temperature, fluids, chemistry and humidity of the body. Microphone placement presented a more difficult problem since flesh is a poor conductor. Eventually the ear canal became the preferred location. An antenna of very fine wire was attached to a transmitter and woven into the cat's long fur. The cat's size permitted only the smallest batteries, a factor that restricted the amount of hours the audio could transmit.

Contemporary technology could easily surmount these barriers, but not the other problem encountered by the CIA:

> Control of the cat's movements, despite earlier training, proved so inconsistent that the operational utility became questionable ... The experimental animals could be directed to move short distances to target locations and people in a known environment. However, outside the experimental laboratory, Acoustic Kitty had a mind of its own.

According to another more colourful (and disputed) account, the CIA tried to overcome this difficulty by putting electrodes into a cat's brain to control it, only to see the cat run over by a taxi during the first field test.

Clearly, this technique was less about understanding or using animals than abusing them, a topic that we consider further in the following chapter. The remainder of this chapter will discuss more conventional and (somewhat) more humane uses of animals that are specifically trained for law enforcement.

Police Animals

The way contemporary police use dogs to enforce criminal law is a relatively recent phenomenon, but it builds on earlier uses of dogs for other purposes. In the late nineteenth century, one of the more significant examples of the use of dogs in a criminal investigation was met with controversy.

On 8 October 1888, one week after the deaths of Jack the Ripper's third and fourth victims, London's *The Times* published a letter from local dog breeder Edwin Brough suggesting that the police enlist bloodhounds to try to catch one of the world's most infamous criminals. The letter began:

> Since the bloodhound ceased to be used in the pursuit of sheep stealers, the breed has become scarce, and he is now chiefly regarded as an ornament to our dog shows and a good model for the artist. I hope that you will allow me a little space to advocate the restoration of this noble hound to his old position in the detection of crime.

The next day, Whitechapel police were told not to remove the bodies of any future victims of the serial killer, so that bloodhounds would have an opportunity to take the scent. *The Times* reported that the police commissioner, Sir Charles Warren, had personally participated in trialling two of Brough's bloodhounds in Hyde Park.

However, when another of the killer's victims, May Kelly, was found a month later, no bloodhounds were brought to the crime scene. There were many prosaic explanations for this: the police had refused to indemnify Brough if the Ripper killed his hounds; Warren inconveniently resigned the day before Kelly was killed; and Kelly's body was found in the daytime, when Whitechapel crowds would have disturbed any scent trail.

But historian Neil Pemberton offers other explanations for this 'curious incident':

> The question of whether bloodhounds could or could not discover and track the scent of the Ripper in the East End raised profound questions about animal–human relationships, smells and culture ... As nineteenth-century cities became cleaner thanks to sanitary reform, this revolution was accompanied by similar changes in personal hygiene, meaning that the middle classes became less tolerant of stench, and, culturally, the sense of smell became increasingly relegated to the realm of the animalistic, irrational and intuitive.

Not only did the prospect of using Brough's hounds to hunt the Ripper suggest an intrusion of the pastoral world of hunting into London's urban one, but Victorians also baulked at the very notion that humans have scents, let alone unique ones; that a dog could distinguish a monster like the killer from the sex workers he killed or the 'slum stench' of Whitechapel; and that a hound might savage an innocent target or incite a revolt among London's East Enders.

Brough had anticipated and tried to dispel several of these objections in his letter in *The Times* ('the Cuban bloodhound, which was used for slave-hunting, was a savage animal, and would pull his man down when he came up to him, but this is quite a different breed to our bloodhound'), but the public's discomfort was evident in how scepticism of Warren's plan dominated London's newspapers between the Ripper's last murders. It was only later that the bloodhounds' proponents claimed vindication, suggesting that the month-long gap between murders implied that the mere prospect of their use had deterred a madman.

The upshot of the public backlash against using bloodhounds to track the Ripper was that it took many more decades for the British public – and citizens of most other Commonwealth countries – to accept a role for animals in policing. Binyamin Blum, a historian of forensic science, explains how South African police were instead among the first adopters of police dogs. The South African police introduced Doberman pinschers into the force for a mix of racist reasons, including what they claimed was the inscrutability of black South Africans' appearance and motives to white police; black South Africans' superstitions about dogs; and an analogy with 'native trackers'. Other British colonies, including Australia, then acquired tracking dogs from South Africa, but it was only the widespread use of dogs during wartime – first by the Nazis and later by the Allies – that led to police dogs becoming mainstream in Britain.

The 1955 article that the US Supreme Court relied on in 2013 to argue about the historical relationship between dogs and humans was actually a screed calling for American police to resume their nation's historical use of tracking dogs:

> If one gives some thought to the subject, there is but little difference between fighting an enemy in a declared war and fighting an enemy, the criminal, at home on the crime front. Both are comparable battles for the very existence of civilization, for without the thin wall of police protecting the people from criminal depredation, the world would soon revert to savagery and bestiality.

The article's author casually asserted that Australian police 'praised their dogs for giving warning when vengeful aborigines have attempted to surround the police camp at night, hurling their spears in the darkness, but the bristling hair of the dogs and their warning growls warned their masters in time to avoid serious casualties'. As Blum notes, it is not clear whether claimed comparisons like these advanced or hindered the broad acceptance of tracking dogs in developed countries.

Using Animals' Noses

In March 1997, over a century after Jack the Ripper's murders and on the other side of the world from Whitechapel, passengers travelling from Adelaide to Sydney were mostly sanguine when South Australian police led a dog to their bus's luggage compartment. The dog was not following a human scent, but rather sat in front of an unmarked suitcase. The driver told the police that the suitcase belonged to a passenger who he recalled had boarded in a northern Adelaide suburb. That passenger, Peter Hoare, at first denied owning the luggage, but relented when challenged by the driver. He soon admitted that it contained over 5 kilograms of cannabis and that he was a drug courier, all before the police even opened the suitcase. But he later challenged the legality of the police's actions and was acquitted by a magistrate who ruled that the police's actions were illegal as they had not obtained a warrant from someone independent of their investigation to 'search' the luggage compartment.

These events prompted more senior courts to ponder when police are allowed to use dogs to detect incriminating scents. At the request of South Australian prosecutors, three appeal judges rejected the magistrate's view that the police used the dog to search the passengers' luggage:

> That word ['search'] is not apt to describe the mere act of detection of an odour generated by the content of the item searched, which is released into the atmosphere surrounding it without any positive acts of a third person to effect that release. If it were otherwise, ridiculous questions would arise as to how close one would need to get to an item generating an odour before one could be said to be searching it. In essence, the situation, apropos the accused, was, conceptually, no different than if he happened to be at the bus depot holding the suitcase and the police officer lawfully, but casually, walked past with a sniffer dog, who reacted positively when it came near the suitcase.

The High Court of Australia refused to consider Hoare's appeal, noting that police officers themselves could use their noses to detect crimes such as drink driving.

Three years later, the High Court's test for the legality of using sniffer dogs in policing was considered in a Sydney case. In the new case, police had used a dog to sniff out cannabis held by people standing in line to enter an Oxford Street nightclub. Supreme Court Justice Barry O'Keefe compared a dog's nose for cannabis to a police officer's:

> Take a situation in which an officer of police has a particularly sensitive sense of smell, or experienced a particular reaction to the presence of a certain substance, for example, cannabis. People who have allergies may well be in the latter category. Such particular characteristics or sensitivities may well cause the officer in question to form a suspicion as to the presence and hence possession of cannabis in a particular place, or on a particular person ... I do not think that it could be said that the search began when he detected the odour of the cannabis ... Nor do I think that the detecting by him of such odour before he formed a suspicion as to the presence of cannabis would render illegal any actions of his in searching the person he had detected as the source of such odour.

The defendant, Glen Darby, sought to turn the analogy against the dog. If all the dog had done was sniff Darby, then that would have left the police accompanying him with no way to distinguish him from the rest of people in the packed nightclub line. Instead, the police conceded that the dog had also nudged, 'bunted' and 'ferreted around' Darby's genitals, before placing his nose on Darby's pocket repeatedly as he tried to walk away, pushed aside the dog's head and told the (plain-clothes) police officer to call off his dog. Darby's counsel told the judge: 'If Your Honour were to do as this dog did and nuzzle the defendant's genitals, it would be an indecent assault.'

Justice O'Keefe questioned the analogy at both ends. First, he wondered whether or not such acts would be an assault or merely 'eccentric' if they were committed by a person. And second, he proposed that the acts

> may well be characterised quite differently if performed by one dog on another, or by a dog on a human ... a 'crotch nuzzle' ... may be no more than a conventional, friendly, social gesture with no hostile intent, and unlikely to constitute an assault – whether indecent or otherwise.

But three appeal judges differed with O'Keefe on both points. They held that whatever might be said about sniffing, touching was another thing altogether, and that whatever might be said about 'an exuberant dog [that] nuzzled a passing pedestrian in one of the "physical contacts of ordinary life"', a dog that is encouraged to act that way is another thing as well. Ultimately, the majority ruled, the legality of what happened depended on whether or not the police had reasonably suspected that Darby was carrying drugs because of the dog's behaviour (and Darby's) *before* the dog touched him – and especially before it nuzzled him. They sent the case back to a lower court to consider this issue further, but the result is not recorded. By then, the New South Wales parliament had already changed the law to permit police to 'use a dog to carry out general drug detection' in certain scenarios, including nightclub queues.

New South Wales and South Australia only protect people's bodies against physical trespass, such as bunting by a dog, but many other jurisdictions also protect people's privacy and draw the line between legal and illegal uses of sniffer dogs in a different way. Decades ago, the US Supreme Court ruled that sniffer dogs do not typically invade anyone's privacy because our general smell is not private and sniffer dogs are only trained to reveal particular, criminal smells. Canada's Supreme Court had a different take on both points. While smells are not private, the Canadians ruled, the source of those smells are. (In other words, there's a difference between 'someone farted' and 'you farted'.) And the ability of trained dogs to sniff out specifically criminal smells means they are more intrusive than, say, a human sniffing someone. (In other words, there's a difference between 'you smell funny' and 'you smell of traces of heroin'.) The upshot is that the United States does not place any general limitations on sniffer dogs, but Canada does. However, even Canada's Supreme Court recognised that sniffing is less intrusive than some other police actions. Accordingly, Canadian police do not need to get a warrant every time they use a sniffer dog, and only need to have a specific reason of their own to direct a dog to sniff a particular person or thing.

In practice, the police often rely on social norms, rather than their legal powers, to use animals to search people. In the South Australian case from 1997 discussed earlier, the passengers on the Adelaide–Sydney bus had left their bags in the bus's luggage compartment and hence – the higher courts in that case ruled – had handed over the choice to let a police dog sniff in the vicinity of their luggage to the bus company. Likewise, many public entertainment venues make submitting to sniffer dogs a condition of entry. Commercial organisations make these choices for a variety of reasons, including a desire to keep drugs off their property or to keep the police onside, especially when they are dependent on public licences to operate. In turn, the public have come to accept the use of sniffer dogs in some locations – such as airports – as routine. Even in less regulated settings, such as nightclub lines, many individuals will agree to be sniffed by a police dog, again for myriad reasons – from having nothing to hide to not wanting to look like they do. The overall innocuousness of dogs in human society likely contributes to the willingness of organisations and individuals to submit to their 'use'.

The innocuousness or otherwise of police dogs was central to the 2013 debate in the US Supreme Court that we discussed at the start of this chapter. The dissenting opinion in *Florida v Jardines* described the police's actions as follows:

> Detective Bartelt and Franky [the police dog] approached the front door via the driveway and a paved path – the route that any visitor would customarily use – and Franky was on the kind of leash that any dog owner might employ. Franky approached the door, he started to

track an airborne odor. He held his head high and began 'bracketing' the area (pacing back and forth) in order to determine the strongest source of the smell. Detective Bartelt knew 'the minute [he] observed' this behavior that Franky had detected drugs. Upon locating the odor's strongest source, Franky sat at the base of the front door, and at this point, Detective Bartelt and Franky immediately returned to their patrol car.

Justice Alito (and three other justices of the United States' top court) ruled that Bartelt had stayed within the implied licence all home owners give strangers to walk onto their porch to knock at their door (unless they put up a sign declaring otherwise). And so did Franky, Alito declared, citing the historical relationship between humans and dogs, and noting that 'the common law allowed even unleashed dogs to wander on private property without committing a trespass'.

But Justice Scalia, who wrote the majority judgment, ruled that Franky's specialised training made the visit anything but innocuous:

> Introducing a trained police dog to explore the area around the home in hopes of discovering incriminating evidence is something else. There is no customary invitation to do that. An invitation to engage in canine forensic investigation assuredly does not inhere in the very act of hanging a knocker. To find a visitor knocking on the door is routine (even if sometimes unwelcome); to spot that same visitor exploring the front path with a metal detector, or marching his bloodhound into the garden before saying hello and asking permission, would inspire most of us to – well, call the police.

Justice Kagan equated a drug detection dog to a different device that could be used to look inside someone's home:

> Here, police officers came to Joelis Jardines' door with a supersensitive instrument, which they deployed to detect things inside that they could not perceive unassisted. The equipment they used was animal, not mineral. But that is of no significance ... Drug-detection dogs are highly trained tools of law enforcement, geared to respond in distinctive ways to specific scents so as to convey clear and reliable information to their human partners. They are to the poodle down

the street as high-powered binoculars are to a piece of plain glass. Like the binoculars, a drug-detection dog is a specialized device for discovering objects not in plain view (or plain smell). And as in the hypothetical above, that device was aimed here at a home – the most private and inviolate (or so we expect) of all the places.

She concluded by pointing out that the Supreme Court's ruling would not stop police using dogs (or, presumably, binoculars) to search for drugs present within people's houses; it would just oblige them to obtain a search warrant first.

Using Animals' Teeth

Justice Scalia's reference to a police officer 'marching his bloodhound into the garden' recalls Londoners' fears of aggressive police dogs during Jack the Ripper's 1888's 'Autumn of Terror'. Indeed, Scalia noted that 'Detective Bartelt had the dog on a six-foot leash, owing in part to the dog's "wild" nature', that he stood back 'so that he would not "get knocked over" when the dog was "spinning around trying to find" the source' and that Bartelt ultimately had to pull the dog away from the property. The Florida Supreme Court had relied on these same details to conclude that Bartelt's use of Franky was not merely a search but 'an intrusive procedure that may expose the resident to public opprobrium, humiliation and embarrassment ... [raising] the specter of arbitrary and discriminatory application'. The justices of the Supreme Court of the United States did not directly discuss this issue.

An instance of an Australian court condemning the police's violent use of dogs occurred the year after the US court ruled on Franky. Early one morning, South Australian police spent an hour pursuing a stolen car around Adelaide, only to lose track of the driver after he crashed into a police vehicle and vanished over a suburban fence. The frustrated police were soon joined by two members of their specialist tactical group, who brought their German shepherds, Riggs and Koda, to join the search. One handler explained their approach: 'Unless we are told by a specific person we cannot enter [their property] then we will continue to enter. That's the way I've done it for the thirteen years I've been handling a police dog.'

That was their first of several mistakes made in the case, Justice David Peek later ruled in his review:

There were some words used by the prosecutor at trial that were cal-
culated to conjure up an image of a bloodhound, with its nose to the
ground, following the course taken by a particular person by detection of a deposited scent. It is important to note that that is exactly
what was not happening in this case. It is quite clear that the police
dogs were not 'tracking' the driver and they were not following any
signs left by the driver along the route he took after the police last
lost sight of him. The words of the Chief Magistrate 'the dog located a
fresh scent' meant no more than that the dog located a fresh scent in
the yard of 10 Clarence Street after being taken by their handlers from
the streets into the yards of a number of house properties, one after
another, in an effort to detect fresh human therein.

That meant that the dogs' actions gave the officers' no grounds at all to enter
any of the premises uninvited (and, given the very early hour, they could
not rely on an implied invitation either).

Alas, the police did not just (mis)use the dogs' noses. After Riggs barked
loudly at a baseball cap in one yard, his handler noticed a man inside a car
parked nearby and yelled, 'Police with a dog! Get out of the car!' The man
inside unlocked a door, but did not get out, most likely, the judge deduced,
because both dogs were barking loudly and lunging at the car. (Two other
police officers present stood well back, later explaining that the dogs 'have
a tendency to bite so we didn't want to get too close'.) Riggs' handler opened
the car door and Riggs bit the occupant's leg before being kicked away.
Koda's handler, claiming that he was worried the man would escape out
of the car's far door, 'used Police Dog Koda to effect the arrest' – that is, he
commanded Koda to bite, and Koda promptly dragged the occupant out of
the car by the leg. The man threw a series of punches at Koda, until the second handler instructed Riggs to 'assist'. After both dogs had bitten the man's
legs, they were called off and the four police officers seized the man, eventually charging him with, among other things, 'resisting arrest'.

Justice Peek held that it was the police, not their target, who broke the
law. Not only had they trespassed on private property and arrested someone without any grounds to do so, they had used very violent means to
make the arrest when less violent means would have sufficed. The judge
threw out the man's conviction for resisting the 'arrest', and he also ruled
that the courts could not take into account anything the man said after he
was pulled from the car.

Peek quoted an American article to explain why police mistakes involving dogs are rarely identified:

> Victims of police dog attacks are usually unsympathetic. Generally, they are persons of color, guilty of some offense, and suffer from disabilities including illiteracy, mental illness or drug or alcohol dependency. Most police dog bite victims are suspects in property crimes such as auto theft or burglary who try to hide or escape from the police, so the police perceive the victims as having defied official authority by attempting to avoid police contact. Furthermore, juries (and judges) are easy prey for the police-inspired myth that letting a police dog attack reduces the probability of injury to the officer or innocent persons while supposedly enabling the police to capture suspects who might have escaped but for the dog attack. The police are also very careful to obscure the reality of dog attacks by such euphemistic and misleading terms as the dog 'apprehended the suspect' or 'placed a bite-hold'. Thus, given our long history of vigilante justice, juries are susceptible to the claim that the victim 'got what he deserved'.

Despite the judge's vehement and compelling criticism of Riggs' and Koda's handlers, the case was a vindication of sorts for the dogs themselves, or at least their noses: the house where the man was found turned out to be the home of the stolen car's passenger, whom the police had successfully arrested after the crash.

Animals as Experts

Earlier, we explained how South Africa's police played a crucial early role in establishing broad acceptance of the use of tracker dogs. South African police were able to leverage their country's racial divisions to convince the public to accept the use of dogs in some settings, which – decades later, and following the widespread use of dogs during World War II – led to the public acceptance of police dogs throughout the developed world. However, the South African *courts* had a different view on the matter. At an early stage, they baulked at relying on evidence from animal tracking in criminal prosecutions. Indeed, they still baulk at it, although now they are almost alone in taking such a stance. Other courts shifted from treating dogs as beyond understanding in legal settings to accepting that their input can justify police action and criminal punishment.

In 1918, an Eastern Cape court assessed the effectiveness of a typical way dogs in that era were used to track evidence. In one of the matters considered by the court, police investigating stock thefts used a dog to track some footprints to the accused's home and then improvised a line-up of sorts. The accused and two others were made to stand 30 yards apart, and the dog was repeatedly instructed to find the source of the footprints and picked the accused each time. The judge in the case, Sir Thomas Graham, a former prime minister of the Cape Colony, endorsed the method as a way to identify possible culprits and encourage them to confess, but drew the line at courts relying on the same method to infer guilt. He ruled that 'it would be a dangerous innovation to allow the introduction of the evidence of irrational animals which were actuated by instincts of which we knew but little and could regulate only in a limited degree', likening the evidence to testimony by 'lunatics and persons in state of intoxication'.

South Africa's courtroom ban was confirmed the following year by the newly formed Union's top court. In this case, a dog had followed the footprints of a prowler to a nearby hostel, sniffed each of the eight occupants and then jumped onto the accused's bed, barking at him. South Africa's most feted jurist, Chief Justice James Rose Innes, pursued the opposite line of reasoning to Graham. The problem with tracker dogs was not their *instinctive* behaviour, Innes ruled, but rather their *trained* behaviour:

> The habit of a dog to resent the entrance of a stranger at night, is independent of instruction or experience; it is based upon the instinct of self-preservation; and it is patent to our observation. But to draw inferences from the actions of a trailing hound as to the identity of a particular individual is to go a great deal further; it is to enter a region of conjecture and uncertainty. We have no scientific or accurate knowledge as to the faculty by which dogs of certain breeds are said to be able to follow the scent of one human being, rejecting the scent of all others. But it is not contended that they act merely on instinct; it is admitted even by their optimistic instructors that they must be carefully trained before they can be relied upon. The discharge of their task and the identification expected of them involve processes closely akin to reasoning.

Accordingly, he declared, 'the whole experiment … contains too great an element of uncertainty to justify us in drawing inferences from it in the course of legal proceedings'.

The South African courtroom ban did not stop the use of tracking dogs by the nation's police. Indeed, the courts themselves encouraged the use of dogs to *investigate* crime, dismissing the complaint of a man who was wrongly identified as a cheese thief during a scent line-up and continuing to rely on the confessions of suspects who had been 'identified' as culprits by dogs.

According to African studies scholar Keith Shear, the courts' approach made life easier for the police and their dogs:

> The sealing off of the investigative domain (in which admissible evidence was procured) from the scrutiny of the legal arena (in which such evidence was proved) shielded the technique from searching adverse criticism and permitted the police to continue to maintain that they were following scientifically controlled procedure.

While South Africa's courts protected themselves from the possible misuse of evidence from sniffer dogs in the cases before them, they did not protect South Africa's people from being wrongly subjected to searches based on such evidence, or even from being wrongly coerced into confessions prompted by spurious suspicions cast by dogs and their handlers.

Although South Africa's stance on keeping dogs out of the 'legal arena' persisted and influenced some other countries – it was reaffirmed by South Africa at the height of apartheid and was recently adopted by India's Supreme Court – it is no longer the norm. Instead, most comparable courts have since decided to take into account evidence from trained animals in some circumstances. This occurs in three ways: letting judges and jurors learn about how particular animal species behave, where relevant; permitting police to use the actions of trained animals to justify searching people and property; and allowing humans to be punished largely on the basis of animal evidence.

Telling Courts How Animals Behave

On the evening of Wednesday, 1 October 1980, Dr Kenneth Brown, a forensic odontologist, dressed a skinned and decapitated goat carcass in a baby's jumpsuit and threw it into an enclosure at Adelaide Zoo. The enclosure held dingoes that had not been fed for five days. It was too dark to see what happened next, but the next day he returned to find the kid devoured and the jumpsuit torn and filthy. This point of this grim experiment was to compare the remains of the jumpsuit with those of a similar article of clothing found six weeks earlier near Central Australia's Uluru, shortly after the disappearance of nine-week-old Azaria Chamberlain. Northern Territory police later used the results of the experiment to argue before coroners and a jury that Azaria was not taken by a dingo, because Azaria's jumpsuit showed no sign of dingo saliva and hair, while both were found on the jumpsuit with which Brown had dressed the goat carcass. Although the utility of the zoo's experiment was hotly debated in court, the Northern Territory judges were happy to receive the evidence. After all, they – like almost everyone else – knew next to nothing about the eating habits of dingoes.

As we have discussed, the courts are willing to hear evidence of how particular animals behave in the presence of familiar and unfamiliar things, such as when a dog greets its owner or barks at strangers, because jurors and judges are acquainted with such reactions and can judge them accordingly. Courts are similarly willing to hear what can be discerned from behaviour that is wholly unfamiliar to them, such as dingoes' eating habits, on the basis that the court can learn about what is otherwise unknowable. To that end, they are willing to hear evidence from trustworthy zoologists or other scientists whose qualifications, professionalism and biases (if not their methods or fields) can also – the argument goes – be usefully judged by non-experts. Since the Chamberlain case, police have formalised the study of how natural environments affect human remains through the creation of 'body farms', which expose donated cadavers to the elements. These elements include animals – ranging from bacteria and insects to larger scavengers – so that their impact on the newly dead can be related to courts in pertinent cases by forensic anthropologists.

However, the way police use tracker dogs to investigate crimes in the field does not easily conform to any of these categories. While most people are familiar with dogs and their noses, they know little to nothing about how dogs track humans. And every instance of dog tracking is an experiment of sorts, as each exercise involves different conditions – different people, environments, times of day and so on. This makes it hard to generalise about the results. Additionally, the dogs' handlers – the ones who tell the courts how the dogs behaved – do not study their dogs, but rather train and work alongside them. As an Indian court put it in 1963:

The tracker dog's evidence cannot be likened to the type of evidence accepted from scientific experts describing chemical reactions, blood tests and the actions of bacilli, because the behaviour of chemicals, blood corpuscles and bacilli contains no element of conscious volition or deliberate choice. Dogs are intelligent animals with many thought processes similar to the thought process of human beings, and wherever there are thought processes there is always the risk of error, deception and even self-deception.

The result, as South Africa's chief justice held in 1920, is that courts risk three errors:

Not only is there the possibility that the dog may fail to distinguish between one scent and another, or may desert one for the other, but also there is the possibility of a misunderstanding between the animal and his keeper. And there is the further consideration arising from the dramatic nature of the testimony and the super-canine sagacity claimed for these animals by those in charge of them, that juries might be inclined to attach to such evidence a dangerously exaggerated importance.

For courts to accept the use of tracker dog evidence, they would have to be confident that each of these risks – of errors made by the dogs, their handlers or the courts – was understood and managed.

It would be a steep uphill battle to convince judges to accept dogs' tracking skills, at least if a 1903 judgment from Nebraska's Chief Justice John Sullivan is any guide:

The bloodhound has, of course, a great reputation for sagacity, and there is a prevalent belief that, in the pursuit and discovery of fugitive criminals, he is practically infallible. It is a commonly accepted notion that he will start from the place where a crime has been committed, follow for miles the track upon which he has been set, find the culprit, confront him and, *mirabile dictu*, by accusing bay and mien, declare, 'Thou art the man.' This strange misbelief is with some people apparently incorrigible. It is a delusion which abundant actual experience has failed to dissipate. It lives on from generation to generation. It has still the attractiveness of a fresh creation. 'Time writes no wrinkle on its brow.' But it is, nevertheless, a delusion, an evident and obvious delusion. The sleuthhound of fiction is a marvellous dog, but we find nothing quite like him in real life.

Sullivan noted that some American courts had admitted such evidence in the past but 'the judicial history of the civilized world is against them'.

Fifteen years later, South Africa's Chief Justice Innes deemed the Holmesian absence of British judgments accepting such evidence 'highly significant' because 'there must be numbers of dogs in England, specially bred and trained, whose services would be available for tracking criminals'. As noted earlier, he was completely wrong about that; the English resisted most police uses of bloodhounds until after World War II.

However, as many scholars of contemporary evidence law now bemoan, courts are typically quick to shed their scepticism of novel investigatory practices once they are widely adopted by the police, whether those practices concern the individuality of fingerprints or the utility of blood spatter examinations. Hence, just a decade after police dogs became widely adopted in the cities of postwar Britain, Scotland's High Court of Justiciary declared: 'I suppose it is common knowledge that people do have different scents and dogs are able to discriminate between one person's scent and another.' That 1960 ruling, which lacked even the American insistence on the dog being a 'purebred' of a known tracking breed, was then adopted in Canada in 1962, New Zealand in 1964 and Northern Ireland in 1966. It was another three decades before England's courts followed suit. In 1994's *Pieterson v R*, copious evidence implicated the defendants in a robbery, including a dog that had tracked them from the crime scene to a broken strap that seemingly matched a bag owned by the accused. Lord Chief Justice Peter Taylor decided to 'follow the approach which has been adopted in the cases already cited from jurisdictions other than that of South Africa'.

Each of these courts initially remained cautious about the dogs' human associates who vouched for their dogs' expertise. In the English case, the handler said the following about her dog:

I have been a dog handler in the Thames Valley Police since June 1985. I have worked with police dog Ben for 18 months, following the departure of Ben's previous handler and the death of my previous police dog. Ben is a German shepherd and will be eight years old in December 1993. He commenced his training at one year old in the Thames

Valley Police Force and had six-and-a-half years' experience of the work required from him in May 1993.

Taylor held that merely stating 'the length of time that the dog had "been on the books"' was not enough; rather, the court needed to know 'the nature of the training that the dog had been given, [and] of the reliability of the dog on any tests that have been carried out in controlled conditions to see whether the training has produced a reliable response'.

New Zealand's Justice Owen Woodhouse initially barred handlers from saying *more* than that:

> Constable Bracey cannot attempt to tell us what the dog was thinking or intending. But provided he is in a position to describe the training of the dog, and the behaviour of dogs generally, in regard to the tracking of persons (what in effect has been discovered they do on these occasions), then in my view he can simply state what happened on the occasion in question. In doing so, he should not translate what he observed into terms, for example, of the dog following some person's scent or track.

Woodhouse's apparent concern was that handlers would exaggerate the significance of their dogs' abilities and actions. New Zealand's Court of Appeal later endorsed this rule, stating that 'care must be exercised lest any over-readiness to admit peripheral testimony should result in unfairness to accused persons', but accepted that a handler could tell a jury that his tracker dog 'was aggressive towards' the accused once they were located.

In the end, presumably because of fears that jurors would find complex tracking evidence hard to understand, the same court relented. In a case where a dog tracked back and forth between a location where the defendants had been seen and another where some items had been concealed, New Zealand's Court of Appeal said:

> Constable Payne was asked to express an opinion, based on the behaviour of the dog, as to the freshness of the track it was following. Likewise he gave evidence as to the habit of tracker dogs to follow the most recent human scent in the area where they are commanded to begin tracking. Both these matters were properly the subject of expert evidence.

Nearly all courts now insist that jurors be specifically warned about the risk that tracking dog evidence may be incorrect. In a 1987 New South Wales trial, which included evidence that a dog had tracked a scent from a rape victim's home to a location where a car (eventually found with the accused) had been stolen, the trial judge told the jury:

> When considering the evidence of Sgt Bell in relation to the activities of police dog Jake, caution must be exercised for the following reasons. Although the evidence of Sgt Bell was capable of being tested in cross-examination and indeed was tested, there is no way by the very nature of things that the dog could be subject to cross-examination. You must also be careful to avoid overestimating the reliability of the operation of a dog's senses, so you must avoid too rapidly arriving at the conclusion which the Crown asks you to draw from the evidence of the dog's tracking activities.

The next year, in what appears to be the first Australian judgment to approve a verdict relying in part on tracker dog evidence, Chief Justice Murray Gleeson declared this 'an adequate warning in the circumstances'.

Using Animals to Justify Police Searches

At Lindy and Michael Chamberlain's trial over the death of their baby Azaria in 1982, the prosecution told the jury why it was significant that no dingo hairs were found on their daughter's jumpsuit:

> I suggest you would think, would you not, that somewhere in some place on some article you would find at least one hair which could be positively proved to have come from a dingo. Remember that Doctor Harding had some 100 dingo hairs from the zoo jumpsuit [in which the goat carcass had been wrapped] to use for comparison purposes.... The Crown says the absence of hairs, like the absence of saliva, is negative evidence pointing to a positive conclusion which is this: that the baby was not taken by a dingo. Therefore she was murdered.

But, as evidence law scholar Gary Edmond observed, Dr Harding had also told the jury that he recognised a fatal flaw in Dr Brown's experiment at Adelaide Zoo:

It occurred to me at the time of thinking about this that the experiment did not show whether these hairs were by direct contact of the clothing with the dingo at the zoo or whether this experiment happened in a pen where there could have been a lot of dingo hairs, and other hairs for that matter, on the ground or floor or whatever you call it and the clothing came into contact with that and picked up hairs, so it could give a false impression. If I might just add to that, I have since learned that there were perhaps problems with the moulting time of the dingo or dingoes. There is a large number of imponderables there, really, which make the interpretation very difficult and probably not of a great deal of value.

The Chamberlain case is now emblematic of how a range of circumstantial evidence – of which the zoo experiment was just a minor example – can generate spurious suspicions of criminality. Almost everyone now accepts that Azaria Chamberlain was in fact taken by a dingo.

The use of trained police animals at the start of a criminal investigation raises a version of this problem. In contrast to court findings in a civil or criminal case – which respectively require a jury or judge to decide whether a claim is more likely to be true than not or whether it is true beyond a reasonable doubt – the only condition a police officer must meet in order to search someone is a good reason to expect that the search will reveal something. In many contexts – notably, personal and vehicle searches – the officer makes this call without prior independent scrutiny. Police in this position have every incentive to read a dog's behaviour as pointing to something suspicious, which permits them to perform a search to confirm or dispel those suspicions, rather than as something ambiguous (which would require the officer to explore more onerous and less fruitful investigative avenues).

In the second Florida sniffer dog case to reach the US Supreme Court in 2013, a police officer pulled over a truck twice in a week, first because its licence plate had expired and then due to a broken tail-light. The officer concluded each traffic stop by letting Aldo, his German shepherd, have a 'free air sniff' of the car (which US law allows, based on the theory that the air around a car is not private). Each time, Aldo alerted the officer to the door handle, prompting the officer to search the truck. The problem for the officer was that neither search turned up any of the drugs that Aldo was trained to detect. The problem for the driver, Clayton Harris, was that one search turned up a set of ingredients – hundreds of loose pseudoephedrine pills, thousands of matches, hydrochloric acid, antifreeze and iodine – that can be used to make methamphetamine. As a result, he was arrested for drug trafficking and eventually sentenced to two years in prison.

There was no doubt that Harris was guilty as charged – he confessed all to the officer after being read his rights – but he could only be punished if the officer's search of his truck was legal. The officer explained that he trusted Aldo's alerts because he and his dog had completed a forty-hour training course a year earlier and did four hours of training a week at a wrecking yard, where he placed drugs on vehicles for Aldo to find. He produced training records that showed Aldo's performance was always 'satisfactory', as well as records showing that Aldo's alerts led to drug arrests around five times a month. But Florida's Supreme Court noticed a flaw in those records: there was no documentation of the times that Aldo's alerts failed to turn up drugs, including both of the occasions that Harris's truck was searched. That meant that there was no way for a court to judge whether Aldo's alerts were reliable: on some of these occasions Aldo may have alerted the officer when he had smelt nothing or had mistaken stale smells for fresh ones; on others, his handler may have misread or even prompted his alerts.

Ultimately, the US Supreme Court ruled that Florida had set the bar far too high for establishing whether tracker dogs are reliable enough to justify an intrusive follow-up search:

> The question … is whether all the facts surrounding a dog's alert, viewed through the lens of common sense, would make a reasonably prudent person think that a search would reveal contraband or evidence of a crime. A sniff is up to snuff when it meets that test. And here, Aldo did.

Justice Elena Kagan dismissed the significance of the lack of any drugs in Harris's vehicle on both occasions Aldo alerted:

> A detection dog recognizes an odor, not a drug, and should alert whenever the scent is present, even if the substance is gone (just as a police officer's much inferior nose detects the odor of marijuana for some time after a joint has been smoked). In the usual case, the mere chance that the substance might no longer be at the location does not matter; a well-trained dog's alert establishes a fair probability – all that is required for probable cause – that either drugs or evidence of a drug crime (like the precursor chemicals in Harris's truck) will be found.

Indeed, adopting the officer's own explanation of Aldo's alert – that Harris was a regular meth user and some of the meth would have been left on the door handle – the court ruled that 'a well-trained drug-detection dog *should* alert to such odors'.

Justice Kagan reasoned that it is wrong to focus on a dog's actual performance in the field for many reasons. First, that standard could never be met by a 'rookie dog'. Second, there is no way to judge the occasions when a dog does not alert, because the officer will never know what might have been found in a search. Third, a record of false positives – when a dog does alert but nothing is found – could also be misleading, because the failure to find any drugs could be the fault of the officer (if the drugs are well hidden) or the circumstances (if the scent was from recently removed drugs). Rather, Kagan ruled, the focus should be on formal training records, because the trainers will know whether the dog had failed or succeeded in any controlled test. Indeed, the police's own assessment of the adequacy of their training programs and records should generally suffice:

> After all, law enforcement units have their own strong incentive to use effective training and certification programs, because only accurate drug-detection dogs enable officers to locate contraband without incurring unnecessary risks or wasting limited time and resources.

As for possible errors in the field – such as a dog being out of its element or a handler being confused or cueing the dog to alert – rigorous cross-examination can be trusted to sniff out such problems, Kagan ruled. In short, like so many others before it, America's top court – the world's most protective court when it comes to scrutinising police searches – put its faith entirely in the professionalism of police, lawyers and judges when it came to assessing whether or not police officers are right to base their suspicions of criminality on the actions of their trained dogs. The result is that the law can now readily rely on the police's understanding of their own dogs to justify further investigations of suspects.

Using Animals to Find People Guilty of Crimes

The 1980 Adelaide Zoo experiment is a minor footnote in a much longer tale of the miscarriage of justice that left a lasting mark on the Australian criminal justice system. Lindy Chamberlain was convicted of the murder of her baby Azaria in 1982 and lost her appeal in Australia's High Court in 1984. In 1986, a chance event freed her from prison: people searching Uluru for a fallen climber came across the matinee jacket she had always insisted Azaria was wearing when a dingo took her.

The discovery not only bolstered the credibility of the convicted murderer's claims of innocence, it also exposed another flaw in Kenneth Brown's experiment: he only tested the *prosecution's* theory of what Azaria was wearing, not the *defence's*. When a new inquiry re-examined the prosecution's evidence the following year, Commissioner Trevor Morling noted that Brown's experiment actually supported the Chamberlains' claim that a dingo attack was consistent with Azaria's relatively undamaged jumpsuit:

> The dingoes used in the experiment managed to remove the meat from the jumpsuit, opening only its top two studs. The jumpsuit suffered considerable damage in the experiment, but perhaps less than might be expected.

Years after the Chamberlains were acquitted, fresh evidence of untrained animal behaviour – in the form of new dingo attacks on Australian children – finally convinced most Australians that Lindy Chamberlain's murder conviction was a horrifying error.

Some of this was foreshadowed in South Africa and Canada many decades earlier. When Sir Thomas Graham first rejected the use of tracking dogs in South African courts, he argued:

> If it is held that evidence of this nature is relevant and thus admissible, the rule will apply to cases of every description, and respectable citizens of every class in life may have their lives, liberty and reputation jeopardised by evidence that a trained police dog had indicated them to be guilty persons.

The British Columbia Court of Appeal agreed a decade later that 'human life or liberty shall not be made to depend upon inferences to be drawn from the actions of dogs'. However, the court's future chief justice Archer Martin dissented:

> the court must also avoid the equally grave danger of being over-cautious and thereby rejecting reasonable evidence which would

enable the guilty to escape that just punishment which is necessary for the protection of the public.

Later that century, it was Martin's view that carried the day. In 1962, the same court overturned a burglary acquittal because the judge had excluded the prosecution's evidence that a dog, given a pair of shoes found at the crime scene, followed a path for two hours through urban streets to a motel connected to the accused. Although the prosecutors initially said that they would not seek a fresh trial, they belatedly changed their mind. The judges assured the defendant that he 'will receive a trial surrounded by all the safeguards an accused person is entitled to under our system of jurisprudence'. The outcome of that retrial, much less its accuracy, is not known.

While the Australian police force's use of South African dogs in the 1920s was short-lived, Australian customs followed the example of other countries and started using dogs for drug detection in the 1960s, and regular police soon followed suit. However, Australia's courts were initially slow to endorse the use of animal evidence in criminal trials.

In a 1980 burglary appeal, the Victorian Court of Appeal acknowledged the many decisions on tracker dog evidence made overseas but excluded the particular evidence before them – a tracker dog had stopped mid-search between the accused and their car near a fence where a witness had earlier seen some burglars climbing – as too equivocal to justify admission.

In 1999, New South Wales' top court similarly baulked at admitting evidence that a dog had followed a trail to a house where the accused had lived a year before the crime, citing the lack of any evidence that he had recently returned to the property.

A decade later, the same court endorsed a jury conviction based in part on evidence that a novice tracker dog – which had received poor grades for work on soft soil – had led a police officer through a forest to two men trying to get away from him. But the court was surely influenced by other evidence suggesting that these men were the burglars an eyewitness had seen entering the forest, including a bag of stolen items found nearby.

In 2013, Queensland's Court of Appeal fulfilled the Nebraska chief justice's prediction of eleven decades earlier: if the evidence of tracker dogs was 'held to be legal evidence, it would, standing alone, sustain a conviction'. The previous year, an eleven-year-old who had woken early one morning to use the toilet interrupted a burglar who had broken into the family home and car. When the child's mother called the police, they arrived with a tracker dog named Jack.

The dog's handler later testified that he had 'cast' Jack at footprints near the house, and the dog had picked up a scent, leading him through easements, roads and council land, and stopping at two locations for some time. Eventually the handler had noticed Jack becoming more excited as they approached a house. There the handler had found a man pulling at the door saying, 'Let me in, let me in.' The man, Eddie Tamatea, told the police he had simply stepped outside for a cigarette and had accidentally locked the door behind him, a claim backed up by the house's two residents, who said that he had been there all night.

The police searched Tamatea and the house and found no stolen property, though a name tag belonging to the eleven-year-old was eventually found near the first location where Jack had paused, and a wallet from the burgled house was recovered from a creek that passed near the second location. However, the child could not identify Tamatea, nor did the suspect's fingerprints match those found at the window where the burglar had entered, on the car he had broken into or on the garage door he had left by. In short, the only significant connections between the burglary and Tamatea were the trail Jack followed to Tamatea's house, the location of the child's name tag and the handler's claim that he saw human footprints in the dew for most of Jack's route.

At Tamatea's trial, the judge told the jury to acquit him if they had 'a reasonable doubt about whether the tracking was true and accurate and correct and reliable'. The prosecution faced the difficulty that Jack and his handler had only been teamed up for a month, a problem they countered with evidence from Jack's previous handler and a senior handler who oversaw the reteaming, both of whom vouched for the reliability of the new human–animal team. The judge also warned the jury:

> In this particular case, you also need to take extra care because the dog, you won't be surprised to know, it can't give evidence, it can't be cross-examined or otherwise scrutinised in the way a person's evidence is scrutinised. You should be careful to avoid overestimating the reliability of the operation of the dog senses.

In the end, however, the jury convicted Tamatea, and the Court of Appeal unanimously ruled that it 'was open to the jury to find that the tracking evidence was accurate and reliable, and it was open to them to be satisfied that the person tracked was the offender'.

For Eddie Tamatea, the consequences of this ruling went beyond his conviction and sentence. He was a New Zealand citizen with a criminal record. In 2018, the twenty-nine-year-old was deported to a country he had not lived in since he was a child. According to a later sentencing report, his 'deportation back to New Zealand . . . was a significant factor in' his subsequent decision to take a woman hostage at an Auckland shopping centre, which led to a two-year sentence for the now thirty-one-year-old. The use of Jack the tracking dog was either vindicated by or to blame for these depressing changes to Tamatea's life.

5.

HARMING ANIMALS

For this was on seynt Valentines day
Whan every bryd comyth there to chese his make
Of every kynde that men thinke may

Geoffrey Chaucer, The Parlement of Foules, 1382

S T VALENTINES DAY, OR 14 FEBRUARY, WAS ONCE THE MID-dle day of Lupercalia, a Roman festival that was said to combine animal sacrifices with fertility rites. Its modern romantic associations took hold over a millennium later, in the decades after Chaucer's dubious observation about the timing of avian mating.

On Valentine's Day of 1641, John Wakeman, one of the seventy 'freemen' who founded the New Haven colony in modern-day Connecticut, had a different connection between animals and humans on his mind when he walked into the colony's courthouse carrying the body of a dead piglet:

Itt had no haire on the whole body, the skin was very tender, and of a reddish white collour like a childs; the head most straing, itt had butt one eye in the midle of the face, and thatt large and open, like some blemished eye of a man; over the eye, in the bottome of the foreheade wch was like a childes, a thing of flesh grew forth and hung downe, itt was hollow, and like a mans instrumt of genration. A nose, mouth and chinne deformed, butt nott much unlike a childs, the neck and eares had allso such resemblance.

The problem was more than skin deep: 'This monster being after opened and compared w'h a pig of the same farrow, there was an aparant difference in all the innards.'

The people of New Haven colony surely knew that Wakeman's 'pdigious monster' was merely a tragically deformed pig, born from a pregnant sow Wakeman had recently bought from Henry Browning, a fellow freeman. What concerned them was what 'some hand of God' had revealed about unseen events – an 'impression' visited first upon Wakeman's wife, 'sadly expecting, though she knew nott why, some strange accedent in thatt sows pigging' and then on the 'many thatt saw the monster, (therein guided by the neare resemblance of the eye), that one George Spencer, late servant to the said Henry Browning, had beene actor in unnatureall and abominable filthynes w'h the sow'.

The law that would be brought to bear on Spencer is *criminal law*. We have already dealt with criminal law several times in this book: It was applied to Tania Isbester, the owner of Izzy the Staffordshire terrier, and it was one of many legal tools we discussed in Chapter 2 that oblige humans to control animals. It was also, of course, the primary means by which animals themselves could be blamed and punished in medieval animal trials or in the criminal trials of their human owners, both examined in Chapter 3.

In essence, the criminal law has three features: a rule (these days, almost always set out in a statute) defining an act (or a failure to act) that in certain circumstances or with a particular result constitutes a crime; a specific procedure for proving that someone has committed a crime (typically beyond a reasonable doubt and, for serious crimes, before a jury); and judges who are empowered to punish proven criminals (including with prison terms or, in certain countries and eras, death).

The first four chapters of this book addressed how criminal law deals with animals that harm humans, variously punishing the owner, the animal or both. The law's approach to humans that harm animals is quite different – it permits humans to perform such arguably 'unnatureall and abominable' acts as killing animals, eating them, caging them or breeding them.

But there are limits to this legal largesse. First, there are a variety of legal protections afforded to some animals, including protections from certain human acts. We discuss these in the following chapter. Second, there is a smaller set of acts that criminal law specifically bars humans from doing to (many, if not all) non-humans. Such acts are the focus of this chapter, which we begin by discussing George Spencer's alleged crime, bestiality – an ancient but continuing prohibition whose *raison d'être* is to protect humans, not animals – and conclude by considering more recently defined crimes against animals, including other forms of human cruelty.

This chapter may be confronting to some, and we recognise that readers may find bestiality and general cruelty to animals hard to read about. We include it for the sake of completeness: these are some of the ways in which humans and animals interact, and the law has a lot to say about that. Bestiality, of course, is not only a crime, but something that remains taboo in many societies to this day, where it is increasingly understood as an extreme form of cruelty to animals and humans alike. Other forms of cruelty to animals are simply awful to read about. We well understand why some readers would skip this chapter, but we also appreciate that others will opt to better understand the law on harming animals by reading on.

One of the jarring things we'll see in this chapter is how the law seems to vacillate between treating these crimes as extremely dangerous and taboo and, in other cases, in an almost in a matter-of-fact way. As we'll see, the latter was not possible for George Spencer.

Sex with Animals

The New Haven colony was founded (and ultimately faltered) on the view that 'the Scripturs doe holde forth a perfect rule for the direction and governm' of all men'. A year before the piglet's birth, George Spencer had already fallen foul of these laws and had been whipped for various offences, including 'being prophaine and disorderly in his whole conversation'. But he faced a graver problem in 1641: the laws set out in the book of Leviticus contain a clear, albeit jarring to contemporary eyes, list of those who men cannot have sex with – close relatives, neighbours' wives, menstruating women, various in-laws, men and animals – and he was accused of violating the latter prohibition.

The English legal system, while largely unbothered by men having sex with their in-laws or the menstruating, followed Leviticus in conflating (and condemning) some very different sexual acts. Church laws initially included a single prohibition on 'buggery comyttid with mankynde or beaste', and this link between same-sex and different-species sex was preserved when secularism wrested control of Britain's law on sexual offences. Even England's *Offences Against the Person Act 1861*, a landmark of modern law, continued the practice by defining 'sodomy and bestiality' as a single crime. The 'abominable crime of buggery, committed either with mankind or with any animal' remained on the books even after the legalisation of 'a homosexual act in private' a century later. England was not alone in this approach. Tasmania, the last Australian state to legalise homosexual sex, likewise maintained a joint prohibition on sex 'with any person against the law of nature' (including oral or anal sex between humans) and 'with any animal'. In 1997, the first prohibition was finally removed, but, as we will see, the latter prohibition remained and defining its meaning proved difficult.

Defining Bestiality

Until this century, legislatures baulked at defining the 'abominable' crime of sex with animals, and court reporters were often reluctant to even name the crime, let alone describe it. Consider this Tasmanian newspaper law report from 1843:

> Charles Wells, was next placed at the bar, charged with the commission of an unnatural crime. This is one of those cases with which we cannot sully our columns. We cannot, however, do other than say, that the address of the Attorney-General to the bench and jury, in opening the case, deserves to be spoken of in terms of high commendation. He said that in discharging his duty, he would strictly follow the example laid down by His Honor in expediting the public business by every possible means in his power; adverting to the crime with which the prisoner stood charged, he said, that the very horror arising in the minds of the jury from the bare mention of the perpetration of such a crime, ought to make it extremely doubtful, and having explained to the jury such points of law as bore on the case, he concluded by again observing, that the very character of the offence ought make them extremely sceptical, unless fully established by evidence.

The refusal to name or describe the crime of bestiality, combined with the way it was conflated with oral and anal sex under the umbrella term 'buggery', poses a challenge to historians trying to work out what historical crimes were actually committed. In this instance, a record in the Tasmanian archives show that Wells 'was found not guilty of buggery with a calf, but guilty of intent at buggery with a calf'.

Such coyness can also have a legal impact, as it obscures the boundaries of the crime. Recently, the police accused a Hobart man of committing various sexual acts with a dog. Had he been charged between 1924 (when Tasmania replaced the colonial-era crime of 'buggery' with a statutory crime of 'unnatural carnal knowledge') and 1987, he would have been acquitted, because 'carnal knowledge' was defined to mean 'penetration to any the least degree of the organ alleged to have been known by the male organ of generation'. Most of the acts the Hobart man was accused of did not involve penile penetration. After Tasmania replaced the term 'carnal knowledge' with 'sexual intercourse' in 1987, the same limitation remained, as 'sexual intercourse' was similarly defined. In 2017, however, Tasmania joined the rest of Australia in defining 'sexual intercourse' in a broader way that included digital penetration, something the Hobart man was alleged to have done to the dog.

Unfortunately, the Tasmanian parliament also opted to replace the offence of 'unnatural crimes' (which until then was defined to include 'sexual intercourse with any animal') with the offence of engaging 'in an act of bestiality', without providing any further definition. Tasmania's attorney-general provided the following explanation for this decision:

> During development of the Bill, it became apparent that the definition of 'sexual intercourse' to the crime of 'unnatural sexual intercourse' under section 122 was not appropriate and did not support prosecution for all acts of bestiality. Accordingly, the Bill amends the crime by retitling the crime as 'bestiality' and removing reliance on the definition of 'sexual intercourse'.

It certainly made sense to avoid the language of 'sexual intercourse' in the context of animals – a term that lay people exclusively use for sex between humans, and that modern statutes carefully define as such. But it made no sense at all to replace it with 'bestiality', a term from biblical times that reflects entirely dated concerns.

The Hobart man was easily able to point the Tasmanian Supreme Court to old cases and statutes that defined bestiality as an act involving penile penetration. Although that definition was not strictly limited to penile penetration by the human – the list of forbidden sexual acts in Leviticus is largely directed towards men but also tells women that they 'must not stand before an animal to mate with it' – it has never included other forms of sexual activity. The Tasmanian prosecutors urged judge Stephen Estcourt to use modern mores to interpret the word 'bestiality' more broadly, but he refused to do so, explaining, 'I am of the view that the word "bestiality" has a well understood legal meaning, that parliament must be taken to have used the word in that sense and that the [Tasmanian attorney-general's] speech cannot be substituted for the text of the law.'

What made Estcourt's ruling almost inevitable was that the Supreme Court of Canada had reached exactly the same conclusion in 2016, a year before Tasmania foolishly adopted the term 'bestiality' in its criminal code. In the Canadian case, a man was charged with inducing his stepdaughter into a non-penetrative act with a dog. The Canadian court observed that broadening the definition of bestiality 'could turn a person such as the victim in this case [that is, the stepdaughter] into a co-perpetrator'. 'That legal conclusion should give us pause,' said the court.

Unsurprisingly, the Tasmanian government has said that it will now consider replacing its bestiality offence with a modern definition. The Canadian parliament paused for two years before unanimously voting in 2019 to define 'bestiality' as 'any contact, for a sexual purpose, with an animal'. The nation's justice minister explained that this language, taken from other laws regulating sexual conduct between humans, applies to acts 'committed for the sexual gratification of the accused' and not the animal – a caveat to address the concerns of those who work in animal husbandry. The Australian Capital Territory and South Australia similarly criminalise any 'sexual activity' with an animal. And the same year the Supreme Court of Canada ruled, Victoria modernised its laws to strike a middle ground of sorts. However, the rest of Australia either continues to use the term 'bestiality' without definition or, like England, expressly limits the crime to penetrative acts.

In 2016, Victoria broadened its general definitions of 'sexual penetration' and 'taking part in a sexual act' – formerly terms used to define crimes against humans (such as rape and the sexual abuse of children) – to include equivalent acts with animals. The legislation specifies that 'in relation to sexual penetration of an animal, a reference to the vagina or anus includes a reference to any similar part' (such as a bird's cloaca). It also criminalises all sexual acts with animals that involve the presence of non-consenting humans, children or other vulnerable people, as does similar legislation in contemporary Canada, South Australia and the Australian Capital Territory. However, Victoria differs from those jurisdictions when it comes to contact between animals and consenting adults. In that context, it only bars adults from engaging in *penetrative* acts with animals, although not nec-essarily penile penetration – such acts can involve any body part or object (with exceptions made for procedures 'being carried out … in good faith for veterinary or agricultural purposes or scientific research purposes'). That leaves consenting adult Victorians, like most other Australians, free to engage in *non*-penetrative sexual acts with animals. There is one impor-tant caveat, however: the law on animal cruelty, which we will discuss later in this chapter.

In late-nineteenth-century England, the issue arose as to whether bes-tiality extended to sex with birds. The problem was not linguistic. While old church law was about 'beasts', which were perhaps distinct from 'fowls', England's 1861 statute referred to 'any animal'. Rather, the problem was that a senior court had, at some point, acquitted a man of attempting to have sex with a duck, without any written explanation for that acquittal. In an 1889 appeal, Lord Chief Justice John Coleridge, after tracking down some of the judges from the earlier case, revealed that their concern was not whether a duck was an animal, but whether it was physically possible to have sex with one. Alas, that concern was not present in the case before Coleridge, who commented, 'it is obvious that as a fact the offence could be commit-ted by the boy'. He had not only confessed to 'habitual' sex with 'domestic fowls' but had left birds 'torn and bleeding apparently from the effects of attempted penetration'.

As is clear from Coleridge's finding, it was a crime both to have sex with animals (bestiality) and to try to (attempted bestiality). The law on criminal attempts expands the law on sex with animals in three ways. First, it reduces (but does not remove) the difficulties of proving exactly what occurred physically. Second, it allows people to be punished even if something – a third party, the animal or their conscience – prevented the bestiality from taking place. Coleridge's ruling itself presaged English and Austral-ian courts' later willingness to extend the general criminal law of attempt to cover people whose crimes failed simply because they were physically impossible, so long as they nevertheless wanted to do them and wrongly believed that they could (which may or may not have covered the man with the duck). This hypothetically broadens the law on sex with animals in a third way: in theory, it covers people who merely imagine that they are having sex with animals, for example by fantasising about sex with animals while engaged in sexual acts without any animals present. However, actual prosecutions of such thought crimes are very unlikely, both because of the difficulty of establishing proof and because such proceedings would surely fail the 'public interest' test in modern prosecutors' charging guidelines.

None of these contemporary issues were a concern in 1641. The witnesses before New Haven's court pointed out that George Spencer, like the piglet, 'hath butt one eye for use' and 'his deformed eye being beheld and compard together w'h the eye of the monster, seemed to be as like as the eye in the glass to the eye in the face'. God's hint was clear: 'The monster shewed, upon wch God from heaven seamed both to stamp out the sin, and as w'h his finger to single out the actor.' When Spencer was 'examined concerning this abominatiō, att first he said he had nott done itt that he knew off, then denyed itt'. Nevertheless, the court committed him to prison to face a charge of bestiality 'partly on strong probabilities of this fact'.

Proving Bestiality

More than a century and a half after Spencer's trial and in a different English colony, a newly arrived convict wrote to Philip King, the third governor of New South Wales, 'imploring permission to state one of the most serious Grievances that an unfortunate female could possibly labour under', one that threatened 'utterly to blast her future prospect in life'. Mary Daniels explained that she had been sentenced to transportation to Australia after she was 'deluded at the early age of thirteen (an unhappy orphan) into the commission of error'. When she arrived on The Experiment in 1804, she found 'her self publickly charged with a crime, at which humanity shudders': Sydney was awash with reports that she had 'been detected by some person in the act of bestiality with a dog'. She faced a formidable evidentiary challenge: how do you prove or disprove an allegation of bestiality?

Disputes about sexual conduct are nearly always about what happened in private places, involving acts that many alleged participants would be reluctant to describe or, in the case of criminal acts, admit. When the sexual conduct involves an animal, one of the participants cannot speak at all. Daniels clearly could never prove that she had not had sex with a dog, but – fortunately for her – the man who was telling Sydneysiders that she had done so could not prove the opposite. When Judge Advocate Garnham Blaxcell questioned him, David Batty revealed that he was merely passing on claims from two of Daniels' fellow passengers on The Experiment. Labelled 'villainous' and 'unmanly', Batty was imprisoned for a month and ordered to make a 'public acknowledgement satisfactory to' Daniels.

Most importantly, Blaxcell found (without going into the details) that 'it appeared upon a very minute scrutiny, that the libel was as false as it was infamous'. Six years later, Governor Macquarie, citing her 'upright & honest character', granted the now twenty-four-year-old Daniels freedom to return to England.

A third-party witness – in the (surely) rare cases that there is one – can solve some, but not all, of the evidentiary problems surrounding bestiality. On 4 April 1796, a labourer returning with his goats from Cockle Bay, New South Wales, heard a noise, approached a shelter the labourers used and looked through an open door. Two days later, he told Sydney's criminal court that he saw George Hyson 'on his knees, with his trousers down; that his private parts were close to the bitch's, close to her backside'. When Hyson saw him, 'he appeared much flurried and immediately buttoned up his Trowsers'. After an exchange of words, a constable was summoned, who told the court that, although the prisoner and witness had known each other for years, he did 'not know of any slight subsisting between' them. But that was not enough to convince the court's officers, given Hyson's testimony that he had merely ducked into the house to 'ease himself' and that the dogs had followed him inside. They acquitted him of buggery, but convicted him of 'assault with intent to commit it'. Hyson was sentenced to three hours over three days on the pillory outside Sydney's Provision Store.

The kind of eyewitness account that constitutes sufficient evidence of bestiality was demonstrated three years later, when another man peered into a dwelling house on a farm and saw 'in the Swine Stye a sow lying therein and the prisoner also lying at her stern in the act'. The resulting trial of James Reece contrasted with Hyson's in several ways. First, the witness claimed that 'he saw the Prisoner withdraw his private parts from out of the Body of the said Sow', and provided other graphic details. Second, the witness immediately called out to his companion, 'Come, here, Dennis, here's a fellow by buggering a Sow', and the companion testified that he saw James Reece sitting beside the pig, 'besmeared'. Third, Reece's denial was a bare one, simply saying that he was employed to take care of the dwelling house. Even though the trial was a private prosecution brought by the sow's owner, the court convicted Reece and sentenced him to death.

In contemporary times, these evidentiary gaps are typically filled by the perpetrator's human victims. For example, in the case that reached the Supreme Court of Canada, the evidence of sexual contact with the dog was strongly supported by the testimony of the abused stepdaughter, her and her sister's horrific accounts of a decade of sexual abuse at the hands of the accused, and his own admission of what he claimed was consensual sex with the older sister as an adult. Most distressingly, evidence was taken from his computer in the form of photos and videos, including media that captured incidents involving the dog.

Of course, no such evidence was available to the New Haven court trying George Spencer in 1641, given that neither the alleged crime nor the accused would have been suspected if not for a supposed supernatural sign (the deformed piglet). Nevertheless, it was the accused himself who filled the evidentiary gap. A magistrate visited Spencer on his second day in prison and, after a conversation about the piglet and its mother, 'apprehending in the prisoner some relenting, as a preparatio to confession, remembered him of that place of scripture, he thatt hideth his sin shall not prosper, butt he y' confesseth and forsaketh his sins shall finde mercie'. Spencer promptly confessed.

Alas, in a pattern that recurred with each of his many confessions, no matter how detailed or to whom they were made, Spencer immediately told others – and later the court – that he had only confessed to gain official favour. Asked by the marshal 'how he durst mock God in putting up a bill desiring the congregation to pray for the pardon of that sinne wch now he denyeth', Spencer 'after some pause, confessed to him that the did comitt the fact, and desired him to looke upon him as one acted by the devil in denying itt'. Spencer later explained that a fellow prisoner, Will Harding, 'had given him councell to deny the fact, and had tolde him thatt the Court could nott proceed against him, butt by his owne confession'.

Harding's advice to Spencer was proved sound five years later. In 1646, a second deformed piglet was born in New Haven, resembling a second one-eyed labourer, Thomas Hogg. When shown the piglet, Hogg 'fetched a deepe sight, fell in his countenance, but denyed it'. However, the case against him was stronger than that against Spencer. Multiple witnesses testified about Hogg's 'filthy nakednesse' around women and girls (something he blamed on a 'trusse' he wore because 'his belly was broake') and even the sow betrayed him. The magistrates took him to her and made him 'scratt' her '& immedyatly there appeared a working of lust in the sow, in so much that she powred out seede before them'. As a control, they asked him to 'scratt' a different sow and it 'was not moved at all'. Nevertheless, the court only sentenced him (to whipping and prison) for his 'filthynesse' around women, 'leaveing that about beastyalytye to be further considred on'. There is no sign of any further consideration, most likely because Hogg never confessed.

Spencer, by contrast, hoped for the 'mercie' the scriptures supposedly offered. He sent for a friend he had known from England, initially to hear his denial. But the friend instead witnessed him asked three times 'whether he did comitt thatt sin of beastiality charged upon him' and answer 'yea ... I did doe itt'. Why say yes, his friend asked, when 'there were none thatt knew of it butt yor owne selfe, and that yor confessio might prove dangerous to you? ... He answered thatt he did doe itt'. Spencer later told a freeman, 'he wondred thatt the people of God did nott come to him, and thatt he feared there was no hope of him, because the people of God did not speake to him as formly they had done'. Alas, the scriptures rejected (secular) mercy when it came to bestiality. The court found 'the prisoner to be guilty of this unnatureall and abominable fact of beastiality, and thatt he was acted by a lying speritt in his denyalls'. His sentence, and the pig's, was fixed by the Bible: 'thatt the prisoner and the sow, according to Levit. 20 and 15, should be put to death'.

Punishing Bestiality

A nonlegal question loomed over the New Haven court's inquiry into Spencer's alleged bestiality: how could he? The colonists did not mean that literally (except for Harding, who asked Spencer 'how he could make the sow stand'). Rather, they wanted to know 'how his conscience wrought while he was acting itt, and whatt pleasure he founde, and how long he was acting itt'. He told them:

> about halfe an hower, and itt was the most terrible halfe hower that ever he had, they asked how he could doe itt if he had no pleasure in itt, he answered he was driven by the power of the devill and the strength of his corruption to doe the thing.

Spencer did not expect execution for his crime, and for good reason. As he explained to his fellow inmate Harding: 'Thomas Badgers sin was worse then his, for Badger lay w'h a Christian, butt himselfe the prisoner, lay butt w'h a rotten sow'. Badger's sin, adjudicated by the New Haven court a year earlier, was indeed far worse – he had confessed to 'defileing him-selfe by divers uncleane passages w'h one of his masters children not above 6 yeares of age' – and yet his sole sentence was to be 'whipped att a carts arce about the towne to make his punishment examplary'. Sadly for Spencer (and New Haven's children), Leviticus only mandates execution for men's sexual misdeeds with animals, men, their mothers (including their stepmothers and mothers-in-law), their daughters-in-law and their neighbours' wives.

Why do people commit bestiality, and how should they be punished for it? Three centuries after Spencer's sentence, these questions still trouble the courts. In 1983, Colin Higson's wife made an 'unexpected return' to their home and discovered her husband committing 'attempted buggery' with a 'Pyrenean-Mountain bitch'. 'Understandably disgusted', she initially took her husband to the Samaritans, but soon decided to leave him. The England and Wales Court of Appeal asked him for 'his account of events' and summarised his 'succinct' one-page statement as follows:

> It seems that the appellant had had an unsatisfactory marital relationship with his wife for some time following the birth some two years ago of their youngest child. Their sexual relationship has been described initially as adventurous, then more prosaic and finally, at the beginning of 1983, it terminated. This was a state of affairs which had caused the appellant considerable tension. He found that the more he made advances to his wife the more she repulsed him and so his frustration increased.

While Spencer blamed the devil for his (self-described) misdeeds, Higson blamed sexual frustration and, on one reading, his wife. Or maybe it was just the court that blamed her. The judges observed that 'she seemed at first to have responded with compassion', and that, but for her later decision to tell the police, his crime 'would never have come to public notice'.

Such explanations for bestiality are not new. In Sydney, thirteen years after James Reece was sentenced to death for having sex with a pig in 1799, a constable came across a convict 'holding a bitch with his two arms round her middle, the hind part of the bitch towards his belly'. After the man 'got off his knees & fell down on his backside', the constable asked him 'if there was no woman in the country'. He 'thruw up his hands & said "Worse, and Worse and bad enough"'.

A few decades later, Sir William Molesworth, the chair of a British parliamentary committee that was created to review the system of transporting convicts to Australia, questioned a Catholic prelate (William Ullathorne) about sexual offences in the penal colony:

[MOLESWORTH:] Do you think that those crimes will ever cease among the convicts not in confinement as long as the proportion of men and women is so great as it is at present in the whole colony; I believe in Sydney it is two and half to one, and in the country about four to one?

[ULLATHORNE:] Yes, I believe that is about the proportion; I think the temptation to crime will be very great as long as the disproportion is so considerable ...

[MOLESWORTH:] Are unnatural connexions with animals, do you suppose, common?

[ULLATHORNE:] I believe that they exist, particularly in the remote districts.

[MOLESWORTH:] To any considerable extent?

[ULLATHORNE:] I believe that the amount of that kind of crime is not inconsiderable.

[MOLESWORTH:] Are there any other species of bestiality common?

[ULLATHORNE:] I believe that when a bad man is under the dominion of a passion of that kind, he will gratify that passion in any manner that suggests itself to his imagination.

Molesworth's committee damned the penal system in multiple respects, and concluded that 'unnatural' crimes are far more common in the penal colonies than would be supposed from the number of convictions for those offences. Transportation of convicts to New South Wales ended three years later.

The criminal courts have always struggled with largely external explanations for individual misdeeds. Colin Higson's plea was that his crime was so out of character that he could supply the necessary condemnation himself:

I would like to say that this has never happened before, I can't explain why I did it. I was disgusted, particularly when my wife caught me.

I ask the court to help as I feel I do need help more than punishment. I've punished myself enough since it happened.

The panel of judges who initially sentenced him were unmoved:

In this country we now live in a society which is permissive and decadent, but that does not mean that the courts which act on behalf of the ordinary decent people in this area will countenance the maligned depravity which causes a man to attempt to satisfy his sexual lust by having intercourse with a dog.

They sentenced Higson to two years' imprisonment, a term that prompted his appeal judges to comment that 'one might have supposed that a woman or a young person, if not a child, was involved'.

Higson's case had a lasting legacy: a strongly and startlingly worded judicial call for a less punitive approach to bestiality. The appeal judges, including England and Wales' lord chief justice, wrote:

Bestiality is repugnant to right-thinking people. It cannot be condoned. But this kind of sentence leads a reasonable man to say with Mr Bumble, 'If the law supposes that, the law is an ass.' If this court were to uphold this sentence, it would be left without any sensible scale by reference to which a person could appropriately be punished for buggery with human beings (other than consenting males of full age in private). The object of sentence in these circumstances should be to avoid so far as possible any recurrence of the offence. When all is said and done, it is the appellant and indeed his wife, and not the dog, who need help.

The latter observation seemingly endorsed the assessment of a probation service doctor who 'stressed the need for helping both the appellant and his wife in their obvious marital and sexual problems' (she and Higson had reconciled). Noting that the thirty-one-year-old's past crimes were non-sexual and largely from his youth, and that he had lost a rare chance at permanent employment because of his prosecution, they resentenced Higson to non-prison supervision.

Legal responses to bestiality, like social ones, are always at the extremes – bemusement or disgust, curiosity or horror, mercy or stringency. Six years after *R v Higson*, the same appeals court decided that the lenient precedent set in *Higson* was limited to 'the case of a person who may be unhappy, distressed and not sexually orientated in the normal way'. They distinguished it from the case before them, *R v Tierney*, on three grounds: Tierney had involved his ex-wife in the crime (in what 'must have been a very unpleasant and degrading experience for her'), he had photographed it (showing that he was 'a person who would enjoy or obtain satisfaction from this form of unnatural sexual' act) and he asserted that he needed no counselling and was simply unaware that bestiality was a crime (corroborated by him giving the film to a camera store to develop). The judges deemed imprisonment necessary but held that a three-month term 'served to mark the disgust which any ordinary person would feel'.

More recently, the majority of Australia's High Court brushed aside a defendant's fears that his jury had been turned against him by the improper inclusion of charges for the possession of bestiality images. The majority of judges deemed this 'of little moment', given that he faced graver charges for child pornography. Justice Michael Kirby, however, was not convinced. 'The response of individual jurors to accusations of the possession of images of "bestiality" is particularly hard for appellate judges to assess and predict,' he said, noting how US justice Antonin Scalia had recently included bestiality in a 'catalogue of evils' alongside adult incest, prostitution, masturbation and same-sex marriage.

Equanimity was never an option in Spencer's New Haven. On 8 April 1641, a cart brought him to a seaside field, where 'upon sight of the gallowes he seemed to be much amazed and trembled'. He once again denied his crimes, but:

> The halter being fastened to the gallowes, and fitted to his neck, and being tolde it was an ill time now to pvoke God when he was falling into his hands, as a righteous and severe judge who had vengeance att hand for all his other sins, so for his impudency and atheisme, he justified the sentence as righteous, and fully confessed the beastiality in all the scircumstances.

Spencer nevertheless disappointed the crowd in his final moments:

> Being desired to express somthing what apprehensions he had of the haynousnes of his sin, as against God, and whatt impressions of

sorrow were wrought in him for itt, and whatt desires of pardon and mercie in Jesus Christ, he could not, though much pressed, be drawne to speake a word to any of those purposes, and in this frame for ought could be discerned, the sow being first slaine in his sight, he ended his course here.

Cruelty to Animals

To modern eyes, the most jarring feature of bestiality law is that it has never been enforced for the benefit of animals. 'The *sow being first slaine* in his sight,' recorded the New Haven court in 1641. 'It is the appellant and indeed his wife, *and not the dog*, who need help,' said England and Wales' appeals court in 1984. As in so much else, Leviticus led the way:

> If a man lies carnally with an animal, he must be put to death. And you are also to kill the animal. If a woman approaches any animal to mate with it, you must kill both the woman and the animal.

The Bible takes the same approach to what it considered to be other sexual crimes, condemning adulterers, homosexuals and fornicating in-laws by the pair, and a man who 'marries both a woman and her mother' by the trio: 'both he and they must be burned in the fire, so that there will be no depravity among you,' goes the relevant passage.

In 1565, in a similar vein, a man was burned at the stake with the mule he had committed bestiality with. The animal was inclined to kick and thus the executioner cut off the mule's feet before burning it. In 1662, Cotton Mather, the Puritan minister later notorious for his involvement with the Salem witch trials, recorded that a man named Potter was hanged along with a cow, two heifers, three sheep and two sows with which he had apparently committed bestiality. Other animals burned or executed with perpetrators of bestiality included mares and female dogs.

Killing an animal that has been subjected to bestiality could be variously explained as punishing the animal for its part in the act, punishing the human (this is seemingly why the animal was slayed in front of its supposed lover) or protecting the community from a supposedly tainted animal (and its offspring). The first rationale may explain what was apparently a historical exception to the custom of killing the animal.

This occurred in 1750, when a French she-ass was reportedly acquitted of bestiality 'on the ground that she was the victim of violence and had not participated in her master's crime of her own free will'. Local dignitaries signed a certificate declaring that they had known the she-ass for four years, 'and that she had always shown herself to be virtuous and well behaved, both at home and abroad, and had never given occasion of scandal to any one'.

The practice of executing the animal victims of bestiality persisted in some societies that were less religious, even ones that saw animals as mere property. Patrick Brannaghan, the farmer who owned the sow that James Reece was found to have assaulted in New South Wales in 1799, soon regretted prosecuting Reece, because the court not only ordered his execution but also the sow's. Brannaghan informed the judges that he was:

> unable to sustain a loss so material as the value of the said Sow, which he estimates at £15, and moreover as it appears that the said sow has ferried since the commitment of this unnatural felony and produced a litter of the 11 pigs, also which must be necessarily lost by condemnation of the said Sow.

Such executions seem not only unfair to animal and owner alike, but are also counterproductive to law enforcement. This was certainly the situation in 1823, when a bricklayer caught an employee having sex with his pig and watched as the employee defiantly continued for a further minute. The furious bricklayer told him that 'I was a poor man and could not afford to lose my Sow, or I would prosecute him to the utmost extend of the law'. In Brannaghan's case, the judges opted to 'submit this poor man's hard case to his Excellency's humane consideration', but the recommendation was only for 'remuneration'. The sow and her piglets, it seems, were beyond both judicial and executive mercy.

The second part of this chapter examines more recent criminal law, which instead of punishing animals, aims to give them 'humane consideration'. Modern law enables courts to punish humans who are cruel in various ways to certain animals, while at the same time permitting more acceptable or arguably unavoidable cruelties. This part looks, in turn, at how human cruelty to animals is defined, proved and punished.

Defining Cruelty

On 2 May 2019, Patrick McElligott asked a Gold Coast Bunnings employee whether there were any cameras in the store's car park. Apparently, there were not. The man turned to his German shepherd dog, Axel, and screamed: 'If you don't find my effing car I'm going to beat you.' Apparently, Axel could not. Another employee saw the dog trying to pull away from the man and later heard more yelling. He returned to the cark park to witness McElligott screaming 'Where's my effing car' and kicking Axel's head 'two or three times'. The German shepherd 'cowered [and] bowed his head', trying to get away. The employees called the cops.

Such random, violent acts seem the epitome of cruelty, but animals often meet much worse fates. Over a decade earlier, neighbours of a dairy farm near Repda in north-west Tasmania found a cow trapped in a tree, groaning. She was one of several Friesians that had been penned on steep, slippery ground that provided far less feed than the animals needed. Over the next few months, animal welfare officers repeatedly found 'downed' or dead cows on the farm, seemingly left unattended and unfed, including a cow with a half-born calf that had an eye and two teats removed by crows as she died. The farmer, Roderic Mitchell, ultimately faced over 150 charges of animal cruelty.

What is animal cruelty? The criminal offence that both McElligott and Mitchell were charged with is a successor to the world's first animal welfare statute, an 1822 UK law that made it a crime to 'wantonly and cruelly beat, abuse or ill-treat' cattle. Within decades, the word 'wantonly' was dropped, and the law was extended to 'any animal', including birds – as Sir William Wightman ruled in a 'cock-fighting' case – and thus the general offence of cruelty to animals was created. At the heart of the new offence was the adjective 'cruelly', which Lord Chief Justice John Coleridge's court authoritatively defined in 1889 – the same year he extended the older offence of bestiality to domestic fowls.

One mark of the laws' impact was Coleridge's decision to read out a detailed description of the abhorrent farming practice at issue in the case before him. He declared the report to be 'utterly disgusting' but conceded that 'in the interests of common humanity it must be read':

> These animals were dishorned on October 15. The animals had no horns on their heads and seemed to be in great pain. There was a discharge coming out of cavities on the top of the heads of two of these

cattle, which was flowing down their cheeks. This discharge was pus. The horn on one of these animals had not been sawn off. Some of the horns were more clumsily sawn off than others; all of the horns were sawn off as close to the head as a flat saw could be made to do it. There was an opening on the top of the heads of some of the cattle large enough for the admission of the thumb; on the heads of others there was a depression like what mechanics would call countersinking. The surrounding parts were very tender, and the animals flinched when they were touched even lightly. The respondent entered freely into conversation with him on the subject, and said the operation added to the value of the cattle when he sold them to the extent of about 30s. to 2l.

The judgment went on to graphically detail the dehorning of a particular animal and the stern condemnations of the practice by nearly a dozen 'eminent men, all of them disconnected with the case ... cattle doctors, not sentimentalists but men of the world, men of sense, men dealing with scientific matters in a scientific way'. Coleridge adopted Wightman's definition of cruelty to declare dehorning 'unnecessary abuse of the animal', and declared that 'we have neither the moral nor the legal right to inflict it, a conclusion not of sentimentalism but of good sense'.

The case's significance, beyond the impact it had on East Anglia's cattle, came from the separate judgment of Sir Henry Hawkins, who set out when it *is* lawful to harm animals. Hawkins listed three conditions for causing harm, none of which were satisfied by dehorning.

First, animal pain can only be inflicted for an acceptable reason. Hawkins ruled that those reasons could extend beyond ones that benefit the animal (such as surgery) to those that benefit humans. He gave breaking horses or castrating male animals as examples of what is acceptable, but drew the line at modifying animals due to 'fashion', 'the whim of the individual' or minor economic benefits, such as the avoidance of occasional stock loss, which was said to follow from dehorning.

Second, there must be no less painful ways to achieve the goal of which harm is the by-product – a test that dehorning failed, given that other approaches were viable, such as removing the tips of horns or breeding hornless cattle.

Finally, Hawkins said, 'Even where a desirable and legitimate object is sought to be attained, the magnitude of the operation and the pain caused thereby must not so far outbalance the importance of the end.' If it did, it should be 'clear to any reasonable person that it is preferable the object should be abandoned rather than that disproportionate suffering should be inflicted'. This last condition, which 'the revolting operation of dishorning' also failed, could potentially criminalise many more uses of animals that would otherwise be permitted, depending on what courts decide is 'clear to any reasonable person'.

Modern law on animal cruelty follows Hawkins' general approach, but also addresses many specifics. Unsurprisingly, contemporary legislatures have opted to define for themselves what is and is not cruel – or at least criminal – in a variety of contexts. Particular treatments of animals – such as causing animals to fight each other – are either specifically banned or deemed to be cruel. In Queensland, humans cannot do the following things to a non-human animal (note that the list starts with a codification of Hawkins' judgment):

(1) A person must not be cruel to an animal.

(2) Without limiting subsection (1), a person is taken to be cruel to an animal if the person does any of the following to the animal –

    (a) causes it pain that, in the circumstances, is unjustifiable, unnecessary or unreasonable;

    (b) beats it so as to cause the animal pain;

    (c) abuses, terrifies, torments or worries it;

    (d) overdrives, overrides or overworks it;

    (e) uses on the animal an electrical device prescribed under a regulation;

    (f) confines or transports it –

        (i)   without appropriate preparation, including, for example, appropriate food, rest, shelter or water; or

        (ii) when it is unfit for the confinement or transport; or

        (iii) in a way that is inappropriate for the animal's welfare; or

        (iv) in an unsuitable container or vehicle;

(g) kills it in a way that –

    (i)   is inhumane; or

    (ii) causes it not to die quickly; or

    (iii) causes it to die in unreasonable pain;

(h) unjustifiably, unnecessarily or unreasonably –

    (i)   injures or wounds it; or

    (ii) overcrowds or overloads it.

We might notice that McElligott's kicking of Axel engages the categories (2)(a)–(c), while Mitchell's treatment of his cattle arguably fits (2)(f)–(h). Mitchell was also charged with the overlapping offence of using 'a method of management of the animal or group which is reasonably likely to result in unreasonable and unjustifiable pain or suffering'. In many areas of animal management – such as farming, breeding, research, sport and entertainment – detailed codes of practice supplement or displace these general cruelty and management offences.

How does criminal law's protection of animals compare to its protection of humans? Queensland's definitions of cruel behaviour covers some acts that are not criminal when directed at humans, such as 'worrying' an animal, which would perhaps cover McElligott's screaming at Axel. But, in other respects, it falls short of the list of crimes against humans, who are protected from deliberate pain or injury in all but a very narrow range of scenarios, including self-defence and emergency, and when consent is granted. The most striking contrast is that the animal cruelty law does not generally prohibit killing animals, even without reason.

In 1978, Quebec's Court of Appeal found that 'the euthanasia of stray and unclaimed dogs, or of dogs at the request of their owner, is justified and that this activity cannot be condemned by reason of the illegality of its purpose'. Canada's future chief justice Antonio Lamer bluntly explained the finding:

> The animal is subordinate to nature and to man. It will often be in the interests of man to kill and mutilate wild or domestic animals, to subjugate them and, to this end, to tame them with all the painful consequences this may entail for them and, if they are too old, or too numerous, or abandoned, to kill them.

As a result, he concluded that 'the legislator did not intend, as in cases of assault among human beings, to forbid through criminalization the causing to an animal of the least physical discomfort'. Rather what is criminalised are *cruel* killings of animals – killings that, as Queensland's law specifies, are either inhumane, slow or unreasonably painful.

The issue before the Quebec court involved the legality of killing dogs by placing them in a small chamber connected to a car engine that forced them to breathe carbon dioxide. Because the heated gas 'would normally have caused pain, suffering or even burns' to the animals, this meant that there were 'at least 30 seconds [when] the animals … definitely suffered'. Lamer heard evidence that the only painless way to kill animals was by using anaesthetic, but he baulked at requiring that method in all cases:

> One does not kill a steer in the same way that one kills a pig. One cannot devote to the euthanasia of animals large sums of money without taking into account social priorities.

Nevertheless, he ruled that the method used by the Quebec euthanasia business was criminal because an alternative was available: a cooling system that 'is relatively simple to install' and the cost of which 'is not prohibitive'.

The criminal law's positive obligations to prevent unnecessary pain to animals that are under the care of humans may sometimes oblige owners to kill them or arrange their deaths. In Mitchell's case, the Tasmanian Supreme Court observed:

> There is no reason to think that [Mitchell] wanted any of his cows to suffer. However, this is an extremely serious case involving sustained and repeated neglect. A number of steps were available … For example, he could have reduced the size of his herd, sold the entire herd, and/or sold the farm.

It is likely that these steps would have led to some or all of the herd being slaughtered, illustrating how even the law on cruelty to animals can permit and even require the killing of those same animals, including by animal welfare officers tasked with protecting the animals and punishing others for their cruelty. The Tasmanian judgment added that many of Mitchell's charges 'related to cows that were neglected and not properly fed for a very long time, with the result that they went down, were unable to get up again, and either died *or had to be destroyed*. Even Axel, the Queensland dog that was kicked by his owner, was reportedly 'euthanised due to a genetic disorder which was causing him pain', presumably by an animal welfare agency that was responsible for providing the care his owner could not. The methods used to kill these victims of crime were not described.

Proving Cruelty

One difficulty with defining a crime in terms of animal suffering is that animals cannot explicitly communicate their feelings to a court. Of course, animals can still communicate through their behaviour, such as the cows' groaning and Axel's cowering, but the meaning of that behaviour is for courts to discern, possibly with the assistance of qualified experts. As Mitchell's barrister reportedly complained, there was 'no evidence from a vet to show that the groaning noises made by the cow wedged in the tree signalled that it was in pain'. McElligott's judge, on the other hand, relied on the testimony of the prosecution's veterinarian, who gave evidence that 'dogs are sentient beings and that they feel pain just like humans do' (the judgment does not set out how the vet knew either of those things).

A less tractable problem is that cruelty to animals, like bestiality, often happens in private. Axel's plight was only detected because McElligott bizarrely carried out his cruelty loudly and in public, which motivated a Bunnings employee to call the police. Concerns about Mitchell's cows were seemingly raised by his neighbours, but were ultimately pursued – to a fault, Mitchell's counsel later argued – by specialist officials who investigate animal cruelty. The RSPCA and other societies devoted to animals are often given a statutory function of investigating or prosecuting animal cruelty offences, and in some instances they are even given access to policing powers, in part because police and regulators such as local councils have other expertise and perhaps other priorities.

Some of the starkest instances of animal cruelty occur in commercial settings out of sight of neighbours, regulatory officials and the public. In early 2015, Australia's flagship public investigation program, *Four Corners*, broadcast an interview with a documentary filmmaker who described a conversation she had just had with Zeke Kadir, a greyhound trainer:

> He talked about how he got live rabbits from a person that he knows and he gets about 30 a week … and then he says he puts those rabbits

in the bull rings with the dogs when he's breaking them in … He said, 'I'll put the animal in there with the dog and get them to give them a bite.'

The filmmaker had told Kadir she was a greyhound owner, but in fact she was a contractor for Animals Australia, a charity devoted to stopping animal cruelty. Her ruse was legal, but New South Wales law barred her from secretly recording her conversation with the trainer. Nonetheless, events at Kadir's property ended up in Australia's High Court because the filmmaker had already broken the law by repeatedly entering Kadir's property late at night without permission and planting a hidden camera to record goings-on there. The resulting footage, broadcast on *Four Corners*, was horrifying:

> A native possum is strung to the lure upside down, terrified, struggling to escape. Two muzzled greyhounds attempt to bite, again and again. Four minutes later, the muzzles come off: the gruesome final moments unseen, but one last, unforgettable cry (sound of possum screaming).

Is it acceptable to commit a crime to expose such cruelty? New South Wales' prosecutors thought so, and granted the filmmaker an indemnity while prosecuting Kadir. So did the state's court of criminal appeal, which ruled that the first secret video could be used against Kadir because without it there was no way for anyone to prove his crimes and little chance of getting official investigators involved. Ultimately, Australia's top court unanimously disagreed with the state authorities, ruling that the lack of lawful ways to prove Kadir's guilt was exactly why evidence obtained through a crime could not be used against him.

The High Court justices did, however, rule that the RSPCA's subsequent investigation was a different matter. The court endorsed the RSPCA's use of Animals Australia's videos to obtain a warrant to lawfully search Kadir's property.

> The undesirability of admitting evidence obtained in consequence of the deliberate unlawful conduct of a private 'activist' entity is the effect of curial approval, or even encouragement, of vigilantism. The RSPCA had no advance knowledge of Animals Australia's plan to illegally record activities at the Londonderry property. There is nothing to suggest a pattern of conduct by which Animals Australia or other

activist groups illegally collect material upon which the RSPCA takes action. The desirability of admitting evidence that is important to the prosecution of these serious offences outweighs the undesirability of not admitting evidence obtained in the way the search warrant evidence was obtained.

The High Court's ruling meant that Kadir's prosecution could proceed, albeit based only on circumstantial evidence turned up by the search (which revealed dead and dying rabbits) and not the video footage that seemingly showed the cruelty itself. But the justices' caveat about there being no 'pattern of conduct' to 'illegally collect material upon which the RSPCA takes action' indicates that the courts will be less sanguine about repetitions of this chain of events in the future.

The best evidence of animal cruelty is often sourced from the alleged perpetrator. The High Court held that the fact Kadir was a victim of subterfuge was not a reason to exclude his apparent admissions of criminality, obtained legally by the filmmaker. Likewise, Mitchell's repeated rejections of instructions from the authorities was part of the case against him and prompted further convictions for obstruction. And as for McElligott, he was his own worst enemy, even re-enacting some of his treatment of Axel for the police, who duly recorded it.

Punishing Cruelty

McElligott and Mitchell each argued that his conduct was less awful than it appeared. McElligott sought to demonstrate to the police that he was simply showing his dog who was the 'alpha'. Mitchell relied on evidence of his repeated consultations with vets, conversations with animal welfare authorities and the possibility that a number of his cattle were supplied to him with a hidden illness. This meant, each argued, that even if their actions were cruel, they did not perceive it that way and accordingly they should not be punished for animal cruelty.

In nineteenth-century England, Hawkins was firm in rejecting such arguments in the dehorning case:

If the law were that any man or any body of men could in his or their own interests, or for his or their pecuniary benefit, cause torture and suffering to animals without legitimate reason, and could, when charged with cruelty, excuse himself or themselves upon the ground that he or they honestly believed the law justified them, though in fact it did not, it is difficult to see the limits to which such a principle might not be pushed, and the creatures it is man's duty to protect from abuse, would oftentimes be suffering victims of gross ignorance and cupidity.

In contemporary terms, the legal issue is whether animal cruelty, like homicide, requires a prosecutor to prove that the defendant had a criminal mind, either wanting to hurt an animal – something open to some question in McElligott's case because he was drunk when he kicked Axel – or grossly negligent – which is open to question in Mitchell's case because he received mixed advice from experts on what everyone agreed was a difficult task of running a dairy farm in a poor paddock.

But the pairs' judges, like nearly all courts, decided that these tests for criminal responsibility did not suit the crime of cruelty, with Tasmania's chief justice explaining:

> If such an interpretation were adopted, prosecutions for mismanagement and cruelty offences based on omissions could only be brought in the most horrendous cases.

The result is that the offence of animal cruelty bundles together two very different sorts of cruelty: McElligott's actions (where causing pain was the means to a particular end of showing he was the 'alpha') and Mitchell's (where causing pain – in vast amounts – was the end of a particular means of managing a dairy farm). Mitchell did escape liability for poor management in the case of two cows (including the one in the tree) who seemingly slipped away to a grim end without his knowledge. As for the rest, Chief Justice Alan Blow held that his excuses – 'that he was in a difficult situation, meant well, and did his very best to care for his animals' – were no defence to a charge of cruelty.

How should the courts punish people who are convicted of cruelty to non-human animals, especially in comparison to crimes against humans? The two crimes are not always distinct. Recent figures in Victoria show that half of the people sentenced (and most of those imprisoned) for animal cruelty were simultaneously sentenced for other offences. The most common non-animal offence for adult offenders, especially men, was injuring other humans, usually in the context of family violence. Indeed, most jurisdictions include threats or harm to animals, when it is 'directed' at a family member, as family violence. But Australia's top court has cautioned against relying on accounts of past cruelty to animals in order to determine whether an offender will be a danger to humans in future.

In 2006, the High Court ruled that Queensland's courts were wrong to order the 'Darling Downs rapist' into indefinite detention to protect the community. The offender had raped three women in the course of fifteen months, but his criminal record before that period was modest, and the courts relied on his admissions of past sex with and cruelty to animals when determining his sentence:

> The details of the sexual activities with animals were unproved. They had never been the subject of any criminal charge .... The appellant was not to be punished additionally in respect of those events. Any feelings of distaste or revulsion concerning such activities should not enter into the sentencing process.

The High Court was undoubtedly influenced by the sentencing judge's misplaced concern that 'on occasions after the act of sexual perversion ... the accused would kill animals', and that this signalled a danger that he might also kill women in future. In fact, the offender had told his psychiatrist that he sometimes shot wild horses in order to have sex with their carcasses, neither of which are necessarily criminal acts.

The difficulty in such cases was underlined a decade later when the offender, seeking parole part way through his twenty-two-year sentence for rape, asserted that he had fabricated the accounts of bestiality on the advice of fellow prisoners who said it would help establish a psychiatric defence. The parole board refused his application, in part because of his evident willingness to lie (one way or the other) to improve his prospects of release from prison.

Should people who are cruel only to animals – such as McElligott and Mitchell – go to jail? In the case of McElligott, who inflicted no visible physical injuries on Axel, he was not jailed but instead ordered to take anger management classes and undergo regular drug and alcohol testing. But Mitchell, whose inadequate farming practices caused numerous cows to suffer, received a harsher sentence. While his cruelty was unintentional, it occurred over a longer period of time, involved more animals and resulted in serious injuries and deaths. Tasmania, like other jurisdictions, treats such outcomes as 'aggravated' cruelty, whether or not the injuries or deaths were deliberate (and, indeed, even if some of the deaths were the result of euthanasia).

The ex-farmer was initially sentenced to fifteen months' imprisonment – a term that other jurisdictions had only ever given to people who had also injured other humans. Mitchell's sentencing judge explained his was a case

> where general deterrence must be the predominant sentencing consideration. It must be made clear to the community and to all those involved in commercial farming that a lack of means or ability or both can in no way abrogate the responsibility to provide appropriate care to the animals in their care.

Tasmania's chief justice agreed that 'the only appropriate sentencing option was imprisonment'. While he reduced Mitchell's sentence to twelve months, he did so only because he thought the magistrate had made too much of the farmer's more minor offences, such as not burying dead cows and obstructing officials. Effectively, he endorsed the most significant part of that one-year sentence, the nine-month term Mitchell was given because of the seventeen cows that died and a further three that were seriously injured as a result of his poor farming.

Deterrence and denunciation of criminal behaviour and the prevention of danger to people are all (heavily contested) goals of the legal system that are meant to directly affect people and that only indirectly protect animals. If the court's goal is to directly protect animals, then there are other sentencing options.

Most jurisdictions permit a sentencing judge to ban an offender from owning animals of a particular kind for many years. The RSPCA recently stated that such 'control orders are a vital component of sentencing for animal cruelty offences and in many instances represent ... the best outcome to ensure animal welfare after the case has concluded'. Such sentences have the (intended) side effect of barring offenders from the future companionship of animals or even their chosen livelihood. These were the unsurprising fates of McElligott, who was barred from owning a companion animal for three years, and Mitchell, who was barred from having the custody of any livestock for ten years.

Recently, the New South Wales parliament enacted a mandatory and permanent ban on anyone who has been convicted of extreme animal cruelty offences owning an animal or having direct contact with animals in their work. The offences covered are killing or seriously injuring an animal while it is engaged in law enforcement (such as the police dogs we discussed in Chapter 5), bestiality (discussed earlier in this chapter), and the unique offence of serious animal cruelty, which we will discuss in Chapter 6. An offender who breaches the ban faces up to a year in prison.

Criminal law is not, however, the sole way of protecting animals, human or non-human. In the next chapter, we will explain a variety of laws that protect – or could protect – non-human animals in myriad ways.

6.

PROTECTING ANIMALS

IN MID-2015, DANIEL BRIGHTON, THE OWNER OF GET WILD Animal Experiences, adopted and trained an 'orphaned wild camel' from South Australia's Flinders Ranges, naming her Alice. 'She was very scared and nervous,' he later told the media. 'Eventually, we were able to gain her trust and train her to try new food, walk on a lead, travel in a horse float, sit down, and attend public events to meet kids.' Brighton later bought two more camels, Ebony and April, to keep Alice company.

Get Wild Animal Experiences provided a mobile zoo catering to schools, shopping centres and parties, but Brighton hoped to create a permanent facility at the premises where he kept his three camels. In April 2016, he applied with his local council to establish the Macarthur Wildlife Park and Zoo in south-western Sydney's Minto Heights. He intended for the zoo to include a camel enclosure, an ostrich enclosure, a dingo yard, a wallaby and emu yard and eight aviaries. 'We aim to house a small collection of native and exotic animals to assist in educating people in the local area about wildlife conservation, environmental protection, Indigenous culture and ecological integrated sustainable living practices,' he told the press, promising locals experiences with crocodiles, lace monitors, snakes, owls, dingoes, monkeys, meerkats and camels, all without needing to travel an hour or more to Sydney's Taronga Zoo.

However, the wildlife park never eventuated, and Brighton faced several setbacks in the years to come. In 2017, two of his crocodiles disappeared from their enclosure, prompting him to plead for their return. Although Brighton suspected theft, the police said there was no sign of forced entry. Soon, one of the crocodiles, Crackle, was spotted in a 'thin and lethargic state' in Sydney's Georges River by a local family, who placed it in their bathtub. Crackle died shortly after returning to Get Wild Animal Experiences; Snap was seemingly never found. Later that year, officers and a veterinarian from the RSPCA seized an alpaca, two chickens and a kookaburra from Brighton's Minto Heights property and laid charges against

Brighton for failing to provide his animals with veterinary treatment and sufficient food. At Brighton's committal hearing in 2018, RSPCA inspector Natalie Will outlined the animals' allegedly 'poor body condition' and expressed concern about their living conditions. However, all charges were dropped on the eve of the two-day trial.

The eventual nadir of Brighton's career had its origin in an earlier event in mid-January 2016. In the middle of the night on a Friday, he was woken by the sound of barking and saw two dogs racing out of his Minto Heights property. A short while later, he was woken again, this time by a 'bizarre screaming noise'. It was Alice the camel, and she was being attacked by the dogs. Brighton managed to scare one dog away, but the other was clinging to the camel's mouth and neck. It refused to let go, even as he beat it with a PVC pipe. He later explained that he had to switch to a shovel, which he used on the dog's head several times, once to dislodge it from Alice and then several more times to stop it growling and snapping at the camel, Brighton and a fellow employee. The two dogs' owners were never located. That meant Brighton had no-one to sue for what happened to Alice, and no-one could sue him for what he did to the dog.

In this final chapter, we will consider how the law protects animals directly, rather than via the humans who own them. As in the introduction, we will discuss many different sorts of laws that could protect animals, albeit often in only narrow ways. First, we detail how private law allows animals to be provided for financially. Second, we consider how public law determines if and when others can speak for animals in court. Finally, we look at how criminal law, in medieval times and today, manages allegations for and against ownerless animals.

Private Law: Providing for Animals

A few months after Alice was attacked, some Sydneysiders found another ownerless animal – a peacock was wandering near an apartment in the city's northern suburbs. A twenty-minute chase ensued, before the residents of the apartment caught the bird with a bedsheet. They temporarily housed him in their bathroom, but they could not care for him long-term, nor could they release the non-native animal into the wild. After contacting several wildlife parks that were unwilling to take a peacock, they appealed for help on a Facebook page for lost companion animals. A respondent eventually pointed them to Daniel Brighton, who took on the bird, named him Peter, and placed him in a 'free-range enclosure' with others of his species.

Brighton was clearly no ordinary zoo owner. In addition to running the mobile petting zoo, he taught vet nursing, zoo keeping and animal care to tertiary students, and – at age twenty-one – he had become a foster carer to a seven-year-old child. His mother described him as having 'a passion for animals and education since he was about ten years old', and described his plans to open a wildlife park as a 'dream ... coming true'. In promoting his proposed permanent zoo, he told the press:

> Having a connection with an animal on a personal encounter can inspire people to really want to make a positive difference in their everyday lives to the environment around them.

His passion for animals and his career also obliged him to make a positive difference to the animals in his zoo, which included campaigning for others to take responsibility for their animals in order to prevent attacks such as the one that Alice suffered:

> We need to change her living arrangements due to this freak incident. She received several deep lacerations to all four legs, lips, neck and her face. It was a bloodbath. We have never had any issues like this and we have smaller animals. People need to be responsible for their own dogs and lock them up so they don't cause havoc.

As we saw in the first half of this book, dog owners have responsibilities to others, including an obligation to compensate people for some or all of the damage their dogs do if they are negligent as owners or if their dog is dangerous. Owners of dogs that attack others can also be prosecuted and punished for criminal offences. And, of course, owners are responsible for the care of their own companion animals as well. Maybe that is why no-one came forward to take responsibility for either of the dogs that attacked Alice (or Peter the peacock for that matter). That left Brighton with the sole responsibility for treating Alice's many injuries and protecting her against future attacks.

His solution was to ask for help via a post on the crowdfunding website, GoFundMe. Brighton might have made this request because he could not afford to properly protect Alice himself, or because he thought that protecting the camels from rogue dogs ought to be a public responsibility. Equally, he could have done it because he wanted to publicise the need for dog owners to be more responsible, or even because he wanted to promote his own business. As we will see later in this chapter, however, he may have had more complex motives.

Just as the law has a lot to say about people who try to hurt animals (as we saw in the last chapter), it also has much to say about people who aim to help them. Brighton would have faced various legal restrictions as to how he used the money raised by his GoFundMe campaign, as others who have used crowdfunding to support various causes have found. What rights did the donors have? What rights and responsibilities did Brighton have to those donors and to Alice? What rights did Alice have?

Many Australians learned about issues of this sort early in 2020, when some of the largest bushfires in the country's history caused widespread property, environmental and economic damage, as well as the deaths of dozens of humans and countless other animals. Donations to those affected poured in, especially via a PayPal account created by comedian Celeste Barber, which received $51 million in donations, exceeding her initial target thousands of times over. The legal problem was that Barber had specified that the money would go to a particular New South Wales rural fire service fund, which was set up to resource firefighting and firefighters. Barber said that she would seek to use the money for other purposes, but in May 2020, the New South Wales Supreme Court ruled that the money could only be used to provide training and counselling for firefighters, and support for injured firefighters and the families of firefighters who had died – it could not be used to support other victims of the fires, including regular civilians and animals.

Brighton's GoFundMe pitch likely bound him to spend what he raised exclusively on his three camels, Alice, April and Ebony (depending on the exact terms of his GoFundMe page). A runaway success similar to Barber's could have meant that he was faced with the task of spending $10 million on each animal. Alas, we do not know the outcome of the campaign, or indeed what eventually happened to Alice the camel.

Providing for a Particular Animal

It is well known that some animals show an amazing degree of devotion to their owners, even after their owners' deaths. The story of 'Greyfriars Bobby', the Skye Terrier who purportedly visited his master's grave for fourteen years until Bobby himself died, is so popular that a statue of the terrier was erected near the entrance to the Greyfriars Kirk graveyard in Edinburgh, Scotland. Similarly, a Japanese dog called Hachikō was said to have waited for his late master at Shibuya Station in Tokyo for over nine years. At first, the station staff tried to shoo Hachikō away from the station, but they let him be when they realised he was waiting for his dead owner, allowed people to bring him food and attended his funeral when he eventually died. Hachikō is remembered by three statutes of his likeness in Japan.

Dogs are not the only animals to show such devotion. In 2020, a cat reportedly went missing after the death of its owners, only to be discovered at their graveyard in Astros, Greece:

> The kitten had lived with [its owners] for a few months before their passing. Following their deaths ... it was nowhere to be seen, until Father Stavros Delimanolis said that the cat appeared out of the blue at the cemetery where his former owners were buried. Cemetery workers immediately recognised the cat, and it now lives permanently at the cemetery. Staff members feed it daily and have created special shelter to ensure that it is safe.

Unsurprisingly, there are no records of animals making wills. However, the Latin priest and historian Saint Jerome (c. 347–420) is reputed to have written a tongue-in-cheek will for a pig after it was sentenced to death by the cook for having smashed some kitchen pots. The 'will' reads as follows:

> I, M. Grunnius Corcotta Porcellus, have made my testament, which, as I can't write myself, I have dictated. I will and bequeath to my Papa, Verrinus Lardinus, thirty bushels of acorns. I will and bequeath to my Mamma, Veturina Scrofa, forty bushes of Laconian corn. I will and bequeath to my sister, Quirona, at whose nuptials I may not be present, thirty bushels of barley.
>
> Of my mortal remains, I will and bequeath my bristles to the cobblers, my teeth to the squabblers, my ears to the deaf, my tongue to the lawyers and chatterboxes, my entrains to tripemen, my hams to gluttons, my stomach to little boys, my tail to little girls, my muscles to effeminate parties, my heels to runners and hunters, my claws to thieves, and to a certain cook, whom I won't mention by name, I bequeath my cord and stick which I brought with me from my oak

grove in the sty, in hopes that he may take the cord and hang himself with it ...

Friends dear to me whilst I lived, I pray you to have a kindness towards my body, and embalm it well with good condiments, such as almonds, pepper and honey, that my name may be named through ages to come.

The German author Johann Alexander Brassicanus purportedly found the 'will' in a manuscript in the sixteenth century.

The oldest written will dates back to 2550 BCE in ancient Egypt; wills have a long history. The desire to take animals with us when we die dates back to a still earlier time. A 12,000-year-old burial discovered in Israel provides early evidence of the domestication of dogs. The burial contained the remains of a human, who was comparatively elderly, with their left wrist under their forehead and their left hand placed on the thorax of a puppy that had been buried with them, indicating a close and affectionate relationship between the dog and the human.

Given that at least some animals appear to remember us after we die, it is natural that we should want our animals to be remembered in our wills if we die before them, in order to provide for their ongoing comfort. However, this is difficult to do because the law does not recognise animals as legal persons but as chattels. Consequently, there are only a few ways to effectively give a bequest to an animal. The first is to leave a friend or family member with money to look after the animal. The animal could also be given to a friend as a gift. However, the friend must be very trustworthy, as such arrangements are not enforceable, and the friend would be under no legal obligation to fulfil the deceased's wishes. The second option is to create a trust to provide for the maintenance of the animal. There is a long history of people doing this, and it has been recognised since the mid-nineteenth century as a valid practice, despite the fact that it is an exception to the general rule that the law does not recognise trusts for non-charitable purposes. The third option is to request that the animals be put down.

This discussion raises the issue of a kind of judge-made law that we have not yet discussed. It developed in medieval England as a response to the rigidity of the common law, which people complained of to the king. At that time, of course, the king had the absolute power to overrule any legal decision, but he did not have the time or inclination to deal with his subjects' complaints and would pass them on to his lord chancellor, typically a churchman trained in canon law (the law of the church). Over time, a new parallel court system grew up, the Court of Chancery, headed by the lord chancellor, who tended to decide matters on the basis of fairness and ethics. This body of law was called 'equity'. Often the Court of Chancery stepped in to ameliorate the common law when it was too harsh or rigid, but it also developed its own institutions, such as the trust, which involved holding property for another. Alongside the common law, Australia inherited this second body of law from the United Kingdom, as did other English colonies.

Eventually, the system of having two different courts became unwieldy, and statutes passed in England and most Australian states provided that one judge could apply both the common law and equity. Despite this, our property law system (and in particular, the law of trusts) still reflects the fact that two parallel systems of law ran alongside each other for hundreds of years. The Court of Chancery developed trusts allowing one person (the trustee) to legally own a thing, but to hold it for the benefit of another (the beneficiary) and use the money derived from it for the beneficiary's benefit. Over time the concept of the trust expanded so that property could be held for a charitable purpose or, exceptionally, for the benefit of an animal.

Leaving Money to a Trusted Person

The most legally straightforward option for providing for an animal after one's own death is to leave money for the purpose to a trusted friend. However, this approach can sometimes backfire. While it is in the interests of the people entitled to the residue of the bequest for the animal to die as soon as possible, the opposite is true for the carer.

In 2014, *The Daily Telegraph* reported that a trustee and guardian became suspicious when a cat called Missy purportedly reached the age of thirty years. Missy's original owner had left a generous payment in her will for a friend to look after Missy for the rest of the cat's lifetime. Upon investigation, it became clear that 'Missy' was much younger than thirty; the friend appeared to have replaced the original Missy with lookalikes in order to keep receiving payments for the cat's maintenance.

Other issues also arise. In 2016, a spat broke out between the executor and the woman appointed to care for a dachshund called Winnie Pooh, after the carer alleged that the executor had not been releasing money for Winnie Pooh's care, and that she had been forced to pay for the dog's orthopaedic surgery out of her own pocket.

Miami Beach socialite Gail Posner left an aide her US$8.3 million mansion and US$3 million to look after her three chihuahuas when she died in 2010. Her only son, Brett Carr, was bequeathed $US1 million. Carr sued his late mother's aides, alleging they had drugged his mother and encouraged her to change her will while she was under the influence. Before her death, Posner apparently told the media that her dog Conchita, the recipient of a Cadillac Escalade, was the world's most spoiled dog. Carr alleged that Posner's aides had encouraged her to make the statement to provide a public pretext for the bequest.

To avoid some of these difficulties, pet owners might look into the possibility of leaving a bequest to a recognised charitable organisation that provides a 'pet bequest' program. Such organisations will look after a companion animal after its owner's death.

Leaving Money to the Animal

The second option for providing for an animal is to leave money to the animal itself. This practice has a long and strange history. Generally speaking, animals have no capacity to own property or to sue or be sued (pigs in medieval France being an exception). Moreover, there is a rule – the 'beneficiary principle' – that a specific person must be the beneficiary of any express trust, and an animal is generally not a 'legal person' in the eyes of the law. However, trusts for animals are an exception to the beneficiary principle.

The first recorded instance of a trust being created for an animal is an English case from 1842. The details are frustratingly brief. The testator provided in his will:

> Having a favourite black mare, I hereby bequeath that at my death, 50l. per annum be paid for her keep in some park in England or Wales; her shoes to be taken off, and she never to be ridden or put in harness; and that my executor consider himself in honour bound to fulfil my wish, and see that she be well provided for, and removeable at his will. At her death, all payment to cease.

The judge, Vice-Chancellor James Knight-Bruce, simply held that a bequest for the upkeep of an animal was valid, that the executor had to report on the state of the mare if requested and that if he failed to care for it, anyone entitled to the money left over after the horse's death should apply to the court to ensure it was cared for going forwards.

Trusts for dogs, horses, a parrot and cats have all been upheld. A man in India, Akhtar Imam, recently upset his wife and children by bequeathing most of his land to two elephants, Moti (Pearl) and Rani (Queen), after they saved his life when armed robbers invaded his property. One must wonder if this will be challenged after the testator dies. In the early 1900s it was even reported that a testatrix (a female testator) provided £70 for the maintenance of three goldfish:

> One is bigger than the other two, and these latter are easily recognised as one is fat and the other lean. If the fish, on quarter-day, are found to be of this description, the money is to be paid; if not it is to be expended on flowers, which are to be placed on the graves of the goldfish after death.

However, it is unclear whether the report was apocryphal: the article in which this story was first reported gives no references, and the testatrix is not named.

While it is understandable that owners want to ensure their beloved companions animals are looked after for the rest of their lives, some bequests to individual animals have been immense.

Leona Helmsley, a real-estate heiress, was notorious for bequeathing US$12 million to her dog, Trouble. The bequest caused a scandal, in part because Helmsley and her late husband had been prosecuted for failing to pay income tax. Helmsley had been jailed for eighteen months for tax evasion, and during her trial, she had become known as 'The Queen of Mean' after her housekeeper reported her saying, 'We don't pay taxes. Only the little people pay taxes.' Helmsley made only a few individual bequests in her will, with most of her remaining estate to go to the Leona M. and Harry B. Helmsley Charitable Trust. However, as *The New Yorker* reported, complications arose when it came Helmsley's bequest to Trouble:

> The will stated that custody of Trouble should go to Rosenthal, Leona's brother, or to her grandson David, and the trust agreement directed them to 'provide for the care, welfare and comfort of Trouble at the highest standard'. But neither man wanted the dog. After the will was made public, Trouble received death threats, which may have had

something to do with their refusal. (Both men declined to comment.) So the trustees had to find the dog a home. Moreover, the bequest to Trouble was so self-evidently excessive for a single, aging dog that the trustees decided to take steps to reduce it.

A judge reduced Trouble's bequest to US$2 million upon application of the trustees, with the residual money left over after Trouble's death to go to the charitable trust. A trusted guardian was also appointed (an employee of Helmsley who had known the dog well). Eventually, in June 2011, Trouble died at the age of twelve, five years after her mistress.

The designer Karl Lagerfeld is also rumoured to have left his substantial fortune to his beloved Birman cat, Choupette. Before Largerfeld's death, he said in an interview that he wanted to marry Choupette, but 'there is no marriage, yet, for human beings and animals ... I never thought that I would fall in love like this with a cat.' As of January 2020, Lagerfeld's estate had not been settled, and Lagerfeld's staff would not disclose how much money Choupette received, although she is apparently living well in Paris and has her own Instagram account.

One of the difficulties with bequests to animals is that it is hard to verify that the executor of the will is actually looking after the animal. Although Knight-Bruce seemed to envisage that the people with an interest in the money left over from a bequest would ensure the animal is being looked after, if their main concern is to maximise the money they receive under the will, it is surely in their interests to keep quiet if the executor is not caring for the animal as required.

Another difficulty is the potential for people to misuse the lifespan of an animal to tie up property. Courts do not want property tied up for generations as it prevents others from using or accessing it. Courts have sometimes tried to deal with this by considering whether the trust would offend 'the rule against perpetuities'. At common law, this rule means that the trust must not extend more than twenty-one years beyond a 'life in being' at the time the trust was created. For instance, if a young mother were to give money on trust for her children, and the residue to her grandchildren, this would likely breach the rule against perpetuities, as she could have another child after she created the trust, and that child could produce her grandchild more than twenty-one years after the trust was created. This would tie up the property for too long and thus it would be invalid.

In an Irish case in 1932, it was said that the 'life in being' had to be a human life, not an animal life. But in an English case two decades later, Justice Danckwerts purportedly took judicial notice of the fact that sixteen years was a long life for a cat and upheld a trust for two cats as a result. In Australia, all states have either extended the perpetuities period to eighty years or abolished it altogether.

The success of a bequest for a parrot in *Re Howard*, a 1903 case, leaves questions of perpetuities unanswered. Some parrots live for a long time – the famous Sydney parrot Cocky Bennett, a sulphur-crested cockatoo, purportedly living to 120 years of age. This has led an American law professor to suggest that parrot owners in particular need to engage in estate planning if they want their parrot to be cared for.

Another strange exception to the rule that trusts must be charitable also concerns animals, but in a less beneficent manner. In *Re Thompson*, a Cambridge don made a bequest to his friend George William Lloyd to promote fox-hunting, which was upheld. It is doubtful that this case from 1934 would be decided in the same way today.

Requiring the Animal To Be Put Down

The ancient burial unearthed in Israel presents a seemingly touching scene of a human and their companion animal united after death, but it has been suggested that the puppy may have been killed for the purpose. Even today, owners sometimes put a clause in their will requiring their pet to be put down. This is obviously problematic when an animal is otherwise perfectly healthy and happy.

Alex Bruce, an Australian animal law scholar, has suggested that it might be possible to argue that such a clause goes against public policy or contravenes a principle of common law or statute – particularly given the existence of animal welfare statutes providing that animals should not be treated cruelly. However, no Australian cases on the issue have occurred yet.

In America, a woman's Shih tzu was recently put down in accordance with the terms of her will, despite the efforts of an animal shelter to save the otherwise healthy dog. After the dog was put down, it was buried with the woman as per her request. In several other cases, American courts have refused to enforce such clauses on the basis that they are against public policy.

Providing for Animals Generally

Another way in which people have attempted to benefit animals is through the creation of charitable trusts or bequests. Australian trusts law recognises four valid charitable purposes, based on the preamble to the 1601 *Statute of Charitable Uses*, which lays out a number of endeavours that were thought to be charitable:

> Releife of aged impotent and poore people, some for Maintenance of sicke and maymed Souldiers and Marriners, Schooles of Learninge, Free Schooles and Schollers in Universities, some for Repaire of Bridges Portes Havens Causwaies Churches Seabankes and Highwaies, some for Educacion and prefermente of Orphans, some for or towardes Reliefe Stocke or Maintenance of Howses of Correccion, some for Mariages of poore Maides, some for Supportacion Ayde and Helpe of younge tradesmen Handicraftesmen and persons decayed, and others for reliefe or redemption of Prisoners or Captives, and for aide or ease of any poore Inhabitantes concerninge paymente of Fifteenes, setting out of Souldiers and other Taxes.

Courts have interpreted the law governing charities by analogising charitable purposes with a named category in the statute. In *Pemsel's Case* in 1891, Lord Macnaughten held that there were four valid categories of charity that could be drawn from that jumble, namely:

- relief of poverty;

- advancement of education;

- advancement of religion; and

- other purposes beneficial to the community.

Note that animals do not explicitly feature in this list. This is because care of animals and the environment was not a central concern in Elizabethan England. As a result, attempts to create trusts for animals (or the environment) have generally had to be shoehorned into 'other purposes beneficial to the community'. While Australian legislation specifies that 'preventing or relieving the suffering of animals' is a charitable purpose, it does not presently cover charitable trusts, only the federal taxation of charities.

The movement to create trusts for the protection of animals occurred in the mid-nineteenth century in England, when judges began to hold that trusts for the good of animals that are useful to humans were charitable. At the same time, concern regarding unnecessary cruelty to animals was on the rise: the Royal Society for the Protection of Animals was founded in Britain in 1824, just after the first legislation preventing cruelty to animals was enacted. Even at the end of the nineteenth century, however, trusts for the prevention of cruelty to animals were not considered charitable. This changed with the English decision of *Re Wedgwood* in 1915. Famously, Lord Justice Swindon Eady said:

> A gift for the benefit and protection of animals tends to promote and encourage kindness towards them, to discourage cruelty, and to ameliorate the condition of the brute creation, and thus to stimulate humane and generous sentiments in man towards the lower animals, and by these means promote feelings of humanity and morality generally, repress brutality and thus elevate the human race.

In other words, the court found that promoting kindness to animals assisted in the moral improvement of humanity, and thus a requisite level of public benefit was met. In *Re Grove-Grady* in 1929, the court found that there were limits to this principle after the testatrix sought a trust to create a refuge for all animals free from human interference. A majority of the court found that the gift was not charitable because without human management, the predatory animals would eat the timid and prey animals, and the sanctuary would not 'denote any elevating lesson to mankind'.

The law has wavered on whether the prevention of vivisection (for the purpose of animal testing) is for the public benefit. Although initially there was some indication that this would be considered charitable, in 1947 the UK House of Lords held it was not, because there was evidence that animal testing was, in fact, beneficial to humanity, particularly in the testing of medication.

Trusts for the general benefit of animals – as opposed to trusts to prevent cruelty to animals – will not be valid. Thus, when a Tasmanian testator left a fund on trust for a veterinary surgeon to use 'for the benefit of animals generally', Justice Zeeman found the trust to be invalid. While gifts to prevent cruelty to animals provide a general benefit to society that is readily understood, this testator's gift was not tied to particular animals or a particular location, and there was no community benefit.

Sometimes the arguable community benefit of a trust for animals is judged insufficient. In *Royal National Agricultural and Industrial Association v Chester* (1974), Edward Chester, a retired poultry farmer and 'pigeon fancier' left the residue of his estate to the Royal National and Industrial Association for the purpose of 'improving the breeding and racing of Homer Pigeons'. To a point, the court accepted the association's argument that there was some evidence that 'homing pigeons have been and can be used in war and peace to carry messages and that their instinctive capacity to return from any point of release to their home lofts is an unsolved problem of scientific interest'. Three judges of the High Court of Australia said:

> It may be that in a general way the breeding of pigeons for racing is a purpose beneficial to the community. It provides recreation for quite a number of pigeon fanciers; it produces birds which are interesting, beautiful, and may at times be useful as a means of communication; it affords opportunity for the scientific study of the birds' remarkable homing instinct.

However, the court ultimately found that the breeding of racing pigeons was *not* within any of the four categories of the *Statute of Charitable Uses*, and did not have sufficient public utility to be charitable.

What happens if someone wants to benefit wild animals, not domesticated animals? The issue of wildlife sanctuaries has provided difficulties for courts. In *Royal Society for the Prevention of Cruelty to Animals (NSW) v Benevolent Society of New South Wales* (1960), Robert Sellar attempted to create a trust over two pieces of land for the benefit of the RSPCA, with the land to be known as the 'The Sellar Sanctuary for Birds' and provision for a manager (initially Sellar himself) to maintain the sanctuary. The residuary property was to go to the Benevolent Society.

Prior to this, Sellar had kept a bird bath at the rear of his house and fed grain to any birds that came to the property (primarily spotted doves, which are not native to Australia). After the 'sanctuary' was established, the manager was to feed the birds three times a day and encourage all native birds (including the 'native' spotted doves) to drink from the fountain at any time. The High Court of Australia held that his was not a charitable purpose, and the trust failed. As a result, that the money went to the Benevolent Society instead:

Many people feed birds. This gives them pleasure and gives the birds satisfaction. But a suburban householder cannot by assuming an obligation to keep a basin filled with water and to put out food for birds convert his home into a public charity of which he can make himself or his nominee the manager.

On the other hand, in *Re Ingram* (1951), a trust to preserve the indigenous animals and birds of Australia was upheld, although it was important to the judge that the trust specified that this was to be for the benefit of the public. Similarly, in *A-G (NSW) v Sawtell* (1978), a judge upheld a trust to preserve native wildlife on the basis that it was in the interests of the public for native flora and fauna to be preserved from extinction.

Public Law: Speaking for Animals

In late 2018, Daniel Brighton had this to say about the RSPCA, which had unsuccessfully prosecuted him for neglecting his zoo animals:

> The work the RSPCA and other animal welfare groups do in the community is incredibly important to ensure that animals are properly cared for, animal owners are educated and that people who are maliciously cruel to animals are prosecuted. Unfortunately, on this occasion they got it wrong and I am glad that we have been cleared of any wrong doing.

It is unclear whether Brighton knew at this point that the RSPCA was interested in him for another reason. A year earlier, its officers had entered his Minto Heights property under a search warrant that allowed them to dig in a particular area of bushland. Their excavation uncovered some towels wrapped around a plastic feedbag, which in turn contained a decomposing dog carcass. The RSPCA were seemingly directed to that spot by two former employees of Get Wild Animal Experiences, who said they had buried the dog there on Brighton's instructions shortly after its attack on Alice the camel. The pair said that they had been woken in the night by another of Brighton's employees, who had been sent for help during the dog attack, but by the time they arrived on the scene, the attack was over.

Brighton would eventually say that he had killed the dog while trying to dislodge it from Alice and to prevent a further attack, but the court also heard two other accounts of its death. One account came from Dr Lydia Tong, a veterinary pathologist from Taronga Zoo, who reported that the dog's remains revealed extensive injuries, including three visible cuts into the bones near its neck and multiple fractures to its skull. The other came from one of the two employees, who testified that Brighton had chased and caught the dog after it had been dislodged from Alice and then, after it was safely subdued, killed it. Challenged as to why she nonetheless continued working at the Minto Heights property and socialising with Brighton's family, she answered: 'I couldn't leave those animals in danger. If I left they would die.'

The magistrate who tried the RSPCA's prosecution of Brighton accepted the ex-employee's account that Brighton brutally attacked the dog on two occasions. The first occasion was shortly after Brighton had tied the dog to a tree and before he drove to a vet to get medicine for Alice. The ex-employee said that Brighton picked up a pitchfork and stabbed the dog multiple times. On his return from the vet, he gave the medicine to Alice and then said 'we should move the dog'. When he started to drag it away, he exclaimed: 'It fucking stood up. It just won't die.' According to the ex-employee, Brighton then used the rope to suspend the dog from the tree and beat its head repeatedly with a mallet, saying 'I'll make sure it's dead.' The magistrate sentenced him to three years and four months in prison; subject to an appeal, he would have to spend at least two years behind bars.

The state RSPCA's chief inspector explained why a forty-month sentence – the longest handed down in a prosecution by the organisation – was apt:

> Animals are sentient. They deserve humane treatment and there is no excuse for the torture of an animal. We would expect a higher level of respect towards animals from someone who owns and operates businesses under licence involving animals.

He added that the dog 'was someone's pet, and he suffered a torturous death'. While he also noted that 'owners have obligations to ensure their pets are securely housed' and that the dog 'caused significant injuries to Alice the camel', he maintained that this 'in no way excuses the actions of the defendant in this matter'. In Australia, the RSPCA can – and is officially encouraged to – initiate such prosecutions, giving it a key role in speaking for animals in formal settings. However, the RSPCA can only perform this role if there is an offender to prosecute and punish. The culprit responsible for Alice's injuries could not be found, but the man responsible for the dog's injuries could.

There is more to discuss about Daniel Brighton's prosecution, but for now we will examine the situations in which courts can be asked to rule on the welfare of animals. In legal systems like Australia's (based on English law), criminal proceedings are the main way that people can bring a case to court. If someone thinks that a crime has been committed, including a crime against an animal, they can start a prosecution, which is known as a 'private prosecution'.

Two decades ago, Mark Pearson, later an elected member of the New South Wales parliament, brought cruelty charges against a circus on the basis that it had allowed its elephant, Arna, to mingle with and then be separated from three other elephants. After a magistrate dismissed the charge on the basis that the circus did not intend any cruelty, Pearson appealed to confirm the precedent that even unintended cruelty can be established as an offence. However, the judge expressed doubt about the circus's guilt either way, given evidence that it did not own the other three elephants. The prosecution ultimately failed due to lack of evidence that Arna was distressed, although it did manage to attract media attention. After Arna crushed a keeper a few years later, she was transferred to a zoo, and died of an unknown cause in 2012, an event the circus owner attributed to 'a broken heart'.

In practice, very few ordinary people initiate private prosecutions, because they are expensive and carry responsibilities and potential liability for the prosecutor, without offering any compensation or gains. Also, official prosecutors can take over and stop prosecutions, and must sign off on many of the more serious ones.

In a 2011 Canadian case, campaigners seeking to move a lone elephant named Lucy from Edmonton's zoo tried to get around these difficulties by simply asking a court to declare that the zoo was committing the criminal offence of keeping an animal 'in distress'. Noting that Canada's public prosecutors had refused to prosecute and would probably stop any private prosecution, the province's chief justice ruled that judges ought to consider whether the alternative of a 'non-criminal declaration' – that is, declaring someone a criminal even though they haven't been prosecuted and therefore cannot be punished – is an appropriate way to enforce that jurisdiction's animal welfare legislation:

The fact that the purpose of Alberta's animal welfare legislation is to protect vulnerable animals invites these questions. Is there no-one who can
intervene under any circumstances no matter how egregious to protect
vulnerable animals from mistreatment by government?

However, the remaining judges ruled that the decision to enforce the criminal law is exclusively one for prosecutors – in particular, the Edmonton
Humane Society, which had the local enforcement role for animal welfare –
not the courts. They also ruled that the organisations bringing the claim
lacked the necessary standing to bring a non-criminal suit.

One difference between criminal law and other parts of the law, such
as private law and government law, is that courts themselves place limits on when people can bring actions to enforce non-criminal laws. The
courts require the enforcers to be people who have 'standing' – that is, they
must show that they have a special interest in the question before the court,
rather than just being generally interested in the law being enforced. The
courts impose that requirement because they do not want to be used for
political purposes by people who are trying to make abstract arguments,
including the sorts of arguments that people trying to protect animals
sometimes promote.

Chapters 1 and 2 of this book discussed the many situations in which
humans can sue other humans over the behaviour of their animals, applying private laws like nuisance and negligence. However, the requirement
of standing means that it is typically only people who are directly affected
by that behaviour who can be involved in private law cases – for instance,
people who say they have been harmed and people who are said to be
responsible for those harms. This section addresses the remaining situations in which arguments can be made in court about the application of a
broader law (such as an animal welfare statute) to a particular animal. As
we will see, the law often limits who can initiate such actions, how they do
so and which animals, if any, the courts can protect.

Suits for Animals

The case of Izzy the Staffordshire terrier was a dispute between people,
even though the sole issue was the life or death of Izzy. Tania Isbester was
able to bring a suit about Izzy because she had an obvious special interest in Izzy's life or death: the dog was hers, in the sense that Izzy was both

Isbester's property and her companion animal. However, it is harder to establish standing in cases where no-one (or at least no litigant) owns the animal that is the subject of a dispute, especially when the laws at issue are concerned not with individual animals but with different or larger issues.

Early in 2020, Phil Maguire, the owner of rural property next to Victoria's Alpine National Park, started an action in the state's Supreme Court aimed at forcing Parks Victoria (which managed the park) to consult with the community about its plan to control the number of wild horses in the park by shooting some of them. However, the court ruled that Maguire could not bring the claim, because he had no special interest in how the government acted in relation to the brumbies. Being a neighbour of the park was not enough, and he could not argue that the way the horses were killed would affect his own land or his use of it for tourism. His very strong views against shooting the animals were not relevant either, because Maguire was just one member of the broader Victorian community who could have weighed in on Parks Victoria's plans. Finally, his emotional attachment to the brumbies themselves – which he said were originally bred on his land, and for which he provided ad hoc care – was also not enough because Australia's High Court had previously ruled that 'a strong emotional and intellectual attachment' to something, including the natural environment, does not establish standing. Maguire lodged an application to appeal the High Court's ruling, perhaps seeking its revision, but dropped it when Parks Victoria promised a community consultation before the next round of culling. However, the existing precedents, if correct, mean that Maguire cannot ask a court to require Parks Victoria to keep its promise.

Rules such as the 'standing' requirement can largely, perhaps wholly, prevent courts from enforcing compliance with laws that generally protect animals. However, Australia's parliament enacted a law in 1999 allowing a wider group of people to ask the Federal Court to stop anyone breaching the national environment protection and biodiversity statute. In addition to people whose interests have been or will be directly affected by such a breach, anyone who has engaged in a series of activities relating to environmental protection, research or conservation within the previous two years are allowed to bring an action as a result.

Notably, this law permitted the Australian Brumby Alliance to seek a federal injunction in 2020 to stop Parks Victoria from culling wild horses in Victoria's national parks on the basis that it would breach the biodiversity treaty. The alliance's action ultimately failed because Parks Victoria had not breached the treaty, but the action nevertheless delayed the proposed cull (which in turn prompted Parks Victoria to consider shooting some horses as part of its cull, a tactic that Maguire, a member of the alliance, would unsuccessfully seek to overturn later the same year).

The upshot is that people seeking to enforce compliance with animal protection laws – notably the compliance of governments – are dependent on governments to enact laws permitting such enforcement. That is also partially true of criminal law – even though prosecutions can be brought by anyone, there are a variety of practical and legal obstacles to prosecuting governments for their alleged crimes. On the other hand, some courts have recognised that certain legal actions against the state can, of necessity, be brought by people who do not have a special interest in a case. The main example is the famous writ of *habeas corpus* (Latin for 'produce the body'), which obliges a court to ask a person who is detaining someone else what legal authority they have to do so. A writ of *habeas corpus* obviously cannot typically be lodged by the detained person, and it would also be invidious to only permit such writs by someone who has a 'special' interest in that person, so it is an exception to the usual requirement that the court action be started by someone with standing.

In a series of recent cases, the Nonhuman Rights Project, a United States civil rights organisation dedicated to securing the rights of animals, sought *habeas corpus* in relation to several chimpanzees and elephants held in zoos or circuses. Relying on *habeas corpus* was advantageous in a number of ways, or so they argued. First, they did not have to establish any special interest in the animals, just their belief that the animals were being detained. Second, because a writ is part of the common law, the question of whether or not it applies to animals was not decided by interpreting a statute, but rather it could be determined – or even altered – by judges, subject to the court's rules on hierarchy and precedents. Third, questions of who owned the animals (if anyone) were not determinative – the issue was whether the animals were being lawfully detained.

On the other hand, the project faced difficult questions about whether its argument would require that the chimpanzees and elephants – and by extension, all companion animals – would have to be freed entirely. The project's lawyers conceded that such an outcome would not be desirable or lawful in most cases, given the dangers posed for and by the animals, but they argued that *habeas corpus* does not guarantee the freedom to go anywhere – a freedom that is unavailable, for instance, to detained adults with disabilities or infants – but rather it guarantees the maximum available freedom of self-determination. Accordingly, they sought a full trial on the capacities and opportunities of the particular animals to self-determine and the release of the animals to better facilities.

So far, the project's writs have all been rejected. Notably, a New York court refused to extend *habeas corpus* to a chimpanzee being held in a circus, because the court ruled that the writ was only suited to beings who have not only legal rights but also legal duties:

> Unlike human beings, chimpanzees cannot bear any legal duties, submit to societal responsibilities or be held legally accountable for their actions. In our view, it is this incapability to bear any legal responsibilities and societal duties that renders it inappropriate to confer upon chimpanzees the legal rights – such as the fundamental right to liberty protected by the writ of *habeas corpus* – that have been afforded to human beings.

Although one senior judge argued that 'whether a being has the right to seek freedom from confinement through the writ of *habeas corpus* should not be treated as a simple either/or proposition', the majority of judges directed the project to the legislature for protection of animals' self-determination rights, noting general US bans on animal cruelty and a specific ban on New Yorkers keeping primates as domestic companion animals.

Suits by Animals

In 2011, photographer David Slater published a series of photos of crested black macaques, including one startling photo of a monkey, said to be named Naruto, baring his teeth in a pose resembling that of a person taking a 'selfie'. More astonishingly, Slater claimed that the Indonesian macaques had been the ones who took the photos:

> They were quite mischievous, jumping all over my equipment. One hit the button. The sound got his attention and he kept pressing it. At first it scared the rest of them away, but they soon came back – it was amazing to watch. At first there was a lot of grimacing with their teeth showing. But then the animals seemed to settle down. He must have taken hundreds of pictures by the time I got my camera back.

Relying in part on this account, several organisations, including Wiki-media Commons, published the photos, concluding that they were not subject to copyright. However, Slater later gave a different account of how the photos were taken. He said he had deliberately set up his camera on a tripod with a remote trigger the macaques could operate, and had optimised various camera settings to obtain successful close-ups – claims he used to support his argument that he owned the images. He eventually self-published the photos.

One of the monkey 'selfies' taken by Naruto

In 2015, Naruto the macaque did something even more surprising than taking a selfie: he sued Slater in the United States District Court for Northern California for infringing his copyright. The fact that Naruto was Indonesian did not bar him from initiating the action – indeed, the fact that the photos were taken in Indonesia removed any requirement for Naruto to have registered copyright. Nor was his species a barrier, or so Naruto's legal counsel argued:

Naruto has the right to own and benefit from the copyright in the Monkey Selfies in the same manner and to the same extent as any other author. Had the Monkey Selfies been made by a human using Slater's unattended camera, that human would be declared the photographs' author and copyright owner. While the claim of authorship by species other than homo sapiens may be novel, 'authorship' under the *Copyright Act*, 17 U.S.C. § 101 et seq., is sufficiently broad so as to permit the protections of the law to extend to any original work, including those created by Naruto. Naruto should be afforded the protection of a claim of ownership, and the right to recover damages and other relief for copyright infringement.

The fact that Naruto himself was suing meant that there could be no argument about standing: obviously a litigant has standing to sue about their own claim in copyright. Rather, the hard questions are how and when a non-human animal can bring a legal suit.

Over a decade earlier, the United States Court of Appeals for the Ninth Circuit (which includes California) had ruled that that the US Constitution empowers the national legislature to permit non-humans (in that case, 'the Cetacean community') to sue humans (in that case, then President George W. Bush) in the nation's courts:

> It is obvious that an animal cannot function as a plaintiff in the same manner as a juridically competent human being. But we see no reason why Article III prevents Congress from authorizing a suit in the name of an animal, any more than it prevents suits brought in the name of artificial persons such as corporations, partnerships or trusts, and even ships, or of juridically incompetent persons such as infants, juveniles and mental incompetents.

However, the appeals court held that the particular action the Cetacean community wanted to bring – a challenge to the US Navy's use of sonar – had not been authorised by Congress, which only allowed 'persons' to bring such challenges.

Naruto's case rested on an argument that copyright law worked differently because it gave rights to 'authors', rather than 'persons'. But the judges who heard and reviewed Naruto's case raised an issue that had not been addressed in the case of cetaceans: how, exactly, could Naruto (and, indeed, other non-humans) initiate a court case, given the obvious barriers a six-year-old crested macaque would face to either starting the case on his own or hiring a lawyer to do so for him. The answer, the judges were told, was that humans had done these things for him, something that all courts permit in the case of litigants who cannot do such things themselves – for example, children, or adults with significant disabilities. The humans who initially claimed to be Naruto's 'next friends' (as they are quaintly termed in such cases) were Dr Antje Engelhardt, a primatologist who had personally studied the Sulawesi macaques (including Naruto himself) and People for the Ethical Treatment of Animals (PETA), a charity that advocates for animal rights (including their legal right to bring court actions).

However, reviewing the District Court's dismissal of Naruto's claim, one judge on the appeals court ruled that humans cannot typically be animals' next friends because they may not understand what animals want:

> Animal-next-friend standing is materially different from a competent person representing an incompetent person. We have millennia of experience understanding the interests and desire of humankind. This is not necessarily true for animals.

The remaining appeals judges decided the issue more narrowly, holding that PETA could not be Naruto's next friend because the charity did not 'claim to have a relationship with Naruto that is any more significant than its relationship with any other animal'.

Why restrict who can act as a party's (including any animal's) next friend? The courts' worry is that a party and their next friend may have different interests. The party may not want to bear the burdens of litigation (including expenses and legal responsibilities), the risks of losing (including costs and having a legal judgment against them) or even the benefits of winning (including possible downsides of victory, or just the impact their win will have on others). The most sceptical appeal judge in the macaque selfie case asked:

> Do animals want to own property, such as copyrights? Are animals willing to assume the duties associated with the rights PETA seems to be advancing on their behalf?

These questions were rhetorical, of course: Naruto could not understand these concepts, or even what a selfie is.

The court's issue was really that PETA, despite its name, was using Naruto – and the court – as a vehicle to further its goal of establishing legal rights for animals generally. The appeals judges saw confirmation of that concern in PETA's attempt to settle the case with Slater on terms that seemed to involve no benefit to Naruto himself. Indeed it is hard to see how PETA's action, even if it had succeeded, could plausibly have helped Naruto, though it is still less likely that it could have somehow harmed him. Most courts resist such tactics because they see the courts' role as resolving individual disputes, not weighing in on abstract questions.

Perhaps in retaliation, the appeals court decided that it also had to determine the issue that had actually caused the lower court to throw out the case: whether animals can be authors under American copyright law at all, even if they were somehow able to bring an action. The judges ruled that Congress had not permitted animals to own copyright, and they pushed for a further step – overruling their earlier judgment that theoretically allowed some animals to bring claims – arguing that those precedents enable groups like PETA to make flawed arguments. However, the judges' calls, which would need to be endorsed by a larger panel of judges to become a new precedent, have not been heeded to date.

Some other jurisdictions have been more open to expressly recognising non-humans as 'legal persons' in some respects.

In 2021, another American animal rights group, the Animal Legal Defence Fund, asked a US court to recognise that animals can sue as legal persons under Columbian law. A 'community of hippopotamuses living in the Magdalena River', descendants of hippos originally owned by drug lord Pablo Escobar, had brought an action in Columbia, seeking a variety of protections against a government plan to kill them. After Columbia's environmental regulator announced an alternative plan to give the hippos contraceptives, a dispute arose about whether the contraceptives were safe. The Animal Legal Defence Fund arranged for the hippos to ask a US court to depose – take testimony on oath – from two animal contraceptive experts to assist in the Columbian case, under a US law that allows any 'interested person' to make such a request in relation to a foreign court case. A federal judge granted the order on the basis that any party to a foreign case is an 'interested person', even a non-human party.

In 2016, New Zealand's parliament enacted a statute that specified that

Te Awa Tupua (the Whanganui River) – 'an indivisible and living whole, comprising the Whanganui River from the mountains to the sea, incorporating all its physical and metaphysical elements' – 'is a legal person and has all the rights, powers, duties, and liabilities of a legal person'. The Act also created the office of Te Pou Tupua as the river's 'human face', exercising the river's 'rights, powers and duties' and its responsibility for its liabilities. The role is carried out by two people, nominees from a collective group of customary rights holders and the New Zealand government. A similar model could be used to allow animals or groups of animals to bring claims in court on the same basis that people and organisations currently can.

Criminal Law: Defending Animals

New South Wales' main law on companion animals expressly allows people to 'seize' or harm a dog in order to protect property, people and, in most cases, other animals. You can seize a dog if that is the only way to protect your property, and you can injure or kill a dog if that is the only way to protect a person or another animal, unless the dog is droving stock or the animal attacked by the dog is considered 'vermin'. If the courts had accepted Daniel Brighton's original story – that he had injured the dog to stop it from attacking Alice the camel – then his actions would have been considered lawful.

New South Wales law also gives the state's farmers a wider ability to injure or kill some dogs:

> If a dog that is not under the effective control of some competent person enters any inclosed lands ... and approaches any animal being farmed on the land, the occupier of the land or any person authorised by the occupier can lawfully injure or destroy the dog if he or she reasonably believes that the dog will molest, attack or cause injury to any of those animals.

This provision seemingly overlaps with the scenario the court ultimately accepted in Brighton's case: that Brighton killed a stray dog that had entered his property, attacked an animal he (arguably) 'farmed' and seemed likely to attack again. However, Brighton did not rely on this provision of the law, most likely because the law only authorises the killing of a dog 'in a manner that causes it to die quickly and without unnecessary suffering', which according to his ex-employee's account he did not do. Instead, Brighton raised a surprising argument: that his action was exempt from the particular offence the RSPCA had charged him with because that offence has a specific exception for the 'extermination of pest animals'.

In Chapter 2, we discussed how the law classifies some animals as pests or nuisances and enables their control in a variety of ways, including through public culling schemes and through private laws allowing landowners to sue people who attract pests or nuisance animals to a particular location. In Chapter 3, we looked at how older societies improvised a different solution to various problem animals, putting the animals themselves on trial for their actions. In this section, we explore how both past and modern criminal law has attempted to manage broader claims that animals are pests. We will start by revisiting the strange history of medieval animals trials, this time looking at attempts to impose religious sanctions on vermin, a practice that generated surprising defences of pest animals. We will then return to the case of Daniel Brighton to see whether New South Wales courts determined that an ownerless dog is a pest animal that can be exterminated by any person despite a new prohibition on serious cruelty.

The Strange Case of the 'Vermin Trials'

Edward Payson Evans' book *The Criminal Responsibility and Capital Punishment of Animals* draws on the analysis of Karl Von Amira, a professor of early German law, to identify two sorts of medieval 'trials' of animals:

> Von Amira draws a sharp line of technical distinction between Thierstrafen [animal punishment] and Thierprocesse [animal trials]; the former were capital punishments inflicted by secular tribunals upon pigs, cows, horses and other domestic animals as a penalty for homicide; the latter were judicial proceedings instituted by ecclesiastical courts against rats, mice, locusts, weevils and other vermin in order to prevent them from devouring the crops, and to expel them from orchards, vineyards, and cultivated fields by means of exorcism and excommunication.

The first sort of trial, which we discussed in Chapter 3, inserted non-human animals into a process designed to detain, test and punish humans for their crimes:

Animals, which were in the service of man, could be arrested, tried, convicted and executed, like any other members of his household; it was, therefore, not necessary to summon them to appear in court at a specified time to answer for their conduct, and thus make them, in the strict sense of the term, a party to the prosecution, for the sheriff had already taken them in charge and consigned them to the custody of the jailer.

Although this practice looks quite odd to modern eyes, the use of criminal processes like arrest, charges, evidence and verdicts, and the typical outcome of those trials (an execution) are at least familiar and intelligible to us. By contrast, the second sort of trial had a process and outcome without any obvious analogue in modern society:

Insects and rodents, on the other hand, which were not subject to human control and could not be seized and imprisoned by the civil authorities, demanded the intervention of the Church and the exercise of its supernatural functions for the purpose of compelling them to desist from their devastations and to retire from all places devoted to the production of human sustenance. The only feasible method of staying the ravages of these swarms of noxious creatures was to resort to 'metaphysical aid' and to expel or exterminate them by sacerdotal conjuring and cursing.

Personalising Pests

At first glance, the oddest thing about vermin trials is their intended outcome: a ritualised pronouncement that the pests were anathema. The purpose of the trials was not to allow the state, or anyone else, to kill or otherwise punish the pests – that was already permitted. Rather, the trials were held because ordinary steps to eliminate the pests had failed:

The fact that it was customary to catch several specimens of the culprits and bring them before the seat of justice, and there solemnly put them to death while the anathema was being pronounced, proves that this summary manner of dealing would have been applied to the whole of them, had it been possible to do so. Indeed, the attempt was sometimes made to get rid of them by setting a price on their heads, as was the case with the plague of locusts at Rome in 880, when a reward was offered for their extermination, but all efforts in this direction proving futile, on account of the rapidity with which they propagated, recourse was had to exorcisms and besprinklings with holy water.

Excommunication, meaning exclusion from the sacraments, was distinct from anathematisation and considered a lesser punishment that no-one thought had any purpose when it came to animals, although Evans notes that many nevertheless used the term interchangeably with anathema.

While Evans is scathing of the use of anathema as a superstition akin to witchcraft trials, its deployment against animals nevertheless fits with our earlier discussion of the various reasons humans have for personifying animals.

First, some kind of 'moral event' may cause humans to give human characteristics to animals. The moral event may be positive, such as the heroic carrier pigeon Cher Ami's delivery of messages while under fire in World War I, for which he was awarded a French Croix de Guerre, and the event may also be negative, such as when pigs killed children in medieval times or when wild animals eat or destroy crops.

Second, there may have been a different attitude to animals in medieval times because of the importance of animals to daily life. On the one hand, St Augustine argued that animals and plants were put on Earth for the use of humans. St Thomas Aquinas also argued that animals and plants exist for the use of humanity, referring to Aristotle, the book of Genesis and St Augustine, and he consequently said that it was lawful to kill animals and eat their meat:

> Dumb animals and plants are devoid of the life of reason whereby to set themselves in motion; they are moved, as it were by another, by a kind of natural impulse, a sign of which is that they are naturally enslaved and accommodated to the uses of others.

On the other hand, the reality of medieval human–animal relations seems to be rather different and more complex than these passages would illustrate. Thus, Sara Butler argues that there is a constant slippage between the categories of the divine, human and animal in medieval times:

The Christian worldview, trumpeted from pulpits and captured grace-
fully in paintings, acted as a constant reminder that humans, animals
and nature are all integral parts of God's creation. The Great Chain of
Being represents the universal hierarchy as a chain extending from the
feet of God down to nothingness, with human beings sandwiched nicely
between angels and animals. Such an integrated view of creation stresses
the co-dependency of each class, as well as their shared attributes. With
angels, humans share the ability to reason, and their spirituality; yet,
the animated bodies of both humans and animals tie them inextricably
together, and to the Earth. This worldview explains much of humanity's
baser behavior: why do some people 'eat like pigs', 'breed like rabbits',
engage in 'cat fights', or act like 'jackasses'? These are moments when the
human capacity for reason is clouded, causing an individual to slip from
one category to another.

Butler also notes that animals were sometimes regarded as better
Christians than humans. A French greyhound – popularly venerated as St
Guinefort – was even worshipped as a patron saint of sick children because
it was said that he had been unjustly slain after saving the local lord's son
from a viper (a myth that bears a distinct similarity with the Welsh story
of Llywelyn and his hound Gelert). In the thirteenth century, the Catholic
inquisitor Stephen de Bourbon attempted to halt the cult of St Guinefort
by taking the bones of the dog and burning them. He was unsuccessful,
and the people continued to worship St Guinefort, although the Catholic
Church never officially recognised him as a saint. In the 1960s, there was
evidence that locals near Lyon still knew of him.

Consequently, the occurrence of medieval animal trials cases may
reflect the possibility that in certain places and at certain times, animals
were regarded as equivalent to (or even better than) humans, particularly
when they committed a positive 'moral act'. Conversely, if one accepts that
animals have an agency that is equivalent to humans', it follows that animals
that behave badly should be punished in equivalent ways. In fact, the criminal trials we describe in Chapter 3 suggest this very phenomenon.

Evans himself rejects such explanations of the trials:

This explanation is very fine in sentiment, but expresses a modern and
not a mediaeval way of thinking. The penal prosecution of animals,
which prevailed during the Middle Ages, was by no means peculiar

to that period, but has been frequently practised by primitive peoples and savage tribes; neither was it designed to inculcate any such moral lesson as is here suggested, nor did it produce any such desirable result. So far from originating in a delicate and sensitive sense of justice, it was, as will be more fully shown hereafter, the outcome of an extremely crude, obtuse, and barbaric sense of justice. It was the product of a social state, in which dense ignorance was governed by brute force, and is not to be considered as a reaction and protest against club-law, which it really tended to foster by making a travesty of the administration of justice and thus turning it into ridicule. It was also in the interest of ecclesiastical dignities to keep up this parody and perversion of a sacred and fundamental institute of civil society, since it strengthened their influence and extended their authority by subjecting even the caterpillar and the canker-worm to their dominion and control.

Somewhat consistently with Evans' view, historian Peter Dinzelbacher has suggested that medieval trials were a product of social and religious upheaval, and were used by authorities to entrench religious and economic control.

Peter Leeson, a professor of law and economics, applies the same reasoning to vermin trials, arguing that they were a way of consolidating religious authority and preventing tithe evasion. During many vermin trials, the obligations of locals to worship and pay tithes were emphasised as preconditions of the vermin's departure. Vermin are usually itinerant, and may move on from an area for a variety of reasons, but if their departure was seen as a positive outcome of a vermin trial, it bolstered church authority. Leeson also identifies an overlap between the timing of witchcraft trials and vermin trials, particularly in those areas where vermin trials occurred. Heresy trials – of such groups as the Waldensians and the Cathars – also took place in these areas at the same time. Leeson hypothesises that this explains the strange geographical distribution and timing of vermin trials: they were designed to reinforce the orthodox faith in those particular areas.

In his seminal book on the topic, Norman Cohn argues that legal trials of heretics and ritual magicians cannot be conflated with later witchcraft prosecutions. According to Cohn, there was a progression from the early prosecution of heretics to the prosecutions of practitioners of ritual magic (also for heresy), and only after that did legal trials for witchcraft occur in the fifteenth, sixteenth and seventeenth centuries. Cohn argues that the notion that witchcraft trials occurred earlier is the result of historical hoaxes and forgeries that were then picked up as fact and repeated. It is true, however, that the stereotype of witches as people who flew by night and attended witches' sabbaths developed in the 1420s in areas where persecution of Waldensians had typically occurred, and that adherence to Waldensian belief and witchcraft were melded. It seems likely that witchcraft and vermin trials did reflect some kind of greater social and religious upheaval that occurred at that time, and to some extent involved an assertion of orthodox religious power.

Representing Pests

While the religious sanctions placed on vermin in medieval times may well be explicable in a variety of ways, the proceedings that led to those sanctions are harder to parse. Evans describes what at first looks to be a wholly religious ceremony:

> In the prosecution of animals, the summons was commonly published from the parish pulpit and the whole judicial process bore a distinctively ecclesiastical character. In most cases, the presiding judge or official was the vicar of the parish, acting as the deputy of the bishop of the diocese. Occasionally the curate officiated in this capacity. Sometimes the trial was conducted before a civil magistrate under the authority of the Church, or the matter was submitted to the adjudication of a conjurer.

However, in many instances, the official would respond to a complaint from those affected by the vermin by appointing two legal representatives – one to make the case against the animals and another to make the case for them. One of the most famed medieval jurists in France, Barthélemy de Chasseneuz, is said to have established his reputation in 1508 through his eloquent defence of the rats of Autun, which had been threatened with anathematisation for destroying the city's barley crop. Chasseneuz was reputed to have represented several other animal clients during his feted career, but no records survive.

Chasseneuz defended the rats of Autun by questioning the summons issued to the rats, arguing that it had been inadequate because the rats were widespread and it may not have been brought to their notice. The judge then ordered a second summons to be read from the pulpits of all the parishes in which the rats lived. When the rats (unsurprisingly) failed to turn up, Chasseneuz argued that this was because of the length and difficulty of the journey, and the dangers of cats along the way, noting that a human would not be required to turn up in court if his life were at risk. The court again adjourned the proceedings. Unfortunately, we do not know the ultimate resolution of the case.

Detailed records, summarised by Evans, exist of another interesting case: a complaint made in 1587 by wine growers in St Julien against a species of green weevils. Two representatives of the wine growers beseeched 'his most reverend lordship, the prince-bishop of Maurienne' to appoint advocates for and against the weevils, to visit and assess the damaged vineyards and then anathematise the pests. Two representatives were duly appointed and exchanged missives for the next five months. Pierre Rembaud, for the weevils, argued that the pests should not be punished for their entirely natural foraging instincts, which accorded with God's expectations. A third lawyer, the wine growers' advocate, François Fay, argued that the weevils were subservient to man and could therefore be punished. Rembaud's blunt response was that the animals' status relative to humans was irrelevant as both are subservient to God.

Despite his earlier advocacy for animals facing anathematisation, Chasseneuz ultimately concluded that the sanctioning of vermin was legally sound. His argument on this matter is the first of fifty-nine essays in a collection of his own legal opinions, *Repertorium consiliorum*, published thirteen years after he defended Autun's rats and ten years before his death. As described by Evans, the jurist's essay focuses on establishing a lengthy history of such practices, dating back to the cursing of the serpent that tempted Adam and Eve, and Jesus' condemnation of a withered fig tree:

> The words of Jesus, 'Every tree that bringeth not forth good fruit is hewn down and cast into the fire', he interprets, not merely as the best means of getting rid of a cumberer of the orchard, but as a condemnation and punishment of the tree for its delinquencies, and adds 'If, therefore, it is permitted to destroy an irrational thing, because it does not produce fruit, much more is it permitted to curse it, since the greater penalty includes the less.'

Chasseneuz's solution to the quandary of how a church can punish animals for their natural instincts was to argue that the purpose of anathematisation is not punishment but precaution: 'Things not allowable in respect to crimes already committed are allowable in respect to crimes about to be committed in order to prevent them.' Such an argument might seem to leave vermin with little answer to a proposed anathematisation. However, Chasseneuz combined his acceptance of religious sanctions as legally apt with an insistence on strict compliance with legal process:

> [Chasseneuz] insists that under no circumstances is a penalty to be imposed except by judicial decision ... and in support of this principle refers to the apostle Paul, who declares that 'sin is not imputed when there is no law'. He appears to think that any technical error would vitiate the whole procedure and reduce the ban of the Church to mere *brutum fulmen* [thunderclap].

Later, when Chasseneuz became president of the Parlement de Provence, the regional Court of Appeal, he was called upon to extend the same clemency to heretics that he had shown to Autun's rats. When parliament issued the *Arrêt de Mérindol* (*arrêt* meaning a sentence or judgment handed down) in 1541, requiring the extermination of the heretical Waldenses of Mérindol and Cabrières-d'Avignon (who rejected the authority of the pope and the Catholic Church), one of the other judges reminded Chasseneuz of his arguments on behalf of the rats and asked if the heretics should not be shown the same courtesy. Chasseneuz agreed and obtained a decree from the king commanding that the Waldenses be allowed to come safely to court and be entitled to legal representation. However, Chasseneuz died shortly thereafter, and his orders were not enforced. It is unclear how many people were killed in the subsequent Massacre of Mérindol in 1545, but historians estimate the number was in the hundreds or thousands.

Whatever Chasseneuz's advocacy achieved for humans facing religious persecution, nuisance animals remained seemingly indifferent and unaffected by their advocates' efforts, as well as the efforts of their opponents. Anathemas were pronounced or (rarely) they were not. Infestations abated or (less rarely) they did not. Tithes were paid or they were not. Connections were drawn between these events or they were not. However, the advocates' 'pettifoggery' (as Evans labelled it) did sometimes prompt those affected by vermin infestations to at least contemplate a middle ground between exterminating them and treating them as victims.

Evans' account of the 1587 trial of the weevils in St Julien is bookended by two cases in which such alternatives were considered. One occurred forty years earlier, in 1546, when the wine growers first sought the pests' anathematisation. Following the advocacy of the procurator and defendant, François Bonnivard, a doctor of laws, declared at that time:

> Inasmuch as God, the supreme author of all that exists, hath ordained that the earth should bring forth fruits and herbs not solely for the sustenance of rational human beings, but likewise for the preservation and support of insects, which fly about on the surface of the soil, therefore it would be unbecoming to proceed with rashness and precipitance against the animals now actually accused and indicted.

During Bonnivard's pause on the extermination of the weevils – enforced through his demands for piety, charity, tithes and a program of mass prayers – the weevils reportedly disappeared from the towns' vineyards of their own accord.

When the pests returned in 1587, there was no formal pause, but the plaintiffs were prompted by the advocates' arguments about natural, human and divine law as it applies to animals – or at least by the resulting length of the proceedings – to find an alternative solution to their dispute with the weevils:

> On the 29th of June, 1587, a public meeting was called at noon immediately after mass on the great square of St Julien, known as Parloir d'Amont, to which all hinds and habitants were summoned by the ringing of the church bell to consider the propriety and necessity of providing for the said animals a place outside of the vineyards of St Julien, where they might obtain sufficient sustenance without devouring and devastating the vines of the said commune.

The inhabitants of St Julien not only settled on a particular location to reserve for the weevils – 'described with the exactness of a topographical survey, not only as to its location and dimensions, but also as to the character of its foliage and herbage' – but voted to appropriate it and convey it 'in good form and of perpetual validity'. The weevils were not, however, granted exclusive possession – the locals reserved their rights to pass through the land, use the springs, mine it for minerals and take refuge there in time of war, albeit without prejudice to the weevils' means of subsistence.

Alas, the litigation continued in a second trial, with the weevils' advocate rejecting the offered land as sterile and insufficient for the weevils' needs, and the plaintiffs insisting that it was full of trees and suitable shrubs, prompting the official to order a survey. Perhaps ominously – there is no record of the litigation's conclusion, at least according to Evans:

> The final decision of the case, after such careful deliberation and so long delay, is rendered doubtful by the unfortunate circumstance that the last page of the records has been destroyed by rats or bugs of some sort.

Evans caps this too perfect outcome by noting that the margins of the final page of the report set out the fees paid to the surveyors and the church official, dated eight months after the action against the weevils commenced.

In later times, these trials ceased, but in Europe and the United States a custom of serving rodents with a letter of ejectment, or even a letter of advice asking them to leave, prevailed. Evans says, 'Lest the rats should overlook and thus fail to read the epistle, it is rubbed with grease, so as to attract their attention, rolled up and thrust into their holes.' In Ireland, Scotland and France, there was apparently a tradition of reciting rhymes to rodents to get them to quit the house. The Scots rhyme is reputed to be:

> Ratton and mouse,
> Lea' the puir woman's house,
> Gang awa' wore by to 'e mill,
> And then and a' ye'll get your fill.

This was sometimes placed on a writ of ejectment that was pasted on a wall.

The Singular Case of Daniel Brighton

We now return to the case of Daniel Brighton, who brutally killed a dog he claimed was a 'pest animal'. While alleged pests were put on trial in medieval times, the issue today is whether the person who killed the pests has committed the particular crime they have been charged with. As discussed

in Chapter 5, laws barring cruelty to animals are a very modern phenomenon. When Brighton killed the dog, New South Wales' two main animal
cruelty offences were cruelty to animals, punishable at that time by up to
six months in prison, and aggravated cruelty, which applies when animals
die or are seriously injured as the result of cruelty, and which had just had
its maximum penalty lifted to two years in prison. But prosecutions had to
be brought within a year of the cruelty, and Brighton's alleged treatment of
the dog emerged years later.

However, the previous decade, after a widely publicised incident of Sydney teens torturing kittens, the New South Wales parliament had created
a new offence of 'serious animal cruelty', which covered people who are
not only cruel to or kill or seriously injure an animal, but who also had an
'intention of inflicting severe pain'. That offence wouldn't have covered the
two examples of cruelty we discussed in Chapter 5 (the kicking of a dog
and the negligent keeping of dairy animals), but it could arguably cover
what Daniel Brighton did. Importantly, there was no time limit on bringing charges under the new offence, and it carried a maximum penalty of
five years in prison. That's how Brighton came to be prosecuted, convicted
and sentenced for killing the dog.

Brighton's hope of avoiding serving several years in prison under the
magistrate's unprecedented sentence turned on the following statutory
defence to the offence of aggravated cruelty:

> A person is not criminally responsible for an offence against this
> section if –
>
> (a) the conduct occurred in accordance with an authority
>   conferred by or under the *Animal Research Act 1985* or
>   any other Act or law, or
>
> (b) the conduct occurred in the course of or for the purposes
>   of routine agricultural or animal husbandry activities,
>   recognised religious practices, the extermination of pest
>   animals or veterinary practice.

Almost everyone agreed that this defence was a peculiar one for an extreme
cruelty offence, as there was little reason to think that any of the activities
exempted by the Act would be carried out with an intention of causing an
animal serious pain. As one judge observed:

One can understand the exemption for recognised religious activities, which, I assume, relates to the slaughter of halal and kosher meat. However, neither process of killing is done with an intention of inflicting severe pain. The whole process, which involves slicing the carotid artery, in one motion, with a sharp knife, along more than half of its length, is designed (albeit at a time when modern slaughtering techniques had not been invented) to avoid inflicting severe pain ... Perhaps, there are still religions that engage in animal sacrifice, but even that practice, albeit ancient, utilises dead animals, not live ones.

Nevertheless, if Brighton could establish that he was engaging in any of these activities when he injured and killed the dog, he would defeat the charge. Brighton did not argue that he had been performing 'routine' farming activities or veterinary practices (or implementing a law or religious practice), so the only issue the court had to decide was whether or not the dog was a 'pest animal' that Brighton had 'exterminat[ed]'.

It is this aspect of the case that is the closest modern analogue to the vermin trials, although there is no equivalent to St Julien's weevils – insects are not covered by the modern offence of serious animal cruelty, which defines 'animal' to mean mammals, birds and reptiles. Nevertheless, the judges realised that the question of whether or not an animal is a pest could determine the criminality of cruelly killing a range of animals that are not commonly thought of as protected in Australia:

The definition excludes amphibians, such as a frog, but includes reptiles, such as a snake, a lizard or a crocodile. On the view expressed by the [RSPCA] in these proceedings, taken to its natural conclusion, a person who saw a snake or a lizard or a crocodile and beat it with a shovel or killed it would be guilty of an offence.

The judge observed that while it was unlikely anyone would attack a crocodile intending to cause it serious pain, snakes or lizards could be another matter. If such a person was charged with serious animal cruelty (which the judge also thought unlikely), then their sole defence would be that they were exterminating a pest animal.

The specific questions the judge who heard Brighton's trial and appeals had to consider were whether a dog can be a 'pest animal' and in what circumstances. Brighton's lawyer argued that this one was a pest:

'This dog came onto the land with another dog and attacked a camel, hanging from its neck,' he said. 'Let's call a spade a spade, this dog went feral, you wouldn't expect a golden retriever to do this or a pet animal. I would not think there's a question that wild dogs can be pests. If a police officer was present at the time of the incident you would expect him to shoot it.'

He added that New South Wales law requires some landowners to destroy a dog that 'is or has become wild', unless it is a companion animal or is kept in a zoo or for research.

The magistrate who tried Brighton cited three reasons to reject his defence: the dog was a domestic breed (a pit bull type); at some point it was someone's companion animal (the remains included a damaged collar and microchip); and, as he was not satisfied that it was a wild animal, he could not be satisfied that it was a pest animal. However, three judges later held that there was enough evidence to suggest the likelihood that the dog had become wild: it was roaming; it was roaming with a second dog; it attacked Alice; and the remains of digested kangaroo were found inside the dog's body. One judge also found that the dog was a nuisance dog and a dangerous dog under New South Wales law, which would place restrictions on it being kept as a companion animal.

The RSPCA argued that the concept of a 'pest animal' is not about the behaviour of an individual animal, such as the dog Brighton killed, but the characteristics of an entire species that could act in 'pest proportions'. While all the judges agreed that entire species (e.g. cane toads) could be pests, none agreed that *only* entire species could be pests, given that they understood 'feral' subgroups of species such as cats and dogs to be pests, even if their domestic siblings were not. One judge accepted that what makes an animal a pest is not its own behaviour but rather a propensity it shares with a group of similar animals. She would have rejected Brighton's defence because there seemed to be just two dogs that were attacking camels or other animals in Minto Heights and a 'class is not constituted by two animals of a kind'. She was also unprepared to deem an animal a pest just because of its behaviour on one occasion. But the remaining judges disagreed. They accepted that a pair of dogs that attack another animal can be 'pest animals', simply because of their behaviour. They said that it was not a question of the dogs being annoying or troublesome; what mattered was that they were destructive. On that basis, the dog Brighton killed was a pest.

But that was not enough for Brighton to avoid conviction for serious animal cruelty. The magistrate had ruled that 'extermination' meant total elimination not the killing of one dog (presumably Brighton would have needed to kill all the stray dogs in Minto Heights to accomplish this), while the RSPCA argued that an extermination is 'a systematic process conducted humanely, embracing concepts of relative "humanity or ethics"'. The first senior judge to review the case thought that both of these views were too restrictive, given that what was at issue was whether and when a person is allowed to kill a particular animal in a cruel way. He would have freed Brighton on the basis that the exception covered any killing of any pest, regardless of how or how many animals were killed.

In the end, the three judges on the state's appeal court disagreed with all of the earlier approaches, drawing instead on the behaviour of insect exterminators, whose job is neither to kill just one or two insects nor to wipe out an entire species or class, but rather 'to eliminate as many pest animals or insects that are exposed to the technique or process of extermination'. Because it requires a systematic process, the judges decided that this definition did not cover Brighton's ad hoc killing of a single dog.

The upshot of the court's ruling is that people in New South Wales can deliberately inflict serious pain on a mammal, bird or reptile – absent the legal authority to do so and not in the course of carrying out a religious, farming or medical practice – if, and only if, more than one animal of its kind has shown a common propensity to be destructive and the person uses a technique or process designed to kill as many of them as possible.

Brighton's prosecution was just a single case about an unusual statute, but it shared with its ecclesiastical counterparts from medieval times a curious mix of technicality, practicality and barbarity. Although Brighton failed to convince the New South Wales courts that his attack on the 'pest animal' was an 'extermination', there are two reasons it is unlikely he will serve his full record-setting sentence of forty months, or even a significant part of it.

First, the one judge who would have accepted Brighton's 'pest' defence also ruled that the prison sentence the magistrate gave him was far too high:

He has an impeccable record; he has not before come to the attention of police or law enforcement agencies. Further, and most relevantly to the current charges, apart from the references that were provided, he has an impeccable record in terms of his treatment of animals, which is his livelihood. The fact that the appellant has an exemplary record in relation to the treatment of animals is a factor which informs not only the sentence to be passed if he were guilty, but also whether it is likely he formed the intention required.

That judge would have lowered the sentence to a maximum of two years, opening the way for Brighton to serve his sentence via community service, which the judge would have augmented with a requirement 'to attend a suitable course on animal cruelty as recommended by authorities'.

Second, the appeal judges who later rejected Brighton's extermination defence nevertheless ordered a fresh hearing on whether he met the main requirement for the offence of aggravated cruelty:

> As unpalatable as the subject matter is, the fact that [Brighton] used a pitchfork repeatedly and then, on the second occasion, a mallet repeatedly to kill the dog may not necessarily be indicative of an 'intention of inflicting severe pain' as opposed to an intention to kill the dog as quickly as possible (perhaps motivated, in the first instance, by retribution for the attack on the camel) and, in the second instance, to put the dog *out of any pain* by killing it quickly, having thought that he had already killed it on the earlier occasion.

It was not enough, the judges stressed, that Brighton knew he was causing the dog severe pain; he had to specifically want to do so for this particular offence to be satisfied, given its high penalty and its purpose of deterring extreme cruelty. Effectively, the judges were suggesting that Brighton may well have been guilty of the less serious animal cruelty offences discussed in Chapter 5, which do not require proof of an intent to be cruel and (as a consequence) have lower maximum penalties. As already noted, though, Brighton could not be charged with those offences because the authorities only learned of them after the statutory time limit had expired. The New South Wales parliament has since made the time limit three years from the point that authorities first become aware of a possible offence.

Views will clearly differ on whether or not Daniel Brighton deserved the painstaking and perhaps generous readings of the criminal law that he received from New South Wales appeal judges. But these developments underline a key point we have made throughout this book: that human laws about animals are almost always motivated by human concerns, and specifically concerns for humans. These include matters like proportionate consequences for wrongdoing and careful attention to clear proof, fair labelling of offending and correct readings of written laws. In the book's conclusion, we will look at the prospects for a partial change of approach, putting concerns for animals either ahead of, or at least equal to, concerns for humans.

CONCLUSION

LAW'S ANIMALS

The Day of the Tentacle

A S WE WERE WRITING THIS BOOK, THE UNDERWATER PHO-tography Guide announced the winners of its Ocean Art 2020 competition. After evaluating 'thousands of entries', the judges awarded its top prize to a Sydney academic engineer, Gaetano Gargiulo, for a photo described by one judge as follows:

The main subject is an octopus, but you don't see the literal octopus. You see suckers and arms, which are arguably the defining characteristics of an octopus. You see the arms and suckers exploring and tasting the dome port, which is quintessential octopus behavior. There is symmetry in placement of the octopus arms. The colors align with R-G-B spectrum. And finally – this is the kicker – there are people visible in the window created by the framing of the octopus's arm. I did not know who the people were when I saw the image, but there is a connotation of mother and child, or other strong bond, with the adult pointing toward the octopus and photographer, child looking on. The interest of the child mirrors the interest of the octopus. In other words, on top of a technically well-executed photo, there is a story there, one that involves both animal and humans.

The judge later learned about Gargiulo's 'story of the shot':

On the day of the photo, I remained in the tide pool as the tide was too low to venture outside of its boundaries. In one of the shallowest parts of the pool I noticed an octopus. I placed my camera near its den and the octopus started interacting with it. It came completely out of the den and to our amazement it started shooting pictures! My son (3 y.o. in the background) was very curious about the octopus.

In other words, the 'adult pointing toward the octopus and photographer' was actually Gargiulo himself, while 'the octopus and photographer' were one and the same. It was actually the photo's 'main subject' that took this 'technically well-executed photo'.

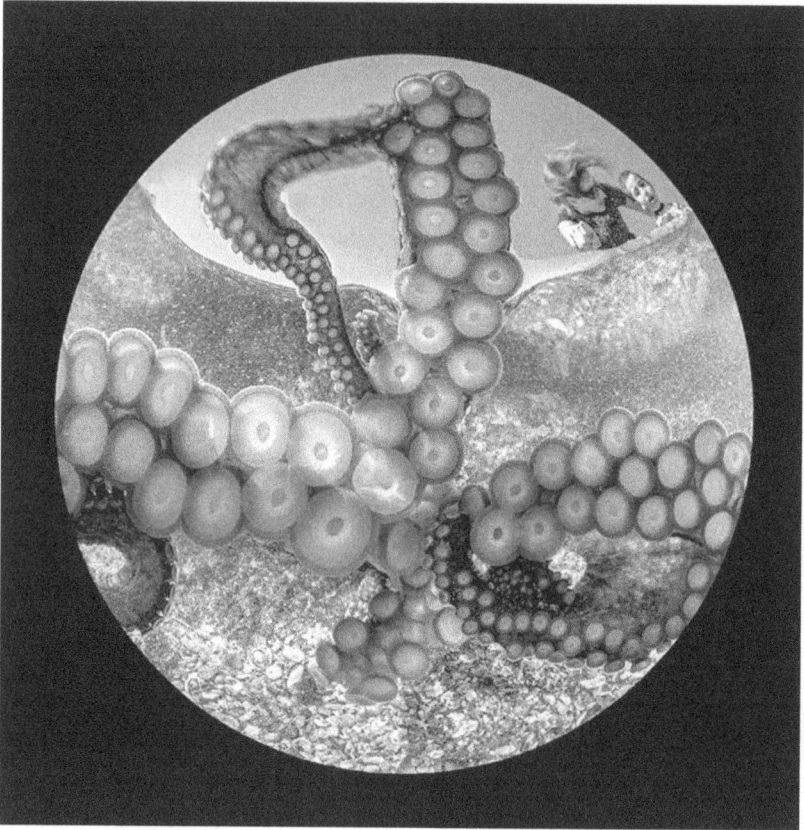

The Day of the Tentacle – an octopus 'selfie'

Readers, we are sure, will notice how these events are similar to a case we have already discussed, in which PETA tried and failed to establish that the copyright owner of a macaque 'selfie' was the macaque himself. But there are three ways that this example differs from its more famous cousin.

One difference is the jurisdiction: the octopus selfie was taken in Kamay Botany Bay National Park, near Gargiulo's home in Sydney, Australia, best known as Captain Cook's landing place on his 1770 voyage. In writing this book, we have often looked for examples from our own jurisdiction, starting with the law of our home state of Victoria, which we set out in the introduction. But, while we continued to cover Australian law in Chapters 1 and 2, we also drew on overseas jurisdictions, especially ones that share the 'common law' that English authorities transported to Australia along with the convicts. No study of animal law could ever be confined to a single country or even a single legal system, which is why, in Chapter 3, when considering how the law blames non-human animals for their actions, we looked at the legal systems of continental Europe (sourced primarily from Roman law), which are quite different to the common law, and at medieval laws, which are indeed very different again. Likewise, in Chapter 4, we trawled nearly every continent for examples of animals being used as legal evidence, while in Chapter 5 we looked back to the precedents set by the Bible and the early European colonies of North America. In Chapter 6 we examined all of these sources again, and more.

Until the Ocean Art 2020 competition prizes were announced, we (like most others, we suspect) had never had cause to wonder how Australian law applies to animal selfies. While Australian copyright law is based on modern legislation, as is US copyright law, both countries have their own statutes, with different wording and potentially different aims. Neither law contains a general definition of who counts as the 'author' of an artistic work, but Australia's *Copyright Act 1986* does define who counts as an 'author' in the case of a photograph: 'the person who took the photograph'. This short phrase, we think, likely settles any question about who the author is (and hence the copyright owner) of the 'Day of the Tentacle' under Australian law: no-one. It cannot be Gargiulo, because he did not 'take' the photo, but it cannot be the actual photographer either, because an octopus is not a 'person'.

There is a second difference between the two cases: the type of legal dispute and the type of law that one would expect to be involved in each. In the introduction, we discussed the three main types of human law that are often engaged by animals: private law, criminal law and public law. Much of Chapters 1 and 2 was concerned with private law, specifically the law on the duties all humans owe to other humans, including respecting one another's property and not foreseeably harming one another. Chapters 3 and 5 were concerned with criminal law, as it is has applied both to animals that harm humans and to humans that harm animals. Chapter 6 examined both of these types of laws again, but looked at specific aspects we had not previously discussed: trust law and criminal process, as well as explaining why public law can (but mostly does not) assist animals. There are many other parts of the law that can also apply to animals – one example being the law of evidence that was discussed in Chapter 4.

The octopus selfie potentially raises yet another part of the law. The Ocean Art competition is not only an art prize, it is also a commercial arrangement between organisers, competitors and sponsors. Each of the 'thousands of entries from 80 countries' involved a US$10 entry fee (with a discount for bulk entries), while the winners of first, second and third place – across twelve categories – are eligible for over US$45,000 in sponsored prizes, making the value of the Ocean Art prize 'among the highest in the world'. Gargiulo, who obtained both first place in the 'wide angle' section and the 'best in show' award, 'won a 7 nights liveaboard diving package for one to the Solomon Islands'. Should that prize have gone to the octopus instead? Or to a different entrant who personally took the photo he or she submitted? That turns on the *law of contracts*, which concerns promises people voluntarily make to each other (such as the promise the competition organisers made to entrants and to their sponsors) in return for giving something of value (known as 'consideration', in this case the $US10 entry fee). It may also turn on any statutes or other laws that regulate competitions, including consumer protection law. Chances are, any legal questions could be resolved by interpreting the contest's own rules, including specific ones. Of course, all of this will only matter if someone – a human someone, for reasons explained in Chapter 6 – decides to sue.

Finally, there's a third difference – the elephant in the room, you could say: an octopus is a very different animal to a macaque. In fact, it is so different that we have not mentioned a single octopus in this book until now – nor any of its 500 fellow cephalopods, such as squids and cuttlefish. Indeed, the sole member of its entire phylum, Mollusca (the second-largest of all the animal phyla), to have been discussed in this book is the snail, and it was only mentioned in passing. A lone snail famously started the modern law of negligence when it somehow ended up in a bottle of ginger beer, and snails were also the subject of several medieval vermin trials.

The vermin trials discussed in Chapter 6 featured several members of the largest phylum (by far), Anthropoda, which includes insects, and Chapters 1 and 2 considered another member of that phylum, the bee. Vast biological differences do not always lead to different legal rules: delightfully, some countries have treated bees in a similar way to a very different beast, the cow, which is in turn grouped within the cryptic category of avers, covering various sorts of livestock. Still, it is no coincidence that nearly all of our examples have been drawn from the Chordata phylum, which includes dogs, cats, fish, frogs, pigs, cows and monkeys – and also humans. Indeed, most of the law's efforts to classify animals – as wild or domesticated, benign or dangerous, trained or natural, companions or ferals, natives or pests – are devoted to a specific class of chordates: Mammalia.

A search of Australia's case law database, *Austlii*, yields a handful of cases that mention octopuses, but almost all are metaphorical, typically referring to corporate or organisational misconduct. However, even though it seems no octopus has had its 'day in court', predicting how the law would apply to interactions between humans and octopuses is still a fairly straight-forward task. A human who captured an octopus would own it, but only for so long as the octopus remained captive (octopuses are notoriously good at escaping from aquariums). An octopus owner would risk being sued if a captive octopus were to attack someone as it escaped; although, as Chapter 2 suggests, perhaps only some species – the extremely venomous blue-ringed octopus, for example – would attract the strict rules that apply to inherently dangerous animals.

For whatever reason, octopuses escaped the medieval animal trials described in Chapter 3, but a Korean man recently blamed his wife's death on a live octopus he had bought, the tentacle of which was found in her throat after she died. Citing her family's claim that she was a reluctant and careful eater of live seafood and her widower's claim on her life insurance, prosecutors later prosecuted him for murder, obtaining a conviction that South Korea's Supreme Court eventually overturned due to lack of evidence.

In the unlikely event that a living octopus witnessed a crime or some other event of interest to the courts, their remarkable expressiveness – including their ability to mimic their surroundings – could perhaps be used as evidence in a human court, as described in Chapter 4 (however, reports of human-trained octopuses appear limited to the instance in which Gargiulo successfully taught one to take photographs).

Sadly, it is much easier to imagine humans harming octopuses, including through crimes of bestiality, which, as Chapter 5 explained, extend in modern statutes to cover all 'animals', including invertebrates (but not necessarily all sexual acts) – octopuses do sometimes feature in erotic art – and crimes of cruelty, which, as we noted in Chapter 6, do not always cover all animals.

One of our main motivations for writing this book is to illustrate the sheer variety of ways that animals, humans and human laws can interact. However, as the example of octopuses shows, our study is skewed by the sort of interactions that have ended up in court to date, something largely determined by human interests and desires.

In this final part of the book, we turn to where animal law might go in the future, and in particular its potential to grant animals various rights. We will look first at the current law on rights, which is almost exclusively about the rights of humans, examining how rights law can sometimes harm non-human animals and sometimes promote their wellbeing. We conclude by examining newer laws and proposed laws that aim to recognise animal rights not on the basis of their humanity but on the basis of their dignity, suffering and sentience.

The Rights of Human Animals

Being Human

Early in 2003, a US judge, Judith Barzilay, was asked to rule on whether myriad beings displayed before her represented 'only human beings' or represented 'animals or other non-human creatures'. This venue for this momentous ruling was as banal as its subject matter: Barzilay sat on the US Court of International Trade and was ruling on the customs duty to be paid on a series of figurines based on Marvel comics characters. The importer, Toy Inc., wanted to avoid paying the higher duty that the United States charged for 'dolls', but it had lost several earlier skirmishes. Previous judges had ruled that the definition of a doll did not turn on whether it 'resembled' a human being; indeed, they noted that humans do not always resemble one other in appearance or capabilities. They also found that the various Marvel figures had too much 'personality' to be dismissed as mere 'tin soldiers' (which are presumptively treated as non-doll toys under US customs law).

To the relief of Toy Inc. but the disappointment of some fans of the X-Men (whose protagonists have long debated whether mutants have more in common with one another or with non-mutant humans), Judge Barzilay ultimately ruled that almost none of the Marvel figures 'represented only humans'. For some of the figures, this was simply a matter of their having bodily parts that no humans have:

> Two of the figures are humanoid, with at least one feature that pre-
> vents them from being representations of normal humans. The figure
> of 'Hobgoblin' has blood red eyes with no pupils and features fangs

and yellow skin. The 'Dr Octopus' figure has four tentacles coming from its back.

For other figures, the call was more difficult:

'Mole Man' is described as both being human and having an 'odd appearance ... extraordinary intelligence, cunning, and fighting prowess with his staff'. The figure is stout and thick, has exaggerated troll-like features, wears a green outfit and cape, and comes with a staff and a small figure of a 'humanoid' creature (yellow in skin with protruding white eyes), symbolizing the fact that the character uses small humanoid creatures to 'do his bidding'. Mole Man lives 'within the earth', and consistent with the character's subterranean nature, the figure has unusually pale skin and wears blue glasses. The character also 'controls a legion of giant monsters'. Given the entire context of the figure's appearance and fantastic story, and the fact that it is part of a series where the characters are described as 'super-human', the court finds that 'Mole Man' is also not properly classifiable as a 'doll'.

Ultimately, Barzilay ruled that describing a figure as a 'mutant' or having 'X-tra powers' amounted to representing it as 'more than (or different than) humans'. Based on this approach, the lone member of the Justice League (a rival comics series) to represent humanity is the one who dresses as a bat.

It is not only trade courts that keep a close rein on what it means to be human. It is likely that the last humans to successfully conceive with a different species lived over 40,000 years ago, around the time that modern humans (or perhaps climate change) drove our Neanderthal cousins to extinction in Europe. (Whether such mating would now constitute the crime of bestiality is a fascinating question that will almost certainly never have to be resolved.) However, scientists have recently reported injecting early blastocysts (fertilised eggs at the pre-embryo stage) from cynomolgus monkeys with 'human extended pluripotent stem cells' (human cells that are genetically reprogrammed to act like egg or sperm cells) to create 'human–monkey chimeric embryos'. While the American and Chinese researchers who created these embryos did not let them develop – their stated purpose was to better understand the potential for cross-species tissue transplants – their work is nevertheless a step towards the theoretical possibility of developing chimeric beings. Among the many profound issues such a development would pose, difficult questions would be asked about how the new beings should be treated by the various laws discussed in this book.

In Australia, both national and state statutes ban the creation or importation of 'chimeric embryos', but these are defined as 'a human embryo into which a cell, or any component part of a cell, of an animal has been introduced'. (The American and Chinese scientists instead seem to have done the reverse, putting part of a human cell into an animal embryo.) Australian laws permit licensed researchers to create a 'hybrid embryo' – a human egg fertilised by an animal's sperm (or vice versa) or an animal nucleus put into a human embryo (or vice versa) – but it bars them from allowing such hybrids to develop beyond fourteen days. Australian law also forbids placing a human embryo into an animal 'for any period of gestation', or an animal embryo in a human, but it does not seem to expressly bar placing a chimeric or hybrid embryo into either (although the rules on creation, importation and development presumably combine to forbid that). Rules like these – which, in Australia, are backed by potential prison sentences of up to fifteen years – aim to strictly preserve what it means to be 'human', while studiously avoiding defining that term. The Australian legislation simply provides that '"animal" does not include a human'. While there is no international treaty governing the creation of embryos, eighty-four member nations of the United Nations General Assembly voted in 2005 for a non-binding declaration that asks that all countries 'adopt the measures necessary to prohibit the application of genetic engineering techniques that may be contrary to human dignity'. In short, lawful humanity is an exclusive club for now.

Human Rights

As discussed in Chapter 6, being human is (usually) a requirement for access to multiple legal regimes, including the protections that statutes offer to 'persons' and the courts offer to those with 'standing'. In general, you must be human to have legal rights. That includes very general sorts of rights, usually known as 'human rights', which are commonly set out in modern international treaties and declarations, constitutions, the judge-made 'common law' and statutes.

The beneficiaries of these general rights are described in a variety of ways. Medieval England's Magna Carta – actually a complex set of narrow rights – is addressed to 'all free men of our kingdom'. France's Declaration of the Rights of Man and of the Citizen is, as its name suggests, explicitly about the rights of 'men' and 'citizens'. The United States' so-called Bill of Rights (the first ten amendments to the US Constitution) is mostly about limits on the power of the nation's government, but it also refers to the rights of 'the people', while its crucial post–Civil War Fourteenth Amendment (on due process and equal protection) applies to 'any person within its jurisdiction'. The United Nations postwar Universal Declaration of Human Rights is more explicit: 'All human beings are born free and equal in dignity and rights. They are endowed with reason and conscience and should act towards one another in a spirit of brotherhood.' In short, human rights laws are only for humans.

Human rights law can sometimes benefit non-humans, including animals, to the extent that it promotes the rights of humans who seek to protect them. One example is the right to protest. In 2017, former Australian senator Bob Brown successfully used one of the few human rights protected by the Australian Constitution to challenge Tasmanian laws that allowed police to stop protests in areas where commercial activities, such as forestry, were taking place. Brown had been arrested under those laws near the Lapoinya Forest, home to various endangered species such as the wedge-tailed eagle, after he refused to desist from protesting when asked. Australia's High Court struck down the anti-protest law because it targeted only protesters, was unclear about where protests could lawfully occur and was unnecessary in light of other laws that protected forestry activities from interference. But the court's sole concern was the rights of the protesters, not of the animals they were trying to protect.

The right applied by the High Court – freedom of political communication – is by no means a blanket protection for protesters, including animal advocates. Two decades earlier, the same court rejected a challenge to laws barring non-licence holders from Victorian duck-hunting sites during the official hunting season. While the judges accepted that protesting hunting on site was a more effective form of political communication than protesting somewhere else, they also agreed with the government that 'there was no greater curtailment of the constitutional freedom than was reasonably necessary to serve the public interest in the personal safety of citizens'. Given the dangers that the protesters might be accidentally shot, they upheld Victoria's law. In light of the court's rulings on the limits to freedom of political communication, several Australian jurisdictions have recently enacted new anti-protest laws aimed at animal rights groups that have been targeting various agricultural businesses.

Human rights law can also harm animals to the extent that it protects the rights of humans to do so. As discussed in Chapter 1, the native title rights provided by Australia's common law and now enforced by a federal statute include the right to hunt animals, overriding contrary state laws in some circumstances. In 1990, the Supreme Court of Canada ruled that a constitutional provision enacted in 1982 that affirms 'aboriginal rights' provides legal protection extending beyond the common law, treaties or past government practices.

In 1984, Ronald Sparrow, a member of the Musqueam Indian Band (a Canadian First Nations community), was prosecuted for using a 45-fathom net to fish for salmon, 20 fathoms longer than authorised by the band's fishing licence under British Columbian fisheries regulations. Expert evidence set out the traditions of the Coast Salish Indian people, including the Musqueam:

> The salmon was not only an important source of food but played an important part in the system of beliefs of the Salish people, and in their ceremonies. The salmon were held to be a race of beings that had, in 'myth times', established a bond with human beings requiring the salmon to come each year to give their bodies to the humans who, in turn, treated them with respect shown by performance of the proper ritual. Toward the salmon, as toward other creatures, there was an attitude of caution and respect which resulted in effective conservation of the various species.

Again, the purpose of the constitutional provision affirming aboriginal rights is to protect the rights of humans, not animals. However, in this case both were protected. The Supreme Court held that Sparrow's prosecution would require proof that the net length restriction did not burden indigenous traditions relating to food or ceremony and, if it did, that 'the brunt of conservation measures would be borne by the practices of sport fishing and commercial fishing'. In response, members of Canada's First Nations who wish to exercise their hunting traditions have been exempted from many animal conservation rules.

By contrast, in 2007, the United Kingdom's top court held that human rights law does not protect the English rural tradition of hunting foxes with dogs, which parliament had banned as cruel. The law lords – the nation's senior judges – held that the general right to respect for private life set out in Europe's human rights treaty does not extend to public activities like hunting.

Seeing Animals

A contemporary example of the mixed impact of human rights law on animals can be seen in videos and photos showing interactions between humans and other animals. Such images can have enormous power. Until recently, octopuses were widely regarded as vicious creatures, based on sailors' tales of octopuses attacking boats. In the mid-twentieth century, the sport of 'octopus wrestling' – in which swimmers would compete to drag octopuses onto boats – was briefly popular, until images revealed it to be an unequal contest. After octopus wrestling was banned and commercial fishing of octopuses was restricted, American divers continued to remove some octopuses by hand to supply restaurants, until photos taken by horrified onlookers in Seattle sparked a backlash.

In Chapter 6, we described how a number of animal rights organisations have tried to initiate cases about the mistreatment of animals in courts. These efforts have mostly failed, but they have been more successful in the court of public opinion, particularly when they can make the suffering of non-human animals visible in some way to humans. Recently, PETA has used the medium of video to campaign against the way octopuses are prepared as food:

> In September 2016, PETA went inside restaurants in Los Angeles that mutilate and serve live animals. At T Equals Fish, our observers watched in horror as chefs held down an octopus – nicknamed 'Pearl' by an observer – and cut off her sensitive limbs with a butcher knife. The severed limbs, which continued to move and react to stimuli, were served, squirming, to diners.

In some instances, PETA's placement of such videos on YouTube – under the headline, 'Can't stomach this video? Then do not stomach an octopus' – has prompted restaurants to take the cephalopods off their menu.

But the making and publication of videos of humans harming other animals can raise complex legal issues. In 2001, Australia's High Court considered whether videos of marsupials being prepared as food can be published without the consent of the human preparers. A Tasmanian company, Lenah Game Meats, which provided possum meat for export to China, sought (and initially obtained) an injunction to stop the national broadcaster from showing videos of brush-tailed possums being killed in its abattoir. The company's complaint was about how the video was obtained, as outlined to the court by its director:

> One camera was placed above the stunning area and one above the sticking area (which is where the throats are cut). I suspect that a third was placed above the boning room. The evidence which I have to support this is that as a result of Tasmania Police investigations I have observed holes which were cut in the roof of the facility. The holes were not cut from the outside. A person would have had to break in to the facility to cut the holes and place video cameras. The cameras were well hidden. They were not noticed by me or any other staff of [Lenah]. In one case the camera lens appeared to be a three millimetre optic fibre cable which had been drilled from one portion of the ceiling to another. Officers of the Tasmania Police have also located a number of items in and about [Lenah's] premises which are consistent with the surreptitious installation of video cameras.

In Chapter 5, we explained how the High Court recently ruled that videos of criminal conduct obtained via trespass cannot be used to prosecute people, but can be used to lead investigators to other evidence of such cruelty. In this case, Lenah Game Meats was not being prosecuted, and, indeed, the court assumed that the possums were killed lawfully and in compliance with animal cruelty guidelines. Rather, the abattoir wished to stop the public from seeing the videos, which had ended up in the hands of an animal rights group and then the national broadcaster. The abattoir feared that the videos would provoke a public backlash against both its business and the laws that permitted it to be carried out.

Broadly, cases like these raise difficult questions about how to strike a balance between the privacy of people carrying out lawful activities on their own land and the ability of others to show the public evidence of those activities. The High Court ruled that while Lenah Game Meats could object to an illegally obtained video being used as evidence against it in a courtroom, it could not object to such a video being shown on television – at least by a broadcaster who had no role itself in the illegality. The abattoir had tried to rely on the part of private law – the action for *breach of confidence* – that can allow a person who told someone something secret to go to court to prevent that secret being revealed to others. But the High Court declared that while commercial animal operations happen on private land, there is nothing secret about them:

> It is not suggested that the operations that were filmed were secret, or that requirements of confidentiality were imposed upon people who might see the operations. The abattoir is, no doubt, regularly visited by inspectors, and seen by other visitors who come to the premises for business or private reasons. The fact that the operations are required to be, and are, licensed by a public authority, suggests that information about the nature of those operations is not confidential. There is no evidence that, at least before the events giving rise to this case, any special precautions were taken by the respondent to avoid its operations being seen by people outside its organisation.

This means that an Australian court would not stop the broadcast of footage of octopuses being killed at a restaurant, even if that footage were taken by a customer sneaking into the restaurant's kitchen. A court may, however, prevent that footage from being shown if it was taken by a guest at someone's private home or by a disgruntled former employee of a restaurant.

Around the same time as this High Court decision was made, the US Congress enacted a law making it a crime to distribute a 'depiction of animal cruelty', defined to mean:

> any visual or auditory depiction ... in which a living animal is intentionally maimed, mutilated, tortured, wounded, or killed, if such conduct is illegal under federal law or the law of the state in which the creation, sale, or possession takes place, regardless of whether the maiming, mutilation, torture, wounding, or killing took place in the state.

This law was not designed to prevent the public exposure of cruel behaviour; indeed, it included an exception for 'any depiction that has serious religious, political, scientific, educational, journalistic, historical, or artistic value'. Rather, its purpose was to stop a new form of animal cruelty: the distribution of videos of animals being abused for human entertainment.

Five years later, Robert Stevens was prosecuted for selling 7000 videos showing dog fights, including pit bull fights in Japan (where the blood sport is legal). Stevens himself had no involvement in the fights themselves, but made money from selling the videos, which he narrated.

Appealing against a three-year prison sentence, Stevens argued that Congress's law breached his right to free speech. In 2010, the US Supreme Court agreed with Stevens. The problem, the court ruled, was that the law went well beyond its purpose of stopping cruel entertainment. First, 'maiming', 'wounding' and 'killing' an animal is not necessarily cruel; such acts also occur in legal, humane forms of killing. Second, such acts are not always cruel even when they are 'illegal', because laws that limit when and how animals can be harmed sometimes have different aims, such as conservation or even the vindication of private rights. Third, modern society's general condemnation of cruelty to animals hides a 'substantial disagreement on what types of conduct are properly regarded as cruel' – for instance, there is a wide variety of views on whether hunting is cruel, the judges noted.

The court's ruling meant that Stevens could not be prosecuted for selling videos of animal fights (even though it is illegal in much, if not all, of the United States to organise such fights). Likewise, no-one could be punished for selling videos of octopus wrestling or instructional videos about how to kill an octopus for food (even if such acts were also banned). It is worth noting that the same right to free speech would also prevent the US government banning depictions of cruelty to animals by hunters or food producers.

A similar approach could well apply to a ban on videos or images of the maiming, wounding or killing of humans. While there are far fewer examples of such acts that are not considered cruel, let alone 'inhumane', a ban preventing the distribution of controversial images such as wartime killings, euthanasia, capital punishment or public violence could also be struck down as infringing free speech, although it is possible that more specific arguments for such bans could be accepted in some instances.

In response to the US Supreme Court's decision to overturn its prohibition on distributing images of animal cruelty, the US Congress speedily enacted a new ban on a narrower range of images and videos, defined as any image or video that 'depicts actual conduct in which [one] or more living nonhuman mammals, birds, reptiles, or amphibians is intentionally crushed, burned, drowned, suffocated, impaled, or otherwise subjected to serious bodily injury' – but only if the image is 'obscene'. This new ban is narrowly targeted at the phenomenon of 'animal crush videos' where animals are seemingly killed for the gratification of a sexual fetish, and it relies on an analogy to bans of sexualised harm against humans that the Supreme Court has upheld.

The court has since rejected a constitutional challenge to this new law, which is notably narrower than its predecessor. It does not seem to cover scenes of animals fighting each other, which featured in the videos distributed by Stevens. Nor does it cover fake images of cruelty, using props, digital recreations or simulated harm. There are also express exceptions for depictions of customary practices and the slaughter of animals for the purposes of food production and hunting. Further exceptions were recently added for pest control, medical or scientific research, defence of life or property and the euthanising of animals. Finally, and most relevantly for octopuses, it does not cover all animals. That means that the new law not only permits the distribution of videos of octopus wrestling and slaughter, but also allows the distribution of 'obscene' images of octopuses being crushed or killed for entertainment. That is because octopuses are not mammals, birds, reptiles or amphibians.

The Rights of Non-Human Animals
Animal Dignity

We have already noted that the UN General Assembly's 1948 Universal Declaration of Human Rights states that 'all human beings are born free and equal in dignity and rights'. And the same body's 2005 declaration urged a ban on 'genetic engineering techniques that may be contrary to human dignity'. When Australia's High Court was considering the relative rights of a Tasmanian possum meat exporter to privacy and an Australian broadcaster to free speech, its chief justice commented that the 'foundation' of the right to privacy is 'human dignity', adding that 'this may be incongruous when applied to a corporation'. Australia, a latecomer to the practice of adopting 'bills' of rights, has, in recent years, seen the enactment of three statutes that expressly declare that 'only individuals' or 'human beings' have human rights. The intention of these declarations is to rule out the position taken by many overseas countries that corporations have some human rights. However, it is likely that these laws also rule out the rights of other categories of non-humans: groups, governments, non-corporate organisations, artificial beings, extra-terrestrials and, of course, non-human animals.

Everyone seems to accept that corporations do not have any dignity, even if most would hesitate to say the same about other groups of humans. But what about animals? Wild creatures (if not domesticated or farmed animals) are 'born free' – perhaps more so than humans. Are they born with 'dignity' too? In 1992, the Swiss Constitution was amended by referendum to address the issue of gene technology, which included requirements for the legislature to 'take account of the dignity of living beings as well as the safety of human beings, animals and the environment', a formulation that seems to potentially ascribe dignity not just to animals, but also to other forms of life, such as plants. Switzerland's top court, commenting on an animal welfare law that was implementing that provision, said, 'Even if [the dignity of other living beings] cannot and must not be equated with human dignity, it requires that living beings of nature, at least in certain respects, be reflected on and evaluated in the same way as people.'

In a famous decision in 2000, Justice Kurup of the High Court of Kerala (a state in India), argued that animals have more dignity than humans:

> Though not *Homo sapiens*, they are also beings entitled to dignified existences and humane treatment sans cruelty and torture. In many respects, they comport better than humans: they kill to eat and eat to live and not live to eat as some of us do, they do not practice deception, fraud, or falsehood and malpractices as humans do, they care for their little ones, expecting nothing. In return, they do not proliferate as we do, depleting the already scarce resources of the earth, for they practice sex restraint by seasonal mating, nor do they inhale the lethal smoke of tobacco, polluting the atmosphere and inflicting harm on fellow beings.

The court rejected an argument that a ban on the training and exhibition of bears, monkeys, tigers and panthers was contrary to the constitutional right of India's circus owners to a livelihood.

When thinking of dignified animals, felines and primates immediately come to mind, and, perhaps more slowly, most other mammals. Other creatures – snakes, slugs, ants – less so. Octopuses, routinely used as a metaphor in court cases when discussing the actions of some human groups, are rarely associated with dignity.

In 1994, when a fish market donated a Giant Pacific octopus it had caught to California's Cabrillo Marine Aquarium, making her the first such octopus to be displayed there, the museum's exhibits director cryptically explained that 'we don't name our animals because they have great regular names'. PETA, which criticised the museum's decision to place the octopus – which had twelve-foot limbs – in a six-foot tank, immediately dubbed her Octavia and publicly fretted that she might engage in self-mutilation. Worse happened three months after she was donated:

> Octavia the octopus was found dead Monday morning at the bottom of her waterless tank. Aquarium officials surmise that she used one of her powerful tentacles to pull off a plastic pipe that served as a water drain. With the pipe removed, water began to flow out faster than it was coming in. The end was inevitable. When a custodian arrived at 6.30 a.m., he found Octavia. On Monday afternoon, animal rights activist Kathy Yandell was in front of the aquarium carrying a sign bearing the word shame.

PETA demanded a necropsy and expressed outrage at the prospect that the octopus's remains would be put on public display.

Animal Suffering

In Chapter 5, we discussed the relatively modern movement to criminalise cruelty to animals. A prominent and early proponent of such laws was legal philosopher Jeremy Bentham, who in 1780 wrote:

> The French have already discovered that the blackness of the skin is no reason why a human being should be abandoned without redress to the caprice of a tormentor. It may come one day to be recognised that the number of the legs, the villosity of the skin, or the termination of the *os sacrum* [bone], are reasons equally insufficient for abandoning a sensitive being to the same fate. What else is it that should trace the insuperable line? Is it the faculty of reason, or, perhaps, the faculty of discourse? But a full-grown horse or dog is beyond comparison a more rational, as well as more conversable animal, than an infant of a day, or a week, or even a month, old. But suppose the case were otherwise, what would it avail? The question is not, Can they reason? Nor, Can they talk? But, Can they suffer?

Which non-human animals suffer? At one level, because of communication barriers, it is hard to know whether any non-humans suffer, though we can readily recognise what seem to be responses to pain in most mammals and many other chordates.

We have seen that in New South Wales, the criminal offence of 'serious animal cruelty' is limited to mammals, birds and reptiles. However, the state's ban on (less serious) 'animal cruelty' covers a broader range of animals, including 'a member of any vertebrate species' (and specifically amphibians and fish), as well as:

> a crustacean but only when at a building or place (such as a restaurant) where food is prepared or offered for consumption by retail sale in the building or place.

This caveat leaves wild crustaceans unprotected (by law, if not habitat) from human cruelty, but limits how creatures such as shellfish and lobsters are prepared and eaten. As David Foster Wallace famously described, the traditional method of boiling lobsters alive, which proponents claim does not cause the creatures pain, is hard to square with their behaviour when placed in the pot:

> If you're tilting it from a container into the steaming kettle, the lobster will sometimes try to cling to the container's sides or even to hook its claws over the kettle's rim like a person trying to keep from going over the edge of a roof. And worse is when the lobster's fully immersed. Even if you cover the kettle and turn away, you can usually hear the cover rattling and clanking as the lobster tries to push it off. Or the creature's claws scraping the sides of the kettle as it thrashes around. The lobster, in other words, behaves very much as you or I would behave if we were plunged into boiling water (with the obvious exception of screaming).

In New South Wales, government guidelines recommend placing lobsters in ice water for twenty minutes prior to speedily cutting their central nervous system, but allows for just the latter step to be taken if the lobster is being eaten raw or boiled. In 2017, a Sydney fishmonger was prosecuted and fined $1500 after RSPCA investigators filmed an employee sawing off a warm, living lobster's tail with a bandsaw.

But what of other invertebrates, such as octopuses? In 2010, the European Union added 'live cephalopods' to its directive on the protection of animals used for scientific purposes, because of 'scientific evidence of their ability to experience pain, suffering, distress and lasting harm'. Experiments (although they themselves raise some fraught ethical concerns) have been used to demonstrate that a variety of animals, including some fish, forego rewards such as food if the costs include pain or the benefits include relief from that pain, although there are no such direct experiments about invertebrates. In the case of octopuses, evidence of their apparent suffering comes from behaviour such as tending to injuries and avoiding being touched near wounds. The killing of live octopuses in restaurants typically involves the speedy, albeit brutal, method of crushing their brains. But even that step may not end the potential cruelty involved, as the majority of octopuses' neurons are in their limbs, which continue to move – and perhaps suffer – well after their brain is destroyed, and even as they are eaten.

Animal Sentience

While Bentham sternly defended the practice of eating animals (so long as they were not kept or killed cruelly), he nevertheless made a far-sighted prediction: 'A time will come when humanity will spread its mantle over everything that breathes.' It is not clear whether he was only thinking of things that breathe air, or whether he would also include animals that breathe by passing water through their gills, including octopuses, whose gills are inside *their* mantle. Whatever Bentham meant, his prediction is yet to be fulfilled. Nevertheless, recent years have seen some jurisdictions extend the mantle of various human laws to cover 'sentient' animals.

Reflecting the animal cruelty statutes of several European nations, article 13 of the current European Union treaty states:

> In formulating and implementing the Union's agriculture, fisheries, transport, internal market, research and technological development and space policies, the Union and the member states shall, since animals are sentient beings, pay full regard to the welfare requirements of animals, while respecting the legislative or administrative provisions and customs of the member states relating in particular to religious rites, cultural traditions and regional heritage.

New Zealand's *Animal Welfare Act 1999* includes, as the first of its several purposes, 'to recognise that animals are sentient'. The part of the statute that addresses the use of animals in research, testing and teaching includes two specific purposes:

(iii) to replace animals as subjects for research, and testing by substituting, where appropriate, non-sentient or non-living alternatives

(iv) to replace the use of animals in teaching by substituting for animals, where appropriate, non-sentient or non-living alternatives or by imparting the information in another way.

New Zealand animal ethics committees are accordingly obliged to examine all research, testing and teaching proposals to check whether consideration has been given to such substitutions.

As noted in Chapter 1, the Australian Capital Territory recently amended its law to provide for, as the first of several purposes, the recognition of animals as 'sentient beings that are able to subjectively feel and perceive the world around them'. However, the statute does not otherwise refer to animal sentience, and the change was not accompanied by broad legal protections for all animals (although new protections were added to prevent dogs from being left in hot cars and to require Canberra residents to report injured mammals).

Such laws do not necessarily recognise that *all* animals are sentient. Both the New Zealand and Australian Capital Territory laws define 'animal' in a narrower way. The Australian Capital Territory law specifies:

Animal means –

(a) a live member of a vertebrate species, including –

(i) an amphibian; and

(ii) a bird; and

(iii) a fish; and

(iv) a mammal (other than a human being); and

(v) a reptile; or

(b) a live cephalopod; or

(c) a live crustacean intended for human consumption.

This definition notably includes some invertebrate species (including octopuses), but crustaceans are limited to those 'intended for human consumption' (as in the New South Wales legislation). By contrast, New Zealand's law, and its goal of recognising sentience, applies to all lobsters and crayfish, not just those that will be eventually eaten by a human.

The word 'sentient' can carry many different meanings, including the ability to feel pain or – as the Australian Capital Territory law indicates – the ability of the animal to 'subjectively feel or perceive' anything 'around' itself. A definition that lands somewhere between these options was suggested in 2005 by John Webster, a professor of animal husbandry:

> A sentient animal is therefore a feeling animal, where the word feeling implies much more than simply responding to sensation. A frog with its head removed but spinal cord intact will respond to a harmful 'nociceptive' stimulus to its foot by withdrawing its leg. A sentient animal, such as a rat, will respond similarly to a similarly nociceptive stimulus such as an electric shock from the floor of its cage. If these shocks are repeated, the rat will learn to associate them not only with the acute sensation of pain but also with an emotional sense of distress and will be motivated to seek ways to avoid receiving further shocks. If it is helpless to avoid repetition of the stimulus it will display anxiety which may progress to profound depression. The sentient animal therefore demonstrates both a physical reflex to the stimulus and an emotional response, i.e. distress.

This definition requires more than just sensing things, which all living things, including insects and even plants, can do to a degree. Webster's shorthand is that 'A sentient animal is one for whom feelings matter,' although he leaves it ambiguous as to whom the feelings matter. The feelings could matter to the animal itself, but it could be enough if the feelings just matter to humans. Such feelings could even cover PETA's outrage about the display of Octavia's remains by the Cabrillo Marine Aquarium. (Bentham himself may not have shared those feelings. His will famously requested that his body be preserved and placed on display, clothed and sitting upright. Indeed, his body – but not his head – is presently on display at the student centre of University College London.)

Webster's shorthand goes some way to explaining why the Australian Capital Territory's definition of 'animal' is limited to 'live' animals. As we have observed, an octopus has neurons in its limbs that allow them to sense things independently of its brain – even if its brain has been destroyed. However, it seems likely, if not certain, that those feelings cannot matter to an octopus whose brain has been destroyed. The position is more complex and controversial for pre-birth animals. New Zealand law's definition of 'animal' includes 'any mammalian foetus, or any avian or reptilian pre-hatched young, that is in the last half of its period of gestation or development', as well as 'any marsupial pouch young', but it expressly excludes any other animal 'in the prenatal, pre-hatched, larval, or other such developmental stage'. The Australian Capital Territory, by referring in a blanket way to 'live' animals, leaves the status of fetuses, pouch young, pre-hatched animals and the early stages of other creatures – such as cephalopods and crustaceans – quite unclear.

Putting these boundary issues aside, what remains clear is that many animals that are not considered sentient are excluded from the protection of Australian and most (perhaps all) overseas animal law. As noted in Chapter 6, among such exclusions are insects and most invertebrates, which can be killed cruelly without legal barrier – be they butterflies having their wings pulled off, salt-covered slugs, or jellyfish, which have their own quiet dignity. Moreover, in much of Australian animal law, and notably in New South Wales law, octopuses are excluded.

The common feature of all of these examples is their biological distance from humans. All mammals have a common ancestor that lived around 100 million years ago (the descendants of which miraculously survived the asteroid strike that killed off the non-avian dinosaurs 50 million years ago) and all vertebrates have a much older common ancestor in a fish that, while probably very odd-looking to modern eyes, was nevertheless probably as sentient as most fish today. By contrast, the common ancestor of humans and octopuses was likely a worm that lived some 600 million years ago and was no more sentient than modern worms are. And yet, it seems that sentience can – albeit perhaps rarely – evolve more than once. As legal scholar Amia Srinivasan observed:

Other creatures that are so evolutionarily distant from humans – lobsters, snails, slugs, clams – rate pretty low on the cognitive scale.

But octopuses – and to some extent their cephalopod cousins, cuttle-fish and squid – frustrate the neat evolutionary division between clever vertebrates and simple-minded invertebrates. They are sophisticated problem solvers; they learn, and can use tools; and they show a capacity for mimicry, deception and, some think, humour. Just how refined their abilities are is a matter of scientific debate: their very strangeness makes octopuses hard to study. Their intelligence is like ours, and utterly unlike ours. Octopuses are the closest we can come, on Earth, to knowing what it might be like to encounter intelligent aliens.

Hence, the growing contemporary view that octopuses are sentient.

The United Kingdom was one of the first nations to (quietly) acknowledge the intelligence of octopuses when a brief regulation was promulgated by Minister Michael Howard (then home secretary, later leader of the Conservative Party in opposition), which included in its definition of 'protected animal' 'any invertebrate of the species *Octopus vulgaris* [the common octopus] from the stage of its development when it becomes capable of independent feeding'. This meant that the octopus was to be treated like vertebrates for the purposes of the law on animal experimentation. With much less far-sightedness or ambition than Bentham, we are confident that the time will soon come when octopuses are included in all animal welfare statutes, whether in Australia or overseas.

Animal Rights

To what end, though? The best-known feature of some human rights laws, most famously the US Bill of Rights, is the empowerment of judges to overrule an elected government on myriad issues, be they questions of life or death, or finer questions of how to balance different people's rights or broader interests. None of the laws recognising the dignity, suffering or sentience of animals give any court such a role, at least generally speaking. Rather, such recognition, if it is not merely symbolic, is expressed through more specific laws, such as criminal offences for animal cruelty or restrictions on animal killing, experimentation, exhibition or captivity. Even these rules are typically hedged by more detailed rules that preserve (in a regulated form) human activities such as eating animals, hunting animals, keeping pets and playing sports involving animals. As discussed in Chapter 6, enforcing such laws requires human support, and courts limit who can provide that, often to the point where questions of enforcement are left entirely to the discretion of government agencies.

There are proposals to change this approach, but only in relation to a few animals. The aim of one of the most prominent of these, the Great Ape Project, is to have the United Nations adopt a World Declaration on Great Apes, extending three human rights to five non-human species:

1. Right to life

The lives of all great primates must be protected. The individuals cannot be killed, with exception for extremely specific situations, such as self-defense.

2. Individual freedom protection

Great primates cannot be deprived, in an arbitrary way, from their freedom. They have the right to live in their habitat. Great primates who live in captivity have the right to live with dignity, in large rooms, to have contact with others of their species, to form families, and must be protected from commercial exploitation.

3. Prohibition of torture

Intentional imposition of intense pain, physically or psychologically, to a great primate, with no reason or to others' benefits, is considered a kind of torture and is an offense from which they must be protected.

Tellingly, this proposal aims to protect humanity's five closest relatives, and of course represents a much narrower list of rights than most human governments have guaranteed to humans.

It is also possible that milder rights protections could be extended more generously to more animals. Australia's approach to human rights law is mostly the opposite of the United States': with a handful of exceptions, Australian judges are not allowed to overrule statutes that breach human rights. Rather, Australian human rights law is mainly about ensuring that human rights are considered at various points in the system: when laws are proposed and enacted, when they are interpreted by courts and others, and when they are applied and implemented by government agencies. While this milder system of rights protection certainly has its downsides, it is a system that could be feasibly extended to sentient animals.

For example, in our home state of Victoria, all proposed laws must now include a 'statement of compatibility' detailing the possible impact of the proposal on human rights, and justifying (or at least owning) any unreasonable restrictions on those rights. One of the authors of this book (Jeremy Gans) has, for many years, advised a parliamentary committee that provides a measure of independent review of the impact of such proposals on human rights.

An elected member of the Animal Welfare Party recently opted to include a statement about the rights of animals in a bill that proposed outlawing duck-hunting:

> This Bill, drafted in order to protect certain birds in Victoria, recognises, and is compatible with, the Universal Declaration of Animal Rights solemnly proclaimed in Paris on 15 October 1978 at the UNESCO headquarters and revised in 1990, which states that:
>
>> All animals are born with an equal claim on life and the same rights to existence.
>>
>> Humans, as a species of animal shall not arrogate to him or herself the right to exterminate or inhumanely exploit other animals.
>>
>> No animal shall be ill-treated or shall be subject to cruel acts.
>>
>> All wild animals have the right to liberty in their natural environment, whether land air or water.
>>
>> Deprivation of freedom, even for educational purposes, is an infringement of this right.
>>
>> The rights of animals, like human rights, should enjoy the protection of law.
>
> This Bill furthers the recognition that non-human animals are sentient individuals with their own intelligence, emotion and subjective experience of life [and] that they have a fundamental right of birth to enjoy without the risk of being hunted, taken and destroyed.

While this law probably won't be enacted, its compatibility statement shows how Victorian human rights law could potentially be extended to allow scrutiny of the impact that all new laws have on the rights of sentient animals.

Courts and government agencies could also be required to consider and, in some instances, minimise such impacts when they interpret and implement statutes. This has occurred on several occasions in India, the Constitution of which states that 'compassion for living creatures' is one of the 'fundamental duties' of 'every citizen in India'. The Supreme Court of India calls this provision (together with another requiring the development of 'humanism') 'the Magna Carta of animal rights', because it can allow mere statutory rules 'to be elevated to the status of fundamental rights, as has been done by few countries around the world, so as to secure [animals'] honour and dignity'. Those rights, the court said, includes rights against 'speciesism' ('a prejudice or attitude of bias towards the interests of members of one's own species and against those of members of other species') and to 'life' ('something more than mere survival or existence or instrumental value for human beings, but to lead a life with some intrinsic worth, honour and dignity').

In 2014, the Supreme Court of India applied those rights to rule that bulls cannot be used in traditional cultural events such as racing, 'since they are basically draught and pack animals, not anatomically designed for such performances'. However, the Supreme Court only did so to determine whether a national statute overrides a local one. The judges added, however, that they expected parliament to strengthen the statute and elevate animal rights as constitutional ones. While using animal rights to interpret human laws in this way still falls well short of what Bentham contemplated – and indeed what a World Declaration on Great Apes would require – it is a step towards a rights law that protects all creatures.

Coda: Being Animals

In 1987, American writer Fleur Cowles published a gimmicky book called *If I Were an Animal*, in which 100 celebrities answered the question: 'What would you choose to be if you could be reincarnated as an animal?' For reasons we will explain, the book is now quite rare and pricey, but we know from book reviews that cats of various sorts were the favourite choice of celebrities, with dogs a close second, and horses and birds the next most popular. Somewhat more interesting choices included a giraffe, an otter and a chameleon. However, as *The Boston Globe* noted, none chose 'that vexatious animal, man'.

The book was a fundraiser for the World Wildlife Fund, so some of the choices were less frivolous: the organisation's director chose an endangered species, the elephant, because 'it doesn't abuse its power', while the head of Nigeria's conservation foundation chose a kudu, 'a rare and uniquely handsome antelope'. British actress Twiggy was likewise influenced by her own campaigning for animal welfare:

> Most entertainers, from time to time, suffer from being misquoted and misused by the all-powerful and inventive press. The animal I would most like to re-enter the world as similarly has suffered from being misunderstood, with a fearsome image far removed from the reality of its gentle, unassuming life pattern. My choice is the gorilla.

Perhaps reflecting an era when cephalopods were still regarded as dangerous, odd and tasty, it seems no-one chose the octopus.

Much more recently, a celebrity chef, Cat Cora, announced to a television host that she would like to be an octopus, but, alas, not for the expected reasons:

> If I was an octopus – if I was a baby octopus … if I was given to a gourmet restaurant, oh, my God – like a three-star restaurant. And I'm on the grill, and I'm so tenderly marinated … Oh, my God, rubbed and massaged before I was cooked and eaten … I mean, hello? Or you want to swim in the ocean all your life?

Suffice to say that we would.

What drew us to Cowles' book, and somewhat restored our faith in our fellow humans, was the book's foreword by Prince Philip, the Duke of Edinburgh, then the president of the World Wildlife Fund:

> It is easy enough to feel an affinity to a particular species of animal, but I just wonder what it would be like to be reincarnated in an animal whose species had been so reduced in numbers that it was in danger of extinction. What would be its feelings towards the human species whose population explosion had denied it somewhere to exist and by sheer indifference had destroyed any chance of it finding a mate and

producing a family? There are not just a few such species, there are a great many and the list is getting longer every day. When I look at the shelf with all the volumes of Red Data Books listing endangered species I must confess that I am tempted to ask for reincarnation as a particularly deadly virus, but that is perhaps going too far. I would much rather see the human species voluntarily restrict its numbers out of consideration for the rest of the living world with which it still has a chance of sharing this planet.

At the start of 2020's coronavirus pandemic, this quote sparked rumours that Prince Philip had died. The quote was widely repeated when the Duke of Edinburgh did in fact die a year later, sparking a run on the available copies of this long out-of-print book.

We enjoyed many of Prince Philip's famous and infamous quotes, but especially this one, for the clear care it shows for all animals, not to mention his willingness to imagine himself as a much smaller and different creature. Like the late prince, we would not go so far as to plump for a virus, but we are motivated to think outside the box and look for many ways to coexist with other animals, big and small. That includes all the laws, big and small, that we have addressed in this book and which we hope will eventually spread humanity's mantle to all of the world's animals.

Authors' Note

This feels like a book that we were fated to write – a book that came about as a result of a series of lucky chances because it wanted (and perhaps needed) to be written.

It all started in 2017, when we were having a lunch meeting and discussing the case of *Isbester v Knox City Council* in our capacity as editors of *Opinions on High*, the Melbourne Law School's blog on decisions made by the High Court of Australia. Conversation then turned to other animal cases we knew about, and because we both have very broad legal interests, there were many.

'Gosh,' said Jeremy, 'we could almost write a book about this!'

'Actually, I've always wanted to write a book about animals and the law!' said Katy. One of her friends, Dave, had been urging her to write such a book for over ten years.

We began to write the sections that later turned into sections of Chapters 3 and 6, and we put together a pitch. One of Katy's former students approached a publisher he had worked for, but the publisher was not interested in the book at all. We were rather crestfallen, and shelved the idea for the time being.

Then, in 2019, matters of academic publishing were in the news again. In a Twitter conversation with another academic, Katy noted that the publisher she had approached about *Guilty Pigs* had been dismissive, which she thought was a pity. Luckily for us, Chris Feik of Black Inc./La Trobe University Press read the tweet and his curiosity was piqued. He asked us to send him our pitch and a sample chapter. We are so honoured by his faith in our idea. We reassembled our pitch and sent it through. Thus, our pet project found a home.

The area of animal law was even more topical and fascinating than we could have envisaged. It turns out that there are not many other books looking at how the law engages with animals as a matter of reality and history – books in this area tend to be written from an animal rights perspective, considering how the law *should* engage with animals to protect their rights. While we do consider this line of thought, along with the legal protection of animals and the ways that humans harm animals, that is not the sole focus of this book.

Our general starting point was Australian law, but we ended up exploring a broad range of legal systems, cultures and eras. It is fascinating what this tells us – about humanity itself as much as about animals.

We are both passionate about making the law accessible to nonlegal people, and hence we want this book to be read by everyone, not just lawyers. To this end, we have tried to explain basic legal concepts in a way that is approachable and understandable. We also decided against footnotes – a ubiquitous feature of legal writing – and instead put all references at the back for those who are interested (along with information on where to look up those resources).

Two notes on terminology: we sometimes use the phrase 'non-human animals'. The fact is, of course, that humans are a species of animal too, although people do not always like to acknowledge this, and the law tends to draw a sharp distinction between us and them. Secondly, we mostly use the term 'companion animal' in place of the more colloquial word 'pet' to reflect the reality that for many people, companion animals are an important part of the family, a fact that the law does not handle well in a variety of contexts (including family breakdown and injury to animals).

The laws and stories described in this book are a strange mixture: sometimes hilarious or ridiculous, sometimes utterly tragic and deeply disturbing. When we examined the tragic and disturbing material we tried to deal with it as sensitively as possible. We have found all the tales invariably fascinating, and we hope you have too.

Katy Barnett and Jeremy Gans, Melbourne, 2021

Acknowledgements

I particularly wants to thank Dave Bath for telling me to write this book over fifteen years ago, after noting my obsession with animals and the law – his insistence that people would love it convinced me it was a worthy idea; Jeremy Gans for joining me in this project; and Lucy 'Tilly' Houghton for her research assistance (I wish so dearly that she could see the final product).

So many people have been enthusiastic supporters of the project, drawing my attention to animal cases and resources from all over the world and throughout history, reading draft chapters and helping me translate and find things: thank you to Jonathan Ainslie, Jennika Anthony-Shaw, Christine Balint-Smith, Lynne Barnett (hi, Mum!), Luke Besse, Ashleigh Best, Philip Britton, Simon Bogli, Sara M. Butler, Geert van Calster, Mat Campbell, Chelsea Candy, John Cannon, Jianlin Chen, Eva Cohen Steiner, David Coombe, Helen Dale, Gillian Dempsey, Chris Devery, Shaunnagh Dorsett, Bronwen Ewens, Debra Franklin, Neil James Foster, William Gelley, Rebecca Giblin, Meg Good, Matthew Harding, Tim Harding, Martin Roland Hill, Amanda Humphreys, Andre Janssen, Anne Kallies, Gabriel Kanter-Webber, Bernard Lane, Tania Leiman, Rachel Leow, Inbar Levy, David Marks QC, Philip Mandie, Andrea Matwyshyn, Joanna McCunn, Jani McCutcheon, Donald McDonald, Paul McGorrery, Julian Murphy, Jenny Ng, Eoin O'Dell, Erin O'Donnell, Pietro Ortolani, Helen Pringle, Paul du Plessis, Michelle Sharpe, Peter Sheppard, Lionel Smith, Joshua Snukal, Tim Staindl Matthews, Bill Swadling, Michael Symons, Mara Tam, Andrew Tettenborn, Rabbi Alex Tsykin, Zeev Vinokurov, 'Lorenzo' M. Warby, Trent Williams, Dominic Villa SC, Derek Whayman, Bill Whitehead and Melissa Wood.

I would also like to thank all my Twitter buddies (many of whom overlap with the list above, and with the people Jeremy names below). I have valued their enthusiasm and support.

Finally, thanks to my family and friends for putting up with 'interesting facts' about animals and the law at random intervals, and to the budgies, Simmer, Flapjack and Duck, for keeping me company in lockdown.

Katy Barnett

I would like to thank my PhD supervisor and co-author, Professor Jill Hunter, for sparking my interest in the law on dogs; Katy Barnett, for turning an idle conversation into a pitch, an initial rejection into a public discussion, and public discussion into a book contract; and Melbourne Law School, for letting me teach criminal law in a way that was less about the wrongs humans can do to each other and more about the way criminal law affects the lives of everyone, including animals.

My colleagues at Melbourne Law School – especially Matthew Bell, Andrew Godwin, Judith Marychurch, James Parker, Andy Roberts, Peter Rush, Stephen Sempill and Dale Smith – have prompted my thinking about the law, and especially statutes, in many ways, as have interactions with many members of parliament through my advisory work for the Scrutiny of Acts and Regulations Committee.

More recently, I have been constantly entertained and challenged by acquaintances on Twitter, many of whom I have not met in person and some whose identity I continue to wonder about, including (in addition to the many we have listed already) @babbyunit, Jarryd Bartle, @CriminalLaw-Aus, Michael Fitzgerald, Sarah Joseph, Chris Kaias, Julia Kretzenbacher, Steve McDonald, Joe McIntyre, Juliette McIntyre, Paul McGorrery, Lisa Parker, Ken Parish and Felix Ralph.

My family, Denise, Zac and Elijah, have, as always, patiently given me time to think and write, not to mention two animals – Mr Moomar and Mahalo – to conduct legal thought experiments on.

Jeremy Gans

Jointly, we want to thank the following people. First, Black Inc./La Trobe University Press for approaching us and taking us on after we had given up on the idea (thanks are due to Chris Feik and Kate Hatch in particular). Second, Carole Hinchcliff and the marvellous staff at the University of Melbourne Library for sourcing sometimes obscure material for us, even during our extended Covid-19 lockdown in Melbourne. Finally, our colleague Christine Parker for being such an invaluable second reader and supplier of sanity in the midst of lockdown. In particular, she organised a daylong discussion of the draft of the book at a critical point, at which we received invaluable comments from her, Nick Ampt, Ashleigh Best, Leo Bromberg, Laura Boehm and Joanna Kyriakakis. As we and everyone else kept pointing out that day, participating in discussions like that is the reason we chose to become academics.

Katy Barnett and Jeremy Gans

Sources

Introduction: Animals' Laws

Law books typically make heavy use of formal footnotes, full of legal and academic abbreviations and the like, but – with our publisher's blessing – we have opted for a less formal and more accessible method of explaining our sources.

Cases

Isbester v Knox City Council has three judgments. The 'citations' for these judgments – a shorthand lawyers use to locate cases, a bit like an internet address – are:

- [2014] VSC 286.
- [2014] VSCA 214.
- [2015] HCA 20.

The first numbers in square brackets are, of course, the years in which the cases were decided. The next set of letters are abbreviations for the courts that made the decisions: Victoria's Supreme Court, Victoria's Supreme Court of Appeal (usually just known as the Victorian Court of Appeal) and the High Court of Australia. The numbers at the end indicate where the cases fall in the relevant court's list of judgments for the year – for example *Isbester* was the High Court of Australia's twentieth judgment in 2015.

All three judgments are freely available online on every Australian lawyer's favourite website, Australasian Legal Information Institute, or AustLII (www.austlii.edu.au). You can find cases on the site by browsing through each court's list for the relevant year or by using the LawCite interface or search bar. This book discuss a lot of cases, and not all of them are so easy to find. Older cases and some overseas cases can only be found in a law library or on commercial databases. Still, it's always worth checking AustLII (or the World Legal Information Institute website).

Another case mentioned in this chapter, which ruled that people injured by dogs must either prosecute or prove *scienter*, is an older one: *Lane v Casey* (1886) 12 VLR 380. In this citation, 1886 is the year, VLR stands for *Victorian Law Reports*, 12 is the volume number and 380 is the page number. But you don't need to go to a law library to read a physical copy of the case: AustLII has it for free in scanned form. If you find it via the website's LawCite interface, you'll also see that other cases that refer to *Lane* are also listed. This is a good way to find more information about the legal issues relevant to a case. For example, *Johnson v Buchanan* [2012] VSC 195 contains a neat history of both *scienter* and Victoria's dog legislation.

Court rulings are important for lots of reasons. One reason is that, while parliaments make statutes, and governments implement them, the courts make the final decision on what a statute means. Courts – especially senior ones – also determine the content of, and sometimes change, the judge-made law (also known as common law and equity). Courts that are more junior are required to follow the lead of senior courts by obeying past decisions those courts have made on how statutes should be read or how judge-made law works. These decisions are known as precedents. However, courts need to decide whether the precedent applies to the dispute before them or whether the dispute is different in some way (the latter is known as 'distinguishing' the precedent). If a parliament disagrees with a court's ruling, it can always change the law itself, although typically that change only applies to future disputes. Parliaments cannot usually change constitutions, so courts – normally the highest court in the land – have the final say on the powers of most parliaments.

Reading this book, you will note that we sometimes have to explain past law in England to explain why the law exists in its current form in Australia today. Upon colonisation, we were initially governed by Britain, and almost all our law was imposed upon us by Australia's colonisers. However, Australian Indigenous groups had a different, pre-existing set of laws, and some have survived colonisation, as can be seen in land rights law and the way Indigenous groups' relationships with the government are defined. In any case, during the twentieth century, the Commonwealth of Australia gradually became legally separate from the UK parliament and England's courts. That separation was formally confirmed in 1986, when both the United Kingdom and Australian parliaments enacted the Australia Acts. The connection nevertheless remains, as the two nations share the same head of state, some English statutes (such as parts of the Magna Carta) continue to apply in Australia and our shared legal history means there are many overlaps and much cross-referencing between our laws.

Statutes

The statute that governed *Isbester* is the *Domestic Animals Act 1994* (Vic.). Note that 1994 is the year the statute was enacted, and 'Vic.' is a shorthand for Victoria, the state parliament that enacted it. You can find Australian statutes on AustLII, but the quickest way to find current statutes is to visit the Legify website (https://legify.com.au). Because statutes are very complex documents that get changed quite often, lawyers often like to use the official version of the statute, which can be found on the relevant government's website. Most government websites provide both the current and older versions of the law. For example, Victoria's website (www.legislation.vic.gov.au) allows you to find the version of the *Domestic Animals Act* that applied in 2012, when Izzy and Jock went to the basin (version 56). When that statute was originally enacted in 1994, it had a different name, the *Domestic (Feral and Nuisance Animals) Act 1994*.

Secondary Sources

Cases and statutes are known as 'primary' sources of law. But lawyers and academics, including ourselves, use a variety of secondary sources, including books, academic articles, newspaper stories and more. There are two ways to locate these sources. One is by going to a major library, such as the state or national library of a capital city, and asking a librarian for help. Another is to search Google. Note that some rare sources can only be found by using a commercial database or going to a very specific library.

For *Isbester*, additional information is available on the High Court's website, where you can read the written submissions each side made and transcripts of the argument before the five judges, and the Knox City Council website, where you can read reports from the second panel that looked at Izzy's fate. The reports of the first panel, if they were ever posted online, are no longer available.

Our discussion of *Isbester v Knox City Council* is mainly based on the courts' reasoning, but it also draws on newspaper reports and other sources. Indeed, the discussion begins well before Isbester sued her council, covering a range of incidents and other legal proceedings that provided a background to the issue that the High Court decided. Many of those earlier incidents were not the subject of official 'reports' issued by the courts or by legal publishers, so most of what we know about them was reported (hopefully accurately) in the press coverage of Isbester's case against Knox City Council. The official reports are not the end of the case either – life goes on, and we do our best in this book, wherever possible, to describe the ultimate outcome of each case beyond the court's decision. *Isbester* received a fair amount of newspaper coverage. Some of this can be found via a Google search, but we largely relied on a commercial database called Factiva, which is available at universities. We especially used reports from *The Knox Leader*, the recently closed newspaper that covered all things in that part of Melbourne.

1. *Owning Animals*

The case of the runaway Japanese macaque, which we use as a running example throughout this chapter, is *Nakhuda v Story Book Farm Primate Sanctuary* [2013] ONSC 5761. Further detail was gleaned from 'Judge: Ikea Monkey Will Not Be Returned to Former Owner', *The Canadian Press*, 13 September 2013.

The quote about the concept of property is from *Yanner v Eaton* [1999] HCA 53, [17] (Gleeson CJ, Gaudron, Kirby and Hayne JJ). The reference to Professor Gray is from Kevin Gray, 'Property in Thin Air', *Cambridge Law Journal*, vol. 50, no. 2, 1991, pp. 252–307.

For information on the domestication of animals, we consulted Melinda A. Zeder, 'Pathways to Animal Domestication', in P. Gepts, T.R. Famula, R.L. Bettinger et al. (eds), *Biodiversity in Agriculture: Domestication, Evolution and Sustainability*, Cambridge University Press, Cambridge, 2012, p. 227, and Fabrice Teletchea, 'Animal Domestication: A Brief Overview', in Fabrice Teletchea (ed.),

Animal Domestication, IntechOpen, London, 2019.

For historical accounts of English law, we used Henry de Bracton, *On the Laws and Customs of England*, ed. G.E. Woodbine, transl. S.E. Thorne, 4 vols, Harvard University Press, Cambridge, MA, 1968–77, and William Blackstone, *Commentaries on the Laws of England*, John Exshaw, Dublin, 1769.

On Roman law, we used Paul J. Du Plessis, *Borkowski's Textbook on Roman Law*, 6th ed., Oxford University Press, Oxford, 2020. We also consulted Alan Watson (ed.), *The Digest of Justinian*, vol. 4, University of Pennsylvania Press, Philadelphia, 1998, specifically 41.1.1–41.1.6, 41.3.2, 41.1.5.2–41.1.5.6, 47.2.37.

Parallels with Slavery

On slavery and the use of Irish slave girls as currency, we consulted Paul Einzig, 'Slave Girl Money of Ireland', in Paul Einzig, *Primitive Money: In Its Ethnological, Historical and Economic Aspects*, Pergamon Press, Oxford, 1966.

The main theorist who equates ownership of animals to slavery is Gary L. Francione in *Animals, Property, and the Law*, Temple University Press, Philadelphia, 1995.

The case in which an offender sought to be released from jail because the prosecutor had compared him to a hornet's nest is *In re Pers. Restraint of Richmond*, 482 P.3d 971 (Wash. Ct. App. 2021).

The slavery cases referred to are: *Pearne v Lisle* (1749) Amb. 76, 27 ER 47 and *Somersett v Stewart* (1772) Lofft 1, 98 ER 499. The two earlier cases that Lord Hardwicke overruled in *Pearne* are *Chamberlain v Harvey* (1697) 1 Ld Raym. 146, 91 ER 994 and *Smith v Gould* (1705–07) 2 Salk. 666, 91 ER 567.

The *Abolition of the Slave Trade Act 1807* (47 Geo III Sess. 1, c. 36) made it illegal to engage in the slave trade in England. The *Slavery Abolition Act 1833* (3 & 4 Will. 4, c. 73) made the purchase or ownership of slaves illegal within the British Empire, with the exception of 'the Territories in the possession of the East India Company' in Ceylon (now Sri Lanka) and Saint Helena.

Research shows that humans don't have genetically distinct races (but that chimpanzees do): Alan R. Templeton, "Biological Races in Humans," *Studies in History and Philosophy of Science Part C: Studies in History and Philosophy of Biological and Biomedical Sciences*, vol. 44, no. 3, 2013, pp. 262–460.

The civilian provisions that say that animals are not property are as follows:

- Civil Code of Catalonia, bk V, art. 511-1(3): 'Animals, which are not considered things, are under the special protection of the laws. The rules of goods only apply to them to the extent that their nature allows.'

- Civil Code of Czech Republic, 2012, s. 494: 'A living animal has a special significance and value as a living creature endowed with senses. A living animal is not a thing, and the provisions on things apply, by analogy, to a living animal only to the extent in which they are not contrary to its nature.'

- Civil Code of Quebec, 1991, bk 4, s. 898.1: 'Animals are not things. They are sentient beings and have biological needs. In addition to the provisions of special Acts which protect animals, the provisions of this Code and of any other Act concerning property nonetheless apply to animals.'

- French Civil Code, Feb. 2014, art. 515–14: 'Animals are living beings endowed with sentience. Subject to the laws that protect them, animals are subject to the regime of tangible goods.'

- General Civil Code of Austria, 1812 (1988 amendment), s. 285a: 'Animals are not things; they are protected by special laws. The regulations applicable to things are only applicable to animals to the extent that there are no other regulations.'

- German Civil Code, 2 Jan. 2002 (revised version), s. 90a: 'Animals are not things. They are protected by special statutes. They are governed by the provisions that apply to things, with the necessary modifications, except insofar as otherwise provided.'

- Netherlands Civil Code, bk 3, title 3.1, art. 3:2a: '1. Animals are not things. 2. Provisions relating to things are applicable to animals, with due observance of the limitations, obligations and legal principles based on statutory rules and rules of unwritten law, as well as of public order and public morality.'

- Swiss Civil Code, 1907, art. 641a: '1. Animals are not objects. 2. Where no special provisions exist for animals, they are subject to the provisions governing objects.'

Animal sentience provisions have also been passed in New Zealand and the Australian Capital Territory:

- *Animal Welfare Act 1992* (ACT), s. 4A.

- *Animal Welfare Act 1999* (NZ).

Theorists who argue that a 'quasi-property' approach to animals is better include David Favre, 'Living Property: A New Status for Animals within the Legal System', *Marquette Law Review*, vol. 93, no. 3, 2010, pp. 1021–70, and 'Animals as Living Property', in Linda Kalof (ed.) *The Oxford Handbook of Animals Studies*, Oxford University Press, Oxford, 2017; Angela Fernandez, 'Not Quite Property, Not Quite Persons: A "Quasi" Approach for Nonhuman Animals', *Canadian Journal of Comparative and Contemporary Law*, vol. 5, no. 1, 2019, pp. 155–232.

Ownership of Wild Animals

For a description of the hunting roles of chimpanzees, see Christophe Boesch, 'Cooperative Roles among Taï Chimpanzees', *Human Nature*, vol. 13, no. 1, 2002, pp. 27–46.

An example of *profits à prendre* is in *Mason v Clarke* (1955) AC 778, in which Clarke had made an oral agreement with Mason for the right to go onto Mason's property and trap rabbits for a year for the sum of £100. The issue was whether an oral agreement was enforceable: in the event it was, because Mason could point to sufficient proof that it arose through the doctrine of part performance. The right to take minerals from the earth is noted in *Case of Mines* (1568) 1 Plow. 310, 75 ER 472 (dating back to the rule of Elizabeth I).

The cases that lay out hunting rights are *Fitzgerald v Firbank* [1877] 2 Ch. 96 (on owning animals which die on the land); *Ewart v Graham* (1859) 7 HLC 332; and *Blades v Higgs* (1861) 10 CB (NS) 713, 142 ER 634 (on animals as a resource to be used by the landowner). Note that in *Blades v Higgs*, a stallholder (Blades) managed to take the case all the way to the House of Lords.

Crocodiles

The case involving crocodile-hunting is *Yanner v Eaton* [1999] HCA 53.

Statutes giving ownership of wild animals in Australia include:

- *Fisheries Act 1995* (Vic.), s. 10.

- *National Parks and Wildlife Act 1974* (NSW), s. 97.

- *Nature Conservation Act 1992* (Qld), s. 83.

- *Territory Parks and Wildlife Conservation Act* (NT), s. 62.

Fish and Shellfish

The two cases involving the open fishing nets are *Young v Hitchens* (1844) 6 QB 606 and *State of Ohio v Shaw*, 67 Ohio St 157; 65 N.E. 875 (1902).

The cases involving the English fishery are *Borwick Development Solutions Ltd v Clear Water Fisheries Ltd* [2020] EWCA Civ 578 (Court of Appeal) and *Borwick Development Solutions Ltd v Clear Water Fisheries Ltd* [2019] EWHC 2272 (Ch), [2020] 1 WLR 559 (trial decision).

For a useful discussion of the Roman law background of the *Borwick* decision, see Jonathan Ainslie, 'Fish, Soil and Industry: Proprietary Interests in *Borwick v Clear Water Fisheries*', *Edinburgh Private Law Blog*, 11 May 2020, and Michael Crawford, 'Wild Things: *Borwick Development Solutions v Clear Water Fisheries* [2020] EWCA Civ 578', *Property Law Blog*, 23 July 2020.

On the public right to fish in Australia, see *Harper v Minister for Sea Fisheries* (1989) 168 CLR 314 ('*Harper's Case*'). For a discussion of the history, see George Kailis, 'Unintended Consequences? Rights to Fish and the Ownership Of Wild Fish', *Macquarie Law Journal*, vol. 11, 2013, pp. 99–124. The High Court of Australia decided that the right to fish in the Northern Territory was wholly overridden by statute in *Northern Territory of Australia v Arnhem Land Aboriginal Land Trust* [2008] HCA 29.

The New South Wales oyster poaching case is *Ex Parte Emerson* (1898) 15 WN (NSW) 101.

The cases about native title and fishing rights are *Mason v Tritton* (1994) 34 NSWLR 572 (native title abalone case); *Karpany v Dietman* [2013] HCA 47 (native title abalone case); and *Sutton v Derschaw* (1995) 82 A Crim R 318 (fish and native title).

Bees

For the history of honey, see Hayrettin Akkaya and Serhat Alkan, 'Bee-Keeping in Anatolia from the Hittites to the Present Day', *Journal of Apicultural Research*, vol. 46, no. 2, 2007, pp. 120–24. For the importance of honey to ancient peoples, see M.J. Gorman, 'The Ancient Brehon Laws of Ireland', *University of Pennsylvania Law Review*, vol. 61, no. 4, 1913, pp. 217–33.

Pottery vessels found in northern China, dating to 7000 BCE, show evidence of a fermented drink made from honey, fruit and rice: see Patrick E. McGovern, Juzhong Zhang, Jigen Tang et al., 'Fermented Beverages of Pre- and Proto-Historic China', *Proceedings of the National Academy of Sciences of The United States of America*, vol. 101, no. 51, 2004, pp. 17593–98.

On ancient Roman bee law, see Bruce W. Frier, 'Bees and Lawyers', *The Classical Journal*, vol. 78, no. 2, 1982, pp. 105–14.

On ancient Irish bee law, see Thomas Charles-Edwards and Fergus Kelly (eds), *Bechbretha*, Early Irish Law Series vol. 1, Dublin Institute for Advanced Studies, Dublin, 1983.

The case of bees swarming to neighbouring land is *Kearry v Pattinson* [1939] 1 KB 471. The case of the theft of bees is *R v Gadd* [1911] QWN 31.

The relevant sections of the German Civil Code, 2 January 2002 (revised version), are ss. 961, 962, 963 and 964. There is a similar section in the Italian Civil Code, 2000 at art. 924.

Foxes

Pierson v Post (1805) 3 Caines 175 (Supreme Court of New York) is the famous US case used to teach property law. For a comprehensive and fascinating description of the history behind the case, see Angela Fernandez, *Pierson v. Post, The Hunt for the Fox*, Cambridge University Press, Cambridge, 2018.

The Canadian cases involving the ownership of semi-wild foxes are *Campbell v Hedley* (1917) 37 DLR 289 (Ontario Supreme Court) and *Ebers v MacEachern* [1932] 3 DLR 415 (PEI Supreme Court).

On taming foxes, see Dor Shilton, Mati Breski, Daniel Dor and Eva Jablonka, 'Human Social Evolution: Self-Domestication or Self-Control?', *Frontiers in Psychology*, vol. 11, no. 134, 2020. The paper questioning the validity of domestication syndrome and Belyaev's experiment is Kathryn Lord, Raymond P. Coppinger and Elinor K. Karlsson, 'The History of Farm Foxes Undermines the Animal Domestication Syndrome', *Trends in Ecology and Evolution*, vol. 35, no. 2, 20, pp. 125–36.

The information about Sydney Fox Rescue was obtained from Chris McLennan, 'NSW Govt Finally Moves to Ban People Keeping Foxes as Pets', *Weekly Times*, 7 October 2014, and Joshua Becker, 'Sydney Charity Wants Ban on Rescuing and Re-Homing Foxes Lifted, Causing Farmer Outrage', *ABC News*, 23 August 2016. The charity seems to have reinvented itself from Sydney Fox Rescue to Sydney Fox and Dingo Rescue and finally to Sydney Dingo Rescue. See Sydney Dingo Rescue website, accessed 20 October 2021, www.sydneydingorescue.com.au, and

'Sydney Fox and Dingo Rescue', Australian Charities and Not-for-Profits Commission website, last modified 17 September 2021, www.acnc.gov.au/charity/80 6a51b894032e8129c2e650ad607660. Thanks to Ashleigh Best for telling us about this issue.

The order declaring foxes to be a pest was the *Local Land Services (European Red Fox) Pest Control Order 2014*, made under the *Local Land Services Act 2013* (NSW).

Peacocks and pigeons

For a description of the idea that you could not steal a peacock, see Krista J. Kesselring, 'Can You Steal a Peacock? Animals in Early Modern Law', Legal History Miscellany blog, 22 April 2020, https://legalhistorymiscellany.com/2020/04/22/can-you-steal-a-peacock-animals-in-early-modern-law.

The case of the escaped racing pigeon is *Hamps v Darby* [1948] 2 KB 311.

The case holding that only lords can put dovecotes on their property is *Boulston v Hardy* (1597) 5 Co Rep 104a, 77 ER 216. The case was also reported as *Bowlston v Hardy* (1597) Cro Eliz 547, 78 ER 794 (note the different spelling of the plaintiff's name).

Swans

The case regarding the swans of Abbotsbury Swannery is known as the *Case of Swans* (1592) 7 Co Rep 15b.

The Chaucer extract is from Geoffrey Chaucer, *The Riverside Chaucer*, ed. Larry D. Benson, Oxford University Press, Oxford, 1988.

On swans and swan upping we consulted:

- 'Abbotsbury Swannery', Abbotsbury Tourism website, accessed 21 October 2021, https://abbotsbury-tourism.co.uk/swannery.

- Emily Cleaver, 'The Fascinating, Regal History behind Britain's Swans' *Smithsonian Magazine*, 31 July 2017.

- Liam James, 'The Ancient Royal Tradition of Counting Swans on the River Thames', *The Independent*, 17 July 2019.

- Sarah Laskow, 'Why the Queen Owns All the Swans in England', *Atlas Obscura*, 14 May 2018.

- Arthur MacGregor, 'Swan Rolls and Beak Markings: Husbandry, Exploitation and Regulation of *Cygnus olor* in England, c. 1100–1900', *Anthropozoologica*, no. 22, 1997, pp. 29–68.

- 'Swan Upping', UK Royal Family website, accessed 21 October 2021, www.royal.uk/swans.

For details of the faithfulness of swans (apart from the Australian black swan!), see Louise Crane, 'The Truth about Swans', *BBC Earth*, 4 December 2014.

Acts regarding swans and other birds include the following:

- *Act for Swans*, 22 Edw. IV. c. 6: *The Statutes of the Realm Volume II* (1377–1504), 474 (UK).

- *An Act against Taking of Feasaunts & Patridgs* (11 Hen. VII c. 17, 1495) (UK).

- *An Acte for the Better Execution of the Intent and Meaninge of Former Statutes Made againste Shootinge in Gunnes, and for the Preservation of the Game of Phesantes and Patridges, and against the Destroyinge of Hares with Harepipes, and Tracinge Hares in the Snowe* (1 Jac. I. c. 27, 1603–4) (UK).

- *Ordinances Respecting Swans on the River Witham, in the County of Lincoln: Together with an Original Roll of Swan Marks, Appertaining to the Proprietors on the Said Stream 1570* (UK). This particular ordinance was described by Joseph Banks, familiar to Australian as the namesake for Banksia flowers and Bankstown.

- *Wildlife and Countryside Act 1981* (UK), s. 1 (s. 2 gives exceptions).

'Royal Fish'

The Act regarding 'royal fish' (some of which remains in force) is *Prerogativa Regis* or *Of the King's Prerogative 1322* (UK) (15 Edw. II. cc. 13-17, s. xiii).

The cases about whale-hunting are as follows:

- *Baldick v Jackson* (1910) 30 NZLR 343.

- *Ghen v Rich*, 8 F. 159 (Mass. 1881).

- *Hogarth v Jackson* (1827) 2 C & P 595, 173 ER 1080.

- *Littledale v Scaith* (1788) 1 Taunt 244, 127 ER 826.

The story of the Welshman who caught a sturgeon is from 'Fisherman Lands £8,000 Catch', *BBC News*, 2 June 2004.

The mock case of the whale washed up on the beach comes from A.P. Herbert, *Uncommon Law: Being Sixty-Six Misleading Cases, Revised and Collected in One Volume, Including Ten Cases Not Published Before*, Methuen, London, 1935. The collection also features a case in which housewives taking revenge on one other by throwing snails into the others' gardens.

Melville's discussion of law can be found in Herman Melville, 'Fast-Fish and Loose-Fish', *Moby Dick*, Claremont Classics, Ringwood, Vic., (1851) 1999, pp. 378–81. The economic explanations for the variations in whaling laws is explored in Robert C. Ellickson, 'A Hypothesis of Wealth-Maximising Norms: Evidence from the Whaling Industry', *Journal of Law, Economics and Organisation*, vol. 5, no. 1, pp. 83–97 (thanks to Jianlin Chen for enlightening us about this research). However, Christopher Tomlins argues that people have taken Melville too literally: 'Animals Accurs'd: *Ferae Naturae* and the Law of Property in 19th Century America', *University of Toronto Law Journal*, vol. 63, no. 1, 2013, pp. 35–52.

Exotic Animals

The case of the escaped sea lion is *Mullett v Bradley* (1898) 24 Misc. 695, 53 NYS 781.

The tale of Yasmin Nakhuda's two new monkeys is described in Jacques Gallant, 'Former Owner of Ikea Monkey Defends Latest Primate Purchases', *Toronto Star*, 21 January 2015. *The Huffington Post*'s story a year later concerns monkeys with different names: see Liam Casey, 'Canada's Animal Laws Allow Canadians to Buy Hippos, Tigers: Owning Exotic Animals Is a Growing Trend in Canada', *The Huffington Post*, 3 March 2016.

Ownership of Domestic Animals

The evidence that the dog in the Chauvet case was actually a dog and not a wolf is discussed in Pat Lee Shipman, 'The Woof at the Door', *American Scientist*, vol. 97, 2009, p. 286.

Evidence that ancient people cared for a sick puppy is presented in:

- Mary Bates, 'Pre-Historic Puppy May Be Earliest Evidence of Pet–Human Bonding', *National Geographic*, 27 February 2018.

- Luc Janssens, Liane Glemsch, Ralf Schmitz et al., 'A New Look at an Old Dog: Bonn-Oberkassel Reconsidered', *Journal of Archaeological Science*, vol. 92, 2018, pp. 126–38.

The ancient burial of dogs with humans is discussed in:

- Silvia Albizuri, Jordi Nadal, Patricia Martin et al., 'Dogs in Funerary Contexts during the Middle Neolithic in the Northeastern Iberian Peninsula (5th – early 4th millennium BCE)', *Journal of Archaeological Science,* vol. 24, 2019, pp. 198–207.

- Marissa Fessenden, 'New Study Looks at Why Neolithic Humans Buried Their Dogs with Them 4000 Years Ago' *Smithsonian Magazine*, 14 February 2019.

Rudyard Kipling's story 'The Cat That Walked by Himself' is in *Just So Stories*, Penguin, London, (1902) 2000.

Justice Hammond's quote is from *Lowe v Auckland City Council HC Auckland AP44/93* [1993] NZHC 238.

Genetic evidence of the domestication of cats is discussed in Claudio Ottoni, Wim Van Neer, Bea De Cupere et al., 'The Palaeogenetics of Cat Dispersal in the Ancient World', *Nature Ecology & Evolution*, vol. 1, art. 139, 2017.

The case in which the cat caught the canary is *McDonald v Jodrey*, 8 Pa.C.C. 142 (1890) 143.

The dispute over Ozzy the cat is described in 'The £24,000 Legal Fight over a Cat: Award-Winning Gardener Is Banned from Feeding Her Neighbour's Moggie after Years of Battling in Courts', *Daily Mail*, 16 January 2020.

Other British legal battles over cats are discussed in Sirin Kale, 'Claws Out! Why Cats Are Causing Chaos and Controversy across Britain', *The Guardian*, 22 January 2020.

Forms of Ownership

The English case involving the mortgage of the dog is *McLean & Anor v Trustees of the Bankruptcy Estate of Dent* [2016] EWHC 2650 (Ch), [2017] Ch 422.

The case involving the mortgage of the horse is *Saltoon v Lake* [1978] 1 NSWLR 52.

Glaister-Carlisle v Glaister-Carlisle, the case involving Springtime Ballyhoo the poodle, was reported in 'Husband Gets Back His Amorous Poodle', *The Times*, 22 February 1968.

The fight over Kobe the Pomeranian took place in *Chow v Chang* [2021] VMC 1. The decision was reported in Tom Cowie, '"He's My Baby": Former Couple Take Dispute over $4000 Dog to Court', *The Age*, 7 April 2021.

The case involving Barry Myrick and Roxy was reported in Doree Lewak, 'NYC Man Chooses to Go to Jail Rather than Give Dog Back to His Employer', *New York Post*, 23 January 2021.

The legislation outlawing the ownership of rabbits in Queensland is the *Biosecurity Act 2014* (Qld).

'Defective' Animals

The sad case of 'Midgeon Supreme' the sterile bull is *Elder Smith Goldsborough Mort Ltd v McBride* [1976] 2 NSWLR 631. Midgeon Supreme was covered by the *Sale of Goods Act 1923* (NSW), s. 19(2).

The case involving the horse with the latent defect was *Vieira v O'Shea* [2012] NSWCA 21.

Monty Python's 'Dead Parrot' sketch appears in John Cleese and Graham Chapman, 'Full Frontal Nudity', season 1, episode 8, *Monty Python's Flying Circus*, BBC, aired 7 December 1969.

The recent case involving Tiberius the sick parrot is *Davy v Kidwai*, 2020 BCCRT 442.

The story of Nala the sick puppy is discussed in:

- 'Our Work: Nala's Matter: Holding Negligent Puppy Farmers Accountable Using Consumer Law', The Animal Law Institute website, accessed 21 October 2021, www.ali.org.au/our-work.

- 'Puppy Farmers Put on Notice after Tribunal Decision'; Maurice Blackburn Lawyers website, accessed 21 October 2021, www.mauriceblackburn. com.au/blog/2018/november/14/puppy-farmers-put-on-notice-after-tribunal-decision.

Australian Competition and Consumer Act 2010 (Cth), schedule 2 (Australian Consumer Law), s. 54, provides for consumer guarantees.

The Welsh case regarding Lady the English sheepdog is *Pendragon v Coom* [2021] EW Misc. 4 CC (22 March 2021). The commentary on the case is Rosalind English, 'What Is the True Value of a Companion Animal?', *UK Human Rights Blog*, 7 April 2021.

The *Consumer Rights Act 2015* (UK), s. 9, provides that goods must be of satisfactory quality. S. 23 of the Act deals with a right to repair or replacement, and s. 24 deals with a right to a price reduction and rejecting the goods.

Harming Other Peoples' Animals

We consulted L.W. King (trans.), 'The Code of Hammurabi', The Avalon Project website, accessed 21 October 2021, https://avalon.law.yale.edu/ancient/hamframe.asp.

St Thomas Aquinas's thoughts on ownership of oxen are available in Thomas Aquinas, *The 'Summa Theologica' of St Thomas Aquinas*, trans. Fathers of the English Dominican Province, Burns, Oates & Washburne, London, 1918.

The case of the rare parrots is reported in James Crisp, 'Hot Air Balloonist to Pay Thousands after Scaring Rare Parrots to Death During Race', *The Telegraph*, 10 September 2020.

The case involving the plane and the mink is *Nova Mink v Trans-Canada Airlines* [1951] 2 DLR 241.

The case involving the shooting of the neighbour's cat is *Davies v Bennison* (1927) 22 Tas LR 52.

Twelve years after *Davies*, the Australian High Court held that a local council was not liable to a mother for the shock and distress she suffered upon finding her son drowned in a trench negligently left uncovered by the local council: *Chester v Waverley Municipal Council* (1939) 62 CLR 1.

The availability of damages for shock and distress caused by negligence was expanded to include situations in which the person who suffered shock did not witness the act of injury, only the aftermath: see *Jaensch v Coffey* (1984) 155 CLR 549.

The case involving the escape and death of Licorice the dog is *Petco Animal Supplies Inc. v Schuster*, 144 SW 3D 544 (2004) (Texas Court of Appeals).

The case involving the injury of Yhani the horse is *Beaumont v Cahir* [2004] ACTSC 97.

The case involving the escape of Harley is *Ferguson v Birchmount Boarding Kennels Ltd* (2006) 79 OR (3d) 681.

Companion Animals and Family Breakdowns

Historical reports of the role of parrots in divorce include:

- 'Parrot Causes Divorce', *Herald Democrat*, 27 September 1920, p. 5 (reports husband divorced wife for teaching a parrot to 'cuss him out).

- 'Parrot in Divorce Case', *The New York Times*, 13 November 1902, p. 1 (reports that a wife divorced her husband for teaching their parrot to say, 'Damn you, get up' in lieu of an alarm clock).

Further descriptions of family law as it applies to animals were gleaned from:

- Tony Bogdanoski, 'Towards an Animal-Friendly Family Law: Recognising the Welfare of Family Law's Forgotten Family Members', *Griffith Law Review*, vol. 19, no. 2, 2010, pp. 197–237.

- Alex Bruce, *Animal Law in Australia: An Integrated Approach*, LexisNexis Butterworths, Chatswood, 2018.

Under the *Family Law Act 1975* (Cth), provisions involving division of property are s. 79(1) (on married couples) and s. 90SM (de facto couples).

For a description of US family law and pets, we consulted:

- Heidi Stroh, 'Puppy Love: Providing for the Legal Protection of Animals When Their Owners Get Divorced', *Journal of Animal Law And Ethics*, vol. 2, 2007, pp. 231–53.

- T.C. Wharton, 'Fighting like Cats and Dogs: The Rising Number of Custody Battles over the Family Pet', *Journal of Law and Family Studies*, vol. 10, no. 2, 2008, pp. 433–41.

For descriptions of Israeli family law and pets, and the *Plonit v Plonit* case, we referred to Pablo Lerner, 'With Whom Will the Dog Remain: On the Meaning of the "Good of the Animal" in Israeli Family Custodial Disputes', *Journal of Animal Law*, vol. 6, 2010, pp. 105–30. Zeev Vinokurov kindly translated the relevant passage of the Hebrew version of *Ploni v Plonit* (Schochet J, Ramat Gan Family Court, FC 32405/01, 18 March 2004, unreported) for us.

The dog custody dispute between the divorcing couple is *Downey & Beale* [2017] FCCA 316. The case in which pet custody was tied to child custody is *Jarvis & Weston* [2007] FamCA 1339. The case where the judge decided she had no jurisdiction to award 'shared custody' of a dog is *Davenport & Davenport (No. 2)* [2020] FCCA 2766.

For US property-based cases dealing with pet ownership upon divorce, see:

- *Akers v Sellers* 54 NE 2d 779 (1944) (Indiana Court of Appeal).

- *Arrington v Arrington* 613 SW 2d 565 (1981) (Court of Civil Appeals, Texas).

- *Bennet v Bennet* 655 So 2 d 109 (1995) (Florida District Court of Appeal).

- *Desanctis v Pritchard* 803 A 2d 230 (2002) (Pennsylvania Superior Court).

- *Nuzzaci v Nuzzaci* 1995 WLR 783006 (1995) (Delaware Family Court).

Conversely, for cases focusing on the 'best interests of the animals', see:

- *Marriage of Stewart* 365 NW 2d 611 (1984).

- *Raymond v Lachmann* 695 NYS 2d 308 (1999) (NYSC App Div).

- *Zovko v Gregory* No CH 97–544 (1997) (Circuit Court of Arlington County, Virginia).

The Singaporean case involving Sasha the dog is *Tan Huey Kuan (alias Chen Huijuan) v Tan Kok Chye* [2011] 3 SLR 960, [2011] SGHC 86. Thanks to Rachel Leow for alerting us to this.

The case involving specific enforcement of the obligation to return the dog is *Houseman v Dare* 405 NJ Sup 536 (2009).

Treating Animals as More than Property

The ultimate fate of Darwin is reported in Maija Kappler, 'Darwin the Ikea Monkey Has a New Baboon "Surrogate Dad"', *HuffPost*, 9 January 2019.

2. Controlling Animals

The Scottish case dealing with the wandering lamb is *Winans v Macrae* [1885] 22 SLR 692. We first became aware of this case through Kate Scarborough, 'Our Legal Heritage: The Lamb that Strayed Too Far from Home', *Scottish Legal News*, 25 August 2020.

Read v J Lyons & Co Ltd [1947] AC 156 was not a case about animals at all. It involved an explosion in an explosives factory.

Glanville Williams wrote the seminal book on animals and tort law in 1939: Glanville Williams, *Liability for Animals*, Cambridge University Press, Cambridge, 1939. We consulted it extensively, particularly on the historical aspects of law.

For Roman law, we again used Paul J. Du Plessis, *Borkowski's Textbook on Roman Law*, 6th ed., Oxford University Press, Oxford, 2020, and Reinhard Zimmermann, *The Law of Obligations: Roman Foundations of the Civilian Tradition*, Oxford University Press, Oxford, 1996.

For ancient Irish bee law, we consulted Thomas Charles-Edwards and Fergus Kelly (eds), *Bechbretha*, Early Irish Law Series vol. 1, Dublin Institute for Advanced Studies, Dublin, 1983.

For some of the cases involving horses, we used Clifford L. Pannam QC, *The Horse and the Law*, 3rd ed., Law Book Co., Pyrmont, 2004.

The poetry of William Blake quoted in this chapter was sourced from *The Complete Poems of William Blake*, ed. Alice Ostriker, Penguin, New York, 1977.

For our discussion of the patchwork of laws covering animals, we consulted Alex Bruce, *Animal Law in Australia: An Integrated Approach*, 2nd ed., LexisNexis Butterworths, Chatswood, 2018.

Domestic Animals

Trespassing animals

Distress Damage Feasant

For Anglo-Saxon laws, including the laws of Ine, we used F.L. Attenborough (ed. and trans.), *The Laws of the Earliest English Kings*, Cambridge University Press, Cambridge, 1922.

John Booth's committal for perjury is reported in *The Sydney Morning Herald*, 16 October 1844, p. 2. Thomas Perigo's surname is misspelt as 'Perigold', but being illiterate, he may not have known how to spell his surname in any case.

The provision allowing someone to seize a dog or cat on private property without permission is the *Domestic Animals Act 1994* (Vic.), s. 23.

The statutes abolishing or limiting the tort of distress damage feasant are:

- *Animals Act 1971* (UK), s. 7.

- *Animals Act 1977* (NSW), s. 5.

- *Civil Law (Wrongs) Act 2002* (ACT), s. 213.

- *Law of Animals Act 1962* (Tas.), s. 7A.

The statute that governs impounding in Victoria is the *Impounding of Livestock Act 1994* (Vic.). In New South Wales, it is the *Impounding Act 1993* (NSW).

The historical statutes allowing the destruction of straying dogs in New Zealand were *The Dog Registration Act 1880* (NZ), s. 13, and the *Dog Registration Act 1908* (NZ), s. 16. The New Zealand cases that involved 'destroying' dogs are *Thompson v Burling* (1890) 8 NZLR 378 and *Robinson v Wagner* (1911) 30 NZLR 367.

The statutes that allow for the destruction of straying goats are the *Inclosed Land Protection Act 1901* (NSW), s. 7, and the *Enclosed Lands Protection Act 1943* (ACT), s. 7.

The historical versions of some of the above statutes include:

- Government Order, 28 September 1811, reported in *The Sydney Gazette and New South Wales Advertiser*, 5 October 1811, p. 1.

- *Inclosed Lands Act 1854* (NSW) (subject to *Angora Goats Protection Act 1873* [36 Vic No. 18 and 19, NSW]).

- *Inclosed Lands Act 1878* (42 Vic No. 4) (Qld), s. 3.

- *Inclosed Lands Protection Ordinance 1915* (PNG), ss. 7 and 8.

- *Pounds Act 1874* (37 Vic No. 478) (Vic.).

The Queensland cases involving the historical version of the *Inclosed Lands Act* are *Kelly v Nufer* (1918) QWN 13 (prohibiting the destruction of trespassing turkeys) and *R v Rogers* (1916) St R Qd 38 (prohibiting the destruction of trespassing bulls).

Cattle Trespass

The legislation abolishing cattle trespass is:

- *Animals Act 1977* (NSW), s. 4.

- *Civil Law (Wrongs) Act 2002* (ACT), s. 212.

- *Civil Liability Act 1936* (SA), s. 18.

The Queensland cattle trespass cases are *Lade & Co Pty Ltd v Black* [2005] QSC 325 and the follow-up case of *Lade & Co Pty Ltd v Black* [2007] QSC 285.

The case that explained why cattle trespass doesn't apply to cats and dogs is *Read v Edwards* (1864) 144 ER 99, 205, 17 CB (NS) 245, 260–61.

The case that said bees cannot be subject to cattle trespass is *Stormer v Ingram* [1978] 21 SASR 93.

The EU case dealing with bees foraging on genetically modified crops is *Karl Heinz Bablok and Others v Freistaat Bayern*, ECJ C-442/09, and it is discussed in Matthias Lamping, 'Shackles for Bees? The ECJ's Judgment on GMO-Contaminated Honey', *European Journal of Risk Regulation*, vol. 3, no. 1, 2012, p. 123. The EU directive that said 'residues' (including GMO pollen in honey) did not constitute ingredients is Regulation (EU) 1169 of 2011 of the European Parliament and of the Council of 25 October 2011 on the provision of food information to consumers, OJ 2011, L304/18.

The US cases on bee trespass we mention are *Lenk v Spezia* 213 P.2d 47 (Cal. Dist. Ct App. 1949) and *Bennett v Larsen Co* 348 N.W.2d 540 (Wis. 1984). They are discussed in Melanie Triplett, 'Torts-Buzz Off! Expanding the Scope of a Land-owner's Duty to Honey Bees Flying along the Fine Line or Trespassing in *Anderson v State Department of Natural Resources*', *William Mitchell Law Review*, vol. 32, no. 4, 2006, p. 1489.

Fencing Animals

The case on fencing is *Searle v Wallbank* [1947] AC 341, accepted as representing the law in Australia by the High Court in *State Government Insurance Commission v Trigwell* (1979) 142 CLR 617.

The Queensland case applying *Searle v Wallbank* is *Smith v Williams* (2006) 47 MVR 248, [2006] QCA 439. *Hutton v ROLX Operating Company Pty Ltd* [2016] QSC 248 is the case in which an exception was made, following *Graham v The Royal National Agricultural and Industrial Association of Qld* [1989] 1 Qd R 624.

Legislation abolishing the rule in *Searle v Wallbank* includes:

- *Animals Act 1977* (NSW), s. 7(2)(b).

- *Civil Law (Wrongs) Act 2002* (ACT), s. 214.

- *Civil Liability Act 1936* (SA), s. 18.

- *Highways (Liability for Straying Animals) Act 1983* (WA), s. 3.

- *Law of Animals Act 1962* (Tas.), s. 19.

- *Wrongs Act 1958* (Vic.), s. 33.

For a suggestion that the rule in *Searle* should be abolished, see Anthony Gray, 'Time to Abolish the Rule in *Searle v Wallbank* for Negligence and Nuisance Claims', *Deakin Law Review*, vol. 13, no. 2, 2008, p. 101.

The Northern Territory, South Australian and Western Australian offences for owners of stray cattle are:

- *Impounding Act 1920* (SA), s. 46 (see also the amendments introduced by *Impounding Act Amendment Act 1967* [SA], s. 6.).

- *Local Government (Miscellaneous Provisions) Act 1960* (WA), s. 484.

- *Pounds Act 1930* (NT), s. 35.

The two South Australian cases on the crime of owning stray cattle are *Snell v Ryan* [1951] SASR 59 and *Norcock v Bowey* [1966] SASR 250. The case about petrol is *Mayer v Marchant* (1973) 5 SASR 567.

The federal exception to criminal responsibility is in the *Criminal Code Act 1995* (Cth), Schedule, s. 10.1.

Trespass, Negligence and Nuisance

The UK statute that covers roaming dogs and other animals is *Animals Act 1971* (UK).

The cat's 'right to roam' is discussed in 'Cats, Trespass and Fouling', In Brief website, accessed 21 October 2021, www.inbrief.co.uk/animal-law/cats-fouling.

The cases involving cats killing birds are *Webb v McFeat* (1878) 22 Journal of Jurisprudence 669 and *McDonald v Jodrey* 8 Pa.C.C. 142 (1890).

In Victoria, cat curfews are provided for in *Domestic Animals Act 1994* (Vic.), s. 25. The provision that provides for fining the owners of nuisance pets is *Domestic Animals Act 1994* (Vic.), s. 32.

The case involving the pigeons creating an annoyance in Sydney is *Fraser v Booth* (1949) 50 SR (NSW) 113.

Annoying Animals

The description of Southampton in early modern times was found in F.J.C. Hearnshaw and D.M. Hearnshaw (trans and eds), *Southampton Court Leet Records Vol 1*, H.M. Gilbert & Son, Southampton, 1905–07, pp. xix–xx.

The famous case of 1610 is *Aldred's Case* (1610) 9 Co Rep 57b, 77 ER. The availability of private nuisance for pig sties is confirmed by *R v Wigg* (1705) 2 Salk 460, 91 ER 397; 2 Ld Raym 1163, 92 ER 209.

The two cases about noisy stables are *Ball v Ray* (1873) 8 Ch App 467 and *Broder v Saillard* [1876] 2 Ch D 692.

The case of the noisy rooster is *Leeman v Montagu* [1936] 2 All ER 1677.

Maurice the cockerel's victory is described in Kim Willsher, 'Maurice the Noisy Rooster Can Keep Crowing, Court Rules', *The Guardian*, 5 September 2019. Maurice's death was reported in 'Maurice the Noisy French Cockerel Dies Aged Six', *BBC News*, 18 June 2020.

Other stories about noisy French animals include:

- Evie Burrows-Taylor, 'Noisy Cows Spark Outcry from British Homeowners in French Alps', *The Local Fr*, 6 September 2017.

- 'End to Eight-Year Battle over Noisy Frogs', *The Connexion: French News and Views*, 19 December 2019.

- 'Holidaymakers Ask French Mayor to Kill Off "Loud" Cicadas in Name of Peace and Quiet', *The Local Fr*, 21 August 2018.

- 'If It Quacks like a Duck: Boisterous Poultry Land French Owner in Court', *The Guardian*, 3 September 2019.

- 'Why Are Dordogne's Noisy Frogs Embroiled in a Bizarre Legal Battle?', *The Local Fr*, 16 April 2018.

The case involving the English publisher and the cowbells is described in Jamie Doward, 'Case of Elgar's Cowbell Concerto Sets Rural France against Townies', *The Guardian*, 9 December 2012.

The law declaring that the sounds and smells of the countryside are part of French heritage is reported in Jack Guy, 'France Has Passed a Law Protecting the Sounds and Smells of the Countryside', *CNN*, 23 January 2021.

The final result in the Grignols frogs case is described in Théo Caubel, 'Dordogne: le bruit des grenouilles agaçait un voisin, la mare de Grignols aura disparu lundi soir', *France Bleu*, 7 March 2021.

The case regarding the Wallum froglets is *Gales Holdings Pty Ltd v Tweed Shire Council* (2013) 85 NSWLR 514, [2013] NSWCA 382.

The cases involving nuisance and bees are:

- *Earl v Van Alstine*, 8 Barb 630, 1 Am. Negl. Cas. 268 (1850), (Sup Ct NY) (on bees as domesticated animals).

- *Parker v Reynolds*, *The Times*, 17 December 1906, p. 12 (on rival beekeepers).

- *Stormer v Ingram* [1978] 21 SASR 93 (Legoe J).

Provisions requiring dog owners to dispose of dog faeces include:

- *Companion Animals Act 1998* (NSW), s. 20.

- *Dog and Cat Management Act 1995* (SA), s. 45A(6).

- *Dog Control Act 2000* (Tas.), s. 45.

- *Domestic Animals Act 2000* (ACT), s. 46.

Other jurisdictions leave these issues to local laws – see *Domestic Animals Act 1994* (Vic.), s. 42(c).

The study of Northern Irish dog walkers is at D. Wells, 'Factors Influencing Owners' Reactions to Their Dogs' Fouling', *Environment and Behaviour*, vol. 38, no. 5, 2006, p. 707.

For a recent discussion of claims about using DNA analysis to identify dog poo offenders, see E. Terzon, 'Local Council in Melbourne's North Will Not Pursue "Innovative" Plan to DNA Test Dog Poo', *ABC News*, 10 October 2019.

Harmful Animals

Dangerous Animals and *Scienter*

On the Roman ban on importing African animals, see Pliny the Elder, *The Natural History of Pliny*, trans. John Bostock and H.T. Riley, Henry G. Bohn, London, 1855, s. 8.24. An account of the exotic animal trade in Roman times is available in Caroline Wazer, 'The Exotic Animal Traffickers of Ancient Rome', *The Atlantic*, 30 March 2016.

The letter from Rufus to Cicero is included in Marcus Tullius Cicero, *Epistulae ad Familiares*, trans. Louis Claude Purser, Clarendon Press, Oxford, 1901, s. 8.6.

The relevant section of the German Civil Code, 2 Jan. 2002 (revised version), is 233a.

For a fascinating discussion of the impact of the Black Death on English law, see Robert C. Palmer, *English Law in the Age of the Black Death, 1348–1382*, University of North Carolina Press, Chapel Hill, 1993.

The case of the biting monkey is *May v Burdett* (1846) 9 QB 101.

The case of the stampeding elephant who harmed the circus performers is *Behrens v Bertram Mills Circus Ltd* [1957] 2 QB 1.

The viciousness of zebras is described in Rory Young, 'Can Zebras Be Domesticated and Trained?', *Slate*, 4 September 2013.

Cases that establish which animals are intrinsically dangerous are:

- *Andrew v Kilgour* (1910) 13 WLR 608, 19 Man LR 545 (raccoons).
- *Behrens v Bertram Mills Circus Ltd* [1957] 2 QB 1 (lions).
- *Buckle v Holmes* [1926] 2 KB 125 (tigers).
- *Filburn v People's Palace and Aquarium Co Ltd* [1890] 25 QBD 258; *Behrens v Bertram Mills Circus Ltd* [1957] 2 QB 1 (elephants).
- *Fischer v Stuart* (1979) 25 ALR 336 (NT) (dingoes).
- *James v Wellington City* [1972] NZLR 70 (chimpanzees).
- *Marlor v Ball* (1900) 16 TLR 239 (zebras).
- *May v Burdett* (1846) 9 QB 10 (monkeys).
- *Stockwell v Victoria* [2001] VSC 497 (wild dogs).
- *Trethowan v Capron* [1961] VR 460, 462 (lions).
- *Wyatt v Rosherville Gardens Co* [1886] 2 TLR 282 (bears).

Cases which establish non-dangerous animals are:

- *Lake v Taggart* (1979) 1 SR(WA) 89 (kangaroos).
- *Nada Shah v Sleeman* (1917) 19 WALR 119 (camels).

The sad tale of Harry the camel was brought to our attention by Mara Tam, Rebecca Giblin and Andrea Matwyshyn on Twitter. See also 'The Introduction of Camels into Australia', Burke & Wills Web, accessed 21 October 2021, www.burke-andwills.net.au/Camels/Introducing_Camels_Into_Australia.htm.

A full extract of Horrocks's final letter is included in 'Expedition to the North-West' *South Australian Gazette and Colonial Register*, 19 September 1846, p. 2.

The account of Harry's execution is taken from 'Early Clare, Interesting Landmarks', *The Register*, 21 October 1920, p. 9, and Clarion, 'Horrocks Centenary; Pilgrimage to S.A. Explorer's Tomb', *The News*, 19 October 1939, p. 7.

We came across the paintings of Samuel Thomas Gill (1818–80) via @artist_s_t_gill on Twitter. The painting of Horrocks recuperating, with Harry in the background, *Invalid's Tent, Salt Lake 75 Miles North-West of Mount Arden* (1846), is held in the collection of the Art Gallery of South Australia.

David Coombe, a historian, has noted that history unfairly blames Harry the camel for what was really an accident – see 'Harry the Camel Who "Shot" J.A. Horrocks', Trove blog post, 21 October 2019, https://trove.nla.gov.au/list/136213. We are inclined to agree with his assessment.

Careless Owners

The South African case involving the *actio de pauperie* is *Van Meyeren v Cloete* [2020] ZASCA 100.

The case of the motorcycle crash involving a kangaroo is *Trend v Trend* (1987) 4 MVR 423 (WASCFC).

Bee negligence cases include:

- *Bauskis v Director General, NSW Agriculture* [2003] NSWADT 228 (Australian case in which beekeeping was restrained).

- *Branezac v Director General, NSW Agriculture* [2003] NSWADT 237 (another Australian case in which beekeeping was restrained).

- *Lucas v Pettit* (1906) 12 OLR 448 (a case involving swarming bees).

- *O'Gorman v O'Gorman* [1903] 2 IR 573 (a tragic Irish case involving death of man after bees stung his horse).

- *Robins v Kennedy* [1931] NZLR 1134 (another cases involving swarming bees).

The *Livestock Disease Control Act 1994* (Vic.) outlines, among other things, the ways in which bees may be kept in Victoria, as does the Victorian Apiary Code of Practice 2011.

The cases involving injuries by horses to passers-by are:

- *Tucker v Hennessy* [1918] VLR 56.

- *Bradley v Wallaces Ltd* [1913] 3 KB 639.

- *Aldham v United Dairies (London) Ltd* [1940] 1 KB 507.

The unfortunate case of the dog who smashed the car window is *Fardon v Harcourt-Rivington* [1938] 48 TLR 215.

The cases involving dog attacks are:

- *Draper v Hodder* [1972] 2 QB 556.

- *Galea v Gillingham* [1987] 2 Qd R 365.

Dangerous Dogs

The crime of failing to control a dangerous dog is outlined in *Crimes Act 1958* (Vic.), s. 319B.

The changes to the restricted-breed legislation can be found in *Domestic Animals Amendment (Restricted Breed Dogs) Act 2017* (Vic.), s. 9.

The case involving the failure to muzzle is *Leichhardt Municipal Council v Hunter* [2013] NSWCCA 87.

The cases involving Axel the pit bull are:

- *Fenech v Wyndham CC* (Review and Regulation) [2015] VCAT 477.

- *Wyndham City Council v Fenech* [2015] VSC 723.

- *Fenech v Wyndham CC* [2016] VCAT 1622.

The story of the death of Ayen Chol was described in S. Farnsworth, 'Man Fined after Child Killed by Pit Bull', *ABC News*, 30 July 2012.

The inquiry into restricted-breed dogs is Legislative Council Economy and Infrastructure Committee, *Inquiry into the legislative and regulatory framework relating to restricted-breed dogs*, Parliament of Victoria, Melbourne, 2016.

Wild Animals

Pest Species

The transmission of the Black Plague is discussed in Katharine R. Dean, Fabienne Krauer, Lars Walløe et al., 'Human Ectoparasites and the Spread of Plague in Europe during the Second Pandemic', *Proceedings of the National Academy of Sciences of the United States of America*, vol. 115, no. 6, 2018, pp. 1304–09.

For the nature of 'pest animals' in modern Australia, see Department of Agriculture and Water Resources, 'Australian Pest Animal Strategy 2017 to 2027', Australian Government, Canberra, 2017, p. 4.

The history of China's disastrous attempt to eliminate sparrows is explored in George Dvorsky, 'Secret History: China's Worst Self-Inflicted Environmental Disaster: The Campaign to Wipe Out the Common Sparrow', *io9*, 18 July 2012.

Tudor laws

The discussion of Tudor laws allowing the culling of 'pest' animals and its lasting impact on British wildlife comes from Roger Lovegrove, *Silent Fields: The Long*

Decline of a Nation's Wildlife, Oxford University Press, Oxford, 2007. The relevant statutes are *An Acte Made and Ordeyned to Dystroye Choughes, Crowes and Roks*, 24 Hen VIII c. 10: *The Statutes of the Realm Volume II* (1377–1504), s. 425, and *An Acte for the preservacion of Grayne*, 8 Eliz c. 15: *The Statutes of the Realm Volume II* (1377–1504), s. 498.

Australian laws

For a history of 'acclimatisation societies' in Australia, we consulted Peter Minard, *All Things Harmless, Useful, and Ornamental: Environmental Transformation through Species Acclimatization, from Colonial Australia to the World*, University of North Carolina Press, Chapel Hill, 2019.

On the sad history of the Thylacine, see 'Tasmanian Tiger', Tasmania Parks and Wildlife Service website, accessed 21 October 2021, https://parks.tas.gov.au/discovery-and-learning/wildlife/tasmanian-tiger, and Thomas A.A. Prowse, Christopher N. Johnson, Robert C. Lacy et al., 'No Need for Disease: Testing Extinction Hypotheses for the Thylacine Using Multi-Species Metamodels', *Journal of Animal Ecology*, vol. 82, no. 2, 2013, p. 366. Details on the introduction of a bounty on the 'native tiger' were obtained from *Tasmanian News*, 5 March 1888, p. 2.

The bizarre history of the 'Emu War' was obtained from Libby Robin, 'Emu: National Symbols and Ecological Limits', in Libby Robin, Robert Heinsohn and Leo Joseph (eds), *Boom & Bust: Bird Stories for a Dry Country*, CSIRO Publishing, Collingwood, 2009.

'The Man from Snowy River' is included in A.B. Paterson, *The Man From Snowy River and Other Verses*, Angus & Robertson, Sydney, 1917.

The case involving brumby culling is *Australian Brumby Alliance Inc. v Parks Victoria Inc.* [2020] FCA 605. The aftermath of the case is discussed in Lisa Cox, 'Victoria to Resume Culling Brumbies in Alpine National Parks after Court Ruling', *The Guardian*, 8 May 2020.

The problem of incentives to cull cane toads is discussed in David Smerdon, 'The Economics of "Cash for Cane Toads" – a Textbook Example of Perverse Incentives', *The Conversation*, 11 January 2019.

Nuisance Animals

The case involving the 'coney boroughs' is *Boulston v Hardy* (1597) 5 Co Rep 104a, 77 ER 216. It was also reported, in more detail, as *Bowlston v Hardy* (1597) Cro Eliz 547, 78 ER 794 (note the different spelling of the plaintiff's name).

The case in which the English judge said flies were a nuisance is *Bland v Yates* (1914) 58 Sol J 612. The series of Australian cases involving the mushroom grower, manure and flies include *Baulkham Hills Shire Council v Domachuk* (1988) 66 LGRA 110 and *Feiner v Domachuk* (1994) 35 NSWLR 485. For a discussion of why Australians complain about flies, and why they are so prevalent here, see: Liam Mannix, 'Why Do We Have So Many Flies in Australia? Here's Swat's What', *The Sydney Morning Herald*, 20 December 2017.

The case involving rats and nuisance is *Stearn v Prentice Brothers Ltd* (1919) 1 KB 394.

For a discussion of Titirangi's problem with feral chickens, see Charlotte Graham-McLay, "Like a Stephen King Movie': Feral Chickens Return to Plague New Zealand Village', *The Guardian*, 10 June 2020.

A.P. Herbert contemplates a spoof neighbourly dispute over slugs between two women called 'Mrs Cowfat' and 'Mrs Wheedle' – arguments over who is feeding wild animals are clearly common enough to generate spoofs. See A.P. Herbert, *Uncommon Law*, Methuen & Co., London, 1935.

The Strange Ambivalence of the Law

One of the main sources on the bizarre history of animal trials that we relied on is Edward Payson Evans, *The Criminal Prosecution and Capital Punishment of Animals*, W. Heinemann, London, 1906.

The trial of the *lutmäuse* (along with tantalising details about local confectionary commemorating the trial of the rodents!) is described in Werner Kräutler, 'Vor genau 500 Jahren: Der Mäuseprozess von Glurns', Tirol Isch Toll website, 11 April 2020, https://tirolischtoll.wordpress.com/2020/04/11/der-maeuseprozess-von-glurns. On the bridge purportedly built for the mice, see 'Der Glurnser Mäuseprozess', *Franz Magazine*, 26 November 2011.

3. *Blaming Animals*

On the history of animal trials, we again we relied heavily on Edward Payson Evans, *The Criminal Prosecution and Capital Punishment of Animals*, W. Heinemann, London, 1906. See in particular Appendix F, in which Evans relates thirty-one instances of pigs being prosecuted.

We also revisit the case involving Izzy the Staffordshire terrier, *Isbester v Knox City Council* [2014] VSC 286; [2014] VSCA 214; [2015] HCA 20.

Domesticated Animals and Crimes

Ancient Times and the Goring Ox

On Mesopotamian laws, see Reuven Yaron (trans.), *The Laws of Eshnunna*, E.J. Brill, Leiden, 1988, and L.W King. (trans.), 'The Code of Hammurabi', The Avalon Project website, accessed 21 October 2021, https://avalon.law.yale.edu/ancient/hamframe.asp.. See also Reuven Yaron, 'The Goring Ox in Near Eastern Laws', *Israel Law Review*, vol, 1, no. 3, 1966, pp. 396–406.

The sections of Exodus that discuss the punishment of goring oxen are 21:28 – 21:31.

We consulted *Bava Kamma*, William Davidson Edition, Sefaria database, accessed 21 November 2021, www.sefaria.org/Bava_Kamma, paras 21 and 22 of 90b.

On Jewish laws and the medical perspective on them, see Jeremy Brown, 'Bava Kamma 46a – Injuries from Cows' and 'Bava Kamma 29a – Injuries from Bull-fighting', Talmudology blog, accessed 21 October 2021, www.talmudology.com. We are grateful to rabbinic student Gabriel Kanter-Webber for supplying us with further information, and for his paper, 'Animals in Court: Do Animals and Other Non-Human Natural Features Have Legal Personality to be Represented before a Beit Din?', June 2020. On his advice, we also consulted W. David Nelson (trans.), *Mekhilta de Rabbi Shimon bar Yohai*, Jewish Publication Society, Philadelphia, 2006, p. 631 (LXVII:IV, 10M and 11J), and looked at the treatment of more vicious animals in the procedural rules laid out in the *Mishnah Sanhedrin* 1:4, Sefaria database, accessed 21 October 2021, www.sefaria.org/Mishnah_Sanhedrin.

On the dangers posed by cattle, see:

- Henry M. Busch Jr, Thomas H. Cogbill, Jeffry Landercasper and Betty O. Landercasper, 'Blunt Bovine and Equine Trauma', *The Journal of Trauma*, vol. 26, no. 6, 1986, p. 559–60.

- Colin G. Murphy, Ciara M. McGuire, Natasha O'Malley and Paul Harrington, 'Cow-Related Trauma: A 10-Year Review of Injuries Admitted to a Single Institution', *Injury: International Journal of Care of the Injured*, vol. 41, no. 5, 2010, p. 548.

On the Irish case of stampeding cows, see John Fallon, 'Frenzied Cows Kill Lucy, 60, in Attack', *The Sun*, 26 February 2015.

On the Irish trial of English cattle, see '1641 Depositions', Trinity College Library Dublin website, accessed 21 October, https://1641.tcd.ie. The depositions are a record of the experiences of the (mostly Protestant) Irish of the 1641 Rebellion. See Thomas Johnson's deposition in particular. We also consulted Keith Pluymers, 'Cow Trials, Climate Change and Causes of Violence', *Environmental History*, vol. 25, no. 2, 2020, pp. 287–309.

There are contemporaneous newspaper reports of the murderousness of Lorenzo the bull. See Francis Scott and Gerard Couzens, 'Horror: Spanish Bullfighter Víctor Barrio Gored to Death in the Ring before a Stunned Crowd', *The Daily Mail*, 10 July 2016. See also Rosa Jiménez Cano, 'Víctor Barrio, una Esperanza Rota', *El País*, 11 July 2016.

The case of Ridgey Didge the rodeo bull is *Smith v Capella State High Court Parents and Citizens Association* [2004] QSC 109.

Other Ancient Legal Systems

On Ancient Greek law see:

- Aristotle, *Constitution of Athens & Related Texts*, trans. H. Rackham, William Heinemann Ltd, London, 1952.

- Karolus Lehmann (ed.), *Lex Alamannorum*, Hahnsche Buchhandlung, Hanover, 1966, s. 96.4 (B Codex s. 99.20), a Merovingian Frankish code from the seventh or eighth century.

- Plato, *Laws*, trans. R.G. Bury, William Heinemann Ltd, London, 1968.

We also consulted:

- Societas Aperiendis Fontibvs (ed.), *Lex Baiwariorum*, Impensis Bibliopolii Hanhniani, Hannover, 1892, s. 19.7 (on pigs eating corpses), a companion Frankish code from the eighth century.

The Late Medieval to Early Modern Era and Killer Animals on Trial

On the history of animal trials, we relied on the following publications:

- Sara M. Butler, 'Persons under the Law? Medieval Animal Rights', Legal History Miscellany blog, 19 February 2018, https://legalhistorymiscellany.com/2018/02/19/persons-under-the-law-medieval-animals-rights.

- Peter Dinzelbacher, 'Animals Trials: A Multidisciplinary Approach', *Journal of Interdisciplinary History*, vol. 32, no. 3, 2002, p. 405–21.

- Edward Payson Evans, *The Criminal Prosecution and Capital Punishment of Animals*, W. Heinemann, London, 1906.

- J.J. Finkelstein, *The Ox That Gored*, American Philosophical Society, Philadelphia 1981.

- Jen Girgen, 'The Historical and Contemporary Prosecution and Punishment of Animals', *Animal Law*, vol. 9, 2003, pp. 97–133.

- Moshe Greenberg, *Studies in the Bible and Jewish Thought*, Jewish Publication Society, Philadelphia, 1995, pp. 25–41.

- Walter W. Hyde, 'The Prosecution and Punishment of Animals and Lifeless Things', *University of Pennsylvania Law Review*, vol. 64, 1916, pp. 696–730.

- Bernard S. Jackson, *Essays in Jewish and Comparative Legal History*, Brill, Leiden, 1975.

- Bernard S. Jackson, *Wisdom-Laws: A Study of the Mishpatim of Exodus 21:1–22:16*, Oxford University Press, Oxford, 2011.

- Philip Jamieson, 'Animal Liability in Early Law', *Cambrian Law Review*, vol. 19, 1988, pp. 45–68.

- Marilyn A. Katz, 'Ox-Slaughter and Goring Oxen: Homicide, Animal Sacrifice, and Judicial Process', *Yale Journal of Law and the Humanities*, (1992) vol. 4, no. 2, 1992, pp. 249–78.

- Peter T. Leeson, 'Vermin Trials', *The Journal of Law and Economics*, vol. 56, no. 3, 2013.

- James McWilliams, 'Beastly Justice', *Slate*, 21 February 2013.
- Glanville Williams, *Liability for Animals*, Cambridge University Press, Cambridge, 1939.
- Steven M. Wise, 'The Legal Thinghood of Nonhuman Animals', *Boston College Environmental Affairs Law Review*, vol. 23, no. 3, 1996, pp. 471–546.
- Reuven Yaron, 'The Goring Ox in Near Eastern Laws', *Israel Law Review*, vol, 1, no. 3, 1966, pp. 396–406.

On the cannibalistic and omnivorous tendencies of pigs, see:

- Simon Worrall, 'Why We Love – and Loathe – The Humble Pig', *National Geographic*, 24 May 2015.
- Mark Essig, *Lesser Beasts: A Snout-to-Tail History of The Humble Pig*, Basic Books, New York, 2015.
- 'Savaging of Piglets (Cannibalism)', The Pig Site, accessed 21 October 2021, https://thepigsite.com.

To our surprise and horror, we found *numerous* news reports from the last ten years of individuals being eaten by pigs:

- 'Five-Month-Old Baby Eaten Alive by Pigs near Hyderabad', *Times of India*, 17 July 2015.
- 'Oregon Farmer Eaten by His Pigs', *BBC News*, 2 October 2012.
- Chris Pleasance, 'Toddler Is Mauled to Death and Eaten by a Pig after Crawling into Its Pen in China', *Daily Mail*, 14 November 2014.
- 'Russian Woman "Eaten by Pigs" after Collapsing', *BBC News*, 7 February 2019.
- Mbulelo Sisulu, 'Pigs Eat Newborn Baby's Head!', *Daily Sun*, 17 August 2018.

For late medieval attitudes to animals, we consulted Thomas Aquinas, *The 'Summa Theologica' of St Thomas Aquinas*, trans. Fathers of the English Dominican Province, Burns, Oates & Washburne, London, 1918.

For early medieval laws regarding pigs, an exhaustive discussion of pig behaviour and pig herding law, and theology regarding pigs, see Jamie Kreiner, *Legions of Pigs in the Early Medieval West*, Yale University Press, New Haven, 2020.

On Lombard law and grazing pigs, see Thom Gobbitt, 'From Grave Robbing to Pastured Pigs: References and Legal Thinking in Lombard Law-Books, c. 1050–1125', *Manuscripta*, vol. 64, no. 2, 2020.

The Motivations behind Animal Trials

While trying to ascertain *why* people might wish to prosecute animals (both wild and domestic), we relied heavily on Geoffrey Goodwin and Adam Benforado, 'Judging the Goring Ox: Retribution Directed Toward Animals', *Cognitive Science*, vol. 39, no. 3, 2015, p. 619–46.

On medieval attitudes to children, see:

- Philippe Ariès, *Centuries of Childhood*, New York Vintage Books, New York, 1962.

- Barbara Hanawalt, *Growing Up in Medieval London: The Experience of Children in History*, Oxford University Press, New York, 1993.

- Nicholas Orme, *Medieval Children*, Yale University Press, New Haven, 2001.

- Shulamith Shahar, *Childhood in the Middle Ages*, Routledge, London, 1990.

English Exceptionalism

The Bracton extract is from Henry de Bracton, *On the Laws and Customs of England*, ed. G.E. Woodbine, transl. S.E. Thorne, 4 vols, Harvard University Press, Cambridge, MA, 1968–77.

The *Queen v Great Western Railway Company* (1842) LR 2 QB 773 is a case in which relatives of people killed in a railway accident sued the train itself in deodand. Obviously the case became notorious, and deodands were subsequently abolished by the *Deodands Act 1846* (9 & 10 Vict. C. 62). The *Fatal Accidents Act 1846* (9 & 10 Vict. c.93) (commonly known as *Lord Campbell's Act*) was enacted to provide remedies for deaths caused by railway accident. In New South Wales a similar, statute abolishing deodands was passed: the *Deodands Abolition Act 1849* (NSW).

On noxal surrender, see:

- Oliver Wendell Holmes Jr, *The Common Law and Other Writings*, Legal Classics Library, Birmingham, 1982.

- Stefan Jurasinski, 'Noxal Surrender, the Deodand, and the Laws of King Alfred', *Studies in Philology*, vol. 111, no. 2, 2014, pp. 195–224.

- Glanville Williams, *Liability for Animals*, Cambridge University Press, Cambridge, 1939.

On deodands, see:

- Sara M. Butler, 'Carts, Ships and Trains: Abusing the Deodand', Legal History Miscellany blog, 29 May 2020, https://legalhistorymiscellany.com/2020/05/29/carts-ships-and-trains-abusing-the-deodand.

- Anna Pervuhkin, 'Deodands: A Study in the Creation of Common Law Rules', *American Journal of Legal History*, vol. 47, no. 3, 2005, pp. 237–56.

For medieval accounts of English coroners' reports into deaths caused by pigs see:

- Sara M. Butler, *Forensic Medicine and Death Investigation in Medieval England*, Routledge, London, 2014.

- H.E. Salter (ed.), *Records of Mediaeval Oxford: Coroners' Inquests, the Walls of Oxford, Etc.*, Oxford Chronicle Co. Ltd, Oxford, 1912.

Several other cases are reported in ancient reports. In all of these cases, the verdict was 'misadventure':

- In 1218 in York, a boy was found dead from a pig's bite, and the pig was deodanded for sixpence: Doris M. Stenton (ed.), *Roll of the Justices of Eyre in Yorkshire in 3 Henry III*, vol. 24, Selden Society, London, 1937.

- In 1248 in Berkshire, a pig bit Alice, daughter of Clement, so that she died at once, and the pig was deodanded for nine pence. The report noted that, 'the first finder [of Alice's body] is not suspected, nor anyone else': M.T. Clanchy (ed.), *The Roll of the Berkshire Eyre 1248*, vol. 90, Selden Society, London, 1979, p. 349.

- In 1256 in Shropshire, a two-year-old boy called Aldith of Bridgnorth was bitten by a pig and died, and the pig was deodanded for eight pence: A. Harding (ed.), *The Roll of the Shropshire Eyre 1256*, vol. 96, Selden Society, London, p. 294.

On how English towns sought to control swine, see Dolly Jørgenson, 'Running Amuck? Urban Swine Management in Late Medieval Europe', *Agricultural History*, vol. 87, no. 4, 2013, pp. 429–51. Rules were made to try to control 'Tantony' pigs and random marauding pigs generally.

The 1329 case of the mare striking the child under the ear can be found at 3 Edw. 3, Fitz Corone 311, Eyre of Northampton (the names and details of the parties aren't known, and only the barest details were recorded). The translation is taken from Donald W. Sutherland, *The Eyre of Northamptonshire, 3–4 Edward III (1329–1330)*, vol. 1, Selden Society, London, 1983, p. 189.

For a discussion of early modern English law, see Matthew Hale, *Historia Placitorum Coronæ – The History of the Pleas of the Crown* and William Blackstone, *Commentaries on the Laws of England*, book IV, In the Savoy, London, 1736.

The case involving the vicious horse let loose on the common by the innkeeper is *R v Dant* (1865) Le & Ca 567, 169 ER 1517.

The 1628 case containing the quote about a pig eating an infant is *Hollowaye's Case* (1628) Palmer 546; 81 ER 1213. The case in fact involved a 'woodward' (a person who guarded his lord's wood) tying a trespassing child to the tail of a horse, causing their death. It is a difficult case to follow because it is written in 'Law French', a bastardised version of Norman French, Latin and English. In the report, Justice Dodderidge notes: 'And thus was a case, where an infant bastard was taken from its mother and hidden in a pigsty, and a sow came and ate the infant, and the woman was hanged for it.' Thank you to Joanna McCunn for the translation.

We have been unable to find an actual case where such an event occurred: we suspect it was an apocryphal story or a hypothetical scenario. However, it is not beyond the bounds of possibility that it reflects a real incident. In India in 2015, a female child was aborted at seven months, abandoned on a rubbish tip and eaten by wild pigs: Gareth Roberts, 'Shock as Pigs Are Caught on Camera Fighting Over Remains of Baby Dumped at Rubbish Tip', *Daily Mirror* 3 March 2015.

On Scottish law and the position of 'head-strang' horses, see A.D.M. Forte, 'The Horse That Kills: Some Thoughts on Deodands, Escheats and Crime in Fifteenth-Century Scots Law', *Tijdschrift voor Rechtsgeschiedenis*, vol. 58, 1990, pp. 95–110.

Prosecutions for Witchcraft

The description of the 'rooster' laying an egg comes from Edward Payson Evans, *The Criminal Prosecution and Capital Punishment of Animals*, W. Heinemann, London, 1906.

For the prosaic explanation of how a 'rooster' laid an egg, we relied upon E.V. Walter, 'Nature of Trial: The Case of the Rooster That Laid an Egg', in R.S. Cohen and N.W. Wartofsky (eds), *Methodology, Metaphysics and the History of Science*, Springer, Cham, 1984.

On the Salem witch trials, see Rebecca Beatrice Brooks, 'Animals in the Salem Witch Trials', History of Massachusetts blog, 20 February 2012, https://historyof-massachusetts.org/animals-in-the-salem-witch-trials.

Domestic Dogs on Death Row in the Modern Day

On Zoroastrian law, see James Darmesteter's translation of the Vendidad in *Sacred Books of the East*, American edition, Christian Literature Co., New York, 1898, available at www.avesta.org/vendidad/vd13sbe.htm.

The Canberra case involving Hodesh and Indiana is *Elliott v Weiss* [2001] ACTSC 127.

The Tasmanian case about Missy is *Pearce, Peter v Kingborough Council* [1998] TASSC 62.

The Victorian case about Jock is *Gubbins v Wyndham City Council* [2004] VSC 238.

The Australian statutes that deal with dog attacks are:

- *Domestic Animals Act 2000* (ACT), s. 55.
- *Companion Animals Act 1998* (NSW), ss. 25–28; Law Reform (Miscellaneous Provisions) Act (NT), s. 32.
- *Dog and Cat Management Act 1995* (SA), s. 66.
- *Dog Control Act 2000* (Tas.), s. 62(3)(g)(ii).
- *Domestic Animals Act 1994* (Vic.), s. 29(11). Compensation under the Victorian Act is only available where the owner has committed an offence under the Act: *Johnson v Buchanan* [2012] VSC 195.
- *Dog Act 1976* (WA), s. 46.

Victoria's provision allowing courts to order the destruction of dogs is *Domestic Animals Act 1994* (Vic.), s. 29.

Tasmania's earlier rules were laid out in its *Dog Control Act 1987* (Tas.), s. 59, and were then replaced by the *Dog Control Act 2000* (Tas.), s. 62.

Canberra's rules on identification can be found in its *Evidence Act 2001* (ACT), part 3.9, and in the *Crimes Act 1914* (Cth), ss. 3ZM–3ZQ. Victoria's additional rules are in the *Jury Directions Act 2015* (Vic.), ss. 35, 36.

Wild and Semidomesticated Animals

The William Shakespeare quote is from *The Merchant of Venice*, Act 4, Scene 1, lines 130–40.

On the strange history of wolf attacks, see Michelle Starr, 'Wolves among Us: Five Real-Life Werewolves from History', *CNET*, 29 October 2015.

The Lynching of Elephants

On the bizarre history of Mary the elephant, see Thomas G. Burton, 'The Hanging of Mary: A Circus Elephant', *Tennessee Folklore Society Bulletin*, vol. 37, 1971.

For details of the electrocution of Topsy, we consulted old newspapers from 1903, including *The New York Herald* and *New York Press*, accessed at fulton-history.com.

On Edison's involvement, see 'Thomas A. Edison Papers', Rutgers University website, accessed 21 October 2021, http://edison.rutgers.edu.

The George Orwell essay is 'Killing an Elephant', *Selected Writings*, Penguin, Harmondsworth, 1957.

Great Apes and Personhood

For more information on the Great Ape Project, see the GAP website, www.pro-jetogap.org.br/en/.

On the aggression of chimpanzees see:

- Chelsea Whyte, 'Chimps Beat Up, Murder and Then Cannibalise Their Former Tyrant', *New Scientist*, 20 January 2017.

- Michael L. Wilson, Christophe Boesch, Barbara Fruth et al., 'Lethal Aggression in *Pan* Is Better Explained by Adaptive Strategies than Human Impacts', *Nature*, no, 513, 2014, pp. 414–17.

- Christopher Flynn Martin, Rahul Bhui, Peter Bossaerts et al., 'Chimpanzee Choice Rates in Competitive Games Match Equilibrium Game Theory Predictions', *Scientific Reports*, vol. 4, 2014, art. 5182.

The case of the chimpanzee that bit off his keeper's finger is *James v Wellington City* [1972] NZLR 70.

For the tragic account of Travis the Chimp and his treatment of Charla Nash, we consulted a number of newspaper articles, including:

- Andy Newman, 'Pet Chimp Is Killed after Mauling Woman', *The New York Times*, 16 February 2009.

- Dan P. Lee, 'Travis the Menace', *New York Magazine*, 23 January 2011.

- Jane Goodall, 'Loving Chimps to Death', *Los Angeles Times*, 25 February 2009.

Modern Prosecution of Wild Bears

The thieving bear was reported in Paddy Clark, 'Bear Convicted for Theft of Honey', *BBC*, 14 March 2008.

On Katya the bear, see Will Stewart, 'Brown Bear Serving Prison Sentence in Human Jail for GBH "Released" after 15 Years', *The Mirror*, 17 November 2019.

4. *Understanding Animals*

The US Supreme Court case concerning Franky the Labrador is *Florida v Jardines*, 569 US 1 (2013).

The 1318 Scottish statute quoted by Alito can be found at K.M. Brown et al. (eds), 'Legislation: Statutes of the 1318 Parliament', The Records of the Parliaments of Scotland to 1707 database, 1318/9, accessed 21 October 2021, www.rps.ac.uk/trans/1318/9.

The 1955 article written by a retired police officer is C. Sloane, 'Dogs in War, Police Work and on Patrol', *The Journal of Criminal Law, Criminology and Police Science*, vol. 46, no. 3, 1955, p. 385–95.

The zoo experiment with a dingo in the Azaria Chamberlain case is described in G. Edmond, 'Negotiating the Meaning of a "Scientific" Experiment During a Murder Trial and Some Limits to Legal Deconstruction for the Public Understanding of Law and Science', *Sydney Law Review*, vol. 20, no. 3, 1998.

Animal Witnesses

The CIA document on trained cats is 'Memorandum for: [deleted], Subject: [deleted] Views on Trained Cats [deleted] for [deleted] Use, March 1967', Document 27, in J. Richelson (ed.), *National Security Archive Electronic Briefing Book No. 54*, George Washington University, Washington, DC.

Reactions to Familiar Things

The Washington, DC, case on the ownership of Prince/Buddy is described in 'A Dog's Tail Cannot Commit Perjury', *The Washington Times*, 4 June 1922, p. 7. Keeley Morse's bankruptcy and sale of his shop is advertised in *The Evening Star*, 8 December 1922.

The Washington State case about the barking dog is *State v Russell*, 141 Wn. App. 733 (2007).

The Namibian case about the disputed cow is S. *v Hepute* [2001] NAHC 23.

Reactions to Unfamiliar Things

The Sherlock Holmes quote is from Arthur Conan Doyle, 'Silver Blaze', *The Memoirs of Sherlock Holmes*, Project Gutenberg, Salt Lake City, (1899) 2019.

The full transcript of O.J. Simpson's trial is available at the Simpson Trial Transcripts website, accessed 21 October, http://simpson.walraven.org. The testimonies of Steven Schwab and his neighbour (Sukru Boztepe), and Nicole Brown Simpson's neighbour (Eva Stein) were given on 8 February 1995. The more distant neighbour, who heard a 'very unhappy animal' and 'plaintive wail' (Pablo Fenjves), testified on 7 February 1995. The 'dog has announced' quip was made by F. Lee Bailey on 21 February 1995. The quotes from Betty Littschwager, Julie Sterling and Carol Gurney are in M. Gelman, 'Quiet Akitas Wail at Trouble, Experts Say – Trial Focus Turns to Nicole's Dog', *The Seattle Times*, 9 February 1995.

The Paris case involving Scooby is described at P. Allen, 'Scooby the Dog Makes Legal History after Appearing in Court as a Witness in a Murder Case', *Daily Mail*, 10 September 2008.

The later French case about Tango is described at M. de Graaf, 'You're Barking Up the Wrong Tree, M'lud! Tango the Labrador Takes the Witness Stand in French Murder Trial', *Daily Mail*, 4 April 2014.

The South Australian case involving Rusty is *R v Lowe* [2016] SASCFC 118.

Mimicking Things

The 1993 parrot case is described in 'Parrot May Have the Answer to a Killing', *The New York Times*, 12 November 1993, p. 20.

The 2010 parrot case is described in D. MacDougall, 'Woman's Daughter Charged with Abuse and Neglect', *Post and Courier*, 7 December 2010.

On the 2014 parrot case, see P. Holley, 'Their Son Was Killed. They Believe His Parrot Is Telling People Who Pulled the Trigger', *The Washington Post*, 6 June 2016. A recording of the parrot Bud is posted on Marty Duram, Facebook, video post, 4 June 2016, www.facebook.com/watch/?v=1108723029169984&extid=eH43 Og8SdDiOtZ4P.

The 2018 parrot case is described in '"¡Ay por Favor Soltame, ay No!", La Frase que Repitió un Loro Testigo de un Femicidio', *Clarin*, 23 May 2020. See also 'Pidieron Prisión Perpetua para los Acusados del Femicidio de Elizabeth Alejandra Toledo', *Télam*, 22 September 2021.

The quotes about Project Acoustic Kitty are from R. Wallace and H. Melton, *Spycraft*, Bantam Books, London, 2009, pp. 200–01. The more colourful account is from J. Richelson, *The Wizards of Langley*, Westview, Boulder, 2001, pp. 147–48.

Police Animals

Edwin Brough's letter was published as 'The East-End Murders', *The Times*, 8 October 1888. For reports on subsequent events, see 'The East-End Murders', *The Times*, 9 October 1888, and 'The East-End Murders', *The Times*, 10 October 1888.

The quote from Pemberton on his use of bloodhounds in the Jack the Ripper case is from N. Pemberton, 'Bloodhounds as Detectives: Dogs, Slum Stench and Late-Victorian Murder Investigation', *Cultural and Social History* , vol. 10, no. 1, 2013, pp. 69–91.

For an account of South Africa's use of dogs, see B. Blum, 'The Hounds of Empire: Forensic Dog Tracking in Britain and Its Colonies, 1888–1953', *Law and History Review*, vol. 35, 2017, pp. 621–65.

Animals' Noses

The South Australian bus case is *In the matter of section 350(2)(A), Criminal Law Consolidation Act 1935; Questions of Law Reserved (No 3 of 1998)* (1998) 71 SASR 223 [1998] SASC 7163.

The High Court application is *Hoare v The Queen* [1999] HCATrans 186.

The Sydney nightclub case is *DPP v Darby* [2002] NSWSC 1157, and the appeal is *Darby v Director of Public Prosecutions* [2004] NSWCA 431.

The NSW legislation was the *Police Powers (Drug Detection) Act 2001* (NSW), ss. 7, 8. See also *Law Enforcement (Powers and Responsibilities) Act 2002* (NSW), ss. 147, 148.

For a US ruling on drug dogs, see *United States v Place*, 462 US 696 (1983). For a Canadian ruling on drug dogs, see *R v Kang-Brown* [2008] SCC 18.

Animals' Teeth

The Florida Supreme Court decision that was appealed to the United States Supreme Court is *Jardines v State* 73 So. 3d 34 (2011).

The South Australian decision about Riggs and Koda is *Police v Williams* [2014] SASC 177. The quote from the American article is at [257].

Animal as Experts

The two 1918 South African cases are *R v Kotcho* and *R v Barley* (1918, E.D.L. 91), and they are described in B. Blum, 'The Hounds of Empire: Forensic Dog Tracking in Britain and Its Colonies, 1888–1953', *Law and History Review*, vol. 35, 2017, pp. 621–65.

The 1920 South African case is *R v Trupedo* (1920 A.D. 58).

The Keath Shear quote is from 'Police Dogs and State Rationality in Early Twentieth-Century South Africa', in L. van Stittert and S. Swart (eds), *Canis Africanis: A Dog History of Southern Africa*, Brill, Boston, 2008.

For South Africa's apartheid reaffirmation of Trupedo see *S. v Shabalala* 1986 (4) SA 734 (A). India's subsequent ruling is *Gade Lakshmi Mangaraju alias Ramesh v State of A. P.* 2001 6 SCC 205.

Animal Inferences

The 1963 Indian ruling is *Abdul Rajak Murtaja Defedar v State of Maharashtra* 1969 2 SCC 234. For the 1920 South African ruling, see *R v Trupedo* (1920 A.D. 58). The 1903 Nebraska ruling is *Brott v State*, 70 Neb 395 (1903).

The 1960 Scottish ruling is *Patterson v Nixon* 1960 SCJ 42. The 1962 Canadian ruling is *R v Haas* (1962) 35 DLR (2d) 172.

The 1964 New Zealand ruling (by Woodhouse J) is *R v Te Whui & Buckland* [1964] NZLR 748, while the later Court of Appeal rulings are *R v Lindsay* [1970] NZLR 1002 and *R v McCartney* [1976] 1 NZLR 472.

The 1966 Northern Irish ruling is *R v Montgomery* [1966] NI 120.

The 1988 New South Wales ruling is *R v Ross Alexander Barnes* (Supreme Court of NSW – Court of Criminal Appeal, No 452 of 1987, 1 December 1988).

The 1995 English ruling is *Pieterson v R* [1994] EWCA Crim 5.

Animal Suspicions

The quotes from the prosecutor and Dr Harding are from G. Edmond, 'Negotiating the Meaning of a "Scientific" Experiment During a Murder Trial and Some Limits to Legal Deconstruction for the Public Understanding of Law and Science', *Sydney Law Review*, vol. 20, no. 3, 1998.

The second Florida sniffer dog case is *Harris v State*, 71 So. 3d 756 (2011) (Florida Supreme Court) and *Florida v Harris*, 568 US 237 (2013).

Convictions Based on Animals' Evidence

Commissioner Morling's quote is from Gary Edmond, 'Negotiating the Meaning of a "Scientific" Experiment, *Sydney Law Review*, vol, 20, no. 3, 1998, pp. 361–401.

Justice Graham's quote is from *R v Kotcho; R v Barley* (1918, E.D.L. 91).

The 1926 British Columbia case and dissent are from *R v White* [1926] 3 DLR 1, while the later case is *R v Haas* (1962) 35 DLR (2d) 172.

The 1980 Victorian case is *R v Joe Saccu* [1980] VicSC 36.

The 1999 New South Wales case is *R v Benecke* [1999] NSWCCA 163.

The New South Wales case a decade later is *Muldoon v R; Carter v R* [2008] NSWCCA 315.

The 2013 Queensland case about Jack is *R v Tamatea* [2013] QCA 399, while subsequent events are described at S. Hurley, '31 Minutes of Fear: Australian Deportee Jailed over Knifepoint Manukau Mall Hostage Situation', *The New Zealand Herald*, 1 July 2019.

5. Harming Animals

Events in the courtroom of the New Haven colony are from Charles Hoadley (ed.), *Records of the Colony and Plantation of New Haven from 1638 to 1649*, Case, Tiffany & Co, Hartford, 1858 – specifically the trials of Thomas Badger (p. 61), George Spencer (pp. 62–73) and Thomas Hogg (pp. 295–96).

The prosecution of Patrick McElligott is described in *Queensland Police Service v McElligott* [2020] QMC 1. See also Lea Emery, 'Attack Left Dog "Terrified"', *Gold Coast Bulletin*, 17 February 2020, p. 3.

The prosecution of Roderic Mitchell is described at *Mitchell v Marshall* [2014] TASSC 43. See also Helen Kempton: 'Two Animal Cruelty Charges Thrown Out', *The Mercury* (Hobart), 1 August 2008, p. 10, and 'Farm Animals "Left for Dead": Cruelty Case Back in Court', *The Mercury* (Hobart), 26 October 2010, p. 12.

Geoffrey Chaucer's poem is *The Parliament of Foules*, ed. T. Lounsbury, Ginn, Heath & Co, Boston, 1853.

The alleged rites of Lupercalia are described in Plutarch, 'The Life of Julius Caesar', *Parallel Lives*, Loeb Classical Library edition, Harvard University Press, Cambridge, MA, 1919.

Sex with Animals

See Leviticus 18:6–23 for prohibitions on various sexual relations.
The English bestiality statutes are:

- *An Acte for the Punysshement of the Vice of Buggerie* (Eng.), 25 Hen. 8, c. 6 (1533).

- *Offences against the Person Act* 1861 (U.K.), 24 & 25 Vict., c. 100, s. 61.

- *Sexual Offences Act* 2003 (UK), s. 69.

The Tasmanian bestiality offence is in *Criminal Code Act 1924* (Tas.), Schedule 1, s. 122.

Defining Bestiality

The Tasmanian case on an 'unnatural crime' is *R v Wells* [1833] TASSupC 3.

The Tasmanian case on non-penetrative bestiality with dogs is *Elnami v Tasmania* [2020] TASSC 54.

The Canadian case on non-penetrative bestiality with dogs is *R. v. D.L.W.*, 2016 SCC 22 (CanLII), [2016] 1 SCR 402.

The Canadian reform statute is *An Act to Amend the Criminal Code (Bestiality and Animal Fighting)*, SC 2019, c 17.

Victoria's provisions on sex with animals are at *Crimes Act 1958* (Vic.), ss. 35A(3), (4) & (5); 35C(a)(ii), (b)(iii); 54A; and 54B.

The English case on bestiality with domestic fowls is *R v Brown* (1889) 24 Q.B.D. 357.

Proving Bestiality

The New South Wales cases discussed are held by the NSW State Archives and Records in the record series 'NRS 3397 Judge Advocate's Bench of Magistrates, Proceedings'. With the archive inaccessible due to Covid-19, we relied on online transcripts. For the Mary Daniels, George Hyson and James Reece cases, see:

- '1804, Mary Daniels', Unfit for Publication: NSW Supreme Court and Other Bestiality, Buggery and Sodomy Trials 1727–1930 website, accessed 21 October 2021, www.unfitforpublication.org.au/trials/1800s/5-1804-mary-daniels.

- 'Violent Crimes and Violent Deaths in Australia and New Zealand 1788–1853', Criminal Justice Research Centre website, accessed 21 October 2021, https://cjrc.osu.edu/research/interdisciplinary/hvd/australia-new-zealand/crimes-and-deaths, 23 April 1796, pp. 12–13 (George Hyson), 31 January 1799, pp. 13–14 (James Reece).

Punishing Bestiality

Leviticus's capital punishments for various sexual acts are at 20: 10–17.

Colin Higson's case is reported at *R v Higson* (1984) 6 Cr App R 20. The case that distinguished it is *R v Tierney* (1990) 12 Cr App R(S) 216.

For the 'worse, and worse and bad enough' case, see: '1812, Daniel Gilmore', Unfit for Publication website, accessed 21 October 2021, www.unfitforpublication. org.au/trials/1800s/14-1812-daniel-gilmore.

The evidence of the prelate (William Ullathorne) can be found in UK Parliament, *Report from the Select Committee on Transportation*, House of Lords, London, 16 August 1838. The findings about 'unnatural crimes' are at p. xxvii.

The High Court case is *Bounds v R* [2006] HCA 39.

Cruelty to Animals

The Leviticus quotes are at 20:14 and 15.

For the 'poor man' case, see '1823, James Ruark', Unfit for Publication website, accessed 21 October 2021, www.unfitforpublication.org.au/trials/1800s/18-1823-james-ruark.

The mule being burned at the stake and the she-ass being spared for execution for bestiality are described in Edward Payson Evans, *The Criminal Prosecution and Capital Punishment of Animals*, W. Heinemann, London, 1906.

Cotton Mather describes animals being executed for bestiality in *Magnalia Christi Americana or The Ecclesiastical History of New England*, vol. 2, S. Andrus and Son, Hartford, 1865, pp. 405–07.

Defining Cruelty

The English statutes are:

- *An Act to Prevent the Cruel and Improper Treatment of Cattle*, 3 Geo. IV c. 71 (1822).

- *An Act for the More Effectual Prevention of Cruelty to* Animals, 12 & 13 Vict. c. 92 (1849).

The cock-fighting case is *Budge v Parsons* [1863] EngR 270.

The dehorning cattle case is *Ford v Wiley* (1889) 23 QBD 203. The Queensland provision is the *Animal Care and Protection Act 2001* (Qld), s. 18.

The case on animal euthanasia is *R v Menard*, 1978 CanLII 2355; 43 CCC (2d) 458.

Proving Cruelty

The interview with the documentary filmmaker is 'Making a Killing', *Four Corners*, ABC, 16 February 2015.

The High Court judgment is *Kadir v The Queen; Grech v The Queen* [2020] HCA 1.

Punishing Cruelty

The Victorian statistics (and the RSPCA quote) are from: Sentencing Advisory Council, *Animal Cruelty Offences in Victoria*, Sentencing Advisory Council, Melbourne, 2019.

The 'Darling Downs rapist' case is *Buckley v R* [2006] HCA 7. See also *Buckley v Queensland Parole Board* [2017] QSC 41.

The new NSW ban is the *Crimes Act 1900* (NSW), s. 31AB.

6. *Protecting Animals*

The cases involving Daniel Brighton are:

- *Brighton v Will* [2020] NSWSC 435.

- *Will v Brighton* [2020] NSWCA 355.

The applicable legislation is *Crimes Act 1900* (NSW), s. 530.

For more information on Alice, including the GoFundMe campaign, see K. Caines, 'Dog Pack Mauls Young Camel', *Macarthur Chronicle*, 2 February 2016.

Details about the proposed zoo and Brighton's background are from K. Caines, 'Zoo Plans Feature Close Encounters with Animals', *Macarthur Chronicle*, 26 April 2016.

The missing crocodiles were reported in:

- C. Ngo, 'Fears for Missing Croc Duo', *Macarthur Chronicle*, 14 March 2017.

- C. Ngo, 'Sad End for Croc Crackle', *Liverpool Leader*, 6 May 2017.

- 'Steve Irwin Version Two', *Country News*, 25 April 2017.

The neglect charges against Brighton were reported in:

- A. Tullis, 'RSPCA Gives Evidence in Cruelty Case', *Campbelltown-Macarthur Advertiser*, 22 August 2018.

- R Dickins, 'Get Wild Mobile Zoo Owner Cleared of Animal Cruelty Charges', *Campbelltown-Macarthur Advertiser*, 4 December 2018.

The case involving the bushfire donations is *In the Matter of the New South Wales Rural Fire Service & Brigades Donations Fund; Application of McDonald & Or* [2020] NSWSC 604).

Private Law: Providing for Animals

Providing for a Particular Animal

The story of Greyfriars Bobby is described in Ben Johnson, 'Grayfriars Bobby', Historic UK website, accessed 21 October 2021, www.historic-uk.com/HistoryUK/HistoryofScotland/Greyfriars-Bobby.

Hachikō's story is told in Jessica E. Page, 'Hachiko Statue University of Tokyo', Japan Travel website, 21 April 2015, https://en.japantravel.com/tokyo/hachiko-statue-university-of-tokyo/20013.

The case of Chatziko the kitten was reported in 'Cat Sits by Owners' Graves at Greek Cemetery Mourning Their Death', *Neos Kosmos*, 8 December 2020.

The will of the pig M. Grunnius Corcotta Porcellus is described in Michelle Lovric, *Weird Wills and Eccentric Last Wishes*, Zondervan, Grand Rapids, 2004, pp. 52–53, and Virgil M. Harris, *Ancient Curious and Famous Wills*, Beard Books, Washington, DC, (1911) 2000, pp. 20–21. Harris also talks of the oldest will being Ancient Egyptian.

The dog burial is discussed in Simon J.M. Davies and François R. Valla, 'Evidence for Domestication of the Dog 12,000 Years Ago in the Natufian of Israel', *Nature*, no. 276, 1978, pp. 608–10.

Leaving Money to a Trusted Person
On the case of Missy the cat, see Adam Bell, 'Trust Fund Pets Are Rolling in It as Owners Leave Huge Inheritances to their Furry Loved Ones', *The Daily Telegraph*, 5 December 2014.

Honey Pooh's story is reported in Julia Marsh, 'Dachshund Robbed of $100K Trust Fund: Lawsuit', *New York Post*, 28 July 2016.

Gale Posner's trust for Conchita the chihuahua is discussed in Kyle Munzenrieder, 'Gale Posner Left a $3 Million Trust Fund and Mansion to Her Dogs and Her Son Is Pissed', *Miami New Times*, 17 June 2010.

RSPCA Australia's pet legacy options are detailed online: 'Pet Legacies', RSPCA website, accessed 21 October 2021, www.rspca.org.au/support-us/pet-legacies.

Leaving Money to the Animal
The case of the black mare is *Pettingall v Pettingall* (1842) 11 LJ Ch 176.

The other cases involving bequests to animals are:

- *Mitford v Reynolds* (1848) 16 Sim 105; 60 ER 812 (horses).

- *Re Dean* (1889) 41 Ch D 552 (horses and hounds).

- *Re Haines* (reported in *The Times*, 7 November 1952, p. 11) (two cats).

- *Re Howard* (reported in *The Times*, 30 October 1903, p. 3) (two dogs and a parrot).

The tale (tail?) of the will for goldfish appears to have originated in 'The Eccentricities of Testators', *Green Bag*, vol. 15, no. 2, 1903, pp. 583–85.

The story of the man who left his land to elephants appears in 'Indian Man Upsets Wife by Bequesting Land to Two Elephants', *The Guardian*, 11 June 2020.

The Irish case stating that the rule against perpetuities has to be about a human life is *Re Kelly* [1932] IR 255.

The case where the English judge took judicial notice of the lifespan of cats is *Re Haines* (reported in *The Times*, 7 November 1952, p. 11).

The Australian legislation extending the perpetuities period is:

- *Law of Property Act* (NT), s. 187.

- *Perpetuities Act 1984* (NSW), s. 8.

- *Perpetuities and Accumulations Act 1968* (Vic.), s. 5.

- *Perpetuities and Accumulations Act 1985* (ACT), s. 8.

- *Perpetuities and Accumulations Act 1992* (Tas.), s. 6.

- *Property Law Act 1969* (WA), s. 101.

- *Property Law Act 1974* (Qld), s. 209.

South Australia has abolished it altogether: *Law of Property Act 1936* (SA), s. 61.

The story of Cocky Bennet was reported in Glenda Kwek, 'Sydney's Old Crock of a Cockie Was a Legend at 120', *The Sydney Morning Herald*, 31 August 2011.

Recently, Gerry W. Beyer noted the issues that might arise from long-lived parrots and suggested solutions in 'What If Your Parrot Outlives You? Preparing for Your Bird's Future', *SSRN*, 8 October 2020.

The case of the fox-hunting trust being upheld is *Re Thompson* [1934] Ch 342.

The full story of Leona Helmsley is told in Jeffrey Toobin, 'Rich Bitch: The Legal Battle over Trust Funds for Pets', *The New Yorker*, 29 September 2008.

Trouble's death was reported in Susan Donaldson James, 'Leona Helmsley's Little Rich Dog Trouble Dies in Luxury', *ABC News* (US), 10 June 2011.

The information about Karl Lagerfeld and his cat, Choupette, was gleaned from:

- 'Karl Lagerfeld: Designer's Cat Choupette "Named in His Will"', *BBC News*, 21 February 2019.

- Liam O'Brien, 'Karl Lagerfeld Says He Wants to get Married ... to His Cat', *The Independent*, 1 June 2013.

- Dana Thomas, 'What Happened to Choupette? Karl Lagerfeld's Cat, and Rumoured Heir, Has Become a Business unto Herself', 21 January 2020, *The New York Times*.

- Choupette Lagerfeld (@choupetteofficiel) Instagram account.

Requiring the Animal to Be Put Down

Lesli Bisgould suggests the dog buried in the Natufian was put down in *Animals and the Law*, Irwin Law, Toronto, 2011, pp. 2–3.

The lack of cases requiring animals to be put down on their owner's death in Australia was noted in Alex Bruce, *Animal Law in Australia: An Integrated Approach*, LexisNexis Butterworths, Chatswood, 2018.

The American case of the Shih tzu that was put down when her owner died is detailed in Rob Bailey-Millado, 'Healthy Dog Euthanized to Be Buried with Dead Owner as Her Will Requested', *New York Post*, 22 May 2019.

The American cases in which clauses requiring animals to be put down were not enforced include:

- *Re Caper's Estate* 34 Pa D & C 2d 121 (1964) (euthanasia of dog).

- *Re Estate of Clive Wishard* ACWSJ Lexis 34836 (1992) (euthanasia of horses).

- *Smith v Azanzino* No 225698 (1980) (Supreme Court of San Francisco County).

Providing for Animals Generally

The Elizabethan statute governing charities was *Charitable Uses Act of 1601* (43 Eliz I, c. 4). It was repealed in England and Wales by the *Mortmain and Charitable Uses Act 1888* (51 & 52 Vict, c.42), s. 13(1), which preserves s. 13(2) of the original Act in the preamble. The English law of charities and charitable trusts is now governed by the *Charities Act 2011* (c. 25) (UK).

Lord Macnaughten's four categories are enunciated in *Commissioners for Special Purposes of Income Tax v Pemsel* [1891] AC 531 at 583.

The Australian statute that holds that 'the purpose of preventing or relieving the suffering of animals' is a charitable purpose is *Charities Act 2013* (Cth), s. 12(1)(i). The purpose of 'advancing the natural environment' is also covered in s. 12(1)(j).

The series of English decisions that held that trusts benefiting both animals and humans were charitable include:

- *University of London v Yarrow* (1857) 1 DeG & J 72, 44 ER 649.

- *Re Douglas* (1887) 35 Ch D 472.

- *Re Vallance* (1876) 2 Seton's Judgments & Orders, 7th ed, 1304, cited in *Re Herrick* (1918) 52 ILT 213.

- *Re Joy* (1888) 60 LT 175.

For the history of the RSPCA, see 'RSPCA: Our History'. RSPCA website (UK), accessed 21 October 2021, www.rspca.org.uk/whatwedo/whoweare/history.

The cases that held that trusts for the prevention of cruelty of animals were not charitable per se include *Armstrong v Reeves* (1890) 25 LR Ir 325 and *Re Foveaux* [1895] 2 Ch 501. However, these cases did contemplate that anti-vivisection aims might be charitable.

Re Wedgwood [1915] 1 Ch 113 held that prevention of cruelty to animals was charitable. The quote is from p. 122 of that judgment.

The case that held that anti-vivisection aims are not charitable is *National Anti-Vivisection Society v Inland Revenue Commissioners* [1948] AC 31.

The case that found that an animal refuge free from human interference would not be charitable is *In re Grove-Grady* [1929] Ch 557.

The case in which the trust for the general benefit of animals was rejected is *Murdoch v Attorney-General* (Tas.) (1992) 1 Tas R 117.

The case for the benefit of the homing pigeons is *Royal National Agricultural and Industrial Association v Chester* (1974) 48 ALJR 304. The quotes are taken from pp. 304 and 305. The court applied Lord Wilberforce's 'public utility' test from *Scottish Burial Reform and Cremation Society v Glasgow Corporation* [1968] AC 138.

They rejected testing 'any purpose beneficial to the community' as suggested by Russell and Sachs LLJ in *Incorporated Council of Law Reporting for England and Wales v Attorney-General* [1972] Ch 73.

The case involving the trust for spotted doves is *Royal Society for the Prevention of Cruelty to Animals (NSW) v Benevolent Society of New South Wales* (1960) 102 CLR 629. The quote is from pp. 648–49 of the judgment. Spotted doves were introduced to Australia in the 1860s, and they flourished: 'Spotted Dove', Birdlife Australia website, accessed 21 October 2021, www.birdlife.org.au/bird-profile/spotted-dove.

The trusts for native animals that were upheld include *Re Ingram* [1951] VLR 424 and *A-G (NSW) v Sawtell* [1978] 2 NSWLR 200.

Public Law: Speaking for Animals

For RSPCA's statement on Brighton's sentence, see 'Record Prison Sentence for Petting Zoo Owner Who Stabbed, Beat, Hanged Dog to Death', RSPCA NSW website, 27 June 2019, www.rspcansw.org.au/blog/media-releases/record-prison-sentence-for-petting-zoo-owner-who-killed-dog.

The Australian case involving the ownership of elephants is *Pearson v Janlin Circuses Pty Ltd* [2002] NSWSC 1118.

The legislation preventing cruelty to animals is the *Prevention of Cruelty to Animals Act 1979* (NSW), s. 5(2).

Arna's fate is described at H. Moore, 'Killer Elephant "Died of a Broken Heart"', *News.com.au*, 13 August 2020.

The cases involving Lucy the Elephant are discussed in Shaun Fluker, 'Lucy the Elephant v. Edmonton (City)', University of Calgary Faculty of Law ABlawg blog, 1 September 2010, https://ablawg.ca/2010/09/01/lucy-the-elephant-v-edmonton-city, and Kathleen Harris, 'Supreme Court Dismisses Case Involving Lucy the Elderly Elephant', *CBC News*, 20 December 2019. The animal welfare legislation covering Lucy is the *Animal Protection Act*, R.S.A. 2000, c. A-41 and the *Wildlife Act*, R.S.A. 2000, c. W-10.

Suits for Animals

The case in which Maguire sought to force Parks Victoria to consult with the community about its plan to control the wild horses in Victoria's Alpine National Park is *Maguire v Parks Victoria* [2020] VSCA 172. The earlier case brought over the brumbies is *Australian Brumby Alliance Inc. v Parks Victoria Inc.* [2020] FCA 605.

The federal law that allows some actions without standing is *Environment Protection and Biodiversity Conservation Act 1999* (Cth), s. 475.

For information about the conclusion of Phil Maguire's case, see 'Feral Horse FAQs', Parks Victoria website, accessed 21 October 2021, www.parks.vic.gov.au/get-into-nature/conservation-and-science/conserving-our-parks/feral-animals/feral-horses/feral-horse-faqs.

The cases brought by the Nonhuman Rights Project are detailed in 'Litigation', Nonhuman Rights Project website, accessed 21 October 2021, www.nonhuman-rights.org/litiation. The case on Tommy is *People ex rel. Non-human Rights Project Inc. v Lavery*, 998 N.Y.S.2d 248 (2014). See also the later unreported case decided on 8 May 2018.

The case on orcas is *Tilikum v Sea World*, 842 F.Supp.2d 1259 (2012).

Suits by Animals

For Slater's initial account of how the monkey 'selfies' were taken, see S. Morris, 'Shutter-Happy Monkey Turns Photographer', *The Guardian*, 5 July 2011. His modified description is at C. Cheesman, 'Ape-rture Priority Photographer Plays Down Monkey Reports', *Amateur Photographer*, 5 July 2011. The 'Monkey Selfie' case is *Naruto v Slater* 888 F 3d 418 (9th Cir 2018). Paul Babie's article on the case is 'The "Monkey Selfies": Reflections on Copyright in the Photographs of Animals: *Naruto v. Slater*, 888 F.3d 418 (9th Cir 2018)' (2018) 52 *UC Davis Law Review Online* 103.

The case on cetaceans is *Cetacean Community v Bush*, 386 F.3d 1169 (2004).

On the Columbian case, see 'Animals Recognized as Legal Persons for the First Time in U.S. Court', Animal Legal Defense Fund website, 20 October 2021, https://aldf.org/article/animals-recognized-as-legal-persons-for-the-first-time-in-u-s-court.

The statute concerning Te Awa Tupua (Whanganui River) is *Te Awa Tupua (Whanganui River Claims Settlement) Act 2017* (NZ).

Criminal Law: Defending Animals

The NSW law is the *Companion Animals Act 1998* (NSW), s. 18.

The Strange Case of the Vermin Trials

In this section, we once again relied on Edward Payson Evans, *The Criminal Prosecution and Capital Punishment of Animals*, W. Heinemann, London, 1906.

The medal awarded to Cher Ami is described in Kayla Webley, 'Top 10 Heroic Animals', *Time*, 21 March 2011.

The views of St Augustine and St Thomas Aquinas are laid out in:

- St Augustine, *De Civitate Dei*, Oxbow Books, Oxford, 2005, book I: 'By a most just ordinance of the Creator, both their life and their death are subject to our use.'

- Thomas Aquinas, *The 'Summa Theologica' of St Thomas Aquinas*, trans. Fathers of the English Dominican Province, Burns, Oates & Washburne, London, 1918, q. 64, art. 2.

Sara M. Butler discusses the more complex aspects of medieval attitudes towards animals in 'Persons under the Law? Medieval Animal Rights', Legal History Miscellany blog, 19 February 2018, https://legalhistorymiscellany.com/2018/02/19/persons-under-the-law-medieval-animals-rights.

Stephen de Bourbon's efforts to stamp out the worship of the saintly hound are described in Étienne de Bourbon, *Anecdotes historiques ... d'Étienne de Bourbon*, Librairie Renouard, Paris, 1877. Passage translated by Paul Hyams available at 'Medieval Sourcebook: Stephen de Bourbon (d. 1262): De Supersticione: On St. Guinefort', Fordham University website, last modified 8 September 2000, https://sourcebooks.fordham.edu/source/guinefort.asp.

The continued veneration of St Guinefort is noted in Colin Dickey, 'A Faithful Hound: How a Dog Came to Be Recognised as a Saint', *Lapham's Quarterly*, 18 June 2013.

The article drawing a link between vermin trials and witchcraft trials is Peter T. Leeson, 'Vermin Trials', *The Journal of Law and Economics*, vol, 56, no. 3, 2013, pp. 811–36.

The most comprehensive account of how witchcraft prosecutions evolved in Europe is Norman Cohn, *Europe's Inner Demons: The Demonization of Christians in Medieval Christendom*, revised ed., University of Chicago Press, Chicago, 1993.

The Scottish rhyme is included in Robert Chambers, *Popular Rhymes of Scotland*, W & R Chambers, Edinburgh, 1858, p. 120 (with note of the writ of ejectment!).

Leslie Megahey (dir.), *The Hour of the Pig*, BBC Films, 1993, starred Colin Firth as 'Richard Courtois', but the character is clearly based on Chasseneuz.

The Singular Case of Daniel Brighton

When Brighton killed the dog, s.34 of the *Prevention of Cruelty to Animals Act 1979* (NSW) required prosecutions to be brought within a year of the cruelty. The *Prevention of Cruelty to Animals Amendment Act 2021* (NSW) changed the time limit for prosecution.

The Day of the Tentacle

For more information on the Ocean Art 2020 contest, see '2020 Ocean Art Contest Winners', Underwater Photography Guide website, accessed 21 October 2021, www.uwphotographyguide.com/ocean-art-contest-winners-2020. It includes links to the winning images (including *The Day of the Tentacle*), the judges' comments (including comments from Tony Wu) and Gaetano Dario Gargiulo's 'story of the shot'. The contest rules are at www.uwphotographyguide.com/ocean-art/competition-details.

The definition of 'author' in the *Copyright Act 1986* (Cth) is provided at s. 10(1).

The octopus-related murder case is reported in 'South Korean Court Upholds "Octopus Murder" Acquittal', *ABC News*, 12 September 2013.

For an account of a photo-taking octopus, see J. Lee, 'Is This Picture-Taking Octopus As Smart as She Seems?', *National Geographic*, 17 April 2015.

The Rights of Human Animals

Being Human

The case concerning the X-Men toys is *Toy Biz Inc. v US*, 248 F. Supp.2d 1234 (2003). The earlier cases are reported at 123 F. Supp. 2d 646 (2000); Supp. 2d 17 (2001); and 219 F. Supp. 2d 1289 (2002).

The research on human–monkey chimeras is Tao Tan, Jun Wu, Chenyang Si et al., 'Chimeric Contribution of Human Extended Pluripotent Stem Cells to Monkey Embryos Ex Vivo', *Cell*, vol. 184, no. 8, 2021, pp. 2020–32.

Australia's statute on hybrid and chimeric embryos (at the federal level) is the *Prohibition of Human Cloning for Reproduction Act 2002* (Cth), ss. 9, 17, 18.

The United Nations *Declaration on Human Cloning* is included in General Assembly, 59th Session, Agenda Item 150, International Convention against the Reproductive Cloning of Human Beings, Report of the Sixth Committee, A/59/516/Add.1, 24 February 2005.

Human Rights

An image and transcript of the original Magna Carta is available at 'Magna Carta 1215', British Library website, accessed 21 October 2021, www.bl.uk/collection-items/magna-carta-1215. For its current form, see Magna Carta (1297) on Legislation.gov.uk, accessed 21 October 2021, www.legislation.gov.uk/aep/Edw1cc1929/25/9/contents.

The first ten amendments to the US Constitution can be viewed at 'The Bill of Rights', National Archives website, accessed 21 October 2021, www.archives.gov/founding-docs/bill-of-rights.

The French Declaration of the Rights of Man and of the Citizen is available at 'Déclaration des Droits de l'Homme et du Citoyen de 1789', Léfigrance website, accessed 21 October 2021, www.legifrance.gouv.fr/contenu/menu/droit-national-en-vigueur/constitution/declaration-des-droits-de-l-homme-et-du-citoyen-de-1789.

For the Universal Declaration of Human Rights, see 'Universal Declaration of Human Rights', UN website, accessed 21 October 2021, www.un.org/sites/un2.un.org/files/udhr.pdf.

The Australian decision on Tasmania's anti-protest laws is *Brown v Tasmania* [2017] HCA 43. The earlier decision on protesting duck-hunting in Victoria is *Levy v Victoria* [1997] HCA 31. An example of a recent law introducing new restrictions that target animal rights protesters is the *Criminal Code Amendment (Agricultural Protection) Act 2019* (Cth).

The Canadian decision on Musqueam hunting rights is *R v Sparrow* [1990] 1 SCR 1075.

The English decision on fox-hunting is *R (on the application of Countryside Alliance and others) v Attorney General & Anor* [2007] UKHL 52.

Seeing Animals

The octopus-hunting incident in Seattle is discussed in M. Hanel, 'The Octopus That Almost Ate Seattle', *The New York Times Magazine*, 16 October 2013. For several contemporaneous accounts of octopus wrestling, see K. Veronese, 'Octopus Wrestling, a Sport That Amounted to Cephalopod Home Invasion', *Gizmodo*, 17 February 2012.

For a description of how live octopus is prepared, see 'Your Food Shouldn't Be Trying to Escape From Your Plate – Watch These Videos and Never Eat Octopus!', PETA website, 6 April 2017, www.peta.org/living/food/eating-octopus-cruel. PETA claims a restaurant changed its menu in response to its campaign against live-animal eating: 'Update: Sik Gaek Restaurant Removes Live Animals from Menu', PETA website, 26 March 2021, www.peta.org/action/action-alerts/octopuses-new-york-restaurant.

The Australian decision on the legality of a video depicting possum slaughter is *ABC v Lenah Game Meats Pty Ltd* [2001] HCA 63.

The US decision on dog fight videos is *United States v Stevens*, 559 US 460, (2010). The revised US law is at 18 US Code, s. 48.

The Rights of Non-Human Animals

Animal Dignity

The three Australian rights statutes that limit their application to individuals or human beings are:

- *Human Rights Act 2004* (ACT), s. 6.
- *Charter of Human Rights and Responsibilities Act 2006* (Vic.), s. 6.
- *Human Rights Act 2019* (Qld), s. 11.

For background on the first two, see J. Gans, 'Denial of Non-Human Rights Protection in Australia', *New Zealand Law Review*, vol. 2011, no, 2, 2011, pp. 229–60.

The Swiss provision is the *Federal Constitution of the Swiss Federation*, art. 120.2. The Swiss decision is *X und Y gegen Gesundheitsdirektion des Kantons Zürich und Mitb.*, Swiss Federal Supreme Court (Oct. 7, 2009) BGE 135 II 384 (Switz.), p. 405.

The Indian decision is *N.R. Nair And Ors., Etc. Etc. vs Union Of India (Uoi) And Ors.* (High Court of Kerala, 6 June 2000, AIR 2000 Ker 340.)

On Octavia the octopus, see J. Antczak, 'Octopus Drains Tank, Dies, Activists Blame Death on Stress in Captivity', *Los Angeles Daily News*, 12 April 1994, and J. Michael Kennedy, 'Octopus Dies as Tank Empties', *Los Angeles Times*, 12 April 1994.

Animal Suffering

Bentham's quote is from J. Bentham, *Principles of Morals and Legislation*, Clarendon Press, Oxford, 1789, p. 311.

New South Wales definition of 'animal' is provided in *Prevention of Cruelty to Animals Act 1979* (NSW), s. 4(1).

David Foster Wallace's lobster essay is 'Consider the Lobster', *Gourmet*, August 2004, pp. 50–64.

The NSW guidelines on humane killing of crustaceans are available at 'Humane Harvesting of Fish and Crustaceans', Department of Primary Industries website, accessed 21 October 2021, www.dpi.nsw.gov.au/animals-and-livestock/animal-welfare/animal-care-and-welfare/other/companion-animal-files/humane-harvesting-of-fish-and-crustaceans.

On the 2017 prosecution of the fishmonger, see N. Zhao, 'Sydney Fishmonger Convicted of Animal Cruelty over Lobster Treatment', *The Guardian*, 15 February 2017.

The European Union directive is *Directive 2010/63/EU of the European Parliament and of the Council of 22 September 2010 on the protection of animals used for scientific purposes*, Official Journal of the European Union, 20 October 2010, L 276/33, 3(b).

Animal Sentience

Bentham's quote is from J. Bentham, *Theory of Legislation*, 5th ed., Turner & Co, London, p. 429.

The European Union provision is the *Treaty on the Functioning of the European Union*, art. 13.

The relevant New Zealand provisions are the *Animal Welfare Act 1999* (NZ), para (a) of the long title, and ss. 80(2)(b) and 100(1)(fa). The definition of 'animal' is at s. 2(1).

The Australian Capital Territory provision is the *Animal Welfare Act 1992* (ACT), s. 4A(1)(a). A definition of 'animal' is included in the Act's dictionary.

Webster's quote is from J. Webster, *Animal Welfare: Limping towards Eden*, Oxford, Blackwell, 2005, p. 11.

On the display of Bentham's preserved body, see 'Auto-Icon', University College London website, accessed 21 October 2021, www.ucl.ac.uk/bentham-project/who-was-jeremy-bentham/auto-icon.

Amia Srinivasan's essay is 'The Sucker, the Sucker!', *London Review of Books*, vol. 39, no. 17, 7 September 2017.

The United Kingdom rule is the *Animals (Scientific Procedures) Act (Amendment) Order 1993* (UK), s. 3.

Animal Rights

The proposed World Declaration on Great Apes is available at 'World Declaration on Great Apes', GAP Project website, accessed 21 October 2021, at www.projetogap.org.br/en/world-declaration-on-great-primates.

The Animal Welfare Party's statement of compatibility for the Wildlife Amendment (Protection of Birds) Bill 2019 is at Parliament of Victoria, *Parliamentary Debates (Hansard)*, Legislative Council, 59th Parliament, 1st Session,

11 September 2019, pp 3019–20.

India's 'Magna Carta of animal rights' is *The Constitution of India*, s. 51A(g) & (h). The Indian decision is *Animal Welfare Board of India vs. A. Nagaraj and Ors.* (2014) 7 SCC 547.

Coda: Being Animals

Fleur Cowles' book is *If I Were An Animal*, Morrow, New York 1987. It was also published as *People as Animals*, Robin Clark Ltd, London, 1986. Without access to the book, we largely relied on the following reviews:

- B. Flanagan, book review, *Star-Tribune*, 16 March 1987.

- R. Lewis, 'Cats, Dogs Top Comeback List', *Los Angeles Times*, 9 June 1988.

- 'Noted with Pleasure', *The New York Times*, 1 November 1987.

- R. Taylor, book review, *Bookmaking*, Boston Globe, 11 October 1987.

The Cat Cora quote is from 'Cat Cora: Her Kitchen Rules', Jonathan Coulton interview with Cat Cora, *Ask Me Another*, NPR, 13 January 2017.

Image Credits

'Examples of swan markings' (p. 43): unknown artist, 'Swan Marks', in W. Yarrell, *A History of British Birds*, vol. 3, John Van Voorst, London, 1843.

Swan upping on the River Thames (p. 45): Henry Robert Robertson, *Swan-Hopping* (1875), courtesy of Chronicle / Alamy.

'A fourteenth-century illustration of beekeeping' (p. 83): unknown artist, beekeeping illustration (1500s), courtesy of CPA Media Pte Ltd / Alamy.

'S.T. Gills' depiction of John Horrocks's "invalid's tent"' (p. 104): S.T. Gill, *Invalid's Tent, Salt Lake 75 Miles North-West of Mount Arden* (1846), courtesy of the Art Gallery of South Australia, Morgan Thomas Bequest Fund 1944.

'The trial of a sow and her piglets' (p. 131): unknown artist, *Trial of a Sow and Pigs at Lavegny*, in *The Book of Days: A Miscellany of Popular Antiquities*, vol. 1, W & R Chambers, London, 1863.

'The wolf of Ansbach' (p. 148): unknown artist, *The Wolf of Ansbach*, in Wolfgang Schild, *Die Geschichte der Gerichtsbarkeit. Vom Gottesurteil bis zum Beginn der modernen Rechtsprechung*, Nikol Verlagsgesellschaft, Hamburg, 1997.

'Operation Acoustic Kitty' (p. 165): unknown artist, 'Operation Acoustic Kitty: How the CIA's Attempt to Turn CATS into Cyborg Spies Ended Abruptly after the Cat Was Run Over by a Cab', *Daily Mail*, 9 May 2013.

'One of the monkey "selfies" taken by Naruto' (p. 240): Monkey 'Selfie' by Naruto (2011), courtesy of David Slater.

'The Day of the Tentacle – an octopus "selfie"' (p. 262): Gaetano Dario Gargiulo, *The Day of the Tentacle* (2020), courtesy of the photographer.

Index

Katy Barnett is a professor of law at the University of Melbourne. She is the author of the young adult novel *The Earth Below* and co-author of *Remedies in Australian Private Law*.

Jeremy Gans is a professor of law at the University of Melbourne. He is the author of *Modern Criminal Law of Australia* and *The Ouija Board Jurors*, a true crime book. He is also the co-author of *Uniform Evidence*.

Lightning Source UK Ltd.
Milton Keynes UK
UKHW040742031122
411568UK00003B/174